A Voice Crying Out in the Desert

A Voice Crying Out in the Desert

Preparing for Vatican II
with
Barnabas M. Ahern
(1915–1995)

Carroll Stuhlmueller
(1923–1994)
and
Sebastian MacDonald
Editors

A Liturgical Press Book

THE LITURGICAL PRESS
Collegeville, Minnesota

Cover: Timna Valley, Negev Desert, part of the Syro-African Rift. Photo by Richard T. Nowitz. Design by Robin Pierzina, O.S.B.

© 1996 by The Order of St. Benedict, Inc., Collegeville, Minnesota. All rights reserved. No part of this book may be reproduced in any form or by any means, electronic or mechanical, including photocopying, recording, taping, or any retrieval system without the written permission of The Liturgical Press, Collegeville, Minnesota 56321. Printed in the United States of America.

1   2   3   4   5   6   7   8

Library of Congress Cataloging-in-Publication Data

Ahern, Barnabas M.
   A voice crying out in the desert : preparing for Vatican II with Barnabas M. Ahern, C.P. / Carroll Stuhlmueller and Sebastian MacDonald, editors.
     p. cm.
   Includes bibliographical references and indexes.
   ISBN 0-8146-2354-9
   1. Bible—Criticism, interpretation, etc. 2. Bible—Theology.
3. Catholic Church—Doctrines. 4. Ahern, Barnabas M.
I. Stuhlmueller, Carroll. II. MacDonald, Sebastian K. (Sebastian Killoran), 1930- . III. Title.
BS511.2.A37 1996
230'.2—dc20   95-41479
                                                                                       CIP

To Bishop Paul M. Boyle, C.P., whose life and ministry has coincided with that of Father Barnabas both in interpreting the work of Vatican II and in sojourning at Rome where they shared much of this task together.

* * *

Fr. Barnabas Mary Ahern, C.P., has been a leading biblical scholar in this country. His phenomenal memory and continual study of Scripture allowed few passages to escape him. A man steeped in the classical tradition, he had a facile ability to speak the trenchant truth in a poetic phrase. The impressive force of his manifest sanctity emerged in his penetrating eyes, the timbre of his voice, the glow of his face, the gaunt, ascetical bearing of his frame. At the council, he exhibited a marvelous manner of connecting the old and the new, seeing conciliar development growing out of Scripture and Church teaching. He conveyed the spiritual implications of proposals for the Christian life. This earned him invitations from the council leaders to conduct workshops in their countries around the world for clergy, religious, and laity. His contribution toward worldwide acceptance of conciliar teaching was tremendous. It is the privilege of one who lived with him for many years, enjoyed his friendship and the fire of his love for Jesus and the Church, to present this book in his honor.

Bishop Paul M. Boyle, C.P.
Apostolic Vicar of Mandeville

Contents

Preface: Bishop Timothy J. Lyne, D.D.   xi

Acknowledgments   xv

Introduction: Sebastian MacDonald, C.P.   xvii

Part I
Barnabas M. Ahern, An Appreciation

1. A Personal Saga   3
    by Roger Mercurio, C.P.

2. Barnabas M. Ahern, Scholar and Spiritual Guide   12
    by Patrick Rogers, C.P.

3. The Prophet's Challenge: Barnabas M. Ahern and Vatican II   20
    by James P. Roache

Part II
Interpreting the Bible

4. New Horizons in Sacred Scripture   33

5. Interpreting the Bible Typologically.
   The Exodus: A Continuous Story of Salvation   46

6. New Light on the Gospels   64

7. Contemplative Interpretation of the Bible in Today's World   74
    A Response by Carroll Stuhlmueller, C.P.

Part III
The Bible and Openness to the World

8. The World, Its Culture, and Church Ministry 95
9. Père Lagrange:
   Pioneer of Modern Catholic Biblical Scholarship 104
10. The Haunting Face of Jesus in the Option for the Poor 110
    A Response by Cassian Yuhaus, C.P.

Part IV
The Church, the Body of Christ

11. Christian Union with the Body of Christ 123
12. Biblical Concept of Church 132
13. Role of Law in the Church 148
14. Ecumenism and Revelation 163
    A Response by Jerome M. Vereb, C.P.

Part V
The Presence of Mary in the Bible

15. The Infancy Narratives 173
16. Mary and the Poor of Israel 183
17. Mary, Prototype of the Church 195
18. Mary in Church Life Today 202
    A Response by Jerome Crowe, C.P.

Part VI
The Cross and Suffering

19. St. Paul and the Apostolate 213
20. Begotten Through the Cross 222
21. Sharing in His Sufferings 238
22. The Death of Jesus and the Birth of a New World:
    Matthew's Theology of History in the Passion Narrative 265
    A Response by Donald Senior, C.P.

PART VII
Mystical Life and Life After Death

23. The Indwelling Spirit: A Foretaste of Heaven   279

24. With Christ After Death   289

25. Christian Perfection, Contemplation, and Purgatory   302

26. Mystical Life Today   311
    A Response by Costante Brovetto, C.P.

PART VIII
In Recognition

27. Barnabas M. Ahern, Churchman   323
    by Bishop Paul M. Boyle, C.P.

Barnabas M. Ahern's Bibliography   333
    Compiled by Kenneth O'Malley, C.P.

Index of Names   341

Index of Topics   343

Index of Biblical Passages   346

Preface

On October 24, 1966, more than a thousand of the priests of Chicago gathered for a historic meeting at McCormick Place on lakefront Chicago. These were the heady days following the close of the Vatican Council. The winds of change and reform were blowing even stronger than the fall breeze wafting off the lake. In the presence of John Cardinal Cody and the bishops of the archdiocese, the priests met to discuss an ever increasing voice in the fulfillment of the decrees of Vatican II and an emerging, more active participation of the clergy in the decisions and programs of the archdiocese. The priests, on that important night, had chosen for their keynote speaker Fr. Barnabas Mary Ahern, C.P., to give the opening talk.

In the 1960s there was a great revival and an increase in the study of Holy Scripture and especially its use in teaching and preaching. This had been fueled originally by the 1943 encyclical of His Holiness, Pope Pius XII, *Divino Afflante Spiritu*. In that encyclical the Holy Father said, "Priests who are charged with winning the eternal salvation of the people should diligently study the sacred pages. They should assimilate them by prayer and meditation and then they should zealously dispense the supernatural power of the divine word in their sermons, homilies, and exhortations. They should support Christian Doctrine with passages taken from the sacred books." For many of the priests, especially those of us who had finished our seminary career before 1943, it meant that there was a whole new way of teaching and thinking about Scripture. In the late forties and early fifties, many priests went away to study Scripture and acquire the degrees, skills, and languages necessary to become, in a real sense, true Scripture scholars.

Barnabas Mary Ahern was one of those, and when he came back equipped with those wonderful talents, he put himself at the service of the priests of Chicago and the nation. He was not only an able scholar but also a very deeply spiritual and understanding man. He quickly won both the recognition and the admiration of the priests. He taught us many of the things of Scripture that had changed since the days of our seminary career. In a special way he gave to the clergy and to those who wished to study a real knowledge of what the texts meant and how they could be applied to the daily life of the people of the Church. More than that, his own spirituality was an inspiration to the priests. And, as a retreat master and speaker, he not only demonstrated how to use the texts, he enabled us to apply them more intimately to our own daily lives. Barnabas Mary Ahern was a real inspiration, not merely for change but also for the furtherance of our own spirituality and for deepening the knowledge of Scripture in a way that would change the lives of the faithful. To him, Scripture was not just knowledge but a drawing ever closer to the God whose word it was that he made part of his life.

The words of the encyclical *Divino Afflante Spiritu* had for priests a very important sentence that he made part of his life, "Their use of scripture should be eloquent, orderly, and clear." Barnabas Mary Ahern was all of those things. He was an eloquent speaker at Mass, in retreats and conferences. His teaching was orderly and well organized and, above all, he made things very clear. He opened new vistas of what the love of God would and should mean in daily life and an ever increasing reliance and dependency on the word of God in forming and developing our own spiritual consciousness.

His influence on those of us who had the opportunity to share both his knowledge and his wisdom was to be an inspiration and guide in the life of priests and the church of Chicago. In his own community, he was a leader in establishing the wonderful Passionist tradition of Scripture scholars that has since been followed by Carroll Stuhlmueller, Donald Senior, and various other members of the Passionist community. We are particularly happy that the Passionists have continued to give us that leadership in Chicago and in the surrounding area.

In controversy he was always a gentleman who wore his learning lightly. So many of the great steps that have been taken in the last twenty years in the widespread knowledge of and devotion to the Scriptures were due to pioneers like Barnabas Mary Ahern. He awakened a hunger for the Word of God that is more and more experienced by modern-day Catholics.

Most of all Barnabas Mary Ahern was first, foremost, and always the priest. To all who faced the struggle for priesthood he was always the rock of thoughtful reason and an oasis in the midst of confusion. He was, indeed, a *sacerdos magnus*.

Bishop Timothy J. Lyne, D.D.

Acknowledgments

The articles of Barnabas M. Ahern, C.P., edited anew for publication in this book, originally appeared in the following publications: *Chapter 4 from a transcript of a clergy conference of the Archdiocese of Chicago, February 1961, similar to an article in *Critic*, August–September 1962; *Chapter 5 from a chapter in *The Bridge*, New York: Herder and Herder, 1955; *Chapter 6 from *Chicago Studies*, Spring 1962; Chapter 8 from *The Passionist*, March 1962; Chapter 9 from *Worship*, March 1962; Chapter 11 from the *Catholic Biblical Quarterly*, 1961; *Chapter 12 from the *Proceedings of the Society of Catholic College Teachers of Sacred Doctrine*, 1961; Chapter 13 from a seminar conducted by the Canon Law Society of America, n.d.; Chapter 15 from *Cross and Crown*, December 1960; Chapter 16 from *Cross and Crown*, September 1959; *Chapter 17 from The Liturgical Conference, *Proceedings*, National Liturgical Week, 1954; Chapter 19 from *Perspectives*, December 1961; Chapter 20 from *Cross and Crown*, March 1949; *Chapter 21 from the *Catholic Biblical Quarterly*, 1960; Chapter 23 from the *Catholic Biblical Quarterly*, April 1947; *Chapter 24 from *Proceedings of the Catholic Theological Society of America*, 1961; Chapter 25 from the *American Ecclesiastical Review*, February 1948. Chapter 22 is adapted from an article that first appeared in *Currents in Theology and Mission* 19 (1992).

Valuable secretarial and editorial assistance came from Marylyn Welter, Virginia Piecuch, and Lissa Romell.

---

*Early copy appeared in *New Horizons*, Notre Dame, Ind.: Fides Publishers, Inc., 1963.

Barnabas M. Ahern, C.P.
1915–1995

Introduction

This *Festschrift* honors Barnabas Mary Ahern. Comprising twenty-seven chapters in eight major sections and a bibliography of his works, it unfolds along lines descriptive of his life: the man, the churchman, the contemplative. Throughout his life trajectory is the man of Scripture.

THE MAN

People have often noted the human quality of Barnabas. Given other features of his character, this is noteworthy. Very much a Chicago Irish Catholic product of the 1920s, he exhibited these typical traits throughout his life. Mentally nimble, adroit, and quick-witted, he managed to "land on his feet" throughout a career of debate, tension, change, and conflict, hardly "the worse for wear" until the end.

His roots nourished him and provided him a recognizable identity over the years for those with whom he engaged. As Roger Mercurio, Carroll Stuhlmueller, and others sketch their appreciation of him as a man, they explore these roots to which he stayed close, even as he branched beyond them.

A striking instance of this was the way his success became the boast of those who remained behind. Rather than separating, it cemented relationship to him, engendering a pride in "one of our own" who has "made good."

THE CHURCHMAN

To describe Barnabas as a churchman is to recognize more about him in this regard than usually accrues to one who has spent his life as a priest and religious.

The essays in Part IV of this testimony suggest the special dimensions of his churchmanship. There was a period in his life during the 1950s when, with a few others of his stature, he expressed his loyalty to the Church in terms of a vision encompassing her openness to the world. A spirit of loving criticism of certain features of Church doctrine and discipline characterized that brief period of time. For the remainder, his was an obedient attitude toward ecclesiastical authority.

The institutional church was the milieu in which he lived and moved. It secured his total allegiance, so much so that at times his friends and admirers wondered whether he ever harbored a personal position on an issue differing from what the "Holy Father," as he always said, or the Vatican Congregations expressed. In his later years, a rigidity regarding official church positions occasionally overtook him, with even his body betraying strong feelings if he perceived opposition to this teaching.

The acme of this churchmanship was the more than twenty years he spent in Rome, as consultor for the Sacred Congregation for the Doctrine of the Faith, and as a member of the International Theological Commission, the Anglican-Roman Catholic International Commission, and the Pontifical Biblical Commission. This total commitment to and regard of the Church facilitated his successfully arguing at the Vatican Council for inserting its Mariological doctrine within the document on the Church.

MAN OF PRAYER

From his early years, Barnabas Mary Ahern was linked to the Congregation of the Passion. He was a Passionist well over fifty years. This fact is revelatory of many traits of his character. A Passionist is a contemplative; prayer underlies his life and activity. This depicted Barnabas in large part—a man of prayer.

His physical bearing suggests that to an observer—the tilt of the head, the stooped shoulders, the pose struck as he pondered a question put to him. The reputation he garnered rests as much on his prayerful contemplation as it does on his conversance with Scripture. His apostolic activity, whether among his Passionist brethren or the clergy, religious, and laity, fed upon his prayer which proved to be his most effective ministry. It is appropriate that a major portion of this book acknowledges his "life in the spirit."

A SCRIPTURE MAN THROUGHOUT

Permeating his person and crowning his accomplishments over fifty years was his expertise in New Testament studies, especially the Pauline writings.

He was among the first American Roman Catholic priests to earn a Doctorate in Sacred Scripture (S.S.D.). The story bears telling of his *tour de force* when undergoing the defense of his dissertation. In the course of that ordeal, the lights of the *aula magna* or great hall went out, leaving everything in total darkness, to the consternation of the many observers. Barnabas, however, carried on before the examiners without a pause. This was an auspicious beginning (he achieved a perfect score on that occasion) to a Scripture career that involved not only scholarship but also teaching, lecturing, and preaching, as he popularized contemporary approaches to Scripture among a broad public. On this dearest of all topics, he spoke eloquently and passionately. These competencies recommended him to Chicago's Albert Cardinal Meyer as a theologian who should attend the Vatican Council. This introduction to another level in serving the church eventuated in a Roman sojourn that was to encompass many of his years.

The Scriptures fed his contemplative spirit. They gave him entree to God's own mind and heart and enriched his religious consecration to the Passionist life he had embraced. He was a Scripture man throughout.

A TIMELY STUDY

As Barnabas reached the end of his scholarly career, he suffered from a condition that effectively impaired further ministry on his part. This *Festschrift* is designed to acknowledge his numerous contributions.

This book appears shortly after the twenty-fifth anniversary commemorating the close of Vatican II. Barnabas played an important role in that assembly which has been a watershed in the life of the contemporary Church. Any prominence that the U.S. hierarchy enjoyed during its proceedings is owed in large measure to Barnabas, who had gained their trust and confidence, not only as a master of the Scriptures but also as a churchman and a man of prayer.

This collection offers him as a model for those engaged in interpreting the council and its aftermath. In recent years this activity has been intense throughout the Catholic world, though marked by rancorous debate and disagreement. We can all learn from this man's adeptness at interpreting the Scriptures for church rank and file, as well as for church leadership. He earned allegiance and respect. The acumen he displayed during the 1950s interpreting the signs of the times helped prepare the way for the new appreciation of God's role both in the world and in the church that would appear at Vatican II.

The calming effect he had on others was not always his personal experience. He endured powerful inner tensions as he pondered the course of action to advise and the meaning to espouse. Nonetheless, he exuded harmony in his humanness, his churchmanship, his Passionist prayer tradition, and his scriptural expertise. The essays in this collection witness this achievement.

This is an example of Barnabas' work from a generation ago, indicating the scholarship of that day. Those contributing to this volume have been asked to address the same issues as Barnabas Ahern did, but from the vantage point of contemporary professional standards. This allows a comparison of the two time periods and provides opportunity to assess interpretations and positions Barnabas put forth, modeling the best of the efforts underway in the 1950s and 1960s. This may help today's scholars using current methods to pursue more critically the task of unfolding the meaning of God's Word.

This book invites those influenced by Barnabas to recall memories of twenty-five or thirty years ago, and to evaluate them in terms of present perceptions of our needs and God's designs for us. Have these lessons of the past proved equal to contemporary demands? How perennially valid are his understanding and exhortations as found in these selections of his writings?

This collection suggests that we consider the role of "heart" and affectivity in religious studies. Barnabas' humanness affected his churchmanship, his prayer, and his scriptural ministry precisely because this intensely emotional man thought, judged, and spoke with "heart." A concern periodically reappears to counter the approach to truth solely through the intellectual activity of generalizing, comparing, remembering, predicting, judging, etc. Today, as the ability of the rational mind to meet all the demands placed on human agency in discovering truth is again called into question, we find other resources for living, dying, and rising with God. "Heart" is such an asset, rich in potential. Barnabas Mary Ahern had plenty of heart.

Piety is a matter of the heart. Though this century had discounted it as part of Victorian superficiality, it is now regarded as helpful to the *humanum* in its relationship to God.

A portion of this collection attends to the piety of Barnabas. He displayed its readily recognizable signs—humility, reverence, respect—in his demeanor, regardless of the setting. No longer seen as a quaint mode of behavior reminiscent of another era, piety is a forecast of things to come and fits well in a setting where the power of God's Word among us is honored. Compatible with his natural temperament, Barnabas' piety was nurtured in the supportive tradition of Passionist spirituality, strongly pietistic in its texture. This accounts for the singularly effective manner in which he preached and spoke of the Scriptures. It was not merely his mental acumen, but also his emotional affect that enabled him to impact his audience. For good reason this combination is prominent in academia today, especially the humanistic disciplines, for the help it gives in attaining the truth.

This *Festschrift* is a timely witness that continuity with and fidelity to one's background guarantee future progress and success. Barnabas moved beyond his early Chicago Irish Catholic roots. But they enriched his endeavors. His churchmanship, prayer life, and scriptural career betray traces associated with his early beginnings. Throughout a wide-ranging mixture of places, persons, and responsibilities, his identity as "Barney" was discernible to his brethren.

THE CONTRIBUTORS

Each contributor to this book fits into the life history of Barnabas Mary Ahern in one way or another.

Timothy J. Lyne, retired auxiliary bishop of the Chicago archdiocese, was ordained a priest two years later than Barnabas, in 1943. Barnabas, for his part, began his priestly ministry in the archdiocese of Chicago as a member of the Passionist community and a Scripture professor. Barnabas was newly degreed in theology from Catholic University in Washington, D.C. Chicago was and remained the scene of his major U.S. accomplishments, especially on behalf of the clergy, into whose ranks Timothy Lyne had just entered. Father Lyne held several pastorates in the archdiocese, culminating at Holy Name Cathedral.

Three years his junior, Roger Mercurio followed Barnabas in the study and teaching of Scripture, specifically the New Testament, to the Passionist students of Holy Cross Province as well as to a larger audience of religious and laity. An ardent promoter of Passionist spirituality and presently provincial archivist, he has held numerous leadership positions, such as provincial, provincial consultor, local superior, pastor, and director of the province mission program.

Carroll Stuhlmueller joined this group of Passionist scriptural scholars a few years later, concentrating on the Old Testament. Like Barnabas, his mentor, he earned his doctorate in the field, taught in the Passionist seminary system and was a member of the faculty at Catholic Theological Union. A prolific author and editor, he was equally prominent as a popular lecturer, especially on the prophets and psalms. He fell victim to a sudden and unforeseen stroke while preparing this manuscript, and died in 1994, shortly before the death of his friend and fellow religious, Barnabas Ahern, who died in 1995.

A fellow worker with Barnabas during the years of Passionist renewal chapters at the Generalate of Saints John and Paul in Rome (during the late 1960s and early 1970s), Cassian Yuhaus has been a proponent of openness to the world on the part of religious, as Barnabas had been at one point in his career. Degreed in church history, Cassian has been at the forefront of religious life renewal in the U.S. Currently executive director of ministry for Religious Research and Consultancy, he has authored several books and held positions of responsibility within his province of St. Paul of the Cross.

Patrick Rogers is a member of St. Patrick's Province, Ireland. Ordained a Passionist priest in 1966, he pursued graduate work in the field of Scripture, thereby joining several other contributors to this volume. He has engaged in the teaching of New Testament studies at the Milltown Institute of Philosophy and Theology in Ireland (Dublin) and at the International Theologate in Nairobi, Kenya, while Barnabas taught there. He occupied the Flannery Chair of the New Testament at Spokane University during 1989–1990. Another popular exponent of the New Testament, he offers his reflections here.

Unlike many of the authors in this collection, Jerome Vereb is of another generation from that of Barnabas. Currently stationed in Jamaica, New York, he is on special assignment. He has been prominent in a field dear to Barnabas, that of ecumenism, as a consultor to the Pontifical Council for Christian Unity. He called on this Roman experience during Pope John Paul II's 1987 visit to the United States. The Pope added an ecumenical dimension to the trip by accepting the invitation of former President Jimmy Carter to visit the University of South Carolina. Arrangements for this event lay in the hands of Jerome Vereb, who comments here on the thoughts of Barnabas about the church.

James Roache is a priest of the archdiocese of Chicago. Ordained in 1960, he came along just at the end of the most productive period of Barnabas' ministry in the archdiocese. A close friend of several Passionists, his position especially in the field of communications (with the U.S. Bishops Conference, with the Secretariat for Social Communications in the Vatican, and as Communications Secretary under Cardinal Cody) cemented these relationships. He reminisces on Barnabas from this vantage point, as well as from his role as founding director of the archdiocesan Center for Pastoral Ministry.

We welcome the contribution of Australian Passionist Jerome Crowe, another New Testament scholar and colleague of Barnabas. Teacher, lecturer, author, he brings an appreciation of Barnabas' accomplishments in Mariology. Particularly attuned to the latter's Vatican II endeavors, Father Crowe joins his fellow authors to provide us a "then and now" perspective on Barnabas' theology. A lecturer on the New Testament at Templegate, he has served as provincial superior of Holy Spirit Province.

Donald Senior, like Jerome Vereb, represents a younger generation of scholars who have witnessed to and profited by the biblical teaching of Barnabas Ahern. A graduate of Louvain, he has excelled as a New Testament scholar, especially in the passion narratives of the Gospels. He is well equipped to comment on the passion motif in Barnabas' writings, starting with the latter's doctoral dissertation on Paul: "The Power of His Resurrection and Fellowship in His Sufferings." A voluminous writer, he has, like Barnabas, lectured and taught widely on the Scriptures to bishops, clergy, religious, and laity. A professor at Catholic Theological Union, he is the immediate past president of that institution. Most recently he has edited the publication of *The Catholic Study Bible* of *The New American Bible* by Oxford University Press.

Costante Brovetto of Immaculate Heart Province, Milan, Italy, also brings welcome competence to this book. The junior of Barnabas by just a few years, his professional career ran parallel, both in the field of theology and also in the area of religious formation of young Passionists. Early recognized as an expert in the spirituality of St. Paul of the Cross, the Passionist founder, he has been an influential figure in the renewal chapters of the congregation and has served as both general and provincial consultor. This background enriches his essay, translated by Frederick Sucher, on Barnabas' mystical theology writings.

Bishop Paul M. Boyle has been friend of and collaborator with Barnabas over the years, having lived and worked with him in various settings. He also served as his provincial and general superior. Relying on his canon law background during the 1960s he guided numerous communities of American religious through the renewal of their life and apostolate. He taught canon law in the Passionist seminary system and is past president of both the Canon Law Society of America and the Conference of Major Religious Superiors of Men. He brings a wealth of experience to bear upon life in the contemporary church which he has diligently served.

Kenneth O'Malley, C.P., has arranged the bibliography for this volume, a particular expertise of his. A professional librarian, he has utilized his library science doctorate on behalf of seminary education. Professionally active in library societies and consultant to library staffs in the religion and theology areas, he currently serves as director of the library for Catholic Theological Union. Like his peers contributing to this volume, he too is pastorally involved. His bibliography details Barnabas' considerable writings, demonstrating again the latter's vigorous ministry.

These authors who comment on Barnabas Mary Ahern's personality and activities have met him on his life journey at some point along the way. Thanks to the editing done by Carroll Stuhlmueller, on Barnabas' behalf, their reflections offer a relatively full view of the man, the churchman, the contemplative, and the Scripture scholar.[1] Their contributions establish the importance of this *Festschrift*. It presents us with a picture of a person whose influence in the contemporary church has been considerable. May this collection continue the inspiration that he provided over the years.

Sebastian MacDonald, C.P.

---

[1] Carroll Stuhlmueller also compiled an earlier collection of Barnabas' articles and lectures in the book *New Horizons* (1963).

Part I

Barnabas M. Ahern
An Appreciation

How different the man who devotes himself
   to the study of the law of the Most High!
He explores the wisdom of the men of old
   and occupies himself with the prophecies;
He treasures the discourses of famous people,
   and goes to the heart of involved sayings;
He studies obscure parables,
   and is busied with the hidden meanings of the sages.
He is in attendance on the great,
   and has entrance to the ruler.
He travels among the peoples of foreign lands
   to learn what is good and evil among them.
His care is to seek the Lord, his Maker,
   to petition the Most High
To open his lips in prayer
   to ask pardon for his sins
Then, if it pleases the Lord Almighty,
   he will be filled with the spirit of understanding;
He will pour forth his words of wisdom
   and in prayer give thanks to the Lord (Sir 39:1-6).

Chapter 1

A Personal Saga

Roger Mercurio, C.P.

My memories of Barnabas go back to 1941. I was then a theological student at our Chicago monastery on Harlem Avenue. Barnabas came there as a newly ordained priest to prepare for two years of study at the Catholic University in Washington. For the next fifty years I either lived with him or remained in close contact with him. At the end of his life, we were together again, I as archivist and he as a resident in Daneo Hall, our retirement wing, as a victim of Alzheimer's disease.

HIS PASSIONIST CALLING

His story begins in Chicago where he was born in 1915 and given the name of James. He was in the seventh grade at St. Patrick's school on Chicago's southeast side when Rev. Stanislaus Geekie, C.P., gave a mission in the parish. One morning, when questioned by the sister in school about the mission, young James Ahern gave the entire sermon by heart! This was his first contact with a Passionist and the beginning of his vocation.

In 1928 he went to the Passionist prep seminary in Normandy, Missouri. He professed his first vows in 1933 in Louisville and was ordained there in 1941.

EARLY YEARS AS SCRIPTURE SCHOLAR

After two years at the Catholic University, he returned with a licentiate in theology and a year of scriptural studies. The war prevented him from going to Jerusalem or Rome for the biblical degree. In Chicago he began teaching Passionist theological students general introduction to the Old Testament and exegesis.

While still a student at Catholic University he attended the meetings of the Catholic Biblical Association (CBA), becoming a member of the association. The following year, 1943, he wrote his first article for the *Catholic Biblical Quarterly* (CBQ) entitled "Staff or No Staff?" In a quite conservative way he summarized various ways scholars had harmonized the narrative in Matthew and Mark. Later he was embarrassed by this article. He once wrote to me that he wished an atom bomb would drop on every copy of that issue of CBQ to obliterate it completely!

In September of 1943, Pius XII issued the landmark encyclical on Holy Scripture, *Divino Afflante Spiritu*. At the August 1944 meeting of CBA, Barnabas gave one of the major addresses entitled "Textual Directives of the Encyclical *Divino Afflante Spiritu*."

In his address he said: "May we not add, too, that in this encyclical in its first and its latter parts, Pope Pius canonizes the principles enunciated in *La Méthode Historique* by Père Lagrange of holy and beloved memory?" But at once he adds a cautious footnote: "This endorsement, of course, would exclude the erroneous view of history *secundum apparentiam* which Lagrange proposed in this book but later restricted." He wanted to distance himself from Lagrange's original proposal to solve historical statements in the Scriptures by proposing that the author did not intend to teach history but wrote only under the appearance or guise of history.

After the 1944 meeting of the CBA, Barnabas was asked to work on the translation of the Old Testament into English. He was given the Song of Songs but later was assigned the Book of Numbers for translation and commentary. At first the translations were from the Latin Vulgate but later from the original languages.

His Scripture studies inspired his prayer. There were, of course, times when he found prayer difficult. I remember how he was challenged riding Chicago's Rapid Transit trains, familiarly called the "L." He usually carried a small book for prayerful reflection. But the cars were too noisy and distracting. He would laugh, saying that all one can do on the "L" is "contemplate with eyes shut!"

After my ordination, while I was studying at the Catholic University, I would return each summer to Chicago. Barnabas was busy teaching and translating. I remember seeing two large desks in his room, one was for his class work, the other for translations! In this way he could immediately work on one or the other project!

In this period after the war America was quickly recovering. It was a time of hope. Passionists had held their first postwar general chapter. For the first time a non-European was elected general superior (Albert Deane of Argentina, later Bishop). There was much talk of our work in the church. The Chicago province was planning to extend our retreat house apostolate to Detroit, Cincinnati, Houston, and Sacramento and, later, to St. Louis. Two of our recently ordained priests were joining a group of missionaries from our Eastern province as the Passionists returned to China. We were at the dawn of a new day!

Barnabas and I would discuss these matters, especially reflecting on the education and formation which our religious would need to face the problems of these postwar years. There was also a growing appreciation of our Passionist history and spirituality. We began to talk about the contemplative and monastic elements of our life. Barnabas was interested in all of this and had much to contribute. He and I shared our many ideals with one another.

IN JERUSALEM AND ROME

In the fall of 1947, Barnabas went to Europe to obtain a degree in Scripture. While there he spent some months in Israel. We received a beautiful letter from Israel. It shows something of the depth of spirituality of this biblical student as he walked the roads of the Holy Land. Several paragraphs deserve re-reading:

> From my window I can see Jerusalem, and best of all, the dome of the Church of the Holy Sepulchre. As you know, this encloses both Calvary and the Tomb. Friday I offered Holy Mass on the very spot where our Lord died; the intention was for the congregation, our province, and especially for you [my students]. That was an experience which one cannot describe. Tomorrow I go to Bethlehem.
>
> The whole city, even with the squalid streets and . . . British soldiers without number, just seems full of His memory. Just think! On my way to and from school I pass the Garden of Gethsemane. I do pray for you. And in one of the streets of the Old City the Franciscans have marked out the Stations of the Cross. It is wonderful to walk there. The streets are still narrow and rough. Every place you walk, you can truly say: "He was here."
>
> . . . the sky at night is so beautiful. It is spangled with stars. The nature psalms and the *Benedicite* means so much more now.

> And yes, I wish you could feel the wind here, as it rushes through the valley. Like the psalmist of old, you know that "He rides the winds"—they are so strong and compelling. . . .
>
> . . . last night you could see the flares and hear the machine guns of the British soldiers against Jewish terrorists. We are perfectly safe, for the Arabs in Bethany are very devoted to the Passionists and would kill anyone who tried to molest us. But just the same, say some prayers that when the British withdraw—which seems certain—the Russians will not swoop down to fill the vacuum. For that would end all the church's work here, and it might mean the ruin of the holy places.

But his stay in Israel was short-lived, for war soon broke out as the Arabs invaded the new nation of Israel. Barnabas returned to Rome to continue preparing for the examination in biblical studies. Barnabas passed the examinations with a perfect grade "plenis votis." He came back and soon took a more prominent part in the CBA, as well as in writing articles for the CBQ and other periodicals.

In the fall of 1948 I left Chicago for Rome. I would not live with Barnabas again until the three years in Louisville, 1959–1962. But during those eleven years Barnabas and I were in close contact. He would encourage me in my biblical studies. In the summer we attended the biblical conventions together. We would also meet on other occasions. We always talked about Scripture, formation, the congregation, the Church.

During this period Barnabas was deeply involved in the biblical apostolate in the United States. He continued translating the Bible and writing articles. Both in Jerusalem at the l'Ecole Biblique and in Rome he became more aware of recent interpretations of the Scriptures by Catholic scholars. He cautiously began to adopt their opinions.

But Barnabas also remained a "minister of the word." It was part of his Passionist calling to preach the Word of God to the learned and to little ones. Barnabas began to give frequent conferences to various communities of sisters in the Chicago area. Over the years he wrote many conferences, many of which are still preserved. He was always ready to go to the parlor to give a word of advice or comfort to a stranger seeking help.

At this time Barnabas frequently spent a free afternoon going to hospitals to visit the sick, especially in the tubercular sanitarium. He found it necessary to minister to God's suffering ones. From such as these he learned the deeper meaning of the poor, the *anawim* of the psalter and prophets.

THE DOCTORAL DISSERTATION

Towards the end of this period Barnabas returned to Rome to prepare for his doctorate. He attended the Pontifical Biblical Institute. There, under Fr. Stanislaus Lyonnet, S.J., he wrote his doctoral dissertation entitled "The Power of His Resurrection and Fellowship in His Sufferings: An Exegetical and Doctrinal Study of Philippians 3:10-11." It is a 349-page manuscript on the beautiful words of St. Paul, "to know him and the power of his resurrection and the sharing of his sufferings by being conformed to his death, if somehow I may attain the resurrection from the dead." [Editor's note: A key chapter of this dissertation is summarized in Chapter 21 of this book.]

In a masterful manner he shows that Paul's account of his personal experiences are in reality a statement of Christian principles, applicable to every Christian:

> This identity of personality and principle must be kept in mind as fundamental to an understanding of this text. It is Paul who speaks; but in his words the universal reality of Christian life finds expression.

Barnabas' fundamental insight is that, for Paul, the expression "in Christ" affirms that "between the *soma*—person of Christ—and the *soma*—person of the Christian—there exists the same intrinsic bond that unites the body and its members, so that whatever life belongs to the one is shared by the other."

This sharing in Christ's life begins with the experience of "the power of the resurrection" in baptismal conversion. But when Jesus shares his risen life with Christians he bestows upon them also a principle of death. The spirit given by "the power of the Risen Christ" grants the Christian "fellowship in Jesus' sufferings."

He adds: "In verses 10-17 Paul's impassioned words rise to a climax . . . for this new life has conferred upon him both the power and the duty 'to know Christ and the power of his resurrection and the fellowship of his sufferings'—words that sum up for Paul the full meaning of the bond that unites him to Christ." He repeated his understanding of Paul in the *Festschrift* paper he wrote in honor of Rev. Edward P. Arbez, S.S., his professor at the Catholic University.

Barnabas also found in this passage the meaning of his own call to become a Passionist. The theme of his dissertation shows the deep inner spirit of the man who chose to join the Passionists and to dedicate his life to proclaiming the memory of the passion.

BIBLICAL MINISTRY IN THE UNITED STATES

He returned to Louisville in 1959 as a doctor of sacred Scripture. In 1965 the Passionist theologate was joined to the theology school at St. Meinrad's archabbey. Three years later, in 1968, the Passionists, together with the Franciscans and Servites, formed the Catholic Theological Union at Chicago. These were his golden years as Scripture professor in the United States.

At the same time he was lecturing to religious all over the country. In the November 1960 issue of *Worship* there was an article by Godfrey Diekmann, O.S.B., the editor, entitled "Welcome, Father Barnabas!":

> With this issue *Worship* warmly welcomes Fr. Barnabas Mary Ahern, C.P., as editor of its "Holy Scripture" section, succeeding Fr. Kilian McDonnell, O.S.B., . . . *Worship* is deeply indebted to Fr. Barnabas Mary Ahern for agreeing to add the full responsibility for the continuation and improvement of the Scripture section to his present heavy schedule. . . . During the summer of 1960 his lectures were enthusiastically received by hundreds of priests who attended the Biblical Institutes at Glen Ellyn, Illinois, and St. John's Abbey. Father Barnabas combines erudition with kerygmatic unction in a remarkable harmony.

In the fall of 1962 Barnabas became co-editor of *The Bible Today* and shortly afterwards was relieved of his duties for *Worship*. He continued as co-editor of *The Bible Today* until 1974.

For many years Barnabas wrote for both scholarly and popular periodicals. His articles appeared in *L'Osservatore Romano* as well as *Our Sunday Visitor*, in the *Gregorianum* and in *The Way*. In the mid-sixties Fr. Carroll Stuhlmueller, C.P., edited *New Horizons*, a collection of eleven essays and addresses that Barnabas had written or given. In the review of *New Horizons* in the CBQ, Fr. J. Frank Devine, S.J., wrote: "This book has all the solid scholarship, spiritual penetration and felicity of expression that we have come to expect in Ahern's writing and which we so admire."

IMPACT UPON PASSIONISTS

In the congregation Barnabas was highly esteemed. At the first election of delegates to a provincial chapter (initiated in the newly revised rule of 1959), Barnabas received the highest number of votes among all the religious of the province. This chapter was held in the summer of 1962. Barnabas played an important part in it and was elected as the delegate of our province to the forthcoming general chapter to be held in 1964 in Rome.

At that general chapter Barnabas was selected as a member of the committee to write an official letter to the brethren of the congregation. The text of that letter is redolent of his style. Of course by the time of that chapter the Vatican Council had already held two sessions.

In 1968 Barnabas was elected as delegate to the provincial chapter and again to the extraordinary provincial chapter of 1969. He was also elected by the provincial chapter to be a delegate to the extraordinary general chapter of renewal for its two sessions, 1968 and 1970.

PERITUS AT THE VATICAN COUNCIL

When the council opened in the fall of 1962, Barnabas was called as a *peritus*. He attended all of the sessions of the council. He assisted the American bishops, especially with the constitution on the church, the constitution on revelation, and in the area of ecumenism.

Each fall he would be in Rome. While in Rome in 1964 Cardinal Spellman gave him the Spellman Award in the name of the Catholic Theological Society of America. During the summers he went to Africa and elsewhere to speak to clergy and religious.

In 1964 Barnabas was elected president of the CBA. He gave the presidential address at the twenty-eighth meeting of the CBA at the University of Notre Dame. In the report of this meeting we read:

> In his presidential address, which opened the meeting [Tuesday, August 31] Father Barnabas spoke of the challenge to exegetes found in the revised schema on revelation that has been prepared for the fourth session of Vatican II. It offers a synthetic, balanced, pastoral view of revelation as the communication of God to humanity and recognizes the social character of inspiration. Exegetes can rejoice to see that it incorporates the best of modern critical scholarship when dealing with the use of scripture. He warned his colleagues not to approach the document with a "selective subjectivism," but to accept their responsibility to make an apt adaptation of all books of the Bible to contemporary needs. Relaying the requests of missionaries to whom he had lectured, the council *peritus* urged CBA members to be alive to the exigencies of their vocation as scholars. This involves communicating the dynamic relevance of the divine word to people of our time.

ROMAN ASSIGNMENTS

After the council he began teaching at the Catholic Theological Union but it was short-lived; in 1969, he was appointed a member of the Pontifical Theological Commission. Two more times his appointment was renewed—until 1984. During these years he remained in Rome, teaching at the Gregorianum and at the Regina Mundi Institute.

He also held several other important posts in Rome. He was appointed to the Pontifical Biblical Commission in 1966 which he served until 1977. In 1976 he became a consultor to the Congregation for the Doctrine of the Faith. In 1982 he was appointed a consultor to the Congregation for the Causes of Saints.

Perhaps his most influential role was as a member of the ecumenical Commission of Anglicans and Roman Catholics, to which he was assigned in 1969. In 1981 the Anglican Archbishop of Canterbury, with the approval of Queen Elizabeth, bestowed upon Father Barnabas the medal of the Order of Saint Augustine of Canterbury. Barnabas was the first Roman Catholic to receive this honor.

Barnabas would return to the United States each summer where he continued to give retreats and workshops to religious. Several times he spoke at meetings of the Passionist congregation. In 1974, when a general assembly of all the religious of our Chicago province was held at Bardstown, Kentucky, Barnabas addressed the assembly with a learned talk on the Passionist charism. In 1980 he addressed a convocation of the eastern province held at Tarrytown, New York. His subject was "The Passion Myth." He talked with all the power of old from the mystical depths of his own soul, quoting many favorite Scripture passages.

In his conclusion he said: "Perhaps the greatest external change to be noted about us is that, like our holy founder, St. Paul of the Cross, year by year we grow somewhat older—with new and unwelcome physical weaknesses. And all the while what is deepest in our life and its secret wellspring—our love for Christ crucified and our effort to find in his passion the unity of our life and our apostolate—this keeps growing stronger and stronger."

LIVING HIS DISSERTATION

He literally lived these words when in 1984 he left Rome to retire to the Passionist House of Prayer and Solitude at Bedford, Pennsylvania. In the early years of the renewal he had written a position paper on the need of such houses in order to preserve the contemplative spirit of St. Paul of the Cross. Now, at 69 years of age, he gave himself to three years of contemplative quiet and prayer.

I would like to repeat words that I wrote to Barnabas in 1983:

> Life does catch-up with us, and I guess there are moments when we should sit back and see where we have come from and what still remains for us to do. . . . Looking back on your life I see that there has been a steady and continuing scriptural thread throughout your life bringing all of your ministries and activities together toward the one great goal which is the Lord. For as you used to quote so often, "to know the scriptures is to know Jesus Christ." . . . You have given years of service to the church and to the province by your wholehearted commitment and dedication to the scriptures. You have assuredly played a very important, vital, and creative role in the development of our province in the 1950s and especially in the crucial 1960s.

In 1987 the general superior, Fr. Paul Boyle, asked Barnabas if he were willing to return to teaching Scripture at the Passionist seminary in Nairobi, East Africa. Little James Ahern of St. Patrick's church, Chicago, would become a Passionist missionary at long last!

After two years it became obvious that his health was failing. His illness was diagnosed as Alzheimer's disease. He returned to Chicago and was assigned to the retirement-nursing wing, Daneo Hall. At first he was able to enter into community life in a limited way, but the dread disease had taken hold of him ever more persistently.

One day I thoughtlessly reminded him that he had written his dissertation on St. Paul's words "The Power of His Resurrection and Fellowship in His Sufferings." He began to cry, for he now knew the fullness of these words, not just in a scholarly manner, but experientially by mystical participation.

His dissertation—yes, his very life—ends with these telling lines: "Finally, these words make clear that the Christian *knows* Christ precisely as savior; for, *through the activity of the Holy Spirit*, he shares in the salvific reality of Christ's death and resurrection, bearing the *form* of his death that one day he may bear the *form* of his glory."

CHAPTER 2

Barnabas M. Ahern, Scholar and Spiritual Guide

Patrick Rogers, C.P.

In his prison letter to the Philippians, St. Paul reassures them that he expects to be released and then return to their service as an apostle, for their spiritual progress and greater joy in the faith (Phil 1:25). Just such a desire to *make a contribution* also played a leading role in the life of Barnabas Ahern, who ardently admired Paul and had made a special study of precisely this epistle. His work, both as a writer and a tireless lecturer, was always targeted towards providing others with solid inspiration for their living.

My personal association with Barnabas was in three quite distinct phases. In 1964, as a student of theology, I was moved and impressed by his series of lectures in Dublin on current trends in biblical studies—material which formed the substance of his book *New Horizons* (1963). A decade later, while I was in Rome completing doctoral studies in 1975–1977, I shared his company at our community of Saints John and Paul, near the Coliseum. Finally, in 1987–1989, I was his friend and colleague on the staff of Tangaza Theological College in Nairobi, Kenya. Although by then at the end of a long and distinguished teaching career, he still maintained regular study habits, with a love for prayer that was very inspirational. It was in this Kenya phase that I got to know him best and really appreciated his influence as a man of God. His contribution to those who knew him well was more through the kind of person that he *was* than through anything he wrote or said.

TEACHING IN KENYA

At least twelve bulky parcels of books preceded him to Nairobi. Clearly he was prepared for a lengthy stay and intended to take his professorial duties with full seriousness! On his arrival some days later, he was full of enthusiasm and questions about the task ahead. What were the African students like? Did they have a good knowledge of English? How open would they be to modern interpretations of the Bible? Would they be able to understand his American accent? Within the coming weeks, he was pleased to find that his services were much in demand, not simply for teaching, but also as confessor, director of retreats, and spiritual guide.

During the next two years, I had many occasions to notice how his commitment to study and prayer went hand in hand with a genuine pastoral concern for everyone who called on him. It is from this strong combination of qualities that he made his special contribution to biblical studies in our time. Many people who had read his books or heard him speak came to him for advice or to ask for his prayers. It was an apostolate not unlike what Luke records of St. Paul in the final chapter of the Acts: "He welcomed all who came to him, . . . teaching about the Lord Jesus Christ quite openly and unhindered" (Acts 28:31).

Despite all this, it was sadly evident that during these Kenya years Barnabas' physical and mental powers were declining. The famous memory, once incapable of forgetting either a Hebrew word or a student's name, was visibly failing. The golden tongue grew silent. Instead of his former effortless eloquence, he was now tightly bound to his prepared scripts—and these he could read only with difficulty because of advancing glaucoma. Toward the end of this period, he would often stop in the middle of a lecture, or while celebrating Mass, quite confused, bereft of words, unsure of where he was. When, in the summer of 1989, he returned to the United States, his last reserves of energy and memory had been spent. Accompanying him on his departure from Nairobi, I took comfort in recalling the solid and generous contribution Barnabas had made in earlier decades, for others' progress and joy in the faith.

HIS CONTRIBUTION AS A WRITER

His publications, although relatively few for a scholar of his international repute, have a quite distinctive flavor. In them, erudition is always at the service of spiritual uplift and encouragement. Even early on this was evident in the theme of his doctoral thesis in Sacred Scripture, "The Power of His Resurrection and Fellowship in His Sufferings," a treatment of the Pauline spirituality of sharing in the passion of Christ. His main concern was to relate the biblical message to a living spirituality for Christians today.

This concern glows consistently through various essays he wrote during the 1950s and early 1960s (while he taught Scripture at the Passionist theology school in Louisville, Kentucky)—essays that were collected into *New Horizons: Studies in Biblical Theology* (1963). This book adopts what John Mackay of Princeton Seminary praised as a "luminous, poetic style . . . to unfold the thrilling reality of the new life in Christ." It radiates a happy confidence in the new insights gained by Catholic biblical scholarship in the years leading up to the Second Vatican Council. Barnabas gave his firm support to reading the Old Testament as the spiritual story of God's people, rather than as strict history. Genesis 1–11 is Israel's mature *meditation* on the human condition rather than a factual, historical description of humanity's earliest phase. The patriarchal stories and the Exodus saga may have a nucleus of fact, but their thrust is to provide background and meaningful promptings for the later life of God's people. His chapter on the *anawim* spirit of the Old Testament saints further highlights this desire to bridge the gap between then and now. Barnabas lauds this ideal of the "humble, lowly ones, steeped in a spirit of utter dependency on Yahweh" and finds it perfectly enshrined in Mary, the most faithful among the descendants of Abraham. In turn, she becomes a guiding ideal for all followers of Jesus, her Son. Each chapter of the book shows an urgency to link the insights of current exegesis to people's urgent need for spiritual ideals. Expressed in a cheerful, animated style, these articles read as freshly today as when they were penned over thirty years ago.

His estimate of current trends in Gospel studies was mainly positive, although he expressed very sensible caution about the skeptical trend in form criticism. Convinced of the value of redactional studies, he shared a great delight in each evangelist's individuality of style and theological emphasis. He was happy to apply the concept of *midrash* to Matthew's infancy stories and to allow a wide measure of creativity to Luke for all material preceding the public ministry of Jesus. On Rudolf Bultmann's project of demythologizing the Gospels, he held a well-nuanced position. While many scholars, Protestant as well as Catholic, were still reacting in shock to this assault on Gospel historicity, Barnabas pointed to some merits in the project. These included its quest for existential relevancy and the role it ascribed to the early Christian community in shaping the message from which the Gospels were written. At the same time, he strongly resisted Bultmann's idea that the community—through its prophets—simply invented stories and sayings and then attributed them to Jesus. In *New Light on the Gospels* [See Chapter 6 of this book.] Barnabas anticipated to a remarkable degree the position taken in the 1964 *Instruction* from the Pontifical Biblical Commission, which was later summarized into no. 19 of the Constitution *Dei Verbum* (on divine revelation) from Vatican II (1965). As a theological *peritus* (expert) at the council, Barnabas had the opportunity to uphold his views before various groups of bishops. He was even able to shape the form of *Dei Verbum*, the most significant Catholic document about the Scriptures and about divine revelation in general.

In other essays following Vatican II, Barnabas often mined the epistles of St. Paul for themes relating to Christian maturity. In one way or another, most of his writing consists of commentary on, and applications of, Pauline spirituality. Troubled by the signs of vocational instability among priests and religious, as well as among married people, he focused attention on Christ's passion as a paradigm for steadfastness and dedication to God. His later writings are all tinged with this anxiety about what he saw as excessive egoism and self-assertion within the Church, a trend so counter to the humble, prayerful, and self-giving spirit that is vital for true Christian community.

A GIFTED AND TIRELESS LECTURER

It was as a speaker rather than as a writer that Barnabas made his main contribution to the love of the Bible among Catholics. His charism of lively, persuasive speech was such that many hearers in many lands truly gained a glimpse of new horizons; "Did not our hearts burn within us, as he opened for us the scriptures?" (Luke 24:32). Already well established by the early 1960s as a lecturer and retreat master within the United States, he gained a much wider audience during and after the Vatican Council, which he attended as theological advisor to Cardinal Meyer of Chicago. Because of his combined qualities of scholarship and sound spirituality, he was much in demand as a speaker to groups of bishops during the council itself. One of his most celebrated, and no doubt influential, talks was to the hierarchy of the United States on the current state of Scripture studies. This address surely helped them to endorse the Constitution on Divine Revelation, with its liberating vision of the Scriptures as a message of salvation.

From 1963 until the early 1970s, Barnabas' lecturing circuit took him several times around the English-speaking world, including Britain and Ireland, Australia and Africa, plus many missionary groups working in places as far afield as Japan, Korea, India, and South America. During that time he did much to promote people's confidence in the changes of emphasis achieved at Vatican II and, especially, to commend the reading of Scripture as a vital aid to a truly Catholic spirituality.

His talks were always well structured, based on a solid scholarly foundation and yet enlivened by all kinds of stories and comparisons from everyday life, from the recent council, and, quite often, from the lives of the saints. Speaking rapidly, in a voice high-pitched with excitement, he linked the biblical world with our own deepest experiences, convinced that despite the gap of centuries and differences of language, culture, and custom, there are certain basic needs and aspirations ("univocal constants") that are shared by all human beings in relation to life and death and ultimate destiny. But to keep the material from becoming dull from sustained intensity, he would often punctuate his talk with a humorous aside about the human foibles of patriarch, prophet, or apostle. When Barnabas began a sentence with "Why, you might always say that . . ." the audience could be assured of laughter to follow, after which diversion their attention could focus afresh on the main theme.

Part of his charm as a lecturer was his unfailing courtesy. He projected love and respect towards his audience, both as a group and as individual questioners. If he called us to dialogue with the biblical story, it was in order to give an extra dimension of meaning to our lives. The scholarly mantle—his familiarity with Semitic languages and literary forms, with Catholic church history and theology, including an impressive grasp of the *Summa* of Thomas Aquinas—was lightly worn, and references to these sources were often prefaced with a phrase like, "as you already know, Fathers. . . ." At question-time, he would treat each query as significant, perceptive, or "acute," and showed great willingness—unusual among academic theologians—to handle the pastoral implications of the biblical themes. This kindly tone extended also to whatever persons he might mention in illustrating a particular point. It would be "dear, kindly Pope John" or "that profound Jesuit thinker, Karl Rahner" or (ecumenically) "my good Lutheran friend, Dr. Krister Stendahl."

On matters ecclesial, his tone was always respectful towards well-established Catholic traditions, and also towards the leadership, including arch-conservative prelates with whose views he might be in strongest disagreement. He even found words of praise for that Irish bishop who flatly excluded Barnabas from lecturing in his diocese because "he might disturb the faith of the simple people in the truth of the Gospel!" At the same time, his enthusiasm for the ecumenical understanding of Scripture was very marked. I remember how well his lectures were appreciated by various Protestant clerics, both in Ireland and Scotland, back in the 1960s. He seemed to enshrine the very spirit of Vatican II in his understanding of the Church.

A LIVING, BIBLE-BASED SPIRITUALITY

His primary aim was to impart to his audiences and his readers not just *information* but a life-enhancing, Christ-centered, and ecclesially loyal *spirituality* grounded in the Scriptures. For him, there was no genuine hearing of God's Word which did not place the hearer's life under judgment and the call to conversion. Accordingly, while based in Rome during the 1970s, he was glad to teach at the Gregorian University's Institute of Spirituality and also at Regina Mundi, a center of spiritual renewal for missionary sisters. Throughout this time, too, he attended numerous meetings of the Pontifical Biblical Commission, where he held the prestigious position of consultor.

His confreres can attest to his unusual commitment to prayer, both the communal recital of the Divine Office and the daily periods of silent meditation that are part of the Passionist tradition. This daily attendance at prayer, even in the midst of so many outward commitments, was eloquent testimony to his personal value system. It lent added moral force to his teaching about a spirituality based in the Scriptures.

PERIOD OF ANXIETY AND SECLUSION

Somewhere along the line during the end of his period in Rome, Barnabas' earlier buoyancy began to yield place to an increasing anxiety about negative trends in the Church and in society. Several factors may have contributed to this darker outlook, among them his failing eyesight and other problems with his health, as well as the increasing incidence of conflict between theologians and the Holy See, to which he was intensely loyal. He was unhappy with the continuing rate of departures from celibacy and the religious life. He was bothered by the ongoing resistance to the encyclical *Humanae Vitae* and the corresponding insistence on personal choice unhindered by papal moral teaching. He was also upset by the growing stress on a "Christology from Below," which seemed to reject belief in the divinity of Christ.

A possible response to this kind of distress might be to mount a campaign of bitter invective, to raise voice and pen in denouncing the trends of which one disapproved. This was not Barnabas' way. Instead, like Elijah, he chose the desert route towards the mountain of God, going to join the Passionist "community of prayer and solitude" in Bedford, Pennsylvania, where he spent the years 1984–1987. It was from there that, aged 72, he was called by his Superior General to join the recently established house of studies in Nairobi and teach Scripture to young African students for the priesthood. With very little hesitation, he left behind the treasured quiet of Bedford and set out for Kenya, where he would spend the last two years of his active ministry. By the end of that period, his health had visibly deteriorated and he began to show the early stages of the dreadful Alzheimer's disease which would gradually carry him away from the awareness of the world about him. One could only trust that even in this distressful situation, he had some experience of that truth he held so dear: "My grace is sufficient for you, for my power is made perfect in infirmity" (2 Cor 12:9).

"HIS MEMORY SHALL BE HELD IN HONOR"

Father Barnabas' contribution to the Catholic biblical revival, from the 1950s onward, was much greater than would appear from the relatively modest quantity of published work. The extracts from his work included in this volume do, however, convey something of the pastoral zeal and communicative skill which he brought to bear in expounding the Scriptures. His unusual flair for words and imagery would compel the reader's attention to the revealed message. More than most theologians of his generation, he succeeded in presenting the Bible as a relevant living and exciting word, addressed to the modern hearer in all the complexities of our late twentieth-century existence. As thousands of listeners can attest, he shared not just information but enthusiasm for the Scriptures. His special mix of scholarship, spiritual fervor, and love of the Church helped to dispel many residual Catholic prejudices that the Bible was somehow a

"Protestant" book, mainly producing doubt and dissension. For him, it was an inexhaustible source of inspiration for life and prayer because it provided a privileged access to the mind and heart of Christ. Even in the somber mood of his latter years, his love for the Word of God remained undimmed. It is this faith-filled, hopeful approach to the Word that should—and will—be remembered of Father Barnabas. May his memory be long held in honor by his many friends among the people of God.

CHAPTER 3

The Prophet's Challenge: Barnabas M. Ahern and Vatican II

James P. Roache

There is a proverb that says: "People shouldn't hope too much for anything. They might just end up getting it!" When I thought of Fr. Barnabas Ahern and his impact on Vatican II and Vatican II's impact on him, this proverb came to mind. I ran it by a few folks. Each one improved on it.

A scholarly Jesuit put it in the framework of St. Thérèse: "Be careful what you pray for. You just might end up getting it." But a biblical Passionist added yet another dimension. "Perhaps it's like the prophet's destiny. You get it—but differently—the way God wants it to be."

Father Ahern set some of the council foundations by years of "pre-evangelization," with sisters and priests especially. He helped build the dream. And when the dream became a reality, he found himself in key positions to help direct the shape and outcomes of the council. Later, he was to have second thoughts and was seen wringing his hands over the "evil that had been unleashed." Was this the blessing and the curse of his destiny? Did God reach through and beyond Barnabas' dreams and ideas? Did God deliver something different than was imagined?

IN THE SHADOW OF MOSES

It has been suggested that the biblical model for Barnabas at the council would be Moses. Barnabas surely would shy away from any such comparison. But both were called upon by God to lead people in a time of transition, to urge people to keep God's Word at the center of their journey.

Each of their lives might be divided into three main segments: preparation and mature years; doubt and disappointments; stopping in frustration, short of their main goal.

In *stage one*, Moses flees from the courts of Pharaoh in Egypt for the rugged lifestyle of the Midianites in the Sinai desert, to prepare for the heroic task of leading God's people Israel out of Egyptian slavery (Exod 2, 3). Moses returns to Egypt, confronts the divine Pharaoh, leads Israel triumphantly through the Red Sea to Sinai the Mountain of God (Exod 14, 15), and there receives the new, liberating covenant of Israel with the Lord (Exod 19–24). Surrounding this moment at Mount Sinai, the biblical text speaks of the murmuring and fears of the people, their longing to return to the way things were, and their serious repudiation of the covenant as told in chapter 32 of the Book of Exodus. For Father Barnabas, *stage one* consisted in his training for the biblical apostolate, his early lectures to priests and religious, and finally Barnabas' strenuous activity at Vatican II—arguing, reasoning, and writing initial drafts for what became a new, liberating charter of life for the Roman Catholic Church and apostolate, the documents of Vatican II.

The *next stage* came unexpectedly: for Moses, when further problems, some wrong directions, and still more murmuring exploded in his face. We read of these in the Book of Numbers, chapters 11 through 14. Here Moses is confronted with jealousy even from his own family; the people long for the leeks, garlic, and onions of Egypt; and everyone rejects the advice of Moses for entering the Land of Promise after scouts had been sent ahead. Moses' source of support collapses with the deaths of his sister Miriam and his brother Aaron (Num 20); and, in this latter chapter, Moses himself, the giant of holiness, doubts and hesitates before following God's advice to strike the rock. For Barnabas, the *second stage* of his conciliar journey came with his disappointment over events and directions in Church life after the council. These turned his own instincts of piety and ministry upside down. This once courageous man became fearful. Some say this once hopeful person became somewhat embittered. Around this time, he also lost a main support with the untimely death of Albert Cardinal Meyer.

The *final stage* in Moses' career comes in Deuteronomy 34. God leads him up Mount Nebo, with a view on a very clear day as far north as Mount Hermon and, in between, the plateau of Gilead. With longing, Moses imagined himself seeing "Ephraim and Manasseh, all the land of Judah as far as the Western Sea, the Negeb, [and immediately below him] the circuit of the Jordan with the lowlands at Jericho, the city of Palms, as far as Zoar." After letting Moses view the entire Promised Land, God says to him:

> This is the land that I swore to Abraham, Isaac, and Jacob that I would give to their descendants. I have let you feast your eyes upon it, but you shall not cross over (Deut 34:4).

No one reads without sadness the pathetic but heroic statement which follows:

> So there, in the land of Moab, Moses the servant of the Lord, died, as the Lord had said (Deut 34:5).

Moses died without reaching the goal of his life. Or better, the goal as he first imagined it in his commissioning by God in Exodus 3. Had Moses hoped for too much, and did he get it, *only differently* than he had dreamed? Barnabas Ahern's hopes for the council turned out differently. Was he again a shadow figure of Moses in the twilight days of his life?

A SCHOLAR AND TEACHER

The proverb quoted above, about hoping for too much and getting it, begins early in the journey of Barnabas Mary Ahern. Like the Barnabas before him in the Acts of the Apostles, a man of generous encouragement (Acts 4:36-37), "a good man filled with the Holy Spirit and faith" (Acts 11:24), Barnabas Ahern was somewhat of a trailblazer. Much of the work of his teaching ministry and scholarship helped pave the way towards the surprise of the Second Vatican Council. He was not only the right person in the right place and time—one of many who helped shape the council; he had also been preparing a cadre of people to be prepared for the startling events set in motion by John XXIII.

Barnabas believed there was nothing to fear in knowledge. He spoke to many priests, religious, and laity in the 1940s and 1950s preparing them for the 1960s. His summer courses for women religious put many sisters in a much better position than their priest contemporaries to understand and accept the new directions resulting from conciliar decisions. But priests and laity as well had been the beneficiary of his efforts to encourage "continuing education." The last exam in the seminary or the last religious education course one had taken was not the final word. The Spirit is still revealing God's presence in new ways. The Spirit interpenetrates the spirit of our times.

A PASSION FOR THE TRULY REAL

To pursue his dream of continuing to open up minds and hearts, Barnabas had to pay a price. In presenting his historical-critical method of approaching the Scriptures, he unsettled many people who thought they "had it all together" when they passed that final exam.

Some of these were people of power and influence in the Church. There was concern that his method of approaching Scripture studies would disturb or destroy faith. How far does one go in demythologizing? When does a "modern" approach become "modernism"?

Barnabas was well aware of the dangers, as we read more extensively in the third part of this book:

> This is our *Zeitgeist*, to feel for the real; it is becoming more and more the spirit of the Church....
>
> The spirit can lead to unwarranted iconoclasm. The devouring flame of passion for the real can destroy not only the rind but the fruit, not only the shell but the nut-meat which it encases. In biblical studies we have had to save the Bible from the devastating fire of *Entmythologiezung* or "demythologization." Under the influence of the existential philosophy of Heidegger, men like Rudolph Bultmann and Martin Dibelius have so demythologized the gospels that they have left us only the shadow of a merely human Jesus and the meaningless memory of a life without content or challenge.
>
> This same spirit, on the other hand, if only it cherishes respect for what is truly real, truly unchanging, truly the teaching of the Church, is bound to bring out what is richest in the Church's life. For the Holy Spirit is breathing in the *Zeitgeist* of our times, giving the power of divine grace to our human search for the real....

Barnabas was equally aware of those who were disturbed by the challenge of change. Here we quote from an article of his in Chapter 8 of this book: "Nothing is too time-honored or too sacred to escape the fire of passion for the real. Authority may still impose the attitudes of yesteryear; it cannot shut the seeing eye nor trammel the piercing mind."

There was a mildness, a meekness in his way of presenting an idea. The same was true of Moses, the biblical model with whom we compared Barnabas at the beginning of this chapter. Moses, as we read in Numbers 12:3, was canonized as "by far the meekest person on the face of the earth." When you turn the words and ideas of Barnabas Ahern around in your mind, when you parse them, test them, it is surprising what fierce strength is contained in that meek and mild presentation. So too it was with Moses.

Though there were enemies out there—some real, some imagined—Barnabas was to find himself aligned with many of his heroes as he participated in various levels at the Second Vatican Council. He was a *peritus*, a learned assistant to Albert Cardinal Meyer. He was also to become part of the International Theological Council. He wrote, as again we find in Chapter 8 of this book, about some of these heroes. He was proud to identify himself with them:

> True theologians like Karl Rahner, Yves Congar, Jean Danielou, Henri de Lubac, and in our own country, John Courtney Murray, Gustav Weigel, Godfrey Diekmann, and George Tavard appear to some as making shipwreck of the faith. The simple truth is that they are people of our time—with a passionate zeal to uncover the real. Dogmatic teaching is the frail human expression of divinely revealed truth. Like everything human, its tone, color, and wording must be perfected if we are to convey to others our new grasp of what is real in the heart of God's mystery.

There was a certain heady atmosphere in the days of the council and shortly thereafter. Issues that were close to Barnabas' heart had become accepted by the universal Church—if not by a number of individuals in the Church—much more swiftly than anticipated. When Cardinal Meyer addressed the clergy of the Archdiocese of Chicago in December of 1963, he predicted that the Breviary would one day be in English—"but not in my lifetime or yours," he added.

A PROPHETIC VOICE FOR REFORM

But within only a few short months, the vernacular was part of the liturgical reform swept in by the council. Perhaps ideas were shifting too quickly. Perhaps there wasn't adequate time for assimilation. Certainly, there were the nay-sayers. "It's always been done the way we've done it. Why change now? And if this can be changed so easily, what do we really have to hold on to?"

To these Barnabas had a ready response:

> Those who find comfort in the old order will shout insubordination, heresy—as the Old Testament priests shouted heresy before the realism of the prophet Jeremiah's preaching (Jer 26:8). But this cry is only the gasp of a dying order. The living power of new wine, the wine of the Spirit, will burst the old wine bags.
>
> Look around our country. The renewal of religious life is here to stay. Liturgical participation is a force which nothing will check. Go to any convention—the biblical, the theological, the liturgical, the mariological—and you will see that the new wine is in ferment. More and more this spirit is coming into seminaries and theological schools which means it is the spirit of tomorrow. Look at the periodicals which are alive to what is best in the Church—*Theological Studies, Theology Digest, Worship, Nouvelle Revue Théologique*. This is the thinking of theologians guided by the Spirit; and the thought of the scholar penetrates inevitably to the people. What our great religious minds are thinking today, our people will be thinking tomorrow.

The words and the spirit echo biblical prophets. In some ways, Barnabas, the student of prophets, would wear that mantle—as we see in Chapter 8 of this book. At times his oblique phrases and hesitant tone make one think of the prophets of old. He spoke in admiration of one of the council fathers, Bernard Cardinal Alfrink, indeed comparing him to the "prophets of old":

> Cardinal Alfrink's words at Strasbourg will stir opposition in people who are suspicious of the new spirit and who prefer to live in the secure mold and comfortable patterns of the past. On the other hand, those who live vibrantly in the spirit of today will hear in the Cardinal's words a truth of deep, solid reality. He asks: "Could it not be that love for the Church and solicitude for non-Catholics require, in our ecumenical era, that we sacrifice certain non-essential things? Could it not be that some things, no matter how precious they might be for the Church, must be swept away because they obstruct a clear view of the Church?"
>
> In these probing questions the heart of Cardinal Alfrink is alive with the spirit of the prophets of old. And to be a prophet is a glorious vocation. Its only requirement is that one have the light of God to see reality as God sees it and the courage to move beyond rigid boundaries as Jesus did for the sake of poor people, for sick and disabled people, for foreign and dispossessed people!

"The light of God to see reality" and the "courage to move beyond rigid boundaries"! Add to that the ability to discern between the essential and "non-essential things." Easier said than done! Perhaps that is why the true gift of prophecy is sparingly given.

Prophets have to remain in place to see if what they have called for is accomplished. If they lose heart, if they have second thoughts, they send tremors into those who would follow them.

BESET BY DOUBTS

As with Moses, likewise with Barnabas. Friends and supporters died. In Numbers 20, Miriam and Aaron, brother and sister of major importance for Moses, died. For Barnabas, Albert Cardinal Meyer succumbed quickly to a brain tumor. In the same chapter 20 of Numbers, Moses, we are told, doubted and hesitated in following God's orders to strike the rock for supplying water to a contentious people. Barnabas shifted into the next stage of his life's ministry, stricken with hesitation, fear, and unhappiness over the course of events in the Church. His attitude towards the council shifted dramatically.

In researching his book *This Confident Church*, Fr. Steven Avella interviewed Barnabas in September of 1984. Barnabas had already left Rome and was residing at a House of Prayer where the daily schedule was almost exactly the same as in Passionist monasteries before the council. Father Avella was interested in the role Barnabas Ahern had when serving as a *peritus* to Cardinal Meyer. Barnabas had aged some, and it is also possible that the aging process had affected that great mind. What Father Avella uncovered was what others also noted in the post-conciliar Barnabas.

Summing up his interview, Father Avella simply says he was struck by the "sadness of Ahern's life. . . . He really did believe he played a major role in unleashing the force of evil in the Church" (Avella, letter to the author, March 31, 1993).

In the interview, Barnabas puts these thoughts sometimes directly, sometimes indirectly. In one response he says:

> I personally felt it was a great mercy that he died when he did because I think poor dear Cardinal Meyer never could have lived through that traumatic agony the Church had to go through and so many of these priests leaving the priesthood—that would have been to him incomprehensible. I think the Lord spared him. . . .

And again:

> As far as Cardinal Meyer and what happened after the council, I think I've already expressed my own view that I wondered if he wouldn't have found it very difficult to cope with the post-conciliar confusion. I may be wrong on that. He maybe would have been able to handle it beautifully—but I just feel he was so committed to a vision of the ministry and the vision of the priesthood, the vision of seminary formation to the priesthood, I wonder if he really would have been able to cope. I don't know—I may be all wrong.

What happened to those earlier words of Barnabas?

> Hence we must open wide the windows of our seminaries and theological schools that the life-giving spirit of the Church may become the breath of our vocation and the vitalizing power of all its sacred forms. If we close our eyes to the light of the Church, and shut off our concern from the interests of the Church, we shall die. We are committed to ecumenism, to the revival of liturgy, to the activation of the laity, to the mission-mindedness of the modern Church, to its yearning for peace, to its sense of realized eschatology, to its awareness of all life as a sacrament. Thus, concerns of the Church must be our concerns. The advance of the Church must be our advance. . . .

The light to see reality—the courage to move—to know what is essential and what is not.

There was a political side to Barnabas that shines through in the Avella interview. Barnabas is quick to point out whether a particular council member or theologian is lined up with the "conservative" or "liberal" wing of the council. He never gives any indication as to where he would position himself. Indeed, he stresses how he wished to be a resource to both sides, a confidante to such disparate figures as Cardinals Ottaviani and Bea. One vignette is especially revealing:

> I remember, at one of these meetings, I remember very poignantly—I had been a very good friend of Msgr. Clifford Fenton and also Father [Francis] Connell, the Redemptorist—he taught moral theology at Catholic University. I had been very good friends of theirs and I was trying to very much keep this friendship, you see, because they were very conservative people as you know—both of them are dead now, the Lord be good to them. Butch Fenton, Butch is what we called him, was on the theological commission; and so it was that I was on this unity secretariat. This particular night it had really come to quite an impasse

and Cardinal Bea had suggested that we, the members of the secretariat staff, leave the hall in order to discuss among ourselves what we thought should be the answer to the difficulties that had been raised and so we got up and walked out through this very narrow door. That was alright because my back remained to the audience in the hall. But then when we came back into the room, we could come out only in single file, one at a time, the door was so narrow. And I remember there was a light, as it were, shining very brightly on this door so when I came I thought, Oh Lord, here I am revealed in all my duplicity. I knew that Butch Fenton would see me, being with what he considered that horrible group of the secretariat community. . . . So the meeting came to an end and I worked my way to the third floor of the Vatican. I went to the elevator and there was Butch. Well, he opened up on me and he said, "Oh, what a traitor. You're nothing but a Judas." He went after me. Well, the thing was, heaven help us, a little voice said, if you can't speak gracefully at least try to act with grace—so I fled. Do you know this staircase in the Vatican? Well, down this gigantic staircase I was taking four steps at a time, leaping down; and I'll never forget, when I got down to the bottom floor I went out and it was pitch dark and all I could think of was that text from John's gospel, "And it was night."

IN SIGHT OF THE PROMISED LAND

Barnabas made many significant contributions to the Church, local and universal. He obviously influenced influential people in the council. He lived to see many of his dreams become reality both for woe and for weal. In some ways he is a paradigm of that pre-conciliar, conciliar, and post-conciliar Church.

Much work had to go into preparations for that which was to become the council. With the surprise of the Spirit, an elderly Pope called the world-Church together. Many who had been outsiders became insiders. Those who had been, as it were, preparing all their life for something that might never happen, were given an opportunity.

Extraordinary things happened in those few years in the 1960s. Karl Rahner, speaking at Cambridge in 1979, described the event as the "coming-to-be of a world Church—a theological break in Church history that still lacks conceptual clarity and can scarcely be compared with anything except the transition from Jewish to Gentile Christianity." For Rahner, there were only two caesuras or breaks in history. The first, when Paul was the protagonist for changing a Church of Jews to a Church of Gentiles. The second, he saw as Vatican II, an epoch of qualitative change, "the Church's first official self-actualization *as* a world Church."

What ramifications does this suggest, what ramblings, what challenges, what fall-out, what shifts! It is not a matter of good housekeeping or tiny steps forward. It *is* a time for courage, vision, and discernment.

THE VISION OF THE PROPHET

What has occurred since then shouts at us from a T-shirt I saw some time ago: "Keep the rumor alive—Vatican II lives!" Beneath the surface, like a great lava flow, there is something still simmering, still bubbling, still alive. What is needed is the vision, the courage, the ability to distinguish the essentials.

The vision lay before Moses as he died on Mount Nebo. We began this chapter comparing Barnabas Ahern with Moses. Each of them in this, the *third and final stage* of their careers, tasted a certain bitterness, a sigh of disappointment, and failure in the heart. Did they think: Perhaps they had hoped for the wrong thing? Is this the way it was to end?

At what point did each decide, "This is essential. This is not"? Is it an issue of judgment or courage? Is there a temptation to constrain a divine plan by a human vision? The surprise of the Spirit will always be that—a surprise! And when it happens, the courageous must discern and stand by what is essential and set aside what is not essential.

Moses, despite his hesitance, remains prophet par excellence. "No prophet had arisen in Israel like Moses," we read in the final lines of Deuteronomy.

This book, too, is a tribute to a prophet who calls us to visions beyond our ability, giving his lifetime toward their accomplishment. He helped the Church in Chicago, the United States, and thus the broader international community to new insights and a new perception of the Bible's message for today's Church.

He planted seeds. He formed disciples. He left a legacy. Somewhere in the sub-soil of the Church there is movement, a shifting, a powerful energy that takes us both backward and forward. And there must be prophets to lead the way with vision and courage.

Part II
Interpreting the Bible

But you, remain faithful to what you have learned and believed, because you know from whom you learned it, and that from infancy you have known the sacred scriptures, which are capable of giving you wisdom for salvation through faith in Christ Jesus. All Scripture is inspired by God and is useful for teaching, for reputation, for correction and for training in righteousness, so that one who belongs to God may be competent, equipped for every good work (2 Tim 3:14-16).

CHAPTER 4

New Horizons in Sacred Scripture

Many pastoral ministers feel a tension between what seems the obvious meaning of Scripture and what they hear of modern biblical advances. The so-called "new-approach," when first discussed, creates wonderment. Only too often the natural reaction of consternation crystallizes into doubt and suspicion.

The first step to be taken in justifying or explaining the change which has taken place is to assess correctly and sincerely both the challenge and the opportunity of the day in which we live. Pope Pius XII clearly recognized the exigencies of our time and wrote of them in *Divino Afflante Spiritu*:

> Quite wrongly, therefore, do some pretend, not rightly understanding the conditions of biblical study, that nothing remains to be added by the Catholic exegete of our time to what Christian antiquity has produced; since on the contrary, these our times have brought to light so many things which call for a fresh investigation and a new examination and which stimulate not a little the practical zeal of the present-day interpreter. As in our day indeed new questions and new difficulties are multiplied, so by God's favor, new means and aids to exegesis are also provided.

To fully appreciate the Pope's words it is necessary to trace the odyssey of biblical studies in the Church since before the turn of the century.

FACING THE AGE OF ENLIGHTENMENT

At the turn of the century, the Holy See faced a critical situation. The age of Enlightenment had flooded the world of thought with a rationalism which traced all religion to merely natural causes. Nineteenth-century philosophy left no room for the God of revelation or the intervention of the truly supernatural. Religious concepts were explained as the emergent of a natural process of evolution and as the expression of merely human sentiment.

This mentality was bound to influence biblical studies. Looking back now on the Graf-Wellhausen analysis of the sacred books, we find some elements which are worthwhile for the study of the text as a piece of literature. Much of this work, however, was spoiled by the pervasive naturalistic postulate that Israel's religion must have begun in the lower forms of animism and totemism and reached its lofty ethos only through the creative activity of the highly endowed prophets.

In New Testament studies it was the same. The Gospel materials were explained in accord with a preconceived plan which excluded the supernatural. How consummately beautiful a life of Christ, Renan would have written were he not Renan the *philosopher*. And what would Strauss not have achieved in his *Das Leben Jesu* had he not followed the Tübingen school. The Hegelian principle of thesis, antithesis, and synthesis ruled biblical theology. Illuminating insights into the mind and doctrine of Paul were twisted out of focus by scholars like Bousset and Loisy who could admit no form of Christianity except an emergent of syncretism.

Both in the nineteenth century and in the first decades of our century, the Church had to ride out a storm of doctrinal error. Therefore, in this age of uncertainty, she did what seemed the most prudent thing she could. She battened down the hatches with disciplinary decrees which imposed obedient conformity to the tested, traditional opinion. One by one the biblical commission issued decrees covering the various literary theses which were being advanced both within and without the Church. As we know today, the commission was concerned not with the literary position as such but with the false doctrinal principles which often prompted or spoiled it. In 1912, for example, the classic "two-source" theory was proscribed not because it is an impossible solution of the synoptic problem but because it had become the facile tool of men like William Wrede who, in his *Messiasgeheimnis*, denied the historical character of the Gospel picture of Jesus.

Unfortunately the commission decrees were sometimes wrongly interpreted by overzealous members of the Church; the carefully worded decree was explained as imposing a greater restriction than it actually did. So too the official prudent attitude of the Church was sometimes gravely exaggerated by subaltern officers who favored a system of inquisitorial surveillance. The Sodalitium Pianum of the pontificate of Pope St. Pius X exercised a vigilance which far exceeded the authority given it by the Pope and showed itself too ready to favor suspicion and turn it into open attack. As a monsignor of the Roman Curia, Giacomo della Chiesa opposed the methods of the Sodalitium and one of his first moves on becoming pope as Benedict XV was to dissolve this group.

DEFENSIVE ATMOSPHERE

In the first decades of the present century, Catholic biblical scholars, according to John L. McKenzie, lived in the "defensive atmosphere of the beleaguered fortress in which creative scholarship was extremely unlikely." That is why a bibliography of representative Catholic works during these years evidences so little productivity. Catholic scholars feared to write about biblical problems except in the defensive spirit of refuting the critics. Those who in the beginning were hardy enough to propose new views—Lagrange, Von Hummelauer, Prat—were called to task. This attitude was bound to limit the advance of scriptural studies.

It also colored the training which many priests received in their seminary courses. In studying Cornely-Merk, for instance, they kept their eye much more to the "adversaries" than to the Bible itself. The four traditions of the Pentateuch, spoken of under the code of JEDP, spelled only one concept: the machinations of modernism. Seminarians thought and studied in a city under siege.

Life, however, was on the move.

During the years when Catholic scholars were maintaining a prudent and respectful silence, advance was being made in areas of scientific discovery intimately connected with the Bible.

ARCHAEOLOGICAL DISCOVERIES

Studies in anthropology and the stratification of the earth's surface led to conclusions which differed from the biblical story of the origin of earth and humanity. At the same time, newly discovered libraries in Mesopotamia yielded the Enuma Elish story of creation and the Gilgamesh epic with its flood story. No one could miss the conceptual and verbal resemblances between these sources and the early chapters of Genesis. The biblical author used the imagery and thought patterns of Mesopotamia, the home of ancestors Abraham and Sarah, to express the transcendent truths of Israel's faith.

The story of Abraham (Gen 12–25) also took on new meaning in the light of modern discovery. Sir Leonard Woolley's excavations at Ur, study of the Code of Hammurabi, the deciphering of the Nuzi tablets and the Mari tablets—all this formed a large context into which the biblical story of Abraham and Sarah fitted.

In 1929, a whole library of Canaanite or Ugaritic literature was unearthed at Ras Shamra along the Phoenician coast. Deciphered by Bauer and Dhorme in 1930–1931, the language of the Ugaritic tablets has helped to explain the meaning of many Hebrew words, while the imagery and legends and psalm patterns have shed light on many places in Old Testament prophecy and poetry.

The history of the conquest of Canaan and the story of Israel's life in the promised land have been progressively illumined by discoveries which amplified, explained, and altered the biblical picture. The excavations at Jericho by John Garstang and Kathleen Kenyon have provided a commentary on the Bible story of Israel's entry into the promised land and the fall of Jericho.

Allusions to the Apiru in the Tell el Amarna letters, the correspondence between Palestine and Egypt prior to the coming of the Israelites, have led scholars to ask whether all twelve Israelite tribes entered Canaan at the time of the conquest. The surprises which Marquet-Krause unearthed in her excavations at Hai and William Foxwell Albright at Tel ed-Duweir have created a problem for those who would find in the Book of Joshua documented history of the Mommsen-Von Ranke style.

Work in ceramics enabled Flinders Petrie to inaugurate a rather elaborate system of pottery-dating which presents an important control for biblical chronology. The discovery of the Moabite stone of King Mesa by F. A. Klein brought a sizable contribution to our knowledge of the style of Semitic war reports.

Egypt also yielded a vast store of literature to contribute new areas of investigation. The Egyptian legend of the Two Brothers bears a marked parallel to the story of Joseph in the house of Potiphar. The Wisdom of Amenemope may have been drawn from the same source as a large portion in our canonical Book of Proverbs (22:17–23:11). The hymn to the Sun of Akhenaton bears its analogies to our Psalm 104. The Merneptah stela (ca. 1220 B.C.E.) sheds light on the period of

Moses, while the inscription of Sheshak I (ca. 930 B.C.E.) illuminates the period of Rehoboam.

LITERARY STUDIES

Together with these advances in knowledge of the biblical world, studies continued on the literary structure of the books themselves. Eminent biblicists, through objective and scholarly application of the principles of literary criticism, found more and more reason to support the thesis that the Pentateuch or five books of Moses was a skillful editorial tapestry of four strands of tradition—the Yahwist source (J) dating from around 950 B.C.E., the Elohist source (E) from around 850 B.C.E., the Deuteronomist source (D) from around 650 B.C.E., and the Priestly source (P) from the period at the end of the Exile. In spite of minor disagreements, there was a growing consensus view on the number and nature of these traditions, their place of origin, and the conceptual and stylistic characteristics of each.

So too authors found more and more reason to support the critical thesis that the books of Isaiah and Zechariah did not come from one author but rather were made up of several parts composed at widely different periods.

This literary study of the Scriptures took on new impetus through increased attention to the Jewish literature which was contemporary with the composition of the later books of the Old Testament and the whole New Testament. Large parts of the Bible were seen to bear striking resemblance to the literary forms in which the contemporary Jewish world gave expression to its history, its doctrine, and its hopes. Both canonical and noncanonical writings offer moral instructions in the rabbinical pattern of *halakoth*; they explain doctrine with pious stories, along the lines of rabbinical *midrashim*.

All these discoveries and new insights forced upon scholars the awareness that the Bible did not originate in a vacuum. Rather, it grew out of an ambient; biblical authors drew both their imagery and their thought patterns from the milieu in which they lived. Scholars knew, therefore, that the Bible had to be studied in the spirit in which it had been written. To try to explain it without attention to its human origin could never pass as true currency in the market of science.

Catholic scholars were aware of this new mentality. Many among them were anxious to utilize the newly discovered material and had even begun to do so. In 1890, Père M.-J. Lagrange, O.P., [Editor's note:

As discussed in Chapter 9] had opened l'Ecole Biblique in Jerusalem as a center for higher Scripture studies; and in 1892 he began the publication of the *Revue Biblique* as an organ for scholarly Scripture writing. For many years, however, Père Lagrange and those with him could not and did not write all that they felt should be said. As it was, Lagrange's writing was always suspect. His own superiors withdrew him from work on the Old Testament, while an ecclesiastical decree withdrew his New Testament commentaries from classroom use in seminaries.

The tension between the ultraconservative element in the Church and the progressive Scripture scholars rose to a crisis in 1941 when Dom Dolindo Ruotolo, an Italian priest, circulated a pseudonymous letter among the bishops of Italy in which he openly attacked the new biblical approach. He criticized Catholic biblical scholars for (1) preferring the Hebrew and Greek originals to the Vulgate, (2) dabbling in historical and literary analysis of the Scriptures instead of resting content with work of the fathers, and (3) seeking a scientific understanding of the sacred books instead of gathering the spiritual meaning of the text as the Church has always done in her liturgical and patristic texts.

The moment of decision had come, and the biblical commission acted promptly. The congregation issued a strongly worded letter, bearing the signature of the Cardinal Secretary of the Biblical Commission, Eugene Tisserant (1941). It rebuked Dom Ruotolo sternly and condemned his reactionary spirit as inimical to true progress in understanding the Bible (see *Rome and the Study of Scripture*, 5 ed. [St. Meinrad, Ind.: The Abbey Press, 1953] 136–45).

MAGNA CARTA FOR BIBLICAL STUDIES

This was not the end. The times and the moment called for a more official pronouncement. Pope Pius XII recognized the urgent need and met it with a Magna Carta for biblical studies. In April of 1943 he issued his encyclical letter *Divino Afflante Spiritu*, in which he wholeheartedly endorsed and fully developed the blueprint laid down in the previous letter of the biblical commission. His purpose was to offer "encouragement" to biblical scholars that they might "continue with ever renewed vigor, with all zeal and care, the work so happily done."

In reference to the biblical text, Pius XII urged that scholars return to the original languages in which the Bible was written. In reference to biblical interpretation, he emphasized that the exegete must study constantly the work of early Christian writers which often shed brilliant light upon the pages of Scripture. At the same time, he pointed out that much remained to be done in the field of biblical interpretation and, for this work, students must use the precision instruments of modern scholarship. Such an approach, he writes, cannot be neglected "without serious detriment to Catholic exegesis."

He indicated, moreover, the nature of these instruments and the areas of investigation in which the modern exegete must work:

> Let the interpreter then, with all care and without neglecting any light derived from recent research, endeavor to determine the peculiar character and circumstances of the sacred writer, the age in which the author lived, the sources written or oral to which the writer had recourse and the forms of expression employed.

But Pope Pius XII was also a realist. He knew well enough that the new activity of biblical students would awaken new criticism. Therefore, he sought to ensure for them the liberty which they deserved as loyal members of the Church who love and treasure the full revelation of God as their most priceless possession. The Pope asked that there be no name-calling:

> Let all the other members of the Church bear in mind that the efforts of these resolute laborers in the vineyard of the Lord should be judged not only with equity and justice, but also with the greatest charity. All, moreover, should abhor that intemperate zeal which imagines that whatever is new should for that very reason be opposed or suspected.

In the light of this Magna Carta students of the Bible have been working in a halcyon atmosphere of peace, deftly employing the scientific instruments which Pius XII urged them to use. They bring to the Bible a familiarity with the thought patterns and customs of the ancient Near East. They are adept in using the recently discovered literature of the Semitic world to throw light on the style of writing and the literary forms employed by the sacred writers. They pay more attention than ever before to the precise spiritual doctrine and the developing theology of each part of the inspired text.

This method of Scripture study received further encouragement from the Holy See in 1948 when, in answer to the question presented by Cardinal Suhard of Paris, the biblical commission affirmed that the first eleven chapters of Genesis must be interpreted in the light of the cultural and religious milieu in which they were written.

TYPES OF CONTROL ON SCHOLARSHIP

It goes without saying that the activity of biblical scholarship is always subject to control. First of all, there is the practical daily control of scholarship itself. Among students of the Bible—both within and outside the Catholic Church—a healthy power of self-evaluation and self-criticism is always at work.

No one was so outspoken against John Allegro's unfounded interpretation of the Qumran material as his preceptor and colleague at Manchester, J. J. Rowley. When Léon Vaganay published his masterful work on the synoptic question, Lucien Cerfaux and X. Léon-Dufour praised it—with noteworthy qualifications. Others, however, like Jacques Lévie and Alfred Wikenhauser, were vocal in faulting it. Whoever follows the book reviews in scientific biblical journals will soon notice that Scripture scholars rarely give unqualified praise, readily sense a fundamental or superficial inaccuracy, and pointedly express their disapproval or disagreement.

Most important of all, there is the control of authority. The same Pius XII who wrote *Divino Afflante Spiritu* composed also the encyclical *Humani Generis* in which he corrected errors into which some authors had fallen. At any point, the Church can and will intervene whenever her action is necessary to insure doctrinal integrity or a prudential safeguarding of the peace and piety of the faithful.

There is also the control of prudence. Many problems and interpretations may be discussed in scientific journals and before trained audiences. This does not mean, however, that the same subjects may be discussed in public or written about in popular magazines. For the latter publicity two conditions must first be met: a sufficient probability in the opinion proposed and an adequate intellectual and emotional preparation in the audience.

There is, finally, the control exerted by the history of interpretation in the Church. Does the interpretation of the fathers and writers of the Church impose a fixed form of exegesis on modern biblical studies? Pope Pius XII himself answered this question. In *Divino Afflante Spiritu* he urges the Catholic exegete to seek constant help from the penetrating vision of truth which the fathers enjoyed:

> The Catholic exegete will find invaluable help in an assiduous study of those works, in which the holy fathers, the doctors of the Church and the renowned interpreters of the past have explained the sacred books. For although sometimes less instructed in profane learning and in the knowledge of languages than the scrip-

ture scholars of our time, nevertheless by reason of the office assigned to them by God in the Church, they are distinguished by a certain subtle insight into heavenly things and by a marvelous keenness of intellect, which enables them to penetrate to the very innermost meaning of the divine word and bring light to all that can help to elucidate the teaching of Christ and promote holiness of life.

TASK FOR SCHOLARSHIP TODAY

The same pope, however, points out that much is left to be accomplished by the scholar of today:

> In the immense matter contained in the sacred books—legislative, historical, sapiential, and prophetical—there are but few texts whose sense has been defined by the authority of the Church, nor are those more numerous about which the teaching of the holy fathers is unanimous. There remains, therefore, many things and of the greatest importance, in the discussion and exposition of which the skill and genius of Catholic commentators may and ought to be freely exercised, so that each may contribute one's part to the advantage of all, to continued progress of the sacred doctrine and to the defense and honor of the Church.

Here we must point out that there is often a marked difference of approach to Scripture on the part of earlier writers and the modern Scripture scholar.

Writers of the past were far more interested in teaching Catholic doctrine than in determining the precise meaning of a given Scripture passage. They were more intent on seeing the text in the whole context of the faith rather than in the context of its origin at a given moment in the developing history of revelation. Time and again, therefore, the fathers used the words of Scripture as a convenient and beautiful vehicle of expression for truths of the faith. In our own day, on the other hand, we seek to determine scientifically the exact content of each part of Scripture and its precise contribution to the corpus of revelation.

Often enough, the rules of biblical scholarship will require the exegete to abandon a longstanding interpretation either because the erudition on which it rests is no longer sound or because earlier use of the text as a carrier of doctrine has clogged its precise meaning. A typical example may be found in Job 19:25: *Credo quod redemptor meus vivit, et in novissimo die de terra surrecturus sum* (I believe that my redeemer lives, and on the last day I will rise from the earth). Many writers, relying on this faulty translation of St. Jerome, made this text the carrier for the Christian concept of bodily resurrection. The fact is that if the author of Job had a concept of bodily resurrection and of reward after death, he never would have written this problem book which owes its origin to ignorance of God's full salvific plan.

The Catholic exegete can and often must depart from certain interpretations which have been customary for a long while. But this will be no loss. For as Pope Pius XII promised, the modern interpreter will often bring to light a doctrinal insight and a wealth of theology which was not glimpsed in earlier ages. An example of this is found in the modern interpretation of the Book of Jonah. To many in times gone by this book, with its fascinating fish-story, was the tale of a great miracle wrought by God and nothing more. Once scholars came to identify its literary form as that of *midrash* (a pious story intended to teach religious truth), then the way was wide open to lighten the emphasis on the incident of the fish and to concentrate attention on the deep religious lesson which the author was trying to teach: showing his chauvinistic fellow-Jews of the postexilic period that God's salvific love embraces all—even the Ninevites, Israel's archenemy and a people ignorant of the true God. This new interpretation of Jonah is a fulfillment of the behest of Pope Pius, who urged the exegete to determine "to what extent the manner of expression or the literary mode adopted by the sacred writer may lead to a correct and genuine interpretation."

ENRICHED INSIGHTS

Such fidelity to the directives of *Divino Afflante Spiritu* has issued enriched insights into the meaning of Scripture for many. It has brought us to see that in the early chapters of Genesis, the sacred writer never intended to play the role of a geologist telling a scientific story of the origin of the world, or of an anthropologist tracing the scientific history of how humans came to be. Rather, under the influence of an enlightened and living faith, the author sought to teach profound truths about the transcendence of God, the evil of sin, the nemesis of infidelity, and the mercy of God who is always ready to retrieve what is lost.

This new approach has brought us to see that all through Scripture the concern of the writer is to give us not a documented history, where everything is seen with the two eyes of time and place, but rather a history with religious significance—what German scholars call *Heilsgeschichte,* a history of God's saving acts and a history which saves us even as we listen to it. We must always remember that much of Scripture took its origin in the liturgy of Israel. The facts recounted in Scripture were first chanted in shrine centers at Bethel and Dan, Hebron and Jerusalem, where the mighty deeds of God were celebrated not as a documented record of the past but as a living challenge to the present. Many events, therefore, would be telescoped in the telling; many irrelevant details would be passed over. God's action, above all else, would be brought to the fore that the story might conclude, "*Today,* if you hear God's voice, harden not your hearts" (Ps 95:7-8). We must learn, therefore, to read the Scriptures in the spirit in which these inspired books came into being.

This is true of the New Testament as much as of the Old. Its materials were used long and vitally by the Christian community—for at least twenty or more years—before at last they were put into writing. And when the evangelists did put these materials into writing in our canonical Gospels, they intended to compose not history in our sense of the word, but a deeply significant religious history, a *Heilsgeschichte.*

The whole spirit of much of our training has been to look upon the Gospels as a life of Christ in the sense of a modern biography. We have grown up in a period which emphasized the strictly historical character of the story of Jesus in order to counter the attack of those who denied its historical reality. The lives of Christ by Prat and Lebreton, Fouard and Fillion, Lagrange and Daniel-Rops have been the Catholic answer to the challenge of those who dissolve the miracles of Jesus and who transform him from what he really was into merely a good man and a deluded eschatologist. The Catholic reaction was a healthy one; in a period of storm it kept our faith intact.

DISCOVERING THE PURPOSE AND MEANING

But we must realize that we are now living in a period when we can measure more accurately the purpose of the gospel and the real meaning of its contents.

The first Gospel was not written until the years of the sixth or seventh decade, when the Christian community had already lived many years of full faith in the risen Lord who is truly the Son of God. To the Christians, his followers, he was the *Kyrios,* the kingly Lord, whose power and person they acknowledged as divine because they believed he had risen from the dead and because they had received his illumining spirit. All during these first years of the Church, Christians loved to recall the words and deeds of Jesus, not only because of devotion to his person but because they needed the light and direction of his truth for their new way of life as Christians.

This very faith in Christ as God was bound to shed its light upon his life of weakness upon earth. This does not mean that faith "created" the Gospel story. There were too many living witnesses during those first thirty years after Christ's death to "create" anything. A lie would have been instantly challenged by those who had everything earthly to lose in accepting Jesus as Messiah-Lord. Scholars, therefore, like Rudolph Bultmann and Martin Debelius, who speak of a "creative" community in this sense of the word will always be embarrassed by an irrefutable argument drawn from the presence in the primitive community of living eye-witnesses who had been with Jesus from the beginning.

At the same time, we must admit that faith did color the believers' attitudes toward Jesus. And, therefore, it gave them power to see and understand what they had not understood during his lifetime, the divine and salvific aspect of all his words and deeds.

This new insight gives light and spirit to our Gospels. The evangelists in writing centered their attention not on the historic circumstances of the events in Jesus' life—the when? where? how? in what succession? in exactly what words? etc.—but on their religious significance, their pertinence to Christian life in the here and now. It was in this way that Jesus' words and deeds were being recounted in the community—in its catechetics, in its liturgy, in its preaching; and it is in this way the life of Jesus is recounted in the Gospel. The evangelists have given us not a documented history of bare facts but a deeply significant religious story of what the words and deeds of Jesus mean in the salvific plan of God. Our English language lacks words with which to distinguish these two kinds of history. The German language is more rich: they describe factual history as *historisch* and religious history as *geschlichtlich*. The Gospels give us *Heilsgeschichte*, a religious history of salvation.

What riches the new approach to Scripture will bring to our world remains to be seen. One thing, however, is certain. We live today in an age in which God has opened to us the treasures of the ancient past. We live also in the full light of a great guiding document, the *Divino Afflante Spiritu* of Pope Pius XII.

Is it heady to augur a future rich with new and deep understanding of God's inspired Word and a new, great love for the Incarnate Word who is its beginning and end, and its whole meaning?

CHAPTER 5

Interpreting the Bible Typologically
The Exodus: A Continuous Story of Salvation

Upheaval stirred the world of Abraham. Dynastic changes at Ur and vast migrations over the Fertile Crescent stirred the stagnant pool of a world that had died. Babylon in the early second millennium boasted, "I am rich and have grown wealthy and have need of nothing"; and all the while the bragging corpse failed to see how "wretched and miserable and poor and blind and naked" it really was (Rev 3:17). All flesh had corrupted its way; God's clean sun shone on a pool of death.

But life still throbbed at Haran in northern Mesopotamia, for Abraham lived there, a newcomer from Ur in the south. All future history would flow from him; he was to become "the father of us all . . . our father in the sight of God" (Rom 4:17). For one day at Haran, in the middle of the nineteenth century before Christ, God spoke to the heart of this tribal chief (Gen 12:1-3) and broke it wide open with a flood of mercy, which gushed forth to cleanse all hearts by faith.

The divine word promised a blessed future, without telling its precise elements or the time of its coming. Long centuries were to pass before this pledge was fulfilled. But the very sound of God's voice is operative, never returning empty, always doing the divine will (Isa 55:10-11). Hardly had God spoken when this promise began to send forth clean water that spread out in ever widening circles of mercy and loving fidelity until it covered the earth (cf. Ezek 47:1-12). The mercy of God touching each generation performs the univocal work of redeeming from death and of invigorating with life, so that all successive moments of history follow the same pattern. The wide outer circle of Christian fulfillment is the same form as the small inner circle of God's promise to Abraham. And all the circles between bear similar shape.

Thus, a vital continuity binds fast the story of salvation. Far from opposing the Old Testament, the New Testament, to use the apt phrase of Père de Vaux, "prolongs it."

It must be so, for God has shaped all to the full measure of Christ. Through him, the waters of divine mercy were to touch all shores. And so the vast outer circle of mercy's worldwide expansion gives form to every inner circle, even to the first circle of the water's origin in the heart of Abraham. Christ's redeeming death is at once the cause and the pattern of every previous deed of divine mercy. Typology, then—mighty deeds foreshadowing mightier to come—inheres in the Old Testament as a necessary consequence of the Christian quality of all God's work. In the great deeds done for Israel, God so kept the Son in mind that Sören Kierkegaard could speak of "the eternal contemporaneousness of Christ." And the Master himself could say, "Abraham your father rejoiced to see my day; he saw it and was glad" (John 8:56).

This living bond between the Old and New Testaments is well exemplified in the vital typology of Israel's exodus from Egypt. The event was of supreme importance for it played a unique creative role in forming the nation, in fashioning its faith and way. Ever afterward Israel commemorated it with the annual Passover feast when the stirring tale of their deliverance was recounted at local shrines and family tables. Its memory was handed down from generation to generation in streams of tradition marked with all the divergences and accretions of oral history often recounted. Thus, even today, the biblical story of the Exodus, carefully wrought as it is, betrays unmistakable signs of sundry threads deftly woven into a single pattern. Yet the basic historicity of the narrative cannot be questioned. It is an authentic witness to real events that marked the birth of Israel as a nation and of the worship of Yahweh. Memory is tenacious in the East; and, in this case, its reliability is certified by the fact that Israel was often tempted to forget the story of its origin and the stern exactions of Yahweh, its God.

THE EXODUS STORY

Here is the story simply told. Some seventeen or eighteen centuries before Christ, a group of Hebrews driven by famine descended into Egypt where they enjoyed favor under the new dynasty of the Hyksos kings, who had recently swept into power on the wave of a vast Semite migration of which Abraham was part. These sons of Jacob were to remain in the Delta four hundred years, not as a nation within a nation but as an ethnic group—Hebrew in blood but Egyptian in sentiment. Life in the foreign land soiled them with pagan ways and practices. They prospered in the world's goods and in its evils. Idolatry came easily and Egyptian manners were to their liking. But at last the long, peaceful sojourn in Egypt changed to a burdensome existence under cruel persecution. Too long had Israel thickened on its lees (cf. Zeph 1:12); and now, through a tyrannical Pharaoh, God poured the oversweet wine from vessel to vessel.

A native Egyptian dynasty stripped the Hebrews of all privileges and shackled them with the burdens of an unwelcome minority. This persecution is the first instance of cruel anti-Semitism described in the Bible. Cries of pain and despair rent the air, and God answered by making ready a man of the hour, whose name was Moses. Native gifts and early training equipped him for leadership. But the forging of bonds between God and humans is more than a human task. First then, God had to temper the mettle of this chosen instrument. Years of exile with the Kenites in the rocky land southwest of the Dead Sea enriched Moses' mind with new traditions and new insights. But, more important still, these years purified him in a flame of fire at Sinai.

Time and again God was manifested to the great patriarchs of Israel—Abraham, Isaac, and Jacob. This time, however, God's word pulsed with new meaning. Truly it was still the great *El Shaddai* of the ancestors who spoke to Moses. Yet now this most high God, the God of heaven and earth, asked for a special bond with Israel. Later, the prophets were to liken this bond to the tie that binds husband and wife. In their eyes this blood covenant made Israel the people of God and God the spouse and master of Israel (Jer 3:1-12; Ezek 16). But, for Moses on Sinai, God's command involved the here and now. For at Sinai God charged him to lead the people out of Egypt, to shepherd them through the desert, and to bring them into the land God had promised to their ancestors.

It was a mammoth task to ask of anyone. Yet God, who was both solicitous and powerful, promised to help Moses. God's new name was a guarantee. For no longer would God be called merely the great *El Shaddai* of the nations but rather Yahweh, the faithful God of their own covenant. Whether Moses first heard this name among the Kenites or whether it was newly revealed to him at Sinai matters little. Its meaning is what counts. "I am who is," God assured Moses. God is always the mysterious "I am," an alien to the shift of human gods from past to future. And so Yahweh—"Who is"—would always be present among the chosen people. God's name would be a prayer on the lips of the people and a promise when spoken by God.

It required centuries for Israel to taste the full flavor of the Sinai revelation and to understand how the name Yahweh was at once the source of all fear and of all hope. Suffering must first bring God's people to wisdom; the prophets must first see their visions. Then, at long last, the Sinai revelation of God's unfailing mercy would become a conviction. Whatever Israel might do, Yahweh will never turn from the mercy and promise of Sinai. God will always be faithful and true; pity and fidelity will rule all God's works (Ps 24:10). When Israel ceased being a child and grew to spiritual maturity, it came to see that even from the beginning of the world God had always been the same, cherishing creatures as a nurse for little ones, with mercy and fidelity. Then it could appreciate the full meaning of Hosea's urgent plea, "The Lord, the God of hosts, the Lord is God's name! You shall return by the help of your God if you remain loyal and do right and always hope in your God" (Hos 12:6-7).

It was the memory of the Exodus that did most to convince Israel of God's power and pity. At the time, they saw it simply as a liberation from the hard oppression of Pharaoh. But later they came to appreciate it also as a liberation from still worse, the evil of defilement by Egyptian infidelity and idolatry. Indeed, the prophetic school looked upon the deliverance as a true redemption, with God as a warrior struggling in desperate conflict with Pharaoh and the dragon power of his gods (Isa 51:9-10). One after another, Yahweh hurled ten plagues against a king's proud heart that only hardened like mud under the burning heat of the divine bolts. But the last plague was a master stroke not softening Pharaoh's heart, but breaking it in helpless defeat. Where flood and storm and hail had failed, the death of the first-born cleaved the rock.

All through the terrors, the family of Jacob was spared; the plagues struck all around them but they were untouched. Their preservation from God's final blow involved the ritual of the paschal supper and a ceremony of smearing blood on the doorposts. The incidents of this last night in Egypt burned a lasting memory in the soul of Israel. The contrast between their security and the anguish of the Egyptians, the change of heart in the obdurate Pharaoh, and the urgent pleadings of their Egyptian neighbors that the Hebrews enrich themselves from previously hoarded treasures—all this forced upon them the recognition of Yahweh's special favor. Ever before, Egypt had shared its riches with Israel's patriarchs, Abraham, Jacob, and Joseph. But the family of

Jacob came out of the darkness of the paschal night with something far better than Egypt's gold and fine linen. They departed from the land under Moses' leadership with a new consciousness that God had carved them out from the heart of an alien race to become God's own special people. Yahweh was with them as their God and the fiery cloud of the *Shekinah* leading them was God's symbol.

The Exodus was only half of God's work. Yahweh had delivered the people from bondage and separated them from the contamination of Egypt. A positive task yet remained: to forge a bond of union and weld Israel to God's self with a covenant of blood. Like all union with God this could be done only in the desert. "I will lead her into the desert," the Lord was later to say of Israel the unfaithful, "and I will speak to her heart" (Hos 2:16). The *Shekinah* therefore diverted the line of march from the *Via Maris*, the direct route to the promised land, and turned southward instead to the region of Sinai.

PARTING OF THE RED SEA

But Israel's problems with Pharaoh were not yet over. Very shortly the king's retainers set out in hot pursuit to bring back the fugitives. And Israel would have gone back readily if God had not intervened with a definitive liberation that once for all swept it out beyond Pharaoh's reach. The story of the miracle is one of the most stirring in the Bible. The fleeing people found itself in a cul-de-sac: on one side the Red Sea, on the other and behind them the mountains, in front the approaching Egyptians. There was no escape save in surrender—or in God. And God intervened. Moses lifted the rod and a driving wind parted the waters for Israel to march across to safety. The Egyptians followed. But once more Moses lifted his rod and the waters returned to destroy them all. Israel could not miss the meaning of the wonder; they sang and danced to honor the merciful Yahweh, their God. In the words of Dom Damasus Winzen, this jubilant song marks "the hour when the divine office was born." It is the seed of the Church's solemn praise of God.

Indeed, Yahweh was always at hand to supply the needs of the child God had found languishing and had mercifully freed. Time and again on this journey God proved to an incredulous people who it was who had really intervened to point their destiny. When they were thirsty God struck water from the rock; when they were hungry God provided bread from heaven. Therefore, when at last this people reached Sinai, they already had ample experience of God's solicitude and power.

They needed these previous love tokens, for Sinai was the scene of espousals that bound Israel to Yahweh forever. The thunder and lightning of the theophany were terrifying. The ritual of covenant was detailed and impressive but a love story was the heart of it all. Yahweh was bound to Israel and Israel to Yahweh in a covenant of blood. God would love and protect Israel and fulfill the rich promises God had pledged. Israel would ever live and act as Yahweh's people, faithfully fulfilling the just and holy house rules of a God who was perfect. Just as in Egypt God's word had delivered the bodies of the chosen people from Pharaoh, so on Sinai the word of God delivered their souls from the darkness of unbelief and evil practice. Israel is thus a people created by God's word. Moreover, its very continuance depended on divine promises and demands.

BIRTH OF THE NATION

Ever after, Israel looked back to the Exodus and to the Sinai pact as the birth hour of the nation. Its history was often marred by infidelities, but no human weakness could obliterate three dominant facts which Sinai burned into the Israelite soul: there is but one God; one chosen people; one country in which to work out the people's destiny. It was especially the yearly celebration of the Passover feast that kept this national memory intact (cf. Exod 12:14). With Israel, the Passover was not a nature feast commemorating the return of spring, as with the surrounding Canaanites. Rather, it was a religious feast to recall the springtime of God's favor when, through the Exodus, Yahweh graciously ended the winter of oppression and at Sinai entered on the bright joyous days of the espousals with Israel.

All memories of these incidents are steeped in praise and thanksgiving. Later generations will sing of the Exodus as of a triumph (Pss 105; 113) and of the covenant of Sinai as espousals in which God chose Israel for God's self. As time passed, the importance of the Exodus grew to full stature in the minds of the people and its profound meaning was richly interpreted in the sweeping poetry of the prophets and the Deuteronomist. All later laws of the priestly code were traced to Sinai and the definitive redaction of the Pentateuch after the Exile rested the authority of its laws on the authority of Moses.

But there was a twofold orientation in Israel's faith. It centered in the historical exodus which had passed, but it looked forward also to an exodus yet to come. The reason is obvious. God had promised a full flowering, and the merciful pledge of Yahweh, the faithful one, is without repentance. Yet daily events brought bitter experience that the deliverance from Egypt and the covenant of Sinai were not definitive. Time and again Israel hankered for the fleshpots of Egypt; and only too often like Gomer, the wife of Hosea, it proved unfaithful to its faithful Spouse.

From the very beginning then, the prophets saw that there had to be a new exodus and a new covenant (cf. Hos 2:16-25). This enduring hope enriched the memory of Israel's deliverance from Egypt and its covenant with God on Sinai. For the prophets, these events of the past were unforgettable historical facts but, even more, they were cherished pledges of a blessed future.

CHRIST AND THE EXODUS

It was Christ who fulfilled all the rich hopes of the prophets. His very name held promise. For as the angel explained to Joseph, this name was at once a symbol and a guarantee that, at long last, Yahweh had come to save the people (Matt 1:31). It was but natural, then, that the writers of the New Testament should find in Israel's exodus from Egypt a leitmotif for their own description of the work of Christ. Steeped as they were in the Scriptures, they tended to locate the Savior in the biblical context of the great deliverance. The word "exodus," as used by them, always resounds with the full meaning of that historic event.

Often enough there is striking agreement among all the evangelists in handling the elements of this typology. Such identifications were probably fixed and made permanent in the oral catechesis which preceded the writing of the Gospels. Yet at the same time there is also marked fluidity. Jesus is variously identified with the God of the Exodus, with Israel itself, with Moses the leader, or with the chief factor in some incident of the Exodus. Such divergence should occasion no surprise, for all these different aspects merely stress that the basic typology of exodus must be sought in the mercy and fidelity of a saving God who, in solicitude for Israel, penetrated every person, event, and thing with divine power. Each element in the story of the Exodus foreshadowed the much greater work of Christian redemption in which divine power penetrated the human nature and human deeds of Jesus to work a definitive liberation from sin and an eternal covenant with God. Therefore, in pondering the many Gospel applications of exodus typology, we come to a new, rich appreciation of the perfect deliverance that God wrought in and through Jesus.

Among the Synoptics, the Gospel of Matthew is especially rich with this typology. The avowed purpose of the author was to stress the continuity between the old and the new law. It is obvious then that he would utilize the widespread Jewish expectation that "in the last days" God must work a new exodus. In developing this theme, Matthew like Mark stresses a similarity between the experiences of Christ and those of the chosen people of God. Thus the return of the holy family from Egypt after the death of Herod is seen by Matthew as a new exodus. And so he captions it with the very words Hosea had used to describe the earlier event: "Out of Egypt I called my son" (Matt 2:15; Hos 11:1). The beginnings of the Savior's public life are also linked to similar incidents in the history of Israel. As Israel was baptized into its new life with God by passing through the waters of the Red Sea, so Christ inaugurates his ministry for God by accepting baptism in the waters of the Jordan (Matt 3:13-17; Mark 1:9-11). Thereafter, both Israel and Christ live through a period of desert life and temptation. The forty days of Christ in the desert has its parallel in the forty years of Israel. His temptation accords with Israel's testing. His food is the word of God that comes down from heaven just as Israel's food in the desert is not the bread of human making but the manna of God's giving (Matt 4:1-11; Mark 1:12-13). It is especially noteworthy that Christ defeats his tempter with texts from the Book of Deuteronomy, all of them summing up the wisdom of God that guided and strengthened Israel.

CHRIST AND MOSES

After this early identification of Christ with Israel, Matthew prefers to emphasize the resemblance between Christ and Moses. Generalizations are of course always a risk. But there is some justification for saying that Matthew's chief concern is to represent Christ as a second Moses, greater by far than the first lawgiver of Israel. The keynote of this identification is sounded in Matthew's representation of Christ's first discourse, the Sermon on the Mount (Matt 5–7). As Moses drafted the law of the old covenant, so Christ presents here the law of the new covenant. This law is perfect in every way and Christ himself is a lawgiver of divine holiness and authority. As a master he handles the earlier law with deft touch, changing at will and fashioning to perfection. God had spoken through Moses. But this new Moses is more than an instrument, infinitely more than the mouthpiece of God. And so "the crowds were astonished at his teaching, for he was teaching them as one having authority" (Matt 7:28-29).

This resemblance between the two lawgivers dominates all the later discourses of Jesus in Matthew. Indeed, the master draws largely from Deuteronomy for the expression of his own thoughts. Moreover, there is likeness even in Christ's method of teaching. His soul, like that of Moses, was a limpid pool reflecting divine truth without distortion. In both men passion was controlled; nothing disturbed their tranquil grasp of truth or marred the clarity of its expression. For God said of Moses, "Moses was by far the meekest man on the face of the earth" (Num 12:3), just as Christ said of himself, "Learn from me, for I am meek and humble of heart" (Matt 11:29).

The wonders and miracles of Christ also point a likeness between himself and Moses. Through both lawgivers God wrought mighty works to authenticate their mission and to win for their law a hearing. It is not the meaning of the miracle that interests Matthew, nor its resemblance in kind to the miracles of Moses. Thus he is content to tell the story of the multiplication of the loaves without referring, as John does, to the profound symbolism of bread coming miraculously from heaven. Matthew's concern is with the fact itself. Miracles are God's own work; as he had wrought wonders through Moses, so now he was working in Jesus. Both were lawgivers mighty not only in word but also in deed.

It is especially in describing the transfiguration that both Matthew and Mark bring into focus the typology of Moses (Matt 17:1-8; Mark 9:1-7). Here the two great lawgivers of the old and new covenants meet face to face; and the bright cloud that once overshadowed Moses (Exod 33:9-10) now descends upon Jesus. Heaven's authentication of the new Moses follows the pattern of its approval of the old.

EXODUS MOTIF IN THE GOSPEL OF JOHN

The author of the Fourth Gospel is even more pointed in showing how Christ fulfilled the typology of Israel's exodus from Egypt. In fact, some have suggested that exodus provides the whole framework of this Gospel and that John follows it step by step to prove that Jesus, as a new Moses and a new lamb of God, came upon earth to lead a new Israel from the oppression of sin to the liberty of a new covenant with God. It is difficult to accept this thesis in its entirety, for in a Gospel of so many themes it is an oversimplification to reduce all to a single unity. But the fact remains that the exodus motif is prevalent in the Gospel of John.

Like Matthew, John too marks a resemblance between Christ and the lawgiver of Israel. But his aim is to evoke all the richness of the exodus typology, for he is not only a witness to the Gospel tradition but, even more, its "inspired exegete." Therefore, in his treatment of the life and work of Christ, many new aspects of similarity appear.

Often enough John is content merely to suggest a point of resemblance. Thus four times in this Gospel Jesus appropriates to himself the divine name first revealed to Moses at Horeb (John 8:24, 28, 58; 13:19). But, in all these instances, the reference to the Sinai revelation is allusive rather than explicit. So too there is passing reference to the new espousals that will bring to perfection the old covenant (John 3:29-30). But, after the brief unadorned words of John the Baptist, this theme too is dropped.

Other points of resemblance, however, are emphasized and developed at length. Chief among these is the paschal lamb motif. It was the blood of the unblemished lamb that saved the first-born of Israel from slaughter and made possible the departure for the promised land. In John's eyes, Christ is the true lamb of God who shed his blood on Calvary to save all people from the death of sin and to liberate them for the promised land of heaven. John's first introduction to Christ was the Baptist's salute "Behold the Lamb of God!" (John 1:36). Ever after, this typology loomed large in the mind of the evangelist. Thus, several times he makes a deliberate effort to connect Jesus' death with the feast of the Passover (John 2:13; 6:4; 11:55). The providential coincidence of time between the paschal celebration and the death of Christ on the cross provided him an opportunity to stress an underlying typology. Perhaps there is also a meaningful play in John's introduction to his account of the Last Supper: "Before the feast of the Passover, Jesus, knowing that his hour had come to pass out of the world to the Father . . ." (John 13:1). Certainly there is a deliberate allusion to the ritual of the paschal celebration in John's remark that no bone of the victim on the cross was broken (John 19:36). It is obvious then, even to a casual reader of the Fourth Gospel, that John found in the lamb of Egypt a memorable type of the later lamb of Israel.

John also finds many other resemblances. For him, Christ is the light of the world (John 8:12). The conflict between this light and the surrounding darkness is a favorite theme with John. But this theme is not his own; its source is biblical. He has drawn it from the beautiful contemplative meditations of the author of the Book of Wisdom, who penetrates the deep truths contained in God's guiding care of the people as God went before them on their journey, lighting the way with the glory of the *Shekinah*. A cloud of divine light led Israel from Egypt to the promised land. This was the visible sign of God's presence with the chosen people. For John, Jesus is the true light of the world for he is the word of God dwelling among people and radiating everywhere the "glory of the only-begotten of the Father, full of grace and truth" (John 1:14). All must follow this light if they would reach their heavenly home safely. They must approach and love this light if they desire divine approval (John 3:19-21). Thus, the evangelist's witness to Christ as the guiding light of all is hardly appreciated unless one sees it against the biblical context of the *Shekinah* of the Exodus.

The manna from heaven was yet another element of Israel's exodus which John utilized as a type of Christ's beneficent action. In this identification the evangelist was not original, for Jewish exegesis itself had already given to the manna an eschatological meaning. Devout Israelites were certain that as God nourished their ancestors with bread from heaven in the desert, so Yahweh would nourish them with heavenly food in the "last days." They were certain that the manna would reappear in messianic times. This Jewish belief is indicated in the questions the crowd put to Jesus (John 6:30-31). John himself relies on this tradition when, in his Book of Revelation, he equates manna and the tree of life as perfect symbols of the divine goods to be shared by the blessed in the world to come (Rev 2:7, 17). It was the precise object of the Fourth Gospel to show that this eschatological food is already given to the Church. It is hers here and now because of the abiding presence of Jesus in the vital and life-giving reality of the Eucharist. If, as some have thought, the component parts of John's Gospel originated as elements of the primitive sacramental catechesis, then it is obvious that the typology of the manna was widely used in the early Church to describe the riches of the Eucharist.

But, in the desert wanderings, God not only fed the people but also provided water for them from the rock. John follows Paul (1 Cor 10:4) in identifying this rock of Sinai as a type for Christ. This theme of refreshing spiritual water is stressed in John even more than the manna. His use of this type reflects its prevalence in the baptismal catechesis of the early Church and also in the catechetical instructions on grace and spiritual life. It is true that the baptismal reference made by Christ in his discourse with Nicodemus (John 3:5) is probably based on Israel's baptism in the waters of the Red Sea and in the cloud, as mentioned by Paul in 1 Corinthians 10:1-2. But elsewhere in the Fourth Gospel the theme of water seems to rest on the typology of the drink provided miraculously by God in the desert. Christ is the true rock from whom all life and all refreshment must come.

The brazen serpent too figures in the Fourth Gospel as a type of the healing power of Christ's redemption: "As Moses lifted up the serpent in the desert, even so must the Son of Man be lifted up" (Num 21:4-9; John 3:14). These words of Christ are a bare allusion to the miraculous cure wrought by God for the people (Num 21:9). But, in the light of Wisdom 16:5-13, this brief sentence crystallizes a rich typology to provide John with a point of departure for his sublime theology of redemption (John 3:14-21). In his pages, type and fulfillment are so intimately interwoven that they mutually interact to aid the mind in penetrating the wealth of each.

All in all, the story of Christ as told in the Gospels is understood when it is read in the biblical context of Israel's exodus; for Matthew, Mark, and John were all true Israelites steeped in the Scriptures and sharing Israel's hope for an ineffable renewal of the divine mercy. That mercy led the chosen people out of Egypt, bequeathed a covenant on Sinai, and made good its pledge of loving devotedness by working wonders to hearten Israel during the desert wanderings. Long before the evangelists appeared, the Jews had seen in the events of the Exodus shadows cast beforehand by a blessed future. It is the merit of the evangelists that they found in Christ the perfect fulfillment of all the Old Testament hopes—the "substance" that had cast out the shadows (Col 2:17).

CONTINUING WORK OF CHRIST

The life and work of Christ are not over. Before he died, the Savior promised to abide with his Church always—ever the same Christ, "yesterday, today, yes, and forever" (Heb 13:8). Strong is the bond between Moses and Israel but stronger still, intimate as no other, is the union which binds Christ to his people in the Church. For the new Moses and the new Israel are joined together as head and members of one mystical body, as bridegroom and bride of a true marriage. In the mystery of his Church, Christ is personally present to every age and renders accessible to every follower the very substance of his life and work upon earth. As St. Leo the Great expressed it: "What was visible in our redeemer during his earthly sojourn has now passed into the sacraments." Though the Church is the Church of pilgrimage, traveling toward the great day of the Lord, though she moves in time, waiting, hoping, and praying, "Thy kingdom come," she stands all through time on an atemporal level. She is the tremendous sacrament that brings the Christ of the first century into every age and into every heart. For "each time the mysteries are renewed, the work of redemption becomes actual once more." What was wrought in Jesus during his earthly life is renewed in the soul of every Christian. Christ's mysteries belong to his Church and to each member, not merely to contemplate and to utilize but also to relive.

The exodus of Israel from Egypt, therefore, does not exhaust its theology in prefiguring Christ's redeeming life, death, and resurrection. By the very fact that it foreshadowed the events of his life, it also prefigured the life of his followers who would be Israel renewed. For the daily life of Christ's mystical body is but the living reproduction and fulfillment of the saving mysteries in the life of Christ himself. This is the reason, according to Henri de Lubac, S.J., why "the typology of exodus is the most classic and constant in our liturgical tradition and in Christian literature."

PATRISTIC SOURCES

The patristic catecheses which formed the Christian mind place the origin of a Christian's spiritual life at the moment when, through baptism, one shares in the liberating death of the true paschal lamb. Like Israel of old, the Christian is thereby delivered from slavery to the devil, becoming a member of "a chosen race, a royal priesthood, a holy nation, a purchased people" (1 Pet 2:9). As the years pass and one journeys through the desert of life, the Christian finds in the mighty activity of Christ a kindliness, a divine mercy supporting in all days and leading to the promised land of heaven (cf. Isa 46:3-4; Heb 1:3). But the passing from the death of sin to the vibrant life of heaven must be accomplished in Christ, through the power of his exodus, in his company, and according to the pattern of his example. For the exodus and desert journey of the Christian involves both a sacramental sharing in the mystery of Christ and a vital imitation of his conduct.

It was natural then for the early fathers to emphasize the biblical foundation of the sacramental signs. Just as John showed how the redemptive work of Christ renewed and enriched the great wonders of the Exodus, so the fathers taught that the Christian sacraments, as living instruments of the passion, continue these wonders and apply them with new divine power and new Christian meaning to every believer. In this they remained true to the primitive symbolism of the sacraments, which was taken directly from Israel's liturgy and the typology of the Old Testament. Humanly speaking there could be no other source, for Christ and his apostles had been schooled only in the traditions of Israel. Afterwards, it is true, writers of Greek background tried to explain the sacramental symbolism in a new way. New meanings were borrowed from the thoughts and customs of a Greek world. And all this has helped to enrich people's appreciation of the sacraments. But their primitive meaning must still be studied in the light of a biblical context.

The early Fathers of the Church were careful to preserve this biblical foundation of the sacramental signs. Thus, their thought on baptism was always controlled by St. Paul's identification of its type in the crossing of the Red Sea (1 Cor 10:2). For him, the exodus from Egypt and the passage through the Sea prefigured the deliverance from evil that comes to the Christian through baptism. The two realities have similar meanings. Each marks, in its own way, the end of servitude and the beginning of a new existence.

Again, this thought is not original with Paul. At the beginning of the Christian era, the initiation of proselytes into the Jewish community included not only circumcision but also baptism in imitation of the exodus from Egypt through the parted waters of the Red Sea. This symbolic act was charged with the redemptive power of Christ to become a true sacrament of the new law. The ritual washing became a vital, dynamic sharing in the deliverance from sin and the birth to new life achieved by Christ's exodus on the cross: "Are you unaware that we who were baptized into Christ Jesus were baptized into his death? We were indeed buried with him through baptism into death so that, just as Christ was raised from the dead by the glory of the Father, we too might live in newness of life" (Rom 6:3-4).

With the fathers, then, the exodus of Israel from Egypt was a type not only of Christ's death but also of Christian baptism. For them, the Old Testament contained both a Christological and a sacramental typology. The baptismal catechesis of Tertullian is especially eloquent:

> When the people, set unconditionally free, escaped the violence of the Egyptian king by crossing over through the water, it was water that exterminated the king himself, with his entire force. What figure is more manifestly fulfilled in the sacrament of baptism? The nations are set free from the world by means of water; and the devil, their old tyrant, they leave behind, overwhelmed in the water.

This passage places in focus the primitive perspective of baptism and redemption. Both were seen, above all, as a victory over the demon. On the cross, Christ crushed his adversary's head to liberate all humanity from the cruel yoke of sin. Each Christian shares in this triumph of Christ at the moment of baptism. The waters of baptism annihilate Satan's power as completely as the Red Sea drowned the forces of Pharaoh. The deliverance wrought by God for the Israelites in freeing them forever through water from an earthly tyrant and in leading them out as a new nation into the desert finds its antitype in baptism, which liberates a spiritual people from a spiritual tyrant and leads them from the world to the kingdom of God. This theme is frequent in the baptismal catecheses of the fathers.

A striking example is this passage by St. Cyril of Jerusalem:

> Needs must you know that the type of baptism is found in Israel's ancient history. Indeed, when Pharaoh, the bitter and savage tyrant, oppressed the free and noble people of the Hebrews, God sent Moses to free them from the evil Egyptian bondage. The doorposts were daubed with the blood of the lamb so that the destroying angel would pass over the houses marked with the sign of blood. Thus, against all hope, the Hebrew people was set free. As the enemy pursued the liberated, however, he saw, marvelous to say, the sea divided for them; he was avidly going after them, treading in their footsteps, when he was forthwith swallowed by the floods of the Red Sea and buried there. Let us move now from things ancient to things new, from type to reality. There we have Moses sent by God into Egypt, here we have the Christ sent by the Father into the world. There it was in order to free the oppressed people from Egypt, here it is to rescue men and women tyrannized in this world by sin. There the blood of the lamb warded off the destroyer, here the blood of Jesus Christ, the immaculate Lamb, puts the demons to flight. There the tyrant pursued that ancient people even to the sea, here the shameless and insolent prince of all evil gives chase even to the very brink of the sacred font. The one was drowned in the sea, the other is brought to nothing in the saving water.

The Exodus provided also a sublime typology for the Eucharist. Here too, the fathers drew largely from the primitive sacramental catechesis reflected in the pages of the New Testament. The inspired authors had seized on two elements in the Exodus story as prefigurements of the nourishing and strengthening presence of Christ. John favored the manna; Paul, the rock of Sinai. Both symbols were eloquent of the solicitous and operative providence of Emmanuel or "God-with-us." It was only to be expected, then, that the manna-rock symbolism would become a dominant element in patristic teaching. Time and again in explaining the reality and effects of the Eucharist, the fathers return to these types as divinely ordained prefigurements of Holy Communion.

Indeed, the fathers utilized all the elements of Christological typology in the Exodus story as an equivalent sacramental typology. Thus, the very liturgy of initiation, because it took place in the paschal period, is charged with reminiscences of the exodus from Egypt. Each factor in that historical event was identified as a type of the exodus achieved by Christ through his way of the cross and shared in sacramentally by each Christian through participation in the Christian mysteries.

But something more than a sacramental share in Christ's Passover is demanded of the Christian, for the sacrament gives grace and grace means immanent activity. All initiation, therefore, into the mystery of Christ must be accompanied by a conversion of morals and by vital Christian living, a duty Paul never tired of insisting on. After recounting all that God had done for Israel in the desert, he warned his converts: "Now these things happened to them as a type and they were written for our correction, upon whom the final age of the world has come" (1 Cor 10:11). The same lessons are stressed in the Epistle to the Hebrews (3:1–4:13). There the typology of the Old Testament points to positive cooperation and demands of the followers of Christ an eager striving for goodness, a hastening toward the promised land.

The fathers were unanimous in repeating these inspired demands. All were enemies of a sacramentary quietism with its contempt for the sweat and toil of moral effort and its search for a rest in God which is not for the pilgrim—a doctrine condemned again by Pope Pius XII in his encyclical *Mediator Dei*. They insisted that the Christian's sacramental share in Christ's passover brought a new vital power which must be exercised in daily Christian living. Christ's exodus traced the way of the cross. The way of the cross then, dying to self, is the only authentic Christian exodus: "For to this you have been called, because

Christ also suffered for you leaving you an example that you should follow in his footsteps" (1 Pet 2:21).

St. John Chrysostom gives pointed expression to this patristic teaching in one of his homilies. This is his thought: The Lord had brought the Israelites out of Egypt and yet, except for a few, they grumbled against God, mistrusted God's might, doubted God's love. Therefore, they were barred from setting foot in the Holy Land and the grace of liberation and safe passage through the Red Sea availed them nothing. Likewise it avails a Christian nothing to have received baptism and to have shared in the spiritual mysteries, unless he leads a life worthy of this grace.

CONCLUDING AND CONTINUING THE EXODUS STORY

Truly, the Exodus is not an event of the past. Though in Christ we are indeed delivered from sin, from idolatry, and from death, we must be ever in exodus, ever passing over, ever leaving behind the servitude of idolatrous Egypt, ever marching through the austerity of the desert, ever doing our utmost to enter the promised land. Until the day of Christ's return we, God's people, remain as it were in the wilderness. There is still the yearning for Egypt's ease, still the crowd murmurs, still leaders sin. Yet God is faithful, chastening, and forgiving and thrusts us forward without fail toward the new heaven and the new earth which Jesus will usher in when he comes again. Thus to be saved one must take the road God showed to Israel, one must walk the stations of the cross. For Israel's route is the route of the whole of God's people and of each one of them.

Christian life fulfills the typology of Israel's exodus because it is a life in Christ and a full sharing in his wondrous mysteries. But the redeeming mission of the Savior does not reach its consummation in this world, and so life here below cannot be the final fulfillment of the types God prepared in the old law. Only heaven can provide that.

It is the privilege of John then to speak the last word in the glorious pages of his Revelation. There he describes the full flowering of all that exodus typology promised, of all that Christ accomplished. The whole heavenly scene is dominated by the victorious lamb. It is his blood that has achieved all; through him the wonders of the first exodus reach their crown. The elect who have crossed the Red Sea of death sing anew the victory song of Moses and Miriam (Rev 15:2-3). The covenant between God and his people is final and perfect. The new

Israel has become God's bride and "God himself will be with them as their God" (Rev 21:3). To the one who thirsts God gives "the water of life freely" (Rev 21:6), to the one who is hungry God gives "the hidden manna" (Rev 2:17). Forever the Israel of heaven shall be "a kingdom, priests for God" and all shall sing with joy the canticle of the lamb: "To him who loves us and has freed us from our sins by his blood, who has made us into a kingdom, priests for his God and Father, to him be glory and power forever and ever. Amen" (Rev 1:5-6).

The exodus of Israel, the exodus of Christ, the exodus of the Christian—all form a vital unity, all compenetrate in perfect harmony. The Israel of old, mindful of God's mercy in the first exodus, prayed ardently for a richer renewal: "Shepherd your people with your staff, the flock of your inheritance. . . . As in the days when you came from the land of Egypt, show us wonderful signs" (Mic 7:14-15). God heard this prayer and granted the "wonderful signs" of Christ's redemption. This second exodus is greater by far than the first; yet consummation follows the pattern of promise. Both are mighty works of God, revealing God's power and person in the concord of a blended minor and major scale. One cannot be appreciated without the other; both scales sound true only in their mighty harmony.

This fact is fundamental to Christian theology. It is no less essential to Christian spirituality. Pascal achieved his supreme mystical experience in that night of prayer in which he glimpsed how truly the God of Abraham, Isaac, and Jacob was his own God. So, too, every Christian who would really live a Christian life must come to realize that the God of Israel at the Red Sea, the God of Jesus on Calvary, the God of every Christian on earth, the God of the glorified Israel in heaven is always one and the same "yesterday, today, yes, and forever" (Heb 13:8).

Chapter 6

New Light on the Gospels

In 1920, at the close of World War I, the German scholars Rudolph Bultmann, Martin Dibelius, Karl Schmidt, and others worked concurrently, though not in concert, to open the Gospels to agnostics dominated by Heideggerian philosophy. As zealous army chaplains, these students of the Bible had come into contact with soldiers whose philosophy denied all divine intervention in the world of human beings. Working within the same philosophic framework, Bultmann and the others devised a means to make the Gospels meaningful to those who could not envision the supernatural.

This new approach viewed the Gospels as the fabrication of the primitive Christian community. "Community" became the password for full access to the Christian message. Whatever riches the Gospels contain derived form and substance from the creative activity of a community which had come to believe that Jesus had risen from the dead. This faith created a message about Christ for the sole purpose of helping people achieve authentic understanding of themselves before God. Here the center of gravity was not the past but the present. The point of interest was not the Jesus of history, who was almost unknown, but the Christ of faith whose words and deeds were created to meet human needs.

FORM CRITICISM

Another thesis was also developing alongside and sometimes in collaboration with the existentialists. Following the method which Hermann Gunkel had used in the Old Testament, scholars studied the Gospels not as unified works of a literary author but as a mere collection of individual units. One by one these units were subjected to careful analysis on the supposition that the form of each would reveal the sociological factor which brought the unit into being. This method, called form criticism, regarded each unit as the product of a need in community life. Preaching, liturgy, controversy—these factors were looked upon as the creative agents of the Gospel forms.

From the very beginning other scholars, like Charles Dodd and T. W. Manson, reacted strongly against the postulates of German form criticism. While acknowledging that large portions of the Gospels were first formulated in the teaching apostolate of the Church, they denied categorically that the community had created these elements. A community creates nothing; it is rather the womb in which the compelling thought of an original genius becomes viable. They pointed out, moreover, that no one in the community could qualify as the originator of a Gospel message which contradicted cardinal tenets of Judaism and ran counter to prevalent Jewish hopes.

Gradually, even the disciples of form critics came to share this adverse reaction. They sensed the embarrassment of Bultmann when he was asked to explain the enigma of a nameless community creating within twenty years a fully formed Christianity without basis in fact. The theory of a definitive Christian Gospel coming to life in so short a time lacks a *raison d'être* if it rests on the obscure figure of a merely human Jesus and on a life without challenge or meaning. The first Christian community was made up of down-to-earth, hardheaded Jews who would have been the last ones to turn Jesus into a "Son of God." They themselves had lived through the events of his public life like the others to whom they preached. Eyewitnesses are not duped by a hoax when they have everything to lose.

Under pressure of this reaction, the pendulum has swung away from an overly rigid application of form criticism. At the end of World War II, another school arose which shifted attention away from the study of individual units in the Gospels to concentrate on the Gospels as unified compositions of literary authors. This school of redaction criticism is represented by scholars like Gunther Bornkamm, Hans Conzelmann, and Willi Marxsen.

LITERARY CRITICISM

The evangelist now became the focal point of interest. The writer's literary activity, theological insights and purpose, and background of personal interests left a distinctive mark on the literary work. Each evangelist contributed so much to each particular presentation of the gospel message that Willi Marxsen wrote, "There are no synoptic gospels." The day of the *Diatesseron* is gone forever; the four Gospels can no longer be stitched together into a single narrative. Each must be studied as the unique work of a literary artist.

The recognition of a unique literary quality in each Gospel is not new. Père Lagrange, for instance, in the masterful introductions to his commentaries studied carefully the special contribution of each evangelist. He was fully aware that the sacred author forged a message in the fire of his own spirit. The text inspired by God involved also a full play of human powers.

The recent emphasis on this aspect is blighted by a certain weakness. The school of redaction criticism gives the impression at times that it has merely shifted creativity from the "community" of the form criticism school to the "evangelist" of its own school. Readers of Hans Conzelmann's *Theology of St. Luke* will find themselves asking, "Is so large a part of the Gospel merely the creation of Luke?"

Weakness as well as strength characterizes the approach both of form criticism and redaction criticism. Biblists of these schools center attention on factors which must be taken into account if the Gospels are to be studied in the spirit in which they were written. Both schools, however, have tendencies which must be corrected if true perspectives are to be maintained. These perspectives have been greatly sharpened by the work of the past seventy years. Gospel study today occupies a vantage point gained by the positive advances of form and redaction critics.

Previously, Gospel study was bi-dimensional. The reader moved from the analysis of the text to the level of the actual words and deeds of Jesus. This procedure rested on the presumption that the Gospels offer a consecutive biography of Christ, a stenographic report of his words, and a chronological record of his deeds. Viewing the Gospels in this light, the evangelists wrote lives of Christ in the same style as modern biographies.

A certain malaise was inevitable. Authors like Lagrange and Lebreton, Fillion and Prat seemed uncertain in their reconstructions. It had to be so. The conflicting reports of the different Gospel writers, the notable lacunae in their accounts, the divergent geography and time computation which set one evangelist against another—elements like these called for constant harmonization. The simple fact is that the evangelists never intended to provide material for a biography in the modern sense of the word.

INSPIRED INTERPRETATION

Their story of Christ centers on the words and deeds of Jesus of Nazareth; but this portrait of him reveals a "likeness" rather than an "image." It is an inspired interpretation of what he really was rather than a photographic reproduction of what he seemed to be. The evangelists present his life as illumined by the revealing light of the Spirit. For after Pentecost that Spirit recalled to the mind of the Church all that Jesus had said and done in order to make known the profound meaning of his words and the eternal import of his deeds.

This intermediary level of the Church's understanding of Christ is essential for full understanding of the Gospel. Something is missing if Gospel study is merely bi-dimensional. Between the inspired text and the actual life of Jesus there intervened thirty years of the Church's teaching. All three levels must be kept in mind if we are to glimpse the luminous Gospel portrait of the Son of God.

Level One — Inspired Text

The first level is that of the inspired text itself. Each Gospel writer as a literary artist has drawn his own portrait of Christ. Native gifts of style and personal theological interests formed the mold into which he cast his materials. Even when using common sources, each evangelist reshaped the data to accord with his own equipment as writer and thinker.

Mark burned with desire to show that Jesus was the Christ or Messiah even though people did not receive him. He reiterates this theme. He heaps up evidence to prove a plus quality in everything Jesus said or did: "Who then is this, that even the wind and the sea obey him?" (Mark 4:40). Mark achieves this portrayal of the divine Christ by dividing his Gospel into two neat parts, each rising climactically to a resounding cry of faith. The first half of his Gospel (chs. 1–8) culminates in the confession of Peter the Jew, "You are the Messiah" (Mark 8:29). The second half (chs. 8–15) rises to the awe-filled cry of the Gentile centurion on Calvary, "Truly this man was the Son of God!" (Mark 15:39).

Mark, however, was hampered by literary shortcomings. His style is pedestrian and repetitious, like that of a beginner. He, therefore, followed the easier course and incorporated source material without retouching it. If his Gospel is vital and colorful it is because he has reproduced exactly the memoirs of Peter. This dependence on his sources brings the Gospel of Mark close to the bedrock of tradition. The Christ of Mark is strikingly human in the play of his emotions, in the earthy color of his deeds, and in the limitation of even his miraculous powers.

Christ in Mark is a study of *chiaroscuro*, truly divine yet wholly human. This development is only one of many distinctive features in this Gospel. To share the full light of Mark's unique vision we must study the mystery of Jesus from this perspective. Full familiarity with his style and purpose, clear knowledge of his plan, painstaking analysis of his Gospel as a personal literary composition—all this is essential if we are to garner full riches on this first level of Gospel study, the inspired text.

Luke, Matthew, and John also present their own distinctive portrait of Jesus. "Mark," writes Père Lagrange, "works in the warm earthiness of terra cotta; Luke sculptures from white marble." For Luke, both in the Gospel and in Acts, geography is theological. His mind is fascinated by the vast sweep of Christianity's universal mission from humble beginnings in Jerusalem to glorious consummation in Rome. Matthew's outlook is colored by a strong interest in ecclesiology; his style is often hieratic and liturgical. John on the other hand is a sacramentalist with a mystic's insight into the mystery of the Word inspiriting flesh.

Level Two — Community

This interpretative activity of the evangelists has long been recognized. Previously, however, the next move was to proceed from the Gospel text to the actual words and deeds of Jesus. Recent form-criticism studies have now focused light on an intervening level: the community. This intermediary stage has always been well known to Catholics. We, above all others, have constantly affirmed that the gospel was first lived and preached before it was written. Today we must face the implications of this thesis.

Whatever the evangelists wrote they had to receive from the Church for none, except John, were eyewitnesses of the ministry of Christ. Mark entered on the scene only after the resurrection; Luke was a Gentile doctor from Antioch; the canonical "Matthew" was an anonymous author of the late first century. The synoptic evangelists had to draw on materials which only the Church could supply. John, too, was markedly dependent on the full faith of the Church for he wrote not a mere reproduction of words and deeds but a profound interpretation of their meaning and mystery.

This dependence of the evangelists upon the Church focuses light on a second level in Gospel study. The materials which the evangelists record were already illumined by the full light of the Spirit.

The Church has never locked up her memories of Jesus in a hermetically sealed box to be opened only when someone wanted to write a documented history with barren references to exact times and places, with static photographic reproductions. On the contrary she constantly interpreted and applied the words and deeds of Jesus that they might play a vital and informative role in her own life. The history of the Man-God was never viewed as a mere incident of the past. It was seen rather as a power always operative, ringing a challenge, and charting a course for Christians in the present.

This daily use of Jesus' words and deeds was bound to shape their telling and to bring out what was deep and rich in every event. The Gospel record, therefore, drawing its material from the Church, often shows an identification tag of community usage.

The miracle stories, for instance, are drawn from the preaching of the apostles. This preaching involved the recital of how Jesus "went about doing good and healing all who were in the power of the devil" (Acts 10:38). Keeping to the demands of oral style and following the rabbinical pattern, the first preachers described the wonders of Christ with careful economy of phrase and with indifference to irrelevant details of time, place, and circumstance. The account was whittled down to brief notes on three phases: (1) the illness and condition of the sufferer; (2) the action of Christ the wonder-worker; (3) the saving effect of his power.

Miracle Stories

The Gospel miracle stories reflect this community use. They are not a candid photo with background and details but a clean etching of what is strictly essential. The story of the cure of Peter's mother-in-law is typical; it presents only the three points listed above and nothing more: (1) a brief indication of her illness—"Simon's mother-in-law was keeping her bed, sick with fever" (Mark 1:30); (2) a terse action photo of what the miracle worker did—"Drawing near, he took her by the hand and raised her up" (v. 31); (3) a cryptic final statement of the effect—"The fever left her at once" (v. 31).

This crisp brevity is explained by Mark's dependence on a previous oral form which centered all attention on Christ's saving action. Details which would be essential for integrating this incident into a biography of Christ have all been omitted. Such poverty of detail and concentration on what is essential characterize most of the Gospel miracle stories.

The community also had a liturgy to prepare for its distinctive rites of baptism and the "breaking of bread." It was natural to incorporate into the liturgy the story of those events in Jesus' life which prepared for the sacraments of the Church or provided a parallel to them. The recounting of these incidents in the liturgical assembly called for a hieratic style and the rhythm of solemnity.

When incorporated into the written Gospels, these readings of the liturgical assembly retain the color and tone of their cultic origin. The description of the Last Supper in the Synoptics is typical. The courses of food, the songs, the conversation—all this is omitted. We find nothing but a sharply etched portrayal of Christ's eucharistic action in a style which is solemn and lapidary.

The early Church also had to answer many questions and to solve bristling problems. As each difficulty arose, memories of Jesus were rekindled and relevant words of his were recounted. There would have been the question about divorce. Was the Church to use the concession granted by Moses? If so, was she to follow the lenient casuistry of the rabbi Hillel or adopt the stern requirements of the rabbi Shammai? The remembrance of a pointed word of Christ ended the whole discussion: "Whoever puts away his wife and marries another commits adultery" (Mark 10:11). This saying became a directive principle in the community and as such was incorporated into the Gospel.

Other problems called for solution. What was to be done with Gentiles who wished to enter the Church? (cf. Acts 10:15). Some urged that they first become Jews. It was helpful to recall how Jesus had dealt with Gentiles. In healing the servant of a Gentile centurion, he offered to enter the Gentile's house even though Jews looked upon this as a defilement. What is more, he gave full praise to the man's peerless faith: "Amen, I have not found so great a faith in Israel" (Matt 8:10). This conduct of Christ directed the Church's attitude towards Gentile converts; she accepted them just as they were. This incident lived in the Church's memory; more than likely it was already in writing when the evangelists inserted it into their Gospels.

The early Church had its conflicts with a hard core of Jewish Christians who wanted to couple observance of the law with the service of Christ. It was encouraging to remember that Jesus had faced similar controversies. His solution to these thorny problems provided data in controversies in which the Church herself was involved. The frequent rehearsal of his conflicts resulted in a clearly defined literary form which we today call the pronouncement story. The pattern is easy to detect in the Gospels. Everything in the narrative is pared down to bare essentials in order to place emphasis on the conclusive pronouncement of Jesus.

Example — Luke 5:29-32

The story in Luke 5:29-32 provides an apt illustration. First a single sentence describes the situation: "There was a great gathering of publicans and others who were at table with them" (v. 29). Next follows the criticism not only as Jesus heard it from the Pharisees but also as the first Christians heard it from their critics: "Why do you eat and drink with publicans and sinners?" (v. 30). This criticism is met with a memorable pronouncement of Jesus which would serve as a principle of action for the whole Church: "It is not the healthy who need a physician, but they who are sick. I have not come to call the just, but sinners to repentance" (vv. 31-32).

This was the kind of material which the Gospel writers had to use in their accounts of Jesus' ministry. The majority of words and events in our Gospels are there not only because they figured in the life of Christ but also because they served some vital need in the life of the early Church.

It is unwarranted, therefore, to look upon the Gospels as a journalist's report of what happened yesterday. Whatever memories of Christ they contain lived a fruitful life in the soil of the community. The narratives do not follow a chronological succession of events; they do not guarantee verbatim quotations of Jesus' words. The very formulas which the Gospels should have treasured in exact reproduction (e.g., the Lord's Prayer, the words of eucharistic consecration) are found in as many different forms as there are evangelists who recount them.

What the evangelists have preserved for us is not a photographic reproduction of the words and deeds of Jesus but an interpretative portrait as the Church herself prepared it under the light of the Holy Spirit. Jesus himself had promised, "The Holy Spirit . . . will teach you all things and bring to your mind whatever I have said to you" (John

14:26). Under the light of the Spirit, both the Gospel writer and the Church came to see not only what Jesus said and did but, far better, what he really meant for later disciples.

Level Three — Historical Jesus

It is only a study of the Gospels from these two levels of the inspired evangelist and the Spirit-guided Church that brings full understanding of the third level on which all else is based. This is the historical level of the earthly life of Jesus, his words and deeds. A casual reader of the Gospel text might see in his miracles merely human beneficence restoring health to the body. When seen, however, through the eyes of the Church and of the evangelist these miracles reveal the saving power of the messianic Son of God.

We ourselves know what "to hear" means in the rite of baptism and in the story of the cure of the man unable to speak or hear. In the light of the Church's application of this miracle to the transformation of the soul, the story comes alive with new meaning. The miracle is now seen as more than mere restoration of speech and hearing. Working as the Messiah, Jesus changed the whole man, giving not only physical hearing but also spiritual power to hear the Word of God. He bestowed not only physical speech but also spiritual power to speak the praises of God. The Church's use of the miracle story in her liturgy brings us to share her own deep understanding of the full meaning of every messianic miracle.

In the same way, the agony in the garden gains new significance when one remembers that it was originally part of the primitive catechesis. The Greek words which the Church employed and the Gospel writers repeated bear the imprint of community use, echoing words frequently repeated in early catechetical instructions: "Watch and pray." "Pray lest you enter into temptation." These were the words with which the first preachers urged their converts to bear trials and to endure struggles as a real share in the messianic tribulation which must precede the glorious parousia or second coming of Jesus.

In the light of the contribution which each Christian must make in "prayer and watchfulness," the Church was able to interpret the true meaning of Jesus' words to his apostles in the garden. His plea, "Watch with me," was not an appeal for human sympathy. It was rather the heartful cry of a father and shepherd urging his own to be faithful to God in the dread "hour" of messianic struggle with the powers of darkness.

IN CONCLUSION

Through this interpretation coming from the first days of the Church and preserved for us in the Gospel's Greek translation of Jesus' Aramaic words, the scene in the garden comes alive with deep meaning which rings resonantly in the heart of every reader. The apostle in the garden and the Christian in the struggle of daily life are one. Both hear the same plea to "watch and pray" that they may be found worthy of the "hour" of Christ's supreme glory.

Gospel study, therefore, means work on three levels. It is only when we view its message from the perspectives of the evangelist's insight and the Church's understanding that we too, under the light of the Holy Spirit, shall come to appreciate the full, rich meaning of Christ's words and deeds during the days of his earthly life.

An example may help to make all this clear. The floor of the ocean is littered with sea shells. Only some of these are swept onto the shore. There, wind and rain smooth away sharp edges. The sunlight brings out rich coloring. A person finds them there, gathers them up, and forms them into a vase, beautiful in shape and color. To appreciate the exquisite beauty of the vase we not only gaze at its whole contour and color pattern but also study the graceful turn and delicate tint of every shell.

It is the same with the Gospels. Our Lord's life was like an ocean bed filled with words and deeds in such abundance that books could not contain them. Only some of these reached the shore of the primitive community. There the wind and light of the Spirit shaped the telling of each deed and illumined its deep meaning. The Gospel writers gathered together these living memories and molded them into Gospels under the light of the Spirit. No two Gospels are the same; each has its own contour and coloring.

To measure the truth and to appreciate the beauty of the Gospel we cannot be content to study merely the formative work of the evangelist and the overall impression of the literary composition. We must also study each unit in the Gospel, as we would study each shell in a vase, to discover what the Holy Spirit disclosed to the Church—the full meaning of each event and the vital significance of each word in the life of Jesus.

CHAPTER 7

Contemplative Interpretation of the Bible in Today's World

Carroll Stuhlmueller, C.P.

The writings of Barnabas M. Ahern are crafted with brilliant, exegetical skill. They also reveal a personal piety unusually deep and strong. He read and studied the Bible with contemplative eyes. Yet, these same eyes saw plainly the hurts and pains of life and so the serene, careful movement of contemplation and study turned at times into a forceful challenge. He possessed a compulsion for integrity and justice. Barnabas Ahern was at once contemplative, scholar, and activist—and in that order. He joined a religious order committed to contemplative prayer. Within that setting he was assigned to teach Holy Scripture. His religious congregation reached out apostolically, with a special vow to keep alive the memory of Jesus' passion and death, and here came Father Barnabas' penchant for ministering to the poor and sick.

Several lines from Psalm 139 prepare us to continue in our appreciation of Father Barnabas' method of biblical study, at once contemplative, scientific, and pastoral:

> Where [O Lord] can I hide from your spirit?
>   From your presence where can I flee?
> If I ascend to the heavens, you are there,
>   if I lie down in Sheol [our common grave], you are there too.
> If I fly with the wings of dawn,
>   and alight beyond the sea,
> Even there your hand will guide me. . . .
> Darkness is not dark for you,
>   and night shines as the day (Ps 139:7-12).

The ancient psalmist did not compose these lines easily. The inspired author of Psalm 139 felt the sting of hatred, prejudice, and betrayal. The psalmist even seems to over-react in verses 19-22:

> Deceitfully [the wicked] invoke your name . . .
> With fierce hatred I hate them.

The darkness of verse 12 then is the dark night of desperation. Or again, such darkness surrounds the agony of peering at the awesome being of God, during long vigils of contemplation, or seeking the absent God while visiting sick people and befriending homeless people.

In order to exemplify the contemplative approach of interpreting the Bible, we turn first to the writings of Father Barnabas and then to the Old Testament prophets.

CONTEMPLATIVE AMID THE AGONY OF INJUSTICE

Contemplation never lifted Father Barnabas into the clouds, shielding him from the *Sturm und Drang*, the distressful gales of life. He was drawn to sick and impoverished people. Back in the 1940s he regularly visited patients with tuberculosis in Chicago hospitals. These were the outcasts or, if you wish, the AIDS patients of their day. During his years in Rome, Italy, he frequently went by trolley car and by foot to the church honoring St. Benedict Joseph Labre, the hobo saint who died as he lived, homeless and penniless. Father Barnabas' writings, therefore, not only moved with the peace and joy of the Holy Spirit (cf. Gal 5:22-23), but even now, at some distance from their composition, they still leap off the page with prophetic fire; they crackle with stern challenge to convert and reform.

Other details about Father Barnabas' background show up in his lectures and publications. He comes from a family not only with close ties to the Democratic Party of Chicago but also with fierce loyalties to the Catholic Church in this midwest city. In the preface to this book, Most Reverend Timothy J. Lyne, Auxiliary Bishop of Chicago, speaks gratefully of Father Barnabas' impact upon this local church. In Chicago, ecclesiastical and civil institutions kept close ties with ordinary people and neighborhood organizations. Chicago is the birthplace of many lay movements of Catholic action in marriage and the family, in the workplace, among youth. Chicago, though a metropolitan center of the United States, continues to be a cluster of small "towns" or precincts. Chicago Catholics frequently identify themselves by their parish church and their precinct or ward. If we add to these facts the Irish ancestry of Fr. Barnabas M. Ahern, then we understand his ability, at one and the same time, to challenge and charm, to focus upon domestic details and sweep across the world scene. He directed this same sharp yet compassionate insight upon the pages of the Bible.

Father Barnabas remembered people's names and family background with elephantine rigor. Once met, never forgotten! Similarly he stored away a treasure trove of biblical data. He summoned at will important facts from Old Testament chronology like the names and dates of kings and the sequence of prophets, or he overwhelmed you with trivia like the single Aramaic verse in the Hebrew text of Jeremiah (Jer 10:11). He knew when to push hard on principles and to compromise on details, to laugh heartily and to be austerely penitential, to rely upon a quick mind and yet to prepare long and diligently for any assignment. Hence his final days with Alzheimer's disease and its concomitant forgetfulness and helpless passivity evoked such pain.

During his active years nothing was left to chance, yet he acted and spoke spontaneously. Spontaneity, in fact, burst loose with memorable and colorful images, with adroit and expansive vocabulary, with down-to-earth phrases sprinkled with arcane, foreign words, with roller coaster ups and downs as quotations from the mystics rush down to citations of Broadway plays. *Le style est l'homme même*—"The style is the very person," wrote Georges-Louis Leclerc de Buffon back in the eighteenth century, and with Father Barnabas all of these personal facets show up in his method of interpreting the Bible.

Father Barnabas, however, was not simply a facile popularizer. Biblical studies flowed from his depth of prayer and from his agony for honesty and justice. His literary output and lectures were born of long and meticulous research. We encounter in him the rage of Old Testament prophets as well as Jesus' agony before suffering and prejudice. Contemplation and social justice, rhetoric and charism, study and memorization prepare scholars like Barnabas M. Ahern to be *objective and scientific*. Only in this way can anyone properly interpret the Bible in the spirit with which it was written.

What Father Barnabas wrote in a handout for students to accompany class lectures on the prophet Isaiah draws the lines of his own portrait:

> No prophet of the Old Testament combined more perfectly than Isaiah earthly wisdom and sagacity, courage and conviction, ver-

satility of gifts and singleness of purpose, on the one hand, with clear vision and spiritual intuition, a love of righteousness and a keen appreciation of Yahweh's majesty and holiness, on the other. [Editor's note: He now quotes from an unknown source.] "Never, perhaps, has there been another prophet like Isaiah (Moses, of course, excepted), who stood with his head in the clouds and his feet on the solid earth, with his heart in the things of eternity and with his mouth and hands in the things of time, with his spirit in the eternal counsel of God and his body in a very definite moment of history."

Later in this chapter we will look among the Old Testament prophets for this extraordinary combination of tradition, contemplative fervor, and burning zeal for justice. A contemporary biblical student needs the same ingredients for intuiting the depths of meaning in the inspired Word of God and for effectively communicating its message today.

Scholarship Within Contemplation

Barnabas M. Ahern did what very few biblical scholars would dare. He began a scholarly article, this one about the reading of a single verse in the Greek text of Paul's letter to the Ephesians, to be published in the *Catholic Biblical Quarterly* (April 1947), with the statement:

> The presence of the Holy Spirit in the souls of the just has ever been a living source of happiness for all men [and women] of good will. In every age earnest Christians have found in this dogmatic truth a sweet foretaste of life in heaven. [Editor's note: See Chapter 23 of this book.]

Is "sweet foretaste," many will ask, a scholarly phrase? Yet this prayerful, contemplative approach to biblical interpretation is exactly the attitude with which the inspired author conceived the Epistle to the Ephesians and transcribed transcendent intuitions into logical sentences. The first part of this epistle, indeed, abounds with ecstatic formulas: i.e.,

> . . . rooted and grounded in love, [you] may have the strength to comprehend *with all the holy ones* what is the breadth and length and height and depth, and *to know the love of Christ that surpasses knowledge*, so that you may be *filled with all the fullness of God* (Eph 3:17-19).

St. Paul is advising us to be so "rooted and grounded in love," as to *know* "with all the holy ones" that which *surpasses our ability to know* and so "be filled with all the fullness of God." Barnabas Ahern's approach as a scholar was to be "rooted and grounded" in the mind and heart of the inspired author, or as Pope Pius XII expressed it in the *magna carta* of Catholic biblical scholarship:

> Let the interpreter, then, with all care and without neglecting any light derived from recent research, endeavor to determine *the peculiar character and circumstances of the sacred writer*. [The] supreme rule of interpretation is to discover and define what the writer intended to express (nn. 33–34).

The "circumstances of the sacred writer" in composing the Epistle to the Ephesians was a posture of contemplative prayer.

Contemplation and Contemporaneity

At the same time, the Epistle to the Ephesians is firmly grounded on planet earth. The inspired author wrestles with very human problems. We read:

> Immorality or any impurity or greed must not even be mentioned among you, as is fitting holy ones, no obscenity or filthy or suggestive talk, which is out of place (Eph 5:3-4).

The Apostle Paul then proceeds to provide "household rules" for the family and other segments of society. Here we find a compromise to ancient culture or societal practice as to admit the dominant role of husbands (to whom wives are to be submissive) and to accept the institution of slavery (in obedience to the master).

Barnabas Ahern too lived finely tuned to daily life, whether its heavy injustices or its cultural riches in the fine arts and theater. Ministers of the Word must be in touch with what he called the *Zeitgeist* or spirit of the times. He refers to Tennessee Williams' *Streetcar Named Desire* and to Stanley, one of its characters. He mentions Gelber's play, *The Apple*, off Broadway in 1961. He writes further in what is now Chapter 8 in this book:

> This is our *Zeitgeist*, to feel for the real; it is becoming more and more the spirit of the Church. Today our Catholic people are seeking true values and brook no substitute. Time-honored customs and long-standing traditions, human pedigrees and platitudinous

cliches, vested interests and the practices of centuries—all these are being tested by fire. The burning heat of criticism dissolves the tawdry tinsel of pretense and the frail facade of make-believe. . . . Authority may still impose the attitudes of yesteryear; it cannot shut the seeing eye nor trammel the piercing mind.

In this same chapter, he courageously declares that religious truths, even those defined at Vatican I, may need to be reinterpreted, yet certainly not to be repudiated or ridiculed. Caution and loyalty, however, do not so much temper his enthusiasm for reform as they provide balance to the statement and give his audience time to absorb what he is saying.

Father Barnabas felt this same way about the documents from Vatican II. He played a prominent role as *peritus* or adviser to bishops. He helped to draft documents on the church and on revelation. Through a lecture to the U.S. bishops gathered in Rome at the time of the council, he swayed them with his reasons for not having a separate document on Mary but rather including this material as a chapter in *Lumen Gentium*, the constitution on the Church. In a letter to me dated May 4, 1966, after the close of the council, he reacts to a theological congress at a large Catholic university, where he was one of the principal speakers. He writes:

> [This congress] was prestigious but ineffectual. The papers and discussions struck me as Conciliar rather than post-Conciliar. Most of the work was historical and analytical rather than progressive and directive of the future. I failed as much as the others to develop the theme that the Conciliar documents are but the opening of the road which should widen and deepen. There is so much danger that the Conciliar documents will be treated as . . . the "last word" to be venerated rather than [a seminal idea] to be developed.

It is the role of a mystic to look upon the sacred as doors opening into further divine mysteries, even into the awesome presence of God (cf. Isa 6). On the other hand, it belongs to the social activist to tackle new problems within the contemporary *Zeitgeist*. "The road . . . should widen and deepen [and] be developed." Father Barnabas' humility, moreover, clothed this negative yet progressive critique with a cloak of genuine holiness and made it worthy of consideration by conservative persons. He wrote: "I failed as much as the others."

Father Barnabas displayed courage and clarity, forward vision and humble self-examination. So often with most of us, one or another of these qualities gets into the way of the other! Father Barnabas' words still ring true in today's world where we tend to treat Vatican II documents historically and analytically rather than progressively directive of the future. Here he joined another influential figure at Vatican II, Karl Rahner, S.J. In one of his final major discourses at Boston College in April 1979, Father Rahner wrote that Vatican II is the *first* major official event in which the Roman Catholic Church experienced itself as a *world* church. If it is the *first major step as a world church*, there is a long way yet to go, persistently and humbly, absorbing the richness of new world cultures beyond European and North American borders.

This same mix of scholarship and contemplation, confidence and humility, brilliant turns of phrase and a stark call for justice show up in the earliest publications of Father Barnabas. Some of these can be found in Part III, Chapters 8 and 9 of this book. Back in the early forties, he prepared mimeographed handouts for Passionist priesthood students. We refer again, as earlier in this chapter, to his notes on the prophecy of Isaiah. He first summarized the historical background, internal to the land of Judah, external across the ancient Near East. After showing the involvement of Isaiah in state politics, Father Barnabas concluded that "[Isaiah's] chief concern was with religious matters; political events are mentioned . . . only because they have a bearing on the religious life of the people." He quotes Isaiah 8:13, "With the Lord of hosts make your alliance—for him be your fear and your awe."

Father Barnabas then offered a portrait of the prophet Isaiah, his aristocratic lineage, his solid educational background that availed itself of the best in a brilliant, cultural period, his marriage with "the prophetess," blessed with two sons (Isa 7:3; 8:1-4). In treating the theological content of the Book of Isaiah, Father Barnabas wrote:

> The single theme which binds all the parts of this great book together is *salvation by faith*. Isaiah is the St. Paul of the Old Testament. His book is a Hebrew edition, so to speak, of St. Paul's epistle to the Romans. For Isaiah, as for St. Paul, "the just person lives by faith" (Isa 7:9b; Rom 1:17).

True, St. Paul is here quoting from another prophet, Habakkuk (Hab 2:4), yet it is Isaiah who developed the doctrine of faith into a complete theology of salvation. Father Barnabas frequently quoted these other lines of Isaiah:

> Thus says the Lord God,
>   the Holy One of Israel:

> By waiting and by calm you shall be saved,
> in quiet and in trust your strength lies. . . .
> The Lord is waiting to show you favor
> and he rises to pity you (Isa 30:15, 18).

Father Barnabas then wove together like warp and woof his own words with lines and ideas of Thomas Merton (*Monastic Orientation*, Series III, Advent 1951–August 1952, pp. 9–11):

> For Isaiah God is most of all transcendent. Hence we must live by faith. The whole book of Isaiah and the Advent liturgy stress the rejection of human methods and earthly satisfactions and consolations in order to transfer all our desire and trust to God alone. Before [Isaiah], we find the Israelites making many acts of faith, but Isaiah is the first one who teaches that faith must be the very LIFE of the people of God. Because God is ALL, their souls must be permanently and completely steeped in faith. . . . Yet it must be *fides formata a caritate*—faith formed by charity. We cannot approach the God of holiness who *is* Charity (cf. 1 John 4:8), unless we ourselves are holy and are transformed by charity.

In order to illustrate and support this method of interpreting the Bible from a contemplative, even ecstatic position, so apparent in the writings of Father Barnabas, we turn to Old Testament prophecy. In both cases we find an exalted form of rhetoric; each are masters in the use of metaphors, in rhythm of sound, in appealing to emotions and to a sense of honesty and justice, with a preferential regard for the sick and defenseless.

After first attempting to clarify prophetic ecstasy, we look at the way tragedy and injustice, particularly that associated with sickness and disability, induced prophetic mysticism in Old Testament times. The parallel with Father Barnabas comes first from our remembrance of his visiting the sick, especially patients suffering from tuberculosis and secondly from his outreach towards the homeless (his devotion to St. Joseph Benedict Labre) and others neglected or even despised by society.

PROPHET-MYSTIC, WHO ARE YOU?[1]

Fr. Barnabas M. Ahern ranks with other contemporary "saints" who provide a setting for studying Old Testament prophecy. While

---

[1] This section is adapted from articles published in *Biblical Research* 36 (1991) 35–60 and in *Priests & People* 5 (May 1991) 178–86.

remaining within contemporary society and involved with its issues, they push us out into uncharted areas. Extraordinary people, heroically dedicated to social justice, like Edwina Gateley (*Psalms of a Laywoman*, 1981; *I Hear a Seed Growing*, 1990), Daniel Berrigan (*The Dark Night of Resistance*, 1971), Dorothy Day (*The Long Loneliness*, 1952), or Ernesto Cardenal (*Apocalypse and Other Poems*, 1977), show up as poets or contemplatives as well as prophets of social justice. Their intense concern for justice envelops them mystically within a dark night of the soul, feeling as keenly as they do (1) about the massive annihilation of young people through war, (2) about physically and mentally impaired persons, strapped in the dark or left to wander dangerous streets, and (3) about women victimized into prostitution. In these unclean, no-God areas, contemporary mystics meet God beyond forms or structures acceptable to Torah or Church. These heroic people show how social justice and mysticism each impact and sustain the other. Father Barnabas too ventured into areas uncharted by theology or canon law. Examples of this outreach occur in Part III of this book as well as in Chapter 13, "Role of Law in the Church."

From this background that blends justice and prayer we initially understand mysticism as an overpowering experience of God that reaches beyond accepted religious structures and explanations and therefore one that leaves the person alone, reaching for God who is present yet wrapped in darkness.

At the Heart and on the Outer Edge

Yet to abide in darkness presumes that the prophet-mystic does not form another structure of life but rather remains loyally within the original community of Israel or Church. Paradoxically such prophet-mystics remain simultaneously at the heart and on the outer edge. They reach back to initial impulses of biblical religion and give these religious positions a central importance, all the while de-emphasizing other positions (like ritual or positions of authority) which may be equally prominent in the Torah or five books of Moses. Likewise with Father Barnabas! No one ever questioned his loyalty to the Catholic Church. In fact, the final chapter of this book, composed by Bishop Paul M. Boyle, a fellow Passionist who knew Father Barnabas certainly as well as, if not better than, anyone else, writes of him as churchman par excellence. Yet Father Barnabas was always startling his audience with questions and challenges from what he called the *Zeitgeist* or spirit of contemporary society, areas yet to be addressed by church ministry and ecclesiastical law.

The peripheral positioning of biblical prophets, according to Joseph Blenkinsopp (*A History of Prophecy in Israel*, 1983) exemplifies for us this way of functioning on the outer edge of society, in many ways defying categorization, yet always a loyal member of the society. We, therefore, encounter difficulties in defining their role or vocation. Even the biblical titles for prophets, like *nabi'*, *ro'eh*, *hozeh*, or *'is 'elohim*, fluctuated in their use, as the well-known passage of 1 Samuel 9:9 shows:

> For he who is now called prophet [*nabi'*] was formerly called seer [*ro'eh*].

Biblical prophecy, therefore, never arrived at a single well-defined, generally accepted job description.

According to John Barton, in his book *Oracles of God* (1986):

> [prophets] fit no categories that were recognized even by very early readers of the . . . scriptures. . . . They were individuals without a status, lone geniuses whom any generic title belittles.

Barton also wrote, even more pointedly:

> . . . the classical prophets were eccentrics, strange and alarming figures who broke the mould of accepted beliefs and values but who, in the process, changed those values and altered the national religion into something scarcely paralleled in the ancient world.

This status of lonely genius, on the outer edge of institutions, afforded the prophets a unique, absorbing awareness of God's presence and a literary style *sans précédent*. Although Father Barnabas remained more visibly at the center of Catholic church life than these descriptions of Old Testament prophecy permit—he was an official *peritus* or adviser at Vatican II and a member of several Roman pontifical congregations or commissions—nonetheless, he maintained a prophetic independence and voiced unique intuitions which lifted him out of the ecclesiastical mold, at least in the time leading up to and during the council.

Ecstatic Rhetoric from the Outer Edge

Prophets, more so than priests or kings, sensed an immediacy of divine presence and divine command. This absorbing sense of God impacted a prophet's literary style and through the thunderous yet patterned roll of sound and imagery stunned and shaped society. In the case of Father Barnabas, his voice rang with a high pitch and at first did not attract. Yet he invested his words with such religious intensity and moral fiber, as well as with creative and colorful imagery and sound, that he swept the audience along.

Turning to Old Testament prophecy we hear Amos declare:

> The lion roars—
>   Who will not be afraid!
> The Lord God speaks—
>   who will not prophesy! (Amos 3:8, NAB).

In this passage the *New American Bible*, unlike other standard translations, uses exclamation, not question marks. Divine compulsion seizes Amos, no doubt about it! God's roaring word must sweep onward.

Besides the immediate impact of divine presence, prophets moved beyond normal human reactions in still other ways. As Guy P. Couturier writes in the *New Jerome Biblical Commentary*, their interior agony for justice, as in Jeremiah 4:19-21, led "to emotional outbursts the diction of which goes beyond anything preserved from contemporary or earlier prophets." This example of ecstatic, prophetic rhetoric occurs in the Isaiah tradition:

> Oracle on the wastelands by the sea:
> Like whirlwinds, sweeping in waves through the Negeb,
>   there comes from the desert,
>   from the fearful land,
> A cruel sight, revealed to me:
>   the traitor betrays,
>   the despoiler spoils. . . .
> Therefore my loins are filled with anguish, . . .
> I am too bewildered to hear,
>   too dismayed to look.
> My mind reels,
>   shuddering assails me;
> My yearning for twilight
>   turns into dread (Isa 21:1-4).

To feel its full pressure, we must shout passages like this one into the boisterous storm at night.

While this literary style may be found occasionally in legal literature of the Old Testament (i.e., Exod 15), it occurs quite frequently in prophecy. In this way prophets keep contact with Israel's official religion, yet ecstatically burst the limits of its style and vocabulary.

Passionate concern for justice, the agony of its betrayal, and the ineffectiveness of Israel's traditional institutions push prophets beyond the borders of orthodoxy set up by religious authorities. They are not satisfied with any false or facile fulfillment of divine laws. Prophets, at least some of them, find an intense awareness of God in a dark no-God land, an awareness so intense at times as to sweep them into outbursts of rage and rhetorical excesses.

Father Barnabas surprised his audience, perhaps himself at times, with the sweep of his oratory. He urged the reform of liturgy, the use of the vernacular, the stripping away of authoritative veneer and the outreach of compassion to sick and destitute people, hungry for new and more adequate forms of prayer and worship. We refer to the chapters in Part III of this collection of his writings.

Prophet-Mystic and Justice for Sick and Disabled Persons

Once again we search for the conjunction of prophetic mysticism and social justice, this time through the prophet's concern for sick and disabled persons. This side of the topic fits in well with what has already been said about Father Barnabas' outreach to tuberculosis patients; in the early years of his priesthood they were the shamed and feared outcasts of family and society.

It has been remarked several times that mysticism leads a person beyond the borders of orthodoxy, into areas where theology is yet to track the presence of God. Yet, in this "atheistic" or "agnostic" mist, prophecy discovers an intense, overwhelming presence of the divine. At times prophets find themselves without the proper language to express it. At other times they are defiant enough to speak out and so to be instrumental in opening and extending the borders of orthodoxy.

We first look at the prophets' willingness to disregard rules of orthodoxy by touching the dead; second, we observe the prophet's way of linking the healing of sickness with religious conversion and the call of sick and disabled persons into the final, glorious reign of God.

The Unclean Domain of Sickness, Disability, and Death

As a basis for our discussion, we note the Torah's position about ritual uncleanness connected with sickness, disability, and death. Leviticus 21 clearly prohibits any of its priests from functioning at the sanctuary if they have become unclean through contact with persons seriously ill or dead, or if the priests show any physical "deformity." This question has been pursued by Mary Douglas ("The Abominations of Leviticus," 1966), with an update and refinement by Robert P. Carroll ("One More Time Leviticus Revisited," 1978). The same prohibition continues after the return from exile, as we see in the prophecy of Ezekiel and Haggai. They concluded that brushing against anyone sick or dead renders one unclean (Ezek 44:25; Hag 2:13).

The laws of Leviticus seek to preserve the holiness of the temple and its ritual, by prohibiting sick and disabled people from entering and "defiling" the holy place. This is summed up in Leviticus 15:31:

> You shall put the Israelites on guard against their uncleanness, lest they die through their uncleanness by defiling my tabernacle which is among them (JPSV).

Deuteronomy also viewed disease as a manifestation of God's wrath (cf. Deut 28:21-24).

The early prophets seem to have completely disregarded these Torah rules about uncleanness, at least judging from the accounts of Elijah and Elisha. Elijah not only touched but extended himself over the deceased son of the widow, three times, till "the life's breath returned to the child's body and he revived" (1 Kgs 17:22). In another example, a corpse was hurriedly buried in the grave of the prophet Elisha. Immediately upon touching the prophet's bones, the dead person sits up alive. In this situation there is a double uncleanness, two corpses; the bones even of a prophet are legally unclean, the corpse of the other person equally so. Within the traditions of the former prophetic books (Josh, Judg, 1-2 Sam, 1–2 Kgs), human bones were not contaminating, as the Torah declared, but were, in fact, a means by which God marvelously restored life. God was actively present where orthodoxy claimed divine absence. The prophets were willing to disregard the rules of ritual cleanliness which separated them from the sanctuary and to plunge into the world of the dead, the world of spirits and demons.

Clearly associated with sickness and death is Yahweh's image as Lord of pestilence and death. Pestilence and death, indeed, were considered demigods that surrounded the throne of God, always at the divine beck and call. A series of passages in the psalms, as well as in 1–2 Samuel, Amos, Hosea, and Ezekiel, supports this position. For instance, in 2 Samuel 24, the Lord sends pestilence to punish David for a census. The passage in Ezekiel 5:11-17 echoes many words and ideas from 2 Samuel 24. See also Amos 4:10; Hosea 13:14; Habakkuk 3:5; Psalms 78:49; 91:5-6. These passages manifest the amoral aspect of divinity: unorthodox if judged humanly, but actually beyond the reach of religious tribunals.

The belief that deceased persons remained alive and could be contacted through necromancers is explicitly condemned in Deuteronomy 18:9-14 and plainly evident in the episode of Saul's tryst at Endor (1 Sam 28:8-25). Here the necromancer was able to summon Saul's ghost back to life. The text speaks, grammatically in the plural, of gods rising up from the earth *('elohim 'olim)*, so that we are in the fearful realm of divine beings.

In these instances, prophets were willing to wait beside those who mourned the dead, to enter the frightening realm of spirits and demigods, and to risk contamination and theological error in order to provide protection against serious dangers, plagues, and pestilences as well as to console sick, bereaved, and disabled people.

Many of these aspects of prophecy reach beyond the life-experiences of Fr. Barnabas Ahern. Yet he entered pell-mell into the controversies and discussions of Vatican II; he encouraged new ministries by which priests and religious more adequately met contemporary needs. In some ways, he was living in areas uncharted by law and theology—as one can read in Chapter 13 of this book.

Healing and Conversion

We consider two other ways by which prophet-mystics responded, still more positively and energetically: first by bonding together healing and conversion; second, by welcoming sick and disabled persons into the final, glorious reign of God. In the latter case, sick and disabled persons may have constituted a metaphor for helpless people, incapable of sustaining a full life, free of suffering and oppression. Yet, the choice of such a metaphor is significant—as though one were to say today that AIDS patients constituted the core group with which God reconstitutes the disciples of Jesus.

Prophets like Hosea and Jeremiah consistently united healing *(rapa')* and conversion *(shub):* cf. Hosea 6:1-2; 7:1; 11:4; 14:5; Jeremiah 3:22; 8:18-23; 30:12-17; 33:6. On the assumption that the Lord would receive unclean persons, Hosea admonishes the people for not going to Yahweh when they were sick with oozing wounds (Hos 5:13-14). In the following chapter Yahweh actually summons sick and disabled people:

> In their affliction they shall look for me:
> "Come let us return to the Lord,
> For this is the God who has rent, but will now heal us, God who has struck us, but will now bind up our wounds" (Hos 6:1-2).

True, in the larger context of this passage God rejects the people's prayer, but not because of what they say but because "their piety is [elusive] like the dew that early passes away" (6:4). While the language is metaphorical, nonetheless, such metaphors presume Yahweh's willingness to receive sick and disabled persons, even to bind up their wounds, actions which would have rendered the temple priests unclean and barred from the temple! Only prophets would be so bold as to describe God as too unclean to enter the temple!

In Isaiah, God inflicts the country with multiple wounds, with welts and gaping gashes, not drained or bandaged, or eased with salve (Isa 1:5-6). Isaiah accepts the common understanding of the Torah that sickness was an apt symbol for a sinful nation. Yet the Lord is not acting to destroy but to move the people to repentance. In chapter 38, the prophet Isaiah has no problem whatsoever of being contaminated religiously by providing a healing remedy for the ailing King Hezekiah. Sickness and healing mirrored the way of salvation.

For his part, Fr. Barnabas Ahern developed many of these ideas in a theological way, showing how configuration with Jesus Crucified was not only the result of intense union with the glorified Lord Jesus but also the way of sharing his resurrection. See the chapters in Part VI of this anthology. In fact, one of these chapters (ch. 21) summarizes the core ideas of his doctoral dissertation and represents the quintessence of his spirituality. In these studies, Father Barnabas looked upon suffering as much more than an ascetical practice. It was a strong and determined, yet also a strange and disorderly way towards full salvation in Jesus. Here Father Barnabas reached beyond traditional asceticism, at times very negative in its attitudes towards life and activity. He recognized the presence of the risen, glorified Jesus, initiating this suffering and bringing it to a perfection beyond our dreams. This fulfillment follows an earthly route, often eschewed by traditional piety.

Citizens of the Messianic Reign of God

We turn now to our last point, in which prophets invite sick, disabled, and even dead people into the messianic reign of God. Because of their mystical bent and religious courage, prophets were willing to enter into the strange, dark, and silent area of Sheol, the grave or underworld. We read, for instance, in the Book of Psalms:

> In utter terror is my soul—
>   and you, Lord, how long . . . ?
> For who among the dead remembers you?
>   Who praises you in Sheol? (Ps 6:4, 6).

Sick and disabled people were only one step away from Sheol. Some, like lepers, were the living dead. Prophecy identifies these people as the ones being called to the final, glorious triumph of God, the very ones whom the Torah prevented from coming near the God of the living. Father Barnabas lived long moments of prayer with the deceased. Purgatory, that interim place of purification and transformation for the dead, turned into an important stepping stone towards contemplation. This position reaches us with marvelous insights in Chapters 24 and 25 of this book. For further guidance we turn to Old Testament prophecy.

The first passage to consider is from the Book of Micah:

> On that day, says the Lord,
>   I will gather those who limp,
> And I will assemble the outcasts,
>   and those whom I have afflicted.
> I will make of the lame a remnant,
>   and of those driven far off a strong nation;
> And the Lord shall be king over them on Mount Zion,
>   from now and forever (Mic 4:6-7).

The sacred area of the messianic Mount Zion throngs with those whom the law declares ceremonially unclean and therefore forbidden to enter the temple!

Zephaniah, likewise, continues in the same spirit, bringing unclean and outcast people into the temple:

> Yes, at that time I will deal
>   with all who oppress you:
> I will save lame persons,
>   and assemble the outcasts.
> At that time I will bring you home,
>   and at that time I will gather you (Zeph 3:19-20).

This passage shows literary bonds with Hosea and Jeremiah, combining the act of healing with that of conversion or restoration. There are other ties with the prophecy of Micah.

Last of all, one of the final editors of the Isaiah tradition acts under the influence of Second and Third Isaiah (Isa 40-55, 56-66), the former with the imagery of deserts and marshlands where the glory of the Lord will appear (Isa 40), the latter with the explicit invitation to disabled or mutilated persons to enter the temple (Isa 56). The passage reads:

> Then will the eyes of the blind be opened,
>   the ears of the deaf be cleared;
> Then will the lame leap like a stag,
>   and the tongue of the dumb will sing. . . .
> Those whom the Lord has ransomed will return
>   and enter Zion singing,
>   crowned with everlasting joy (Isa 35:5-6, 10a).

Earlier in verse 2 the prophet unites ecstatic visions of the glory of God, a glory that transforms unclean, foreign, desert lands into a temple of the Lord's presence. Surrounding the throne of the Lord is the heavenly host of unclean disabled persons!

In concluding this section, we recognize prophecy's dare to extend the boundaries of the sacred to embrace unclean or profane areas, inhabited by demigods, by sick, disabled, and deceased persons. Here, in this dark abyss according to the Torah, prophets discovered the glory of the Lord and heard the call to worship. The mystic bent of prophecy allowed them to venture beyond the set categories of where God ought to be. Their compassionate spirit for social justice led them to discover healing and salvation for the religiously unclean.

IN CONCLUSION

Biblical prophets were frequently mystics, gifted by a discovery of God beyond the borders of what was generally considered acceptable for God, at least as priests and Levites officially interpreted the Torah or five books of Mosaic law. In these instances, prophets did not have the language or the restraint, proper to orthodoxy, and so were swept by passion and rhetoric, even into amoral situations. What moved prophecy outside Torah boundaries was a strong passion for justice among people who were ostracized.

Torah legislation declared foreigners as well as sick or disabled persons to be unclean and incapable of representing Yahweh, the God of life. Prophets reached out to bond with sick and disabled persons, even if it meant at times dealing with demigods. The "remnant" whom they summoned into the eschatological reign of God consisted of sick and disabled people.

Prophet-mystic is the term we use to describe those moments of prophetic preaching where they paradoxically reached to the depth of covenant-faith in a God, compassionate and faithful towards the poor and oppressed (cf. Exod 34:6-7), yet peered beyond the ways in which the covenant was being understood and implemented. Prophets persevered long by a faith which left them without clear answers, often ostracized and persecuted, in a state which later mystics described as the dark night of the soul.

A strong concern for social justice kept the prophet down-to-earth, capable of interacting with practical demands of life. Prophets reacted strongly against some of the Torah prohibitions about clean and unclean. And in their reaction they became passionately involved, eloquently rhetorical, sternly and even stridently obedient to their conscience. For these reasons we link them with modern prophets like Thomas Merton or Ernesto Cardenal, where poetry is translated into everyday life, lived exaltedly, intensely, often in isolation. Yet, these prophets eventually claim their place in the daily life of Israel and the Church.

Several times this chapter referred to the dark night of the prophet-mystic's soul. Fr. Barnabas M. Ahern plunged to the depths of this dark night after the end of the Vatican Council II. As obscurity closed in on him, he became ever more fearful. Without anyone knowing it, the first ravages of Alzheimer's disease had gripped his mind. As the darkness descended, only God knew the mystic visions within his soul.

Part III
The Bible and Openness to the World

Finally, my brothers [and sisters], whatever is true, whatever is honorable, whatever is just, whatever is pure, whatever is lovely, whatever is gracious, if there is any excellence and if there is anything worthy of praise, think upon these things. Keep on doing whatever you have learned and received and heard and seen in me. Then the God of peace will be with you (Phil 4:8-9).

CHAPTER 8

The World, Its Culture, and Church Ministry

We address the objectives and norms to train for priesthood and other forms of religious ministry in our contemporary world. We reach beyond the norms of the American bishops for priesthood preparation. Our aim centers rather in the exigencies and existential situation for carrying out these norms in our contemporary age.

FEELING FOR THE REAL

The existentialism of Heidegger, Sartre, and Kierkegaard, as a philosophic system, is on the wane. But people of our day are living existentialists. For one reason or another they are men and women with nerve ends exposed to reality, but they feel the real not through the convoluted wrappings of reflection but through the immediate touch of experience.

They are living the spirit of existentialism, allergic to feeling keenly the very heart of experience in the here and now. People of our times are intuitive rather than reflective, with a sharp sense of what lies deep, beneath the surface and beyond the facade. Feeling and realism—these are focal points in thought and in life. This is our *Zeitgeist*—the spirit of earthly men and women, of spiritual men and women; no one escapes it.

In American drama, Tennessee Williams was a great playwright because he felt exquisitely and makes his audience feel what is deep and real in sordidness. We loathe the cruel, lustful Stanley in *Streetcar Named Desire*; but our loathing is an authentic feeling, touching the strength of passion in a man who is half-brute.

In the year of 1961, one of the off-Broadway theaters was running Jack Gelber's play *The Apple*. Reviewers cried out against its "nightmarish frenzy" and "vast perversity." The fact was that Gelber had broken the bottle of experience and jabbed his audience with its jagged edges. The whole absurdist theater, like the "beatniks" of our country and the "angry young men" of England, is always feeling for the real. Whatever may be our personal attitudes, we are blind if we do not see in these phenomena symptoms of the age to which we belong.

Modern art forces the same conclusion upon us. Surrealism and the cult of impressionism cannot be explained simply by the fact that art has yielded to the camera full superiority in the field of life-like portrayal. The artist is par excellence a person of his or her time. Dedicated to expressing insight and emotion, artists are dependent on contemporary experience for the measure of their intuition and the depth of their feeling. If we fail to understand what surrealists are doing, it may be that we are too close to ourselves to understand what we ourselves are always doing, feeling for the real.

The same spirit breathes in our novels. Ernest Hemmingway was a master novelist, so too Graham Greene and J. F. Powers, because they accomplished with consummate artistry what men and women of our day are always doing, cracking shells and tearing down facades to uncover what is deep within and so to touch reality.

It is true, the reality which the average man and woman seeks is a thing of flesh and human emotion alone. Kazan's *Splendor in the Grass* gives the feel of love and its tensions in a young boy and girl. But "the splendor of the grass withers and its flower fades" (Isa 40:7). The love of boy and girl in Kazan's play is a perfect symbol of the bent of mere humanness; its end is dissolution. "The bent of mere humanness," St. Paul writes, "is death; the bent of spirit is life and peace" (Rom 8:5-6).

Some of our artists, it is true, have come to seek an integral reality, probing what is deepest in humanity, not only in *physis* and *psyche* but in God-given *pneuma* which unifies and can even make divine man and woman. The earthly artist seeks what is real in a frail person doomed to die; the spiritual artist seeks what is real in the whole person made to live. But both artists, the earthly and the spiritual, are feeling for what is real.

Albert Camus, I believe, had begun to reach for *pneuma* when his groping hands were stilled by untimely death. Dame Edith Sitwell, I am sure, has found it. It is significant that her discovery of the whole real coincided with her entry into the Church.

BREATH OF THE HOLY SPIRIT

This is our *Zeitgeist*, to feel for the real; it is becoming more and more the spirit of the Church. Today our Catholic people are seeking true values and brook no substitute. Time-honored customs and long-standing traditions, human pedigrees and platitudinous clichés, vested interests and the practices of centuries—all these are being tested by fire. The burning heat of criticism dissolves the tawdry tinsel of pretense and the frail facade of make-believe. Nothing is too time-honored or too sacred to escape the fire of passion for the real. Authority may still impose the attitudes of yesteryear; it cannot shut the seeing eye nor trammel the piercing mind.

The spirit can lead to unwarranted iconoclasm. The devouring flame of passion for the real can destroy not only the rind but the fruit, not only the shell but the nutmeat which it encases. In biblical studies we have had to save the Bible from the devastating fire of *Entmythologiezung* or "demythologization." Under the influence of the existential philosophy of Heidegger, persons such as Rudolph Bultmann and Martin Dibelius have so demythologized the Gospels that they have left us only the shadow of a merely human Jesus and the meaningless memory of a life without content or challenge.

This same spirit, on the other hand, if only it cherishes respect for what is truly real, truly unchanging, truly the teaching of the Church, is bound to bring out what is richest in the Church's life. For the Holy Spirit is breathing in the *Zeitgeist* of our times, giving the power of divine grace to our human search for the real. It is the action of the Holy Spirit as much as the spirit of our times which has forced Roman Catholics to measure up to tested standards of excellence. Facing squarely the compelling requirements of vital needs in our day, the church in America has prepared a thorough-going plan for the formation of religious sisters and has launched singular advances in the fields of education, social work, and hospital administration.

The spiritual life of our people and the apostolic work of religious men and women are becoming more and more an expression of a passionate feeling for the real.

At the liturgical convention in 1962 it was obvious to all that our best Catholics are seeking *direct* contact with the mystery of faith. Through the medium of their own language they want to reach the heart of the mass—just as many priests through an English breviary want to tear down the facade of mumbled words to reach the heart of inspired prayer. The clamor for the vernacular is a ground-swell which is always mounting.

LIVING ENCOUNTERS WITH GOD

The spirit of our time is creating a new emphasis. Our Catholic laity has turned to the Bible in Catholic Family Movement (CFM) groups, Mr. and Mrs. Clubs, and Adult Study Circles. Papers on Scripture are featured in every major convention—in the liturgical, the mariological, the theological, in the congress for the priest-directors of CFM, the Congress for Major Religious Superiors, the Convention of the College Theology Society and many others. All this is proof that our people are seeking to be nourished no longer by crumbs which fall from the table but by substantial food which God has provided in word and in worship. In the spirit of our time American Catholics seek the rich fullness of God's revelation.

The whole revision of our catechetical method is witness to this. Men and women experience a *malaise* over previous patterns of religious instruction. During January 1962, I went through six manuscripts of new catechisms. Under the influence of the Eichstätt Conferences and of scholars like Hofinger, Goldbrunner, and Danielou, and under the impact of catechetical schools like Lumen Vitae in Belgium and its ideals and methods, teachers of sacred doctrine in colleges and high schools as well as leaders of CCD work are driving for a new presentation of the faith. They are convinced that the deepest reality of religion is not a speculative dogmatic system and a detached moral code. These things lack full, dynamic realism until they are seen as part of living encounters between humanity and God. The "Thou" and "I" dialogue of Gabriel Marcel the philosopher and of Martin Buber the theologian is the authentic aim and sure guarantee of religious instruction. The new catechisms present the truth of the faith and the demands of morality in a *kerygmatic* framework. Everything is integrated into the *Heilsgeschichte* or "salvation history" of God's saving interventions in the world to claim for us an immediate loving response in the body of Christ.

PROPHETIC SACRIFICE OF NONESSENTIALS

It is this same drive for the real which impels us to hew down walls of human making, separating people whom God would join together in one fold and under one shepherd. This year our Holy Father, Pope John XXIII, did what no pope before him would have dreamed of doing. For the moment he laid aside his office as pontiff to speak as a fellow human being, as Joseph Roncalli. To a group of Jews who came to him, he spoke the greeting, "I am Joseph your brother" (cf. Gen 45:3). In our country, the spirit of seeking the real is tearing down walls between white and black. In the Church, the same *Zeitgeist* is surging beyond the tentative directives of the *Immortalium animos* of Pius XI to tear down walls of separation and to forge that real global unity which God planned. "There is neither Jew nor Gentile, there is neither slave nor free person, there is not male and female; for you are all one in Christ Jesus" (Gal 3:28).

Diffident spirits are sometimes shocked by this passion for the real which burns in the heart of many modern Catholics. Cardinal Alfrink's words at Strasbourg will stir opposition in people who are suspicious of the new spirit and who prefer to live in the secure mold and comfortable patterns of the past. On the other hand those who live vibrantly in the spirit of today will hear in the Cardinal's words a truth of deep, solid reality. He asks:

> Could it not be that love for the church and solicitude for non-Catholics require, in our ecumenical era, that we sacrifice certain non-essential things? Could it not be that some things, no matter how precious they might be for the church, must be swept away because they obstruct a clear view of the church?

In these probing questions the heart of Cardinal Alfrink is alive with the spirit of the prophets of old. And to be a prophet is a glorious vocation. Its only requirement is that one have the light of God to see reality as God sees it and the courage to move beyond rigid boundaries as Jesus did for the sake of poor people, for sick and disabled people, for foreign and dispossessed people!

AT THE HEART OF DIVINE REVELATION

Nothing in the life of the church is escaping this process of being re-thought and re-expressed. The old presentation of the virtues—the meaning of obedience, the concept of virginity, the relation between active and contemplative life—these thought-patterns are all being probed, not to discard the virtues but to understand them truly by seeing their place in humanity's living encounter with God.

Even theological truth knows the same sifting. In the schema which Yves Congar presented to the preparatory session of the Second Vatican Council he asked not only for the consideration of important truths which the First Vatican Council left untouched but for a reconsideration and restatement of truths which Vatican I defined. The work of Geiselmann and Tavard on the relation between Scripture and tradition is typical. The new explanation of our Lord's action at the Last Supper proposed first by the non-Catholic Joachim Jeremias and seconded by Père Benoit and Dom Dupont would greatly strengthen our presentation of the Eucharist as a sacrifice. The work of Lyonnet and Durrwell on the resurrection is bound to alter our own concept of the passion of Christ and our preaching of this mystery. True theologians like Karl Rahner, Yves Congar, Jean Danielou, Henri de Lubac, and in our own country, John Courtney Murray, Gustav Weigel, Godfrey Diekmann, and George Tavard appear to some as making shipwreck of the faith. The simple truth is that they are people of our time—with a passionate zeal to uncover the real. Dogmatic teaching is the frail human expression of divinely revealed truth. Like everything human, its tone, color, and wording must be perfected if we are to convey to others our new grasp of what is real in the heart of God's mystery.

This spirit is modern through and through, but it is not "modernist." Contemporary theologians are persons of faith who accept the full domain of God's revelation. Yet the very richness of the revelation urges them:

> to penetrate it ever more deeply,
> to express it ever more exactly,
> to communicate it ever more convincingly.

Theologians seek to do what the Church herself has done at early ecumenical councils at Chalcedon, at Nicea, at Ephesus, constantly perfecting the human expression of the divine mystery of Christ.

"Modernists," on the other hand, are not believers. We use the term here in its technical sense. Modernists recognize little or nothing divine or revealed in the deposit of faith. For them, theological truths of faith are the projection of the human mind expressing its own inward drives. If modernists alter previous teaching, they do so in order to express more clearly their interpretation of themselves and to perfect what is their own fabrication.

A feeling for the real is the spirit of our times—both among earthly people and spiritual people. Those who find comfort in the old order will shout insubordination, heresy—as the Old Testament priests shouted heresy before the realism of the prophet Jeremiah's preaching (Jer 26:8). But this cry is only the gasp of a dying order. The living power of new wine, the wine of the spirit, will burst the old wine bags.

Look around our country. The renewal of religious life is here to stay. Liturgical participation is a force which nothing will check. Go to any convention—the biblical, the theological, the liturgical, the mariological—and you will see that the new wine is in ferment. More and more this spirit is coming into seminaries and theological schools which means it is the spirit of tomorrow. Look at the periodicals which are alive to what is best in the Church—*Theological Studies, Theology Digest, Worship, Nouvelle Revue Théologique*. This is the thinking of theologians guided by the spirit; and the thought of the scholar penetrates inevitably to the people. What our great religious minds are thinking today, our people will be thinking tomorrow.

PULSING WITH THE *ZEITGEIST* OF THE CHURCH

If, then, we are to prepare men and women for a living apostolate, we must prepare them to meet the challenge of the future. Students in our theological schools are our future ministers who will preach retreats to priests and sisters who know the meaning of liturgy, who know that the resurrection as well as the passion is to the fore, who have learned to see the sacraments as moments in the *Heilsgeschichte* or "salvation history" and as thoroughly eschatological in their frame of reference. Our future priests and religious ministers will be preaching to laymen and laywomen who have grown intelligent in the faith through competent religion courses in high school and college, through the zeal of enlightened pastors and religious educators and through CFM discussions which have made them see the role of the laity in the church, the power of the liturgy, the sacramentalism of all that is human.

To send out religious leaders with a kit of sermons which could have been written in 1910 is to send "hewers of wood" to people who cook on electric stoves and use microwave ovens. To send out future priests and religious ministers with minds insulated to the vital life of the Church is to miss the providence of the times in which God has placed us. The saving riches of the Church are wide open to everyone. The worth of apostolic laborers will not be the worth of blind confidence in their ordination as priests or their diploma from theological schools. It will be the worth of their authentic life vitalized by the dynamism of the Church within the *Zeitgeist* of our contemporary age.

VITAL FORMATION FOR MINISTRY

How shall we achieve a formation which is vital and contemporary? What practical expedients will secure the full formation of students as dynamic apostolic laborers in the world of 2000?

First, lest there be any misunderstanding, I shall reiterate what I said in the beginning. This is not an *Ersatz*. The first requirement we must meet is to fulfill the ecclesiastical and educational norms not only in the things we teach but also in the spirit we inculcate. Our very *Zeitgeist* requires now, more than ever before, that our students be solidly anchored in obedience to the Church, in respect for the magisterium, in the power of criticizing the merely modern, the novel, the bizarre in addition to a fine sense for what is real and for what is best—all this we must foster both by our own attitudes and by the directives of our training. This we must do, but we must not leave other things undone.

The "other things" were my whole concern in this presentation. Their practical implementations would involve the following:

1. We must make seminarians and theological students "church-conscious." We want to share fully the spirit of the Church in our own day. Hence we must open wide the windows of our seminaries and theological schools that the life-giving spirit of the Church may become the breath of our vocation and the vitalizing power of all its sacred forms. If we close our eyes to the light of the Church, and shut off our concern from the interests of the Church, we shall die. We are committed to ecumenism, to the revival of liturgy, to the activation of the laity, to the mission-mindedness of the modern Church, to its yearning for peace, to its sense of realized eschatology, to its awareness of all life as a sacrament. Thus, concerns of the Church must be our concerns. The advance of the Church must be our advance, if we are to meet the challenge of our vocation—to preach in the Church the compelling relevance of the passion of Christ. A withdrawn blind obedience in this day is a flaunting of the providence of God which has called us to live dynamically not in the eighteenth century but in the third millennium.

2. Seminarians and theological students must, therefore, become "periodical conscious." It is chiefly through the periodicals that they

will grow in the mind of the church, for it is here that we find the living thought of the Church. For college students I urge as required reading *Worship* and *America.* Later *Philosophy Today, Cross-Currents, Thought, The Modern Schoolman, The Thomist* should join the list. *Theology Digest, Theological Studies, New Testament Abstracts, Nouvelle Revue Théologique,* and *Worship* are "musts" during the period of graduate theological studies. [Editor's note: New periodicals he would have added would include *Old Testament Abstracts, New Theology Review,* and *The Bible Today* which he was influential in founding.] Through this reading they will become aware of new realities in the Church's vision of herself.

3. We must make provision that at every stage of development the minds of seminarians and theological students are as wide open to the vital thought of the Church and the world as are the minds of the best students in other Catholic universities.

4. To secure this development we must provide regular cultural programs in every area of modern life: social, religious, political.

5. We must bring our students into contact with the methods, the interests and the personalities of men and women living in the world. Seminary life where students are cut off from opportunity to meet others and to measure their views is not a preparation for the challenge of the ministry. Such students go out smugly self-complacent, yet talking on a level which a living world does not understand.

6. Professors in seminaries and theological schools must be vitally alive to the Church in action, conscientious in attending those congresses and conventions which will help bring the spirit of the Church into theological departments. What is more, I think we ought to sacrifice some of our vacation time to attend one of the great conventions—the liturgical, the CCD, the CFM—that we might keep in contact with people who are seeking the real.

If only we as professors or as future priests and future ministers of the Church are fully alive to the rich values which the Church in our day is constantly finding, then—and only then—shall we share with others the life-giving reality which we have discovered.

CHAPTER 9

Père Lagrange:
Pioneer of Modern Catholic Biblical Scholarship

To every student of the Bible, the month of March brings a memory which will never fade. On March 10, 1938, death came to Père Marie-Joseph Lagrange, O.P., whom Father Vaccari, S.J., himself a veteran biblical scholar, called the "master of masters" in biblical science. As Père Lagrange lay dying at St. Maximin near Marseilles, his last whispered words were for the city he loved and the school he founded, "Jerus—, Jerus—." Jerusalem.

The memory of Père Lagrange is more needed today than ever before. We owe him a lasting debt of gratitude for the unique role he played in the resurgence of modern biblical studies. Even more, we owe him the loyal tribute of following his example, so timely in our day. For we also live in a period when Catholic biblical scholarship must move with great prudence and courage, not merely to avoid the errors of science without faith but also to calm the fears of people with faith "who imagine that whatever is new should for that very reason be opposed or suspected." These are the words of Pope Pius XII in his 1943 encyclical on biblical studies, *Divino Afflante Spiritu*.

Few persons have matched Père Lagrange in the labors and sufferings of his untiring scientific study of Scripture. Fewer still have weathered this stormy sea of Galilee with such humility, peace, and positive gain.

BORN IN A STABLE

When Père Lagrange entered the Dominican community at St. Maximin in 1879, he brought to God's service a mind sharpened by the study of law and a heart burning with love for Scripture—the fruit of his training at the Sulpician seminary of Issy. Ordained a priest in 1883, he taught history for a while and then studied Oriental languages under Miller and Reinisch at the University of Vienna.

In 1890, the superior general of the Dominican Order sent Père Lagrange to Palestine to open a center for the study of Scripture at Saint-Etienne, the shrine of the martyrdom of St. Stephen, just north of the ancient walled city of Jerusalem on the Nablus Road. This commission laid upon him a work of creation, of making something out of nothing. When he arrived, the only books in the library were the few volumes which he brought with him.

Discouragement and feelings of helplessness, however, melted away under the Palestinian sun which shone upon him as he toured the Holy Land and Transjordan during the first months after his arrival. Walking in the footsteps of his master, Père Lagrange came alive with a warm glow of enthusiasm for the task which his superiors had assigned him. On November 15, 1890, he delivered an address before the civil and religious dignitaries of Jerusalem to inaugurate the program of the new school which ever after would bear the familiar name *l'Ecole Biblique.*

The full title of the school, *l'Ecole Biblique practique d'études bibliques*, indicated that the school was to function as a center for the study of the Bible, not only as a sacred and inspired text but also as a literary work to be illumined by the extensive discoveries in archaeology, philology, and contemporary literature. Père Lagrange was convinced that it was time for the Catholic Church to move competently in a field which up to then had been the almost exclusive preserve of non-Catholic scholars. Beginning around 1850, many scholars from a liberal and rationalist position had used their scientific findings to dissolve supernatural truth within Scripture. Père Lagrange was bent on employing the same methods and discoveries to substantiate the claim of the inspired word and to bring out its full theological riches.

The beginnings of this work were very humble. Library facilities and instruments of scientific research were lacking. Of the four professors who constituted the staff only one had received previous technical training. The first students of the school were a group of three Dominican seminarians.

GROWING IN AGE AND WISDOM

Under the direction of Père Lagrange, l'Ecole Biblique was bound to grow. The most potent factor in its development was the launching of *Revue Biblique* in 1892. This periodical was to serve as an official organ for the scholarly work carried on at the school. The high scientific level of the articles, most of them from the pen of Père Lagrange himself, drew promises of collaboration from other Catholic scholars like Vigouroux, Cornely, Batiffol, and Knabenbauer.

The number of students increased, courses expanded, and research intensified. The sacred sites in Palestine, Egypt, Transjordan, and Syria were visited and explored, inscriptions and excavations were studied at firsthand. All this heightened the scientific calibre of the articles which appeared in the *Revue Biblique*.

Urged on by a well-founded sense of accomplishment, Père Lagrange projected another venture, a series of biblical commentaries which would incorporate not only the doctrinal insights of patristic tradition but also the new knowledge which was arising from scientific investigation. He himself wrote a commentary on the Book of Judges, the first volume of the series, *Etudes bibliques*.

NAILED TO A CROSS

Storm clouds, however, lowered on the horizon. The times were perilous. Within the Church itself some had been infected by the new thought. Fascinated by the methods and findings of rationalist scholarship, these Modernists accepted also the principles and conclusions of the rationalist school. Writers like Alfred Loisy denied to the religion of Jesus and of the Old Testament a true historical foundation.

Père Lagrange and his school were bound to fall under the cloud of criticism voiced by ill-informed "defenders of orthodoxy." Critics with good intentions but little understanding failed to distinguish between philosophic postulate and scientific method, between literary style and theological content. To individuals of this character, made fearful by the eighth capital sin of ignorance, Père Lagrange and the Jerusalem school appeared to be cast in the same mold as those who were using science to destroy the supernatural truth of the Bible.

The attack resounded violently in Europe. Jerusalem, however, was far away; and Père Lagrange never permitted the rumblings to ruffle the peace of his own soul. Lightning bolts of denunciation were aimed at his doctrinal integrity, yet he continued to work placidly, making steady advance along the broad, deep lines which he had followed from the beginning. In moments of great tension he would slip away to follow the devotional practice of the way of the cross.

One will search long in his writings to find a single word of bitter complaint against Catholics who were questioning his orthodoxy. His only acknowledgment of their attack was a more explicit effort to show the chasm which separated him from the unbelieving biblical scholar. Never did he permit fear of attack to impede his work. Articles and books followed one another in quick succession. He strode along like a giant, quietly stepping over hurdles of criticism and intent only on positive advance.

At last the tide of controversy grew so strong that it swept him away from l'Ecole Biblique for a whole year, to teach mathematics in France. When at last his superiors authorized him to return, they did so on condition that he confine his work to the less contested field of the New Testament. God writes straight with crooked lines. The fruit of the recommendation matured in the wonderful commentaries which Père Lagrange prepared on the Gospels and Epistles. He might never have composed these if the raging controversy had not forced him to change his course from the Old to the New Testament.

RISEN IN GLORY

The years which followed were comparatively free of criticism. For Père Lagrange, the night had passed and day had come. Catholic authorities were now able to see clearly the merit of his work, the soundness of his positions, the need for using his methods. L'Ecole Biblique enjoyed worldwide prestige; *Revue Biblique* became the outstanding Catholic periodical on Scripture, the one read and quoted by non-Catholic scholars.

More than all this, however, Père Lagrange was forming at l'Ecole Biblique a living witness to his aims, his method, and his spirit. Scholarship coupled with loyal devotion to the Church, dedication to study joined with versatility and warm humanness, analysis of the text implemented by practical work in the field of archaeology. All this was his legacy to the school he founded.

The last thing he wanted was blind loyalty to himself. Nothing would grieve him so much as loyalty which only looks back and refuses to let the spirit face the challenge of the present. He knew well enough that the backward glance of Lot's wife had turned her into a pillar of salt (Gen 19:36)! It is the glory of l'Ecole Biblique that it is alive, like Père Lagrange, to each new finding and to all new knowledge. Today, class work is carried on often enough without any mention of his name and frequently with a contradiction of some of his views. This is just what he wanted: a living search for truth and not a mummification of his suggestions and conclusions.

PÈRE LAGRANGE STILL LIVES

When I studied at l'Ecole Biblique in 1947, the faculty counted a roster of Scripture scholars of worldwide fame: Pères Vincent and Abel, De Vaux and Benoit, Lavergne and Savignac, Couroyer and Steve. Most of these had been formed by Père Lagrange himself; all bore the cachet of his spirit.

They are memorable equally for their scholarship and for their warm Christian goodness. The spirit at l'Ecole Biblique is a family spirit. Everyone who has studied there is called ever after an *ancien élève* (an "old student"); they always belong to l'Ecole.

Père Abel was not only the erudite lecturer on the period of the Maccabees, he was also the devoted sacristan and the friendly *cicerone* of our Thursday afternoon promenades. How the old man gleamed with joy as he led us to some site in the old city and explained its every nook and cranny as only he could who knew by heart every inch of Jerusalem and every detail of its long history. Père Vincent was too old to teach but young enough to give hours of advice on every point of biblical scholarship and to regale us with rollicking stories of the bright and dark first days of the school.

Père Benoit, always brilliant in the classroom, guided our monthly tour of the countryside and our excursions to more distant points. The day before, he worked out an ample bibliography and posted it on our board that we might know everything about everything he would show us. Benoit added the golden tones of his voice to the singing of the divine office.

With all this warm friendliness, the professors at l'Ecole Biblique were even more alive with plans, projects, and work. The first finds were already coming in from Qumran. Materials had to be classified from the school's own excavations at Tel-el-Farah. Pères De Vaux and Benoit were busy editing *Revue Biblique*. Plans were shaping up for the vast project of the *Jerusalem Bible,* a new French translation of the whole Bible with introductions and notes to each book. Each professor was writing articles and books, as peaceful in the melee of the Arab-Jewish war as was Père Lagrange in the war of criticism which constantly flailed him.

THE TRIBUTE OF A BOOK

At that time, Père Roland De Vaux, O.P., was the director of l'Ecole Biblique. Many count him the equal of Père Lagrange in versatility of talent and accomplishment.

Père De Vaux was then preparing material for a monumental work which has now appeared in English under the title *Ancient Israel. Its Life and Institutions* (New York: McGraw-Hill, 1961). Dr. William F. Albright has declared this book "without a peer in its field." There is no hyperbole in this word of praise. Père De Vaux has covered every feature of Israel's life: religious, civil, social, and military. He has carved each unit like a cameo, sharp, clean, and brilliant. He has covered each theme with a competence which seems effortless simply because each theme is the result of years of research.

This work, like so many others, is the fruit of the spirit of l'Ecole Biblique. It is the fair flowering of the work of Père Lagrange who labored so earnestly and suffered so keenly to safeguard for the Church a biblical scholarship which is at once thoroughly scientific and profoundly doctrinal in its study of the word of God.

We need his spirit of devoted love for the Church and of fearless search for biblical truth now, as never before, in this our day. [Editor's note: Readers may want to refer to *Père Lagrange. Personal Reflections and Memoirs* (New York: Paulist Press, 1985) with the subtitle, "The Founder of Modern Catholic Biblical Studies and the Struggle for Theological Freedom in the Modernist Crisis."]

CHAPTER 10

The Haunting Face of Jesus in the Option for the Poor

Cassian Yuhaus, C.P.

Long before Barnabas Ahern became an international celebrity, his tall, gaunt figure was loved and acclaimed by all in the slums of Rome. Before I ever met him and welcomed his powerful personality to reshape my life, I heard what he was doing unseen and unheralded to lift, in whatsoever small way, the oppressive burden from the backs of the powerless poor in the shadows of the imposing basilicas of Rome. It is right as it is a privilege to dedicate this brief reflection in his memory.

It is also significant that this tribute should be offered as the Church and world commemorate a great anniversary: a turning point in history.

CENTENNIAL OF *RERUM NOVARUM*

Certainly among the more momentous decisions made by the Church in the last five hundred years, we must place the daring decision made by a man of unusual courage in the face of violent opposition. One hundred years ago Leo XIII, following the inspiration and great example of Emmanuel Wilhelm Von Ketteler, Archbishop of Mainz, turned the face of the Church away from the controlling grip of the landed aristocracy and arrogant nobility toward the working poor and powerless. It was courageous in the extreme. The Church, but twenty years before (1871), had lost its lands, its armies, its political power, and its invested wealth in the bloody revolt of the Italian States against the papacy. Cavour from the north and Garibaldi from the south put the irremovable pincers on the famed Papal States. Now this daring pontiff imprisoned inside the walls of a tiny Vatican garden dared to risk what support he had from the remaining, dominant heads of states and manipulators of financial destinies in his straightforward address to the "utter misery of the masses."

On May 15, 1891, Leo XIII declared in *Rerum Novarum:* "The momentous gravity of the current state of affairs fills every mind with painful apprehension." He readily admitted, "The discussion is not easy, nor is it void of danger. It is no easy matter to define the relative rights and mutual duties of the rich and the poor."

For one hundred years the Church has struggled to defend those "relative" rights and to clarify those "mutual" duties. But that defense and those clarifications somehow always came from the side of the rich. The subject was the rich. The poor were object, and at times, abject.

It was not until our day and the raising up of yet another prophet, more courageous still, that the Church made a far more momentous decision. The Church declared its place by preference and destiny—on the side of the poor. The option for the poor in the life and teachings of Pope John XXIII and in his council may well be the greatest event of our times. The poor become the subject. The rich the object. The renewed Catholic social doctrine begins and proceeds from the side of the poor. We have yet to grasp the significance of this inversion.

Impeding this grasp are three dangers we face both in the Church at large and within dioceses, parishes, and religious communities, especially of men. They are indifference, confusion, and escape.

The first and perhaps greatest danger is indifference which leads to apathy. This is seen in the light–handed treatment the profound and revolutionary statements of Catholic social doctrine receive at the hands of many Church leaders. If they were uneducated, their stupidity could be excusable. Inexcusable are attitudes contained in expressions such as, "We've heard it all before" or "Here we go again—the poor, the poor. . . . There are so many other items on the agenda. Let's get on with it."

The second danger is confusion, confusion about the very premises of social doctrine. Was Jesus political? What right has the Church to interfere in the world of business? Are we not to keep the temporal and the spiritual orders distinct and separate? Should not the Church be concerned about souls and their salvation? This argument is raised to its highest level when we call God to arbitrate. Do we trust in providence? Is not sacred Scripture enough? The confusion is multiple: scriptural, theological, and social.

And the third danger is the best cover up of all: Who are the poor? We are all poor! And, can we not say that the poorest of the poor, without doubt, are the spiritually poor—all those nice people with their furs and their Porsches who mean so well? Furthermore, what about the most difficult of all in an affluent society—the bewildered middle-class people. Someone must care for them. And after all "the poor you always have with you" to quote an eminent rabbi. There are so many, many concerns. The great escape.

The utter emptiness of these three approaches is self-evident. The truth is: There *is* no other business on today's agenda. The preferential option for the poor *is* the agenda. Let's get on with that. To do so we need a new look.

There are at least five ways in which the preferential option for the poor should strike us as new and bold, daring and prophetic. We need to catch its freshness, its vigor, its challenge.

First, the option is new in the way it emerged in our day. It was as unexpected and as unseemly as its proponent, John XXIII. It shook the council profoundly and reversed its trend. But we should have known this from Pope John's opening words to the Second Vatican Council in 1962: "The church is and desires to be the church of all but principally the Church of the Poor." And that startling remark of Cardinal Larcaro at the close of the first session (December 7, 1962): "The central theme of this council should be the church of the poor."

Second, it is new in its approach. The option dramatically reverses the traditional approach to the problems of poverty, want, and destitution. That approach was always from the side of the rich. That approach was one of compassion, almsgiving, reaching out and caring for the Lazarus at our door, all of it wonderful and good. Somehow we felt we could reverse it all if only the rich would be converted. That approach utterly failed. There is a limit to the number of Band-Aids you can put on a wound. The problems of poverty, want, and misery must be seen not only from the side of the poor but with the eyes of the poor. Only this will lead to pro-active not re-active concern.

Third, it's new in its extent. We are no longer talking about the poor man, the poor woman and child. We are talking about the classes of poor, entire peoples and populations, races and social groups. We are not talking about "pockets of poverty." We are talking about systemic oppression, unjust laws, oppressive policies, outright criminal discrimination, and social degradation. We are focusing on social sin, the sins of a nation, the sins of a Church, the sins of international conglomerates. Our vision is not only local but global and we see these as interconnected. We cannot attend to one without the other.

Fourth, the option is new in its demands. The task facing all of us is prophetic and imperative. The situation in which we live and to which we contribute is immoral. No one can remain indifferent and claim Christ as Lord. Our task is no less than the transformation of the world: calling forth a new humanity, a new way of thinking, acting, sharing in life on this planet—the Christ-revolution.

Fifth, the option for the poor is new in its urgency. We cannot continue to live in a society where, as Pope John Paul II has repeatedly warned us in *Sollicitudo Rei Socialis*, "the rich become richer at the expense of the poor who day by day become poorer." Clearly we are on a collision course. We rightly wonder with Marcel Proust about the glass wall and the dark people: "whether the glass wall will everlastingly protect the celebrations of the wonderful animals within and whether the dark men who look on avidly in the night will not seize them from their aquarium and devour them." Just a few years ago the Holy See ended its appeal to address the question of international debt with these words, "May our appeal be heeded before it is too late."

In his final word to us before his death, the greatest theologian of our day, Karl Rahner, reflecting in *Faith in a Wintry Season* declared ". . . if Christianity really possessed that degree of radical consistency which by nature it demands, then it would be a springtime in the Church. . . . Each one of us should (instead) see these times as a personal challenge to work so that the inner core of faith becomes alive. Then, of course, the Church itself will shine radiantly again and it will again become clear that the Church is what it was intended to be, a sacramental sign of the world's salvation."

WHO ARE THE POOR?

I wish to make a rather simple, declarative statement as the basis for any further discussion about the poor. Shortly I will respond directly to the question that seems to irritate everyone once discussion turns to the option, namely, "Who are the poor?" But, before attempting an answer to that question, let it be said that whatever further truths may be explored, whatever attitudes are shaped or reshaped in the dialogue, whatever action we shall engage in or disengage from will depend upon our perception and acceptance of a truth at once fresh and bold, stark and alarming, before which there is no hiding:

> For the contemporary church as well as for the world of our day the central issue is the poor.

Our success or failure as church depends upon our perception and our response to this issue. More startling still, our success or failure as human beings upon this planet depends upon our perception and response to the poor. Here is "the" survival issue. Church and Church leaders, states and state leaders, all are divided by the stand they take toward the poor.

Let us now address the question, "Who are the poor?" We may escape the issue by the abstract philosophical answer which is very true, "We are all poor." We could hide the issue in the equally true theological statement, "The rich themselves are most frequently the poorest of all." No. A direct straightforward response must be unequivocal.

"Who are the poor?" By the poor we mean the real not the analogous poor; the actual not the theoretical or symbolic poor. By the poor, we mean indigent and suffering humanity. We mean the economically needy. We mean all who are deprived of the material goods necessary to live with dignity and hope. Above all we mean all those classes of people who are the victims of injustice in whatever form. The exploited, the oppressed, the marginalized. This includes not only the wretched, the beggars, the outcasts, abandoned children, but also the exploited workers, the immigrants, the homeless, the unemployed, drug addicts, people with physical and mental disabilities, as well as the minorities, in particular, the African Americans, the aboriginals, women.

RADICAL APPROACHES

So much has changed in a hundred years. Our approach, our understanding, and our response to the poor have all been radicalized. This radical difference moves in both directions: the way we look upon the poor and the way the poor look upon us. In this look is our response.

In times past it was the individual poor person about whom we were concerned. We "treated" the poor case. We "looked after" the poor family across the tracks. Not that we shall ever cease to be concerned about a particular poor person—the entire context has changed. We will never resolve the problems of destitute poverty case by case.

Today we must look upon entire classes of poor: masses of destitute and marginalized peoples, entire groups, whole nations.

And that leads us directly to a second radical approach. The poor are not poor because they want to be poor, despite the absurd references of a recent President of the United States. They are not poor because they are lazy and obnoxious by the standards of the wealthy and well-to-do. They are poor because they are *made* poor and they are poor because they are *kept* poor. The masses of poor people are victims of unjust laws and unjust systems. And these laws and systems lock them out of the mainstream of human life and development and lock them into their prisons of wretchedness while some of us pass by, look in, and feel, for a few moments at least, "It's too bad."

Well, it is too bad. It is too bad for the rest of us. We may not be so cavalier without grave danger to ourselves and to our children's children. Lazarus of old did sit alone at the gate. Lazarus of old did beg for a crumb. He trusted in God and hoped for a better world after a mean life here. Some few of us were moved to pity. But today Lazarus is not alone. There are simply too many of them. And they are no longer whimpering for a pittance. They are rising up. They, too, read the gospel, the gospel of justice and human rights. They, too, read the papers. They see the commercials. They feel the inequity and they demand justice. While we seem powerless to change the situation, they are becoming empowered to take things into their own hands joined with countless others on both sides of the track. They strive for a better life for all, here and here after. And they shall overcome.

There is yet another way of getting a handle on all this. In their insightful and challenging study *The Bible, the Church and the Poor,* Pixley and Boff, eminent scholars and theologians, urge us to approach the almost incomprehensible situation of massive poverty and destitution by seeing the poor in three categories.

Of the first we are all very well aware. Medellin and Puebla gave us the new terminology to better understand their plight. In the first category are the "marginalized," "the exploited poor"—all those who are forced to live outside the prevailing economic system or who are excluded from participation in it.

Marginalized are the outcasts, the abandoned children, the unemployed, the starving lost people, the beggars, the wretched. "Exploited" are so many migrant workers, tenant farmers, immigrants, service people of all kinds who must accept part-time work with no benefits whatsoever. Of these, too, we are all aware.

There is a second very large category of poor. We experience them daily but of these we do not want to be aware. These poor are victims of unhealthy attitudes, unjust practices and policies; victims of our discriminatory laws and customs; victims of discrimination by reason of race or creed or sex or ethnic origin. Our aboriginal people belong here, our deprived African Americans and, above all, women.

There is a third category of poor where the radicalization of our approach, our understanding, and our response to the poor is immediately evident. Unlike times past, in our day a new class of poor has arisen. They make clear to us that the poor are not only the people "out there," in other lands or in the ghettoes and slums of our urban centers. They are everywhere—in our homes, in our overcrowded prisons, in our hospitals, in our streets. They are the drug addicts, the handicapped, physically or mentally, the suicidally depressed, the homeless, the aged, the unemployable. And these "new poor" are spewed up everyday as the social economic system proves itself increasingly inept and unable to respond to the injustice. Without radical transformation from within we shall never be able to respond.

TWO BASIC TRUTHS

The closer one gets to the problem of the poor in our day, the more overwhelming it becomes. There is the danger, all too prevalent among us, of giving up all hope of changing the situation. "What can *I* do?" "Would that there were some ways I could help. But what can one person do?"

As this attitude prevails, the complexity increases. There is much we can and we must do. Permit me to offer a few suggestions about where we might begin and how we may proceed.

I propose we begin with two truths with which every effort to address the issue of the poor should begin. They are foundational, intrinsic, and indispensable.

In a way the common complaint referred to above—what can one person do?—is quite right. Individually and alone, there is not much that we can do in any area of life. But the attitude itself is mistaken. It fails to recognize the most important truth about ourselves: We were never intended to live alone. By our very nature we are dialogical and relational. Our life is fulfilled only in, with, and through one another. The dominant American individualism is not only erroneous, it is extremely dangerous. It not only dis-enables us from addressing the most urgent problems of our time but erodes the very foundations of our society as Robert N. Bellah tells us in *Habits of the Heart*.

Our mutual interdependence (permit the redundance) is not just a matter of family structure. We are interdependent socially, politically, and economically. This interdependent nature is the foundation for the realization of our own worth and personal dignity. It is the assurance of our freedoms. By God's design we are essentially social. We are necessarily and irrevocably interconnected. We belong together. We have power over one another.

For the first time in human history, science and technology have enabled us to relearn in unforgettable ways the basic oneness and unity of the human family. What we are relearning is that essentially we are undifferentiated. Increasingly we are commingled. Critically, we are interdependent. This may well be the most significant feature of our day.

Solidarity is the reality of human existence and its first hope for survival. We are tightly bound together across and around this small village-home which no one of us owns; all of us receive coequally; each calls this home; and all must share justly. This is the first and the basic truth with which we begin our valiant effort to resolve the grave situation which the Church sums up as "the preferential option for the poor."

The second truth upon which we base every effort to understand and to respond to the problem of the poor is a matter of gospel teaching. More, it is the substance of gospel morality. The distinguishing mark of the disciple of Jesus, his/her foremost characteristic, is a deep love for others expressed in a willing and preferential response to the need of the other in the concrete experiences of life. The follower of Jesus, obedient to his gospel, becomes a "whatsoever person." When all is said and done in my life, only one thing matters, "Whatsoever you did to the least of these, you did unto me." Christian love, Christian justice, human rights, and human dignity are the "seamless garment." They are all of a piece and are the basis of peace and happiness here and hereafter.

The recognition of these two basic truths, the interdependence of the human family and the primacy of love in Christian life, leads us directly to the affirmation of further illuminating principles. They are contained in the truths just enunciated and flow from them.

The first is the priority we assign to spiritual values over material ones. While beautifully and inseparably united in the oneness of the human person, spiritual needs and spiritual values are distinguishable from physical needs and physical values. The primacy belongs to the spiritual: love, freedom, justice, truth. These endow the physical with meaning and value. They control, direct, and enable the physical. The physical needs of all can be achieved only when and if the spiritual needs of each are respected and sustained.

The second principle follows: Created by God, created for God, in the very image and likeness of God, each person is eternally sacred—of whatever color, creed, race, or sex. Each is endowed from the moment of conception in this world to the moment of inception into the next with a certain inalienable dignity, with human rights that are to be sustained at every stage of life. Hence, the single unchangeable regard within a wide spectrum of differing expressions for the unborn, the babies, children, youth, the middle aged, the old and infirm.

The third principle addresses the context of this entire reflection. Not only are we essentially interdependent as human beings, we are also interdependent as village dwellers with all the other animals and with the living earth itself. The integrity of creation means precisely that we live together within the earth systems in a respectful and harmonious relationship. All life is held sacred and the life-giving systems upon which we all depend for happiness, growth, and development are safeguarded for all.

CHALLENGE FOR CHANGE

In addressing the foundational truths and principles for the Christian response to the poor, the Church appeals not only to the highest truths of divine revelation but to the highest and noblest instincts of the human heart. It all sounds very utopian, overly optimistic. Not so. The Church and Church men and women have been around too long to fall into the trap of idle dreaming. We acknowledge the fearful reality. We are on a collision course. Our world is divided between the few and the many; between the have and the have not; between the privileged and the deprived; between the rich who daily become richer at the expense of the poor, and the poor who daily become poorer; between the powerful and the powerless.

The super struggle today is not between superpowers. It is between two great sociocultural systems in severe tension and in dread of each other: (1) the superculture of high technology and sophisticated science and (2) the much larger and more traditional culture of the poor throughout the world.

Neither can exist without the other. A threat to one is a threat to the other. Little success has been made in working out a suitable equation for the well-being of both. The issue is whether we shall form a renewed vision of life as sacred and noble for all, as possible and achievable for all, or continue to widen the gap between us.

We shall not attain this vision unless, as Pope John Paul II so poignantly reminds us, we name the devils that afflict us, unless we identify the root of the evils that threaten to destroy us. These are seen to be two: "The all consuming desire for profit and . . . the thirst for power with the intent of imposing one's will upon others." He further states in *Sollicitudo Rei Socialis*, ". . . not only do individuals fall victim to this double attitude of sin, nations and blocs can do so too . . . it is a question of moral evil, the fruit of many sins which lead to structures of sin."

This, then, is really the heart of the matter. Our situation today is entirely different. The challenge is to change the structures that maintain systems of injustice, exploitation, and inequity. The challenge is to utilize the amazing new powers of resource and discovery to find a valid and creative response for the transformation of society, the reshaping of our world. The challenge is to overcome apathy and indifference, fear and ignorance, and dare to create from among examined alternatives a better world for all people, rich and poor alike.

In embracing and proclaiming a preferential option for the poor, the Church and Church people oblige themselves to repudiate any alliance, political or social, with those who unjustly hold power or privilege in society. It means, as Pope John Paul declares explicitly, "to be in solidarity" with all categories of people to effect structural change that alone will eliminate systems of injustice.

The Church courageously accepts the challenge for herself in the first place. In *Justitia in Mundo* the bishops state: "*Anyone* who ventures to speak to people about justice must first *be just* in their eyes. We must undertake an examination of the modes of acting and of the possessions and lifestyle found within the Church itself."

Each of us who accepts discipleship with Jesus must take our stand as he did on the side of the poor. As Pope Paul VI proclaims in *Octogesima Adveniens*, "Today more than ever the word of God will be unable to be proclaimed and heard unless it is *accompanied by the witness* of the power of the Holy Spirit, working within the actions of Christians in the service of their neighbors."

Part IV
The Church, the Body of Christ

As the body is one though it has many parts, and all the parts of the body, though many, are one body, so also Christ. For in one spirit you were all baptized into one body, whether Jews or Greeks, slaves or free persons, and we were all given to drink of one Spirit (1 Cor 12:12-13).

CHAPTER 11

Christian Union with the Body of Christ

Today there is a growing trend towards strong realism in explaining St. Paul's theme of the body of Christ. Far from interpreting it as a mere metaphor signifying the collectivity of Christians as an organization, many Pauline scholars explain it as a literal designation of the risen Christ in all his concrete reality. This contemporary insight into Paul's thought has led J.A.T. Robinson to complain, "One could heartily wish that the misleading and unbiblical phrase the 'mystical' body had never been invented."

A biblicist, however, may never forget that other norms besides Scripture determine the formulation of doctrine. The fact is that the encyclical *Mystici Corporis* presents cogent reasons to show how aptly this phrase expresses the full theological content of the Church's teaching. However, the absence of this expression from Scripture, plus the fact that contemporary formulae do not always square with Pauline thought patterns, urges a reinvestigation of the scriptural source of our present doctrine. As Pope Pius XII pointed out in *Divino Afflante Spiritu,* much is to be gained for understanding a dogma by pressing the sources of revelation for their precise literal contribution.

The following pages present a summary review of pertinent allusions to the body of Christ in Paul's letters: First Corinthians, Galatians, and Romans. It is in these epistles that this concept first receives explicit expression. Here too we find the principles which underlie all later development of this theme in the letters to the Colossians and Ephesians.

EXPONENTS OF REALISM

Much work has already been done to demonstrate the dynamic realism of Paul's thought. Canon Cerfaux has affirmed time and again that, in using the words "Christ" and "body of Christ," Paul never speaks of a pneumatic or mystical Christ but always of the real historic person who rose from the tomb and ascended into heaven. Departing from the earlier position of authors like Prat and Allo, he insists that Christians do not form a mystical Christ but rather belong to the real organism of his risen person. Père Benoit, after several shifts of view, has also endorsed this thesis, asserting that the body of Christ is not a suprapersonal collectivity but the full organism of the animated body-person who now reigns gloriously in heaven. It is, above all, the monograph study of J.A.T. Robinson, *The Body: A Study in Pauline Theology*, which presents a fully rounded coverage of this theme. In this slender volume, Robinson proceeds from a careful study of Hebrew monistic anthropology to its influence on the Pauline theme of the body of Christ "as the physical complement and extension of the one and the same Person and Life." Needless to say, this realistic thesis has not won universal acceptance. But opposition to it is generally due to the influence of a philosophic postulate or to a misunderstanding of the thought patterns involved.

DIRECTIVE PRINCIPLES OF PAULINE THOUGHT

This fresh approach to St. Paul's thought rests its case on two principles which consistently govern his treatment:

1. As a Hebrew writing on religious themes, Paul speaks of the body not as a neutral element in the body-soul composite of Greek anthropology but rather as an animated and corporeal person whose thoughts and desires are contained and revealed under the sensible aspect of somatic experience. Though it is an exaggeration to say that the Hebrew mentality knew nothing of the body in a restricted and neutral sense, it is quite correct to say that a Hebrew using the word body in a religious context includes in that term the whole person with emphasis on what is sensible and somatic. This Semitic thought pattern is also our own. For though in abstract speculation we divide persons into component parts, still in practical life we are always aware of a person's unity—the inseparable bond between psychic experience and somatic reaction. We deal with one another as corporeal persons. Love and hate, hope and fear involve an automatic somatic experience and inevitably seek sensible expression.

2. As an Israelite, Paul thinks of Christ as a corporate personality. This concept which probably stems from the role of the chief in Israel's

tribal and national life is found frequently in the Old Testament and must be kept in mind if one is to understand the eponymic character of its history, the continuity of God's favor recorded in its sacred literature, the existence and permanence of its messianic hope. This concept is equally important for understanding Paul's presentation of Christ as the new Adam and his teaching on the efficacy of sacramental contact with Christ. Because he is a corporate personality, the Savior died and rose again with vicarious efficacy: "Since one died for all, therefore all died" (2 Cor 5:14). Herein lies his power to share with others the salvific effects of his death and resurrection.

These two notions of the body as a person and of Christ as a corporate personality are essential for correct and full understanding of Paul's teaching on the meaning and efficacy of the body of Christ.

THE BODY THEME IN 1 CORINTHIANS 6:14-17

Paul's first allusion to this theme introduces it not so much as a master principle of his system but as the emergent of a particular context. He writes of it because he chooses to challenge an ugly problem on the level of its own realism.

Christians of Corinth had fallen back into fornication, into the commingling of body with body not merely as a physical experience but as a full personal and psychic interchange of thought and affection. Paul opposes the sin by appealing to another bond which the Christian has already contracted, the well-known bond between his *soma* and the *soma* of the glorified Christ, which is as real as the union between a man and a prostitute: "Do you not know that your bodies are members of Christ? Shall I then take the members of Christ and make them members of a prostitute?" (1 Cor 6:15). In both cases the full person is involved. *Soma* is not merely the physical element in the body-soul composite; for Paul the Hebrew it is the whole self as an animated body vital with the fullness of personality.

It is true, the union between a man and a prostitute has in it only the weakness and earthiness of *sarx:* "Anyone who joins himself to a prostitute becomes one body with her. 'For the two,' it says, 'will become one flesh.'" On the other hand, the union between the Christian and the glorified Christ is vital with the strength and holiness of *pneuma:* "Whoever is joined to the Lord becomes one spirit with him" (1 Cor 6:17). Nevertheless, whether the union be in "flesh" or in "spirit" (in the Pauline sense of apart from God or in God), it is always the full body-person that is involved. It is significant that the "joining" of the Christian to Christ in this text is the *kollasthai* of man cleaving to his wife in God's decree of permanence in marriage of the Greek Septuagint (Gen 2:24).

THE BODY THEME IN ROMANS 7:4

Again in Romans 7:4 it is obviously the course of context which leads Paul to speak of Christians belonging to the risen body of the Savior in language which is uncompromisingly physical. In treating a Christian's relation to the law and to Christ, he has introduced the example of a woman free to marry another after the death of her husband. On the basis of this example, he goes on to describe the Christian's new relation to Christ as physically real and personal as that of man and wife: "You also were put to death to the law through the body of Christ, so that you might belong to another, to one who was raised from the dead in order that we might bear fruit for God" (Rom 7:4).

These first allusions to the body of Christ are thus incidental, the emergent of a given context. Yet they have a validity all their own because they express so aptly the realism of the Christian's union with Christ as Paul sees it and as he, or his disciple, will express it later in the consummate synthesis of his thought in Ephesians 5:25-32 where he likens the union of Christ and his Church to the bond between a devoted husband and his wife. No union could be more intimate because no dependence could be more complete. All that the Christian has as a Christian is received in the total surrender of the body-person to the body-person of Christ: "You are in Christ Jesus, who became for us wisdom from God, as well as righteousness, sanctification, and redemption" (1 Cor 1:30).

INCORPORATION THROUGH BAPTISM

This union begins at baptism, as Paul indicates in Galatians 3:27. Though shifting his thought pattern, he maintains the dynamic realism of the Christian experience: "All you who have been baptized into Christ have put on Christ." The analogy is drawn from the action of putting on a garment; but, as G. Duncan points out, "In Scripture it denotes that the wearer becomes in a subtle way identified with what he puts on." Thus God is clothed with majesty (Ps 92:1); the arm of the Lord puts on strength (Isa 51:9); the wicked are clothed with shame and disgrace (Ps 34:26); Job puts on justice (Job 29:14). The same use of *endyesthai* is found also, though rarely, in classical Greek where it signifies similarly entering into another's dispositions. Paul employs this figure fifteen times. The present text shows how intimate is the identification which it evokes. For he goes on to affirm that in the psychosomatic rite of baptism the body-person of the Christian is so totally surrendered to Christ that whatever is merely *sarx* disappears, so that "There is neither Jew nor Greek, there is neither slave nor free person, there is not male and female; for you are all one (*eis*—masculine) in Christ Jesus" (Gal 3:28).

In speaking of the Apostle's conversion, Wikenhauser has posed the question whether it was his faith at the Damascus theophany or his baptism a few days later that made him one with Christ. Probably it never occurred to Paul to differentiate the two moments since, in his mind, both elements formed but one experience. For the Jew, one acts always as a body-person, with an ambit of activity which necessarily includes a physical and sensible aspect. Hence, faith in Christ involves, by inherent necessity, the concomitant resolution to join one's whole self to the whole self *(soma)* of Christ in the physical rite of baptism. Paul's inward experience on the road to Damascus had a radical exigency to be consummated in baptism that his whole self might be engaged in full union with the body-person of Christ. Through baptism, the surrender of faith which he had elicited previously found expression in the psychosomatic rite which completed the surrender of his whole self *(soma)* to the body-person of the Savior.

Paul, therefore, teaches clearly that Christian life involves a real and personal union between the individual *soma* of the Christian and the individual *soma* of the glorified Christ, a union so intimate that the body-person of the Savior alone functions as the directive spiritual force. If they are two in one spirit, there is no doubt to whom the spirit belongs: "I live, no longer I, but Christ lives in me" (Gal 2:20).

BODY UNION THROUGH THE EUCHARIST

This same realism prevails when Paul comes to speak of Christians as a collectivity in his discussion of the Eucharist. Once more the point of departure for his memorable statement is a particular problem, the danger of syncretism arising from sharing in the banquets of pagan worship. He declares that such conduct is incompatible with the celebration of the Christian supper which joins the Christian to Christ: "The bread that we break, is it not a participation *(koinonia)* in the body of Christ?" (1 Cor 10:16).

As proof of this real presence of Christ in the Eucharist, Paul appeals to a fact which carried a barbed thrust to the disunited Corinthians. He recalls the truth which was recognized from the beginning (Acts 2:42). The remarkable *koinonia* of Christian fellowship—the unity of many with one another—has its total cause in the *koinonia* of each individual with Christ in the breaking of the bread: "Because the loaf of bread is one, we, though many, are one body, for we all partake of the one bread" (1 Cor 10:17). In this text the "one body" is still the individual body-person of the risen Christ. There is nothing here to urge that Paul is beginning to use the Stoic analogue as a metaphor for the social organization of the Church. The "many" are "one body" because communion makes each one concorporeal with Christ. In the realism of Paul's thought, both baptism and Communion enable the risen Savior to become "all in all" (cf. 1 Cor 12:13). Indeed, Dr. Rawlinson is on firm ground when he emphasizes the importance of the Eucharist as a prime element in shaping Paul's doctrine on the Church as the body of Christ.

BODY THEME IN 1 CORINTHIANS 12

Here one is more tempted to find a metaphorical sense in Paul's extended discussion of the body of Christ. Familiar as he was with the expression and thought patterns of the Stoa, he could have used their classic body theme as a metaphor to describe the unity in diversity which characterized the Church as a social body with its distinct functions and members.

But several reasons militate against this. First of all, F. de Visscher has shown that the Greek noun *soma* never denoted a collectivity or social group but always a real physical body. If, therefore, Paul identifies Christians as the body of Christ, he cannot mean that Christians are merely an organization. Secondly and more important, throughout this chapter Paul rests his argument not on the diversity which was obvious and provocative but on the unity which is "the first conviction of his faith and theology." There is only one body, one spirit, one Christ: For Paul, this is the perfect answer to the problem. Though he describes the diversity at length (and here he may be following the language of the Stoa), still he constantly brings back the thoughts of his readers to the fundamental fact that each one is *syssomos* with Christ. This Greek word occurs only with Christian writers. Baptized into his body-person, they are constantly preserved in union with him by drinking of one spirit in the Eucharist (1 Cor 12:13). If, then, like any real body, the body of Christ must be differentiated into many members, this only corroborates the truth that all Christians together are really the body of Christ, member for member, ruled and vivified by his spirit.

The question immediately arises, "Is Paul then speaking of the risen body of the personal Christ, or is he speaking of a body apart from Christ yet vivified by him? *Tertium non datur*" (A third [possibility] is not given). But even today this type of question is fair and valid only when both the questioner and the one giving answer are both thinking in the same thought patterns. It would not be right to press Paul with this query for the simple reason that his thought here rises eminently above our thought and includes formalities which our thought patterns tend to differentiate. He knows and he has said clearly that every Christian is united really and corporally to the risen body of Christ. Concentrating on this thought of the allness and uniqueness of Christ, he has nothing left to say except that all Christians together must be the body of Christ. How this is possible is not his concern at this point. Canon Cerfaux is content to translate Paul's words with the noncommittal, "You are a body, a body which is that of Christ." It will be the later controversy with the Colossians which will render his expression precise in describing the nature of the bond as the relation of head and members. At the stage of First Corinthians, his thought is moving at a level of eminence and realism which is all-inclusive.

BODY THEME IN ROMANS

In this epistle, Paul simply presumes that his readers are familiar with the truth that Christian life has united them—body-person to body-person—with Christ. In developing his thought he is much more concerned to show the dynamic involvements of this union. In becoming a member of Christ's body one lives by his life and shares in all the salvific activity of him who died and rose again as the corporate person par excellence. In the first part of this epistle, Christ is seen at work in his task of dying and rising for humanity. In the second part, the Christian shares dynamically in all that Christ is and has. So intimately is the Christian united to the body-person of the Savior that the person's whole spiritual life becomes the death-life of Christ (Rom 6:3-11) through the activity of the spirit who vivifies and glorifies the whole body (Rom 8). In a word, life *in Christ* is inseparably connected with and provides foundation for life *with Christ*.

This conclusion emerges clearly from the inadequacy of P. Bonnard's effort to present a definitive explanation of Paul's *syn-* or with-phrases on the score of merely forensic justification. After reviewing and pointing out the weaknesses of various explanations of this Pauline expression, he makes his own suggestion that Paul has borrowed the use of *syn* (with) from the Hellenistic liturgies, even though Bonnard must admit that there is nothing so far discovered in the literature of the Greek mysteries to substantiate his claim. As for the reality contained in the *syn*-phrase it consists totally in the mere assent of the individual living in the present, to the unique and definitive fact of Christ's death and resurrection.

This proposal, however, carries the sign of its own weakness. The very fact that Bonnard traces the Pauline *syn*-phrase to the mystery literature (though confessedly without actual verification) shows his awareness that in the Pauline corpus this phrase is essentially dependent upon the believer's real and present share in the life of the Savior, an element which is common to the teaching of Paul and the liturgy of the mystery cult.

Moreover, unless Paul's teaching on life *with Christ* is founded upon the realism of life *in Christ,* then Christian experience, as described in the Pauline epistles, is merely the human psychological effort of Jewish striving for justice. Indeed, the salvific event of Calvary is no more effective in the life of the individual than the divine intervention at Sinai unless the believer shares by real participation in the action of the Savior. In ruling out this real contact and in explaining Romans 6:3-11 as descriptive of a mere mental attitude on the part of the believer, Bonnard is forced to reduce the baptismal liturgy to the commemorative value of the Passover regulations in Exodus 13. This is precisely what he does.

The actual words of Paul, on the other hand (especially *ebaptisthomen eis Christon* [baptized into Christ] in Rom 6:3 and *symphytoi* [literally, grown together] in Rom 6:5), plus the whole background of Pauline doctrine, make clear that he teaches a true and intimate union between the Christian and the risen Christ in virtue of which the baptized actually shares all that Christ has accomplished as his representative. This truth is succinctly stated by S. Lyonnet:

> Strictly speaking, the Christ to whom St. Paul declares us united is always the glorious Christ; but, since he is a Christ who died and rose again, we, by the very fact of our union with him, share in the effects of his death and resurrection. It is in this sense that we are plunged into his death, are crucified and rise with him.

CONCLUSION

The teaching of Paul on the body of Christ is eminently simple. For him, all union is the surrender of the body of the Christian in the Semitic sense of self to the body-self of the risen Savior, thus forming with him only one body. The conclusion is inescapable. This union is an existential contact and a dynamic identification between the faithful and the body charged with power. This is especially true in baptism (Rom 6:3-11; Gal 3:27-28) and in the Eucharist (1 Cor 10:16-17; 11:24-30). The life that is in the body becomes the life of those who are its members. Whether in the first moment of union or in the moment of parousia consummation, both the Christian and Christ are inseparably united: "We know that Christ, raised from the dead . . . lives for God. Consequently, you too must consider yourselves as . . . living for God in Christ Jesus" (Rom 6:9-11).

Seen in this light, Paul's doctrine in the great epistles gives strength and meaning to contemporary doctrine on the mystical body. By placing emphasis on the realism of the union between the individual Christian and Christ, he contributes a clear insight into the nature of the bond which unites all Christians to one another. Because each one has all in Christ and because Christ is all in all in each one, therefore, the bond which unites one to the other is the dynamic presence of Christ himself. For, if Paul's words have any meaning at all, they affirm that between the *soma*-person of Christ and the *soma*-person of the Christian there exists a bond so real that the Savior could say to Paul in the moment of his conversion the very words which sum up all his doctrine on the body of Christ: "Saul, why do you persecute me? . . . I am Jesus whom you are persecuting."

Chapter 12

Biblical Concept of Church

Biblical scholars today are coming to see that the Church has deep roots in the soil of the New Testament. To many this may seem like the discovery of a truism. It is rather a significant advancement on the level of scholarship.

It was a previous fashion in some circles to treat the Church as a foundling, fathered by an ingenious primitive community and laid on the doorstep of an unsuspecting Christ. For Adolph Harnack, the gospel was set foursquare within the highly personal framework of God the father, his providence, humanity's kinship, and the infinite worth of the human soul. There was little room even for Christ in a gospel like that—much less for the Church. For Albert Schweitzer, Jesus' message centered in the imminent breakthrough of the heavenly kingdom by a divine *coup d'état*. So, too, most other liberal scholars in the first quarter of the twentieth century found it difficult to ascribe to Jesus of Galilee any idea of founding a Church.

Today, however, a change is notable. As Anton Fridrichsen has observed, "The discovery of the Church's role in early Christianity is the greatest event within exegetical science in our generation." This is due in great part to the influence of the German form-criticism school. Scholars like Rudolph Bultmann and Martin Dibelius have so emphasized the creative power of the primitive apostolic community that, unwittingly, they have made it difficult to accept their parallel thesis on the Church's spontaneous origin. An anonymous source for such a dynamic group as the early Christian community constitutes a vexing problem.

The disciples of Bultmann, therefore, are coming to see why their master has always shown signs of embarrassment when asked to explain the community itself. The primitive Church is a total anomaly unless one accepts its claim to intimate dependence on the person and ministry of Jesus. It is not surprising, then, that the works of Gunther Bornkamm and Harald Riesenfeld show the pendulum swinging back to center.

This return is inevitable. The Church looms so large and clear in the apostolic writings that it provides its own best proof of foundations which are solid and deep. When the eminent Pauline scholar Heinrich Schlier became a Catholic in the early 1960s, he wrote, "The insights which led me into the church developed for me gradually through my constant appraisal of the New Testament. . . . They furnished me with reasons so powerful that I felt myself impelled and commanded to go off into that strange land in which my real home seemed to lie."

This is the confidence which every Catholic must possess. They must share Schlier's conviction that the image of the Church is so clear and consistent in the apostolic writings that this very image offers perennial proof of deep roots in the earthly life of Jesus.

This does not mean that we are to search the Scriptures for anachronisms. The Church is not monolithic; it is living. It has grown from a seedling to a worldwide organization, with a viability which permits adjustment to changing times and places. In the beginning it was a family where everyone knew everyone else, where Peter was a brother among brothers and sisters, and where those who had lived with Jesus and spoken with the risen Lord enjoyed prestige and authority everywhere. To seek identity between our local bishops and the *episcopoi* of Acts is to seek an anachronism. To look for what is Roman in Peter and to try to equate Pope John XXIII with the lean fisherman of Galilee—this is like trying to fit the Roman office of the Passionist Generalate into the little hut where St. Paul of the Cross founded the congregation in the eighteenth century.

It is not our purpose to search the apostolic writings for anachronisms which we shall never find there. What we are looking for are the basic elements of the Church's organization, the rationale of its disciplinary activity, and the pre-eminent source of its divine life and teaching.

PENTECOST EVENT

Let us start at the beginning. Something happened at Pentecost—just as something happened at Sinai—to bring new people into being. Looking back years later, St. Luke illumines the full significance of the event by developing in a highly literary form all the involvements of the coming of the Spirit. His midrashic description of the "tongues of fire," his rich use of the Old Testament prophecies in the Petrine discourse—all this emphasizes the truth that on Pentecost itself the followers of Jesus knew clearly that they had received from God God's own Spirit. The risen Savior, therefore, was truly the messianic son of God (cf. Acts 13:33) and they the messianic community.

This faith of Pentecost needs no proof. Though the opening chapters of Acts owe much to the insights of Luke and to his power of evoking impressions through a literary use of rabbinical and scriptural themes, this section also shows a consistent fidelity to the Spirit and contents of its source material. Whatever may have been the penetrating power of his own developed theology, Luke often presents the thoughts of Peter and Stephen just as they thought them in that first burst of Pentecostal light.

There is the telltale mark of primitive Christian thinking in Peter's words when with full conviction, he announces the ringing challenge: "Let the whole house of Israel know for certain that God has made him both Lord and Messiah, this Jesus whom you crucified" (Acts 2:36). When this statement is brought next to Pauline theology with its more careful precision, we almost suspect an adoptionist color to Peter's formulary. Luke, however, lets it stand even though it sounds so close to the heretical position that Christ was not the consubstantial but only the adoptive son of God. This same spirit of originality flavors Stephen's discourse in Acts 7. For this witness to the faith, the risen Christ is everything while his passion and death are crucial problems calling for apology. The substance of the sermon, therefore, comes from the first days of Christianity, from a level which was not yet enlightened by Paul's profound insight into the real efficacy of Christ's death.

One truth especially emerges from these first pages of Acts. The followers of Jesus believed that the "last day" promised by the prophets had come. He whom they had seen risen from the dead had himself given them the Spirit of God. He, therefore, was the Messiah; and they were the messianic community.

Their life flowed along smoothly in the channels of Jewry because they looked on themselves as its perfect fulfillment. They felt no sharp cleavage with their own people since they were simply enjoying the privileges planned for all in Israel who would believe. When, after the resurrection, they chose Matthias to fill out the number of the twelve apostles, they had in mind that judgment over the twelve tribes which the "last days" would bring. Now that this time had come, they recognized themselves as the perfect Israel (Acts 3:24ff.). Their sense of having arrived filled these first days with a peace and overflowing joy which left a deep impression on their fellow Jews (Acts 2:46-47).

Their belief that Jesus had risen from the dead as the messianic son of God was bound to bring clashes, especially with the Sadducees (Acts 4:1-22; 5:17ff.). Jesus as dead Messiah, however, did not create the same problem as Jesus the living reformer. Whatever tensions existed were not sufficient to cause a full rift. Conflicts could be smoothed over in the same way in which Pharisees and Sadducees agreed to disagree over resurrection and life after death and the number of inspired books. We can speak, therefore, of a true continuity between Jewry and the primitive community. Just as Jesus had found a place in the life of his people, so the followers of Jesus sensed no compelling reason in the Pentecostal experience to break with their background. They had simply entered upon the age for which Israel had always yearned.

NEWNESS OF HOPE FROM THE MESSIAH

There was, however, something dynamically new among Jesus' followers. Their attraction was that of vital youth. All around them was the shadow of aging hope; they, however, possessed the glorious substance of hope and the newness of life which only the Messiah could give. The community was strong with the vigor of the spirit. Many elements of their life made them different from their fellow Jews.

First of all, their preaching (the *kerygma*) set them apart. Their one message to all was the startling truth that the crucified Jesus had risen from the dead and had bestowed the messianic gift par excellence, the Holy Spirit (cf. Acts 2:29-36; 3:12-16). This made him truly Messiah and Lord, the only source of salvation for all humanity (cf. Acts 4:8-12; 5:29-32). For those who accepted this truth there was always further instruction drawn not from Jewry but from Jesus. This was known as the "teaching *(didache)* of the apostles" (Acts 2:42).

This brings to light a second distinctive characteristic of the new community. It was no longer the doctors of the law or the Jewish leaders who taught and directed this group but rather the followers of Jesus who were in a special way the qualified "witnesses of his resurrection" (Acts 1:22; 5:32). The Twelve were now the acknowledged leaders, the chosen chiefs who spoke for the community and suffered for it and proclaimed intransigently all for which it stood.

The distinctiveness of the community was emphasized by a third special mark, its rite of initiation and its central mystery, "the breaking of bread." Even a circumcised Jew could not belong to this new group unless he professed faith in Jesus as the messianic son of God and accepted baptism which resembled the rite of heathen admission into the fold of Israel (Acts 2:38). Continuance in the community meant frequent sacramental contact with the Messiah Lord through the "bread" which he had provided. This was the one mystery which the community kept for itself as its special treasure and as the foretaste of the Lord's imminent return (the parousia). For though the followers of Christ prayed in the temple, they "broke bread" in their own homes (Acts 2:42, 46). While awaiting the glorious return of the Messiah Lord they found strength and joy in the bread which was himself. This was what held them together; sharing in the body of Christ, they became themselves that body which is the Church (cf. 1 Cor 10:16-17).

For the primitive community, Christ was all in all. The belief of all centered in him (cf. Rom 10:9-10); their leaders were people chosen by him; their very worship meant a sharing in the mystery of his body and blood. Now they awaited anxiously the days of refreshment, the parousia, when their judge and king would return to them in glory that they might rejoice with him forever (Acts 3:20). They had much yet to learn of God's plan.

The next move was precipitated by the Hellenist Christians. As Oscar Cullmann has shown, these Greek-speaking Jews had always irritated the homelanders by their disdain for the physical elements of Israel's worship. Living in the diaspora, they had found God away from the temple and had worshipped him with a spiritual devotedness which spurned the smell of blood and burning flesh. In coming to know Jesus, these Hellenists found the way of spiritual worship wide open to them in the "temple not made by hands." When Stephen the Hellenist, therefore, spoke of Jesus, his hearers had ears only for that irritating sentence which echoed the old anti-temple polemic: "Solomon built a house for him. Yet the Most High does not dwell in houses made by human hands" (Acts 7:47-48).

PERSECUTION IN JERUSALEM

That sentence was the signal for persecution. If the Jews could tolerate within their own fold those who followed Jesus as the Messiah, they could not stomach fellow Jews who cast aspersion on the most sacred element of Jewish worship. And so "a great persecution broke out on that day against the church in Jerusalem" (Acts 8:1). Yet not against all the Church. Persecution left the Galilean apostles untouched. Only Stephen the Hellenist was martyred; and only the Hellenist Christians were driven from their Jerusalem home.

This was a stroke of providence. By it, the Church was forced to seek a home on earth outside of Jewry. The messianic community was to become in fact what it was in nature—the community of the world.

Philip the Hellenist went to Samaria and preached Christ there (Acts 8:4-6). It was a likely place of refuge for the Samaritans shared the Hellenist opposition to the Jerusalem temple (John 4:20). Other Hellenist Jews went to Antioch where, for the first time, they extended their apostolate to full-blooded Greeks (Acts 11:19-20). This new move away from Jewry served to emphasize the stress which had been present from the beginning. Christ was all in all for the new community: "They preached the Lord Jesus" (Acts 11:20). People sensed the emphasis. They took from it their cue in giving a name to this new group which had arisen in their midst. If Jesus were the Christ, the Messiah, they were Christian, the messianic community. "It was in Antioch that the disciples were first called 'Christians'" (Acts 11:26).

The Church of Christ was expanding. For "Church of Christ" it truly was. Israel of old was called the *Qahal* (Septuagint—*ekklesia*) because it was the assembly of God's chosen people. For the same reason, the new Israel was also the Church of God *(ekklesia tou theou)* and even more the Church of Christ, for he was its very life.

As it expanded, this Church remained true to itself, taking direction from its leaders, drawing life from its word and sacrament. The story of Philip in Samaria is typical. "Philip went down to [the] city of Samaria and proclaimed the Messiah to them. . . . once they began to believe Philip as he preached the good news about the kingdom of God and the name of Jesus Christ, men and women alike were baptized" (Acts 8:5, 12). The preaching of the Word and the acceptance of the sacrament are both essential in the life of the new community.

Quite as important, however, is the seal of approval from the only ones who could give approval and a full share in the riches of the community's life: "Now when the apostles in Jerusalem heard that Samaria had accepted the word of God, they sent them Peter and John. . . . Then they laid hands on them and they received the Holy Spirit" (Acts 8:14, 17).

It is noteworthy how large Peter looms in this whole picture of expanding Christianity as Luke presents it in Acts. He seems to move always in first place as spokesman and representative of the community (cf. Acts 1:15ff.; 2:14-36; 3:1-11; 4:8ff.; 5:3-11; etc.). There is, however, no blatant note in his claim to authority. He lives and works in a family where everyone knows and loves everyone else. In such surroundings he could fulfill perfectly the behest of Jesus that the one who is first should be as the one who serves: "Now when the apostles in Jerusalem heard that Samaria had accepted the word of God, they sent them Peter and John" (Acts 8:14).

The new Israel threatened the old; the Christ-Lord of Christianity introduced a discordant note into the *Shema's* profession of faith: "Hear, O Israel! The Lord is our God, the Lord alone!" (Deut 6:4). The soul of Paul, therefore, seethed with bitterness and the eradication of the Church became the burning passion of his life. He would stamp out this blasphemy; if need be, he would drown it in the blood of his fellow Jews.

PAUL, THEOLOGIAN OF THE CHURCH

All this was only the darkness before dawn. On the way to Damascus sunlight burst upon him in a blaze of glory and he heard the stunning words, "Saul, Saul, why are you persecuting me?" (Acts 9:4). In the twinkling of an eye Paul the hater of Christ became a Christian. The persecutor of the Church became its theologian.

Scholars like Lucien Cerfaux and Alfred Wikenhauser have written long, penetrating analyses of Paul's doctrine on the Church. It would be endless to rehearse their meticulous erudition. We desire, instead, to center attention on Paul's contribution not as a theologian but as a witness. When he entered the Church, it was already in existence and fully self-conscious. In his letters, therefore, we touch the flesh and blood Church of the first-generation Christians. These earliest writings of the apostolic period bear glowing testimony to the life of the Church just as Paul found it, just as he knew it must remain.

There is no doubt that this man was a rugged individualist, the keen-sighted theologian of the early Church. In his letter to the Galatians he is at his unique best, boasting flagrantly that his are the penetrating insights and the God-given message of liberty. The other apostles, including Cephas or Peter, seem merely to plod along in a pedestrian way: "What they once were makes no difference to me; God shows no partiality" (Gal 2:6). Indeed, "When Cephas came to Antioch, I opposed him to his face because he clearly was wrong"

(Gal 2:11). Restricting their view to texts like these, Baur and Strauss created the image of a Paul who opposes his gospel to the limited teaching of Peter and the Jewish element in the early Church.

Long ago, however, the Tübingen view of Paul was discounted as myopic. It was based on Galatians and overlooked the other letters. And even in Galatians it read only chapter 2 and conveniently forgot that there was also chapter 1.

There is no doubt that Paul was always conscious of his God-given authority; he is "an apostle sent not from human beings nor through a human being but by Jesus Christ and God the Father" (Gal 1:1). This confidence rings in the salutation of all his letters. In making this claim, however, Paul has only one purpose—to validate his right to preach the gospel of Christ.

He considered it his first duty to deliver to others the *kerygma* which had been in the Church from the beginning. Like all the apostles, he presented everywhere the saving truths of the gospel (cf. 2 Tim 2:8). Paul could say to all his converts what he wrote to the Corinthians: "I handed on to you as of first importance what I also received" (1 Cor 15:3).

He knew well that every preacher would try to present the Church's teaching in the most attractive and compelling way they could. Paul himself theologized to his heart's content. He used the juridical and cultic thought patterns of Jewry; he gave full rein to his knowledge of Stoic diatribe and utilized its antithesis in presenting the Christian message. He insisted, however, that these elucidations were valid only insofar as they presented the authentic Christian message. The preacher might build with gold, silver, precious stones, wood, hay, straw; but the essential factor consisted always in the foundation of the Church's saving message (cf. 1 Cor 3:1ff.).

SAFEGUARDING THE TEACHING

This teaching about the Church must be safeguarded at any cost. When people showed too much concern with human philosophizing, Paul went out of his way to center attention on the fundamental teaching itself. The Corinthians loved a display of "wisdom"; they listened delightedly to the brilliant phrases of Apollos and to his finely spun Alexandrian allegories. Paul sensed danger. People might come to prefer the tangible beauty of human words to the ineffable power of God's deeds. Paul, therefore, deliberately avoided the brilliance of "wisdom" to present the simple truths which Peter and James and John had recounted on the morrow of Pentecost: "When I came to you, brothers and sisters, proclaiming the mystery of God, I did not come with sublimity of words or of wisdom. For I resolved to know nothing while I was with you except Jesus Christ, and him crucified" (1 Cor 2:1-2).

In every letter Paul shows his reliance on the traditional teaching which is everywhere the same. Writing to people like the Romans and Colossians whom he has never seen, the Apostle takes it for granted that they are thoroughly familiar with the truths which he himself is preaching. How often he bases his own doctrinal development on this presumed knowledge: "Do you not know?" "Have you not heard?" "Do you not remember?" Writing to the Romans, Paul takes it for granted that their primitive creedal formulary (Rom 1:3-4) contains the same faith which he himself would express with greater theological exactness (cf. Rom 9:5; Phil 2:5-11). Writing to the Colossians, who had been evangelized not by himself but by Epaphras, he simply presumes that they know the Church teaching from which he himself draws the contents of his instructions (cf. Col 1:5-7; 2:6-7).

This reliance on the traditional teaching made Paul suspicious of new customs (cf. 1 Cor 11:16) and intransigently hostile to distortions of the primitive gospel. He was speaking of false teachers when he wrote: "If anyone destroys God's temple, God will destroy that person; for the temple of God, which you are, is holy" (1 Cor 3:17).

This witness to the unchanging teaching of the Church is the first factor one must reckon with if one wishes to share Paul's mind on the Church. He who is looked upon as the most creative of the apostles, the artisan of Christian theology, places his chief glory in being "approved by God to be entrusted with the gospel" (1 Thess 2:4). In the traditional teaching which is always and everywhere the same, Paul sees a dynamic power to save (Rom 1:16-17). Through the Church message the risen Christ entered the heart of every person to save and to sanctify.

Paul, therefore, could write to the Thessalonians in the first letter of his long correspondence: "We give thanks to God without ceasing, because when you heard and received from us the word of God, you welcomed it not as a human word but, as it truly is, the word of God, which works in you who have believed" (1 Thess 2:13). So long as the message was presented accurately and integrally Christ could do his work. When the imprisoned Paul learned that others were busy preaching the gospel in order to curry favor with the new converts, he cried out, "What difference does it make, as long as in every way, whether in pretense or in truth, Christ is being proclaimed. And in this I rejoice. Indeed I shall continue to rejoice" (Phil 1:18).

His mind is crystal clear. Christian life comes from a gospel message which is fixed and creedal and dynamically powerful. For Paul, faith is not the fideism of blind surrender to an unknown God. Paul's faith, instead, is dependent on the spoken word and reaches God truly through surrender to its conceptual element. For the gospel is a mirror held up to the heart of God that it may reflect God's thoughts into the heart of the human (cf. 2 Cor 3:18). As an apostle, Paul considered it his prime duty to witness and to transmit, not to create: "Thus should one regard us: as servants of Christ and stewards of the mysteries of God. Now it is of course required of stewards that they be found trustworthy" (1 Cor 4:1-2).

PAUL ON SACRAMENTALITY

The Apostle's concept of sacramentality is a second factor which one must keep in mind in order to share his understanding of the Church. Scholars of the Lausanne school have suggested that, for Paul, salvation consisted in a mere psychological assent to the salvific deed of Calvary proclaimed by the gospel. In that event, God's intervention at Calvary would have no greater efficacy than his divine intervention on Sinai; and, once more, people would be left to themselves and to their own devices.

Paul's teaching, on the other hand, presupposes that the believer is really and effectively united to the risen Christ as one body-person to another *(soma* to *soma)* in the sacramental rites of baptism and the Eucharist. [Chapter 11 further develops these ideas.] For Paul Christ did not speak in a metaphor when, on the way to Damascus, he complained, "Saul, Saul, why are you persecuting me?" (Acts 9:4).

For Paul, in discussing the Church as the body of Christ, the Hebrew word "body" does not have the same meaning as in our twentieth-century Western vocabulary. Instead of denoting the physical part of the body-soul composite (as with us), the word "body" in Paul's vocabulary signifies the whole reality of the person as an animated and personalized body living a fully human life. When he speaks of the Christian's union with Christ his thought is very realistic. He sees all Christians as completing and extending one and the same person and life, Christ himself.

In the consummate synthesis of his thought in Ephesians 5:25-32, Paul or a later disciple likens the union of Christ and his Church to the bond between a devoted husband and wife. No union could be more intimate because no dependence could be more complete. All that the Christian has as a Christian one receives in the total surrender of one's body-person to the body-person of Christ: "You are in Christ Jesus, who became for us wisdom from God, as well as righteousness, sanctification, and redemption (1 Cor 1:30-31).

This union begins at baptism, as Paul indicates in Galatians 3:27-28. Though shifting his thought pattern, he maintains the dynamic realism of the Christian experience: "All you who have been baptized into Christ have put on Christ." The analogy is drawn from the action of putting on a garment; but, as G. Duncan points out in his commentary on Galatians: "In Scripture it denotes that the wearer becomes in a subtle way identified with what he puts on." The present text shows how intimate is the identification it evokes. For Paul goes on to affirm that, in the psychosomatic rite of baptism, the body-person *(soma)* of the Christian is so totally surrendered to Christ that whatever is merely "flesh" disappears, so that "There is neither Jew nor Greek; there is neither slave nor free person; there is neither male nor female. For you are all one in Christ Jesus."

PERSONAL UNION WITH CHRIST

Paul, therefore, teaches clearly that Christian life involves a real and personal union between the individual Christian and the glorified Christ, a union in which the Christian depends so completely upon Christ that he alone functions as the directive spiritual force: "The one who cleaves to the Lord is one spirit with him" (1 Cor 6:17).

This same realism prevails when Paul comes to speak of Christians as a collectivity in his discussion of the Eucharist. The celebration of the Christian supper joins the Christian to Christ: "The bread that we break, is it not the partaking of the body of the Lord?" (1 Cor 10:16).

As proof of the real presence of Christ in the Eucharist Paul recalls the truth which was recognized from the beginning. The remarkable fellowship *(koinonia)* of Christians with one another has its total cause in the fellowship *(koinonia)* of each individual with Christ in the breaking of the bread: "Because the bread is one, we though many are one body, we who partake of the one bread" (1 Cor 10:17). In this text the "one body" is still the individual body-person of the risen Christ. The many are one body because the "one bread" makes each one concorporeal with Christ.

In the realism of Paul's thought, both baptism and the Eucharist enable Christ to become "all in all," the one source and the only center of Christian life.

For Paul, the Church was not merely a society founded by Christ to endure forever as the best way of saving all. It was far more the enduring sacrament of Christ's abiding presence among humans, the real and permanent means he has chosen to fulfill his promise, "And behold, I am with you always, until the end of the age" (Matt 28:20).

The Apostle constantly witnesses to this reality and permanence of Christ's presence in and through the Church. He likens the Church to a temple where God dwells and where the son gives God ceaseless praise (cf. 1 Cor 3:16-17; 2 Cor 6:16).

For Paul, Christ is "all in all." Whether he speaks of the individual Christian, the local congregation, or the whole Church, Paul sees all as belonging to the body of Christ, as completing and extending the person and life of the risen Christ himself. For the Savior living gloriously in heaven is himself the body-person, the one central figure with whom all Christians are intimately united and on whom they totally depend. In Paul's classic phrase they are "in Christ Jesus" precisely because he is in them as the total source of all spiritual life in the Church. "Here [in the Church] there is not Greek and Jew, circumcision and uncircumcision, barbarian, Scythian, slave, free; but Christ is all and in all" (Col 3:11).

The Apostle's doctrine on the Church as the body of Christ gives special force to his teaching on authority. From the very beginning of his epistolary correspondence Paul shows a vital awareness of the function of authority in the Church.

APOSTLE SENT BY CHRIST

He glories in his apostleship and boasts of his power because he knows well that the apostle is a *shaliah*—one sent by Christ with the fullness of his authority: "So we are ambassadors for Christ, as if God were appealing through us" (2 Cor 5:20). This consciousness of bearing the authority of Christ was with Paul always and everywhere. He acted with complete liberty and aplomb whether he enjoined commands on those who were present or leveled threats against those who were absent. This confidence never failed him for he looked on himself always as the representative of Christ: "I warned those who sinned earlier and all the others, and I warn them now while absent, as I did when present . . . I will not be lenient, since you are looking for proof of Christ speaking in me. He was not weak toward you but powerful in you . . . we shall live with him by the power of God" (2 Cor 13:2-4).

Paul recognized this same authority in other leaders of the Church. For it is clear in his letters that others ruled the local churches during the absence of their father and founder. As in Judaism itself, elders *(presbyteros)* were chosen to direct the conduct of the community. Besides this group—and probably selected from among them—certain administrators *(episcopoi)* were empowered to watch over the needs of the community and to preside at its liturgical assemblies. From the very beginning Paul enjoined obedience to those in authority (cf. 1 Thess 5:12-13). The fact that they discharged their duties in the Church, the body of Christ, made the exercise of their authority a function of Christ himself (cf. 1 Cor 12:27-28; Rom 12:4, 8).

As time went on, Paul would share more and more of his own power with subordinates, like Titus and Timothy. What belonged to the apostles eminently, the unique power of theirs which shaded all lesser authority, became more and more the possession of the local overseers. Yet even in the period of the pastoral letters, the local authorities had not yet received the full power of the monarchical bishop as present in St. Ignatius' letters. This transfer would become necessary only when death brought an end to Paul's overall regency.

AUTHORITY OF PETER

There is also the crucial question of Peter's authority. What did Paul think of it? He never answered this question, simply because he wrote out of a living tradition where Peter's role was taken for granted. His casual remarks, however, shed an aura of light about Peter as someone special in the ruling body of the Church.

After his conversion, Paul paid a courtesy visit to Jerusalem to see Peter (cf. Gal 1:18). Later in his apostolate at Antioch he was greatly disturbed when Cephas (or Peter), of all people, placed a principle in jeopardy by discrimination against the Gentiles (cf. Gal 2:11-14). At Corinth, Paul had to accept the fact that one of the dissenting groups centered its loyalty on Peter, as though he had as much right to that loyalty as Paul and Apollos, the founders of the Corinthian church (cf.

1 Cor 1:12). For Paul, as for the others, Peter stands in a category of his own; "Have we not the right to take about with us a woman, as do the other apostles, and the brethren of the Lord, and Cephas?" (1 Cor 9:15; cf. 15:5).

Paul's letters reflect authentically what the rest of the Church thought about Peter. If he has left no formal proof of Peter's authority it is because, as Père Benoit has pointed out, this truth was a universally accepted part of the Church's life.

This long discussion of Paul's witness to the existence and nature of the Church finds its warrant in the uniqueness of his testimony. First, his letters stand as the earliest extant record of everyday life in the Christian community (between 50 and A.D. 67). Second, they come from a man who first knew Christianity as an unbeliever and a persecutor and who forfeited many privileges to accept its claim (cf. Phil 3:3-8). Third, the Church life he describes was being lived in persecuted communities which, like Paul himself, would have had everything to gain by reverting to earlier Judaic loyalties. Fourth, Paul's value as a witness is all the more significant since it is so easy to distinguish it from his role as an original and creative thinker. His testimony, therefore, is not only a faithful transcript of life and practice in the Church but also a guarantee of its historical claim. A man of Paul's character and background would have been the last one in the world to "create" Christianity.

Other apostolic writings come from a later period, but their witness to the constituent elements of Church life matches the pattern of Paul's testimony. The Johannine writings, for example, are in agreement with many aspects of Paul's portrait of the Church. In them we find the same tenacious emphasis on the unchanging word (cf. 1 John 1:3; 2:27; 3:11) and on the true authority of those who watch over the Church: "Anyone who knows God listens to us, while anyone who does not belong to God refuses to hear us" (1 John 4:6). The whole Johannine Gospel is a witness to the sacramental sources of the Church's life.

Another independent witness may be found in the Greek Gospel of Matthew. Coming from the latter part of the first century, the distinctive mark of this Gospel is its delineation of the Church. It emphasizes the role and authority of the Petrine office—even at a time when Peter was himself already dead—(Matt 16:17-20), the power of the Church leaders (Matt 18:15-18), the presence of Christ in the liturgical assembly (Matt 18:19-20), the unchanging firmness of the Church's word (Matt 7:24-27). Moreover, as David M. Stanley writes, "by transposing a saying of Jesus regarding the mystery of the kingdom (cf. Mark 4:11), Matthew shows the awareness that the Church in his day already possessed a body of doctrines which had been entrusted to the apostolic teachers: 'Because knowledge of the mysteries of the heavenly kingdom has been granted to you'" (Matt 13:11).

APOSTOLIC WRITINGS AS WITNESS TO THE CHURCH

Acts, Paul, John, Matthew—all the apostolic writings witness to the Word, the sacrament, and authority as constituent elements in the life of the Church. What connection does it all have with the Jesus of history? Some find it difficult to read the thought of the Church back into the mind of Jesus; the really impossible thing is to read it out of his mind. For if the Church did not come from Jesus, we are faced with the anomaly of an effect without a cause.

It is true that all we know of Jesus comes from the Church of the first century, from writers who already believed in him as the risen Savior and the messianic son of God. These records and memories, however, come not only from those who believed in him as the risen Savior and the messianic son of God, but also from disciples who had lived with him. They were well qualified to judge whether the *kerygma* of the apostles misrepresented the facts of history. If, therefore, they became members of the Church and accepted its teaching, sacraments, and leaders, it is only because they were convinced that the structure of the Church rested foursquare on the foundation which the apostles affirmed was of Jesus' own making.

During his lifetime, Jesus presented himself in the role of Daniel's son of man (Dan 7) and of Isaiah's suffering servant (Isa 53). He was therefore—in the light of this composite picture—a corporate personality, a son of man who embodies the "saints of God" (cf. Dan 7:13-14 with Dan 7:25-27), a suffering servant who gives his life "for the many" (Isa 53:11-12). His death and glorification involved all; his fate would have weighty meaning in the lives of others. In the days of his earthly life, therefore, he took care to provide for the world-family which would come into being through the power of his resurrection.

If he had not actually made such preparations, the Jews of Jerusalem (who were eyewitnesses of his life) would have been the first to reject the apostles' false claims. They had everything to lose and nothing to gain in accepting a merely fabricated Pentecostal message. This first generation of Jewish Christians offers an irrefutable argument for the intimate bond between the Church of Pentecost and the Jesus of history.

It is only Jesus' choice and preparation that can explain why these first Christians turned from the learned doctors of the law, whom they had always venerated, to accept the religious leadership of ignorant Galilean fishermen whose very background disqualified them from all doctrinal or religious authority. It is also only an act of Jesus that can explain why these same Jews chose the Christian "breaking of bread" as their true and only Passover celebration.

In his lifetime, therefore, Jesus prepared for the future life of the Church by choosing its leaders, by providing it with sacraments, and by ministering the Word which would form the heart of its teaching. Were this not so, the image of the primitive Church which looms so large and clear in the apostolic writings would remain forever an inexplicable anomaly.

CHAPTER 13

Role of Law in the Church

When the fullness of time had come, God sent the Son, born of a woman, born under the law, to ransom those under the law, so that we might receive adoption (Gal 4:4-5).

In these few words St. Paul sums up his doctrine on the work of Christ. The son of God came upon earth to change the whole status of humanity, to transform us from the law-ridden servants of a master into beloved children. Paul, it is true, affirms that the child of God is still governed by law, "the law of Christ" (Gal 6:2). But the whole tenor of his letters shows that the word "law," as applied to Christian life, is used only analogously. The "law of Christ" differs essentially from every other form of law. Paul, therefore, constantly draws a sharp contrast between life under law and life according to the gospel. In this he interprets authentically the mind of Christ.

To grasp the meaning of this contrast and, more pointedly, to understand the unique character of Christian law, it is necessary to see clearly the radical difference between life in the old and in the new covenants.

THE OLD COVENANT: LIFE UNDER A LEGAL SYSTEM

To the chosen people, God was manifested primarily by intervening at Sinai to unite them to God's self through a covenant and to prescribe for them a consequent way of life as the people consecrated to Yahweh, the God who is changeless in holiness and love (cf. Exod 19–24). As Israel grew in appreciation of what God had done at Sinai, it assigned an ever more important role to the five books of its sacred literature which set forth in detail the history and contents of the Sinai pact. The Sadducees of our Lord's day accepted no other books as truly inspired. Other groups in Judaism, while believing in the inspiration of the prophets' words and the sacredness of the "other writings," always regarded the Pentateuch with unique esteem. The Council of Trent's blanket definition of the inspiration and canonicity of all the books of the Old Testament, as well as our own leveling of the prophets and Wisdom literature with the first five books of the Bible, would strike a devout Israelite as offensively cavalier.

The five books of the law were, for the Jew, supremely revelatory of God and normative for human life. The very prescriptions of the law manifested the character of Yahweh, God of Israel: "Since I, Yahweh, brought you up from the land of Egypt that I might be your God, you shall be holy, because I am holy" (Lev 11:45). Everything God did for Israel, in creating it to be the chosen people, in prescribing its unique way of life, in shepherding it through the events and vicissitudes of a providential history—all this taught the people of God both who God is and what God wanted of them. Israel, therefore, named the first five books of its scripture the *Torah* (i.e., the teaching), for, in these books, God's people found not only the laws which were to govern their lives but also a sublime teaching about God and God's wondrous way with people.

Seen in this light the law of Moses was a real boon for Israel, a divine guide for the nation's conduct. As Paul was to affirm, "The law is holy, and the commandment is holy and just and good. . . . We know that the law is spiritual" (Rom 7:12, 14). Its regulations so ordered the life of Israel that its morality and observances were to shine luminously as a sign of the nation's consecration to Yahweh, the uniquely holy God. In the Torah, the prophets of Israel found the substance of their message, the truths about God and the divine ways which they unfolded with clarity, unction, and abundance in words which God inspired. The law, therefore, was the real *Ner Tamid* (i.e., perpetual light) shining brightly and constantly on the paths which the nation was to walk.

Especially after the Exile (586–536 B.C.E.), when people had come to appreciate fully the riches of the Torah as explained by the prophets, Israel built up a whole literature to celebrate the preeminence of the law and to inculcate the need for responding to it generously. This Wisdom literature stresses the truth that Israel's holiness involves constant pondering on the law (cf. Ps 1), esteem for its divine contents (cf. Ps 18), and constant fidelity to its prescriptions (cf. Ps 118). The best commendation of a true Israelite was the oft-repeated formula which

Luke uses to describe Zachary and Elizabeth: "Both were righteous in the eyes of God, observing all the commandments and ordinances of the Lord blamelessly" (Luke 1:6).

No one knew better than Christ himself the spiritual value of the Torah and so he insisted, "Do not think that I have come to abolish the law or the prophets. I have come not to abolish but to fulfill" (Matt 5:17). He saw clearly that the revelation of God and of the divine will through the law provided humanity with a perfect preparation for Christ's own coming. The Apostle Paul, therefore, faithfully interpreting the mind of Christ, has written that "the law was our instructor who had charge of us until Christ came" (Gal 3:24). For Paul, the good work of the "tutor"—the insights into God which Torah provided and the holy way of life which it prescribed—were not abolished by Christ but ineffably perfected, "Christ is the fulfillment of the law" (Rom 10:4).

Old Testament Value to the Church

The perennial value of the Torah and of all the Old Testament writings has once more been authoritatively affirmed, this time by the Church of Christ. The fathers of Vatican II have written:

> The books of the Old Testament, in accordance with the state of humanity before the time of salvation established by Christ, reveal to all people the knowledge of God and of humans and the ways in which God, just and merciful, deals with all. These books though they also contain some things which are incomplete and temporary, nevertheless show us true divine pedagogy. These same books, then, give expression to a lively sense of God, contain a store of sublime teachings about God, sound wisdom about human life, and a wonderful treasury of prayers (*Dei Verbum* 15).

The fact remains, however, that life under the law labored under an enervating weakness. In Paul's polemic writings (especially Romans and Galatians) directed against those who would cling to law as a primary source of holiness and salvation, the Apostle details with biting invective every feature of weakness in lives which are based on law alone, even if it be God's law.

Though the problems of his own apostolate constrained Paul to argue against reliance on the law of the old covenant, it is nonetheless evident that his diatribe is directed against reliance on any kind of law or legal system as a source of salvation.

Because law in itself lacks all power to give life and strength, it is but the "shadow" of the life and strength which it presumes (cf. Col 2:17). A written or oral code with its obligatory regulations can only chart a course and impose corresponding sanctions for failure. The fact is that in the actual history of Israel the law served to bring condemnation upon the nation; here as in every case, reliance on the letter of the law "kills" and imprisons in a "dispensation of death" (2 Cor 3:6-7).

Paul and the Inadequacy of Law

St. Paul marshals many reasons to emphasize the inadequacy of law to sanctify humans when, like the Israelites, they neglect the substance for the shadow (cf. Col 2:17). His arguments, though many, may be summed up under two heads.

First, the God who gave the law to Israel was only a voice to the people. They never saw or heard God or had any immediate contact with God. God was "veiled" to Israel (cf. 2 Cor 3:14); the divine commands and precepts came only from afar. Though the people spoke of God as father, they uttered the word like slaves speaking of a master who deals with servants only through intermediaries.

The law, therefore, required Israel to love and serve God with an unfailing faith which was beyond the power of most to give. Hence, all through its history, Israel continued to make its molten calves (cf. Exod 32), trying to find tangible substitutes for a God they could not see and for the divine will which they could not understand and would not obey.

Second, even if God were visible, Israel would still have found the law inadequate for securing holiness; the nation's moral fibre was not tempered strongly enough to bear the law's burdens. Humanity, weakened by universal sinfulness, lacks the strength to follow always the dictates of moral nature.

Because the Spirit had not yet been given (John 7:39), the will of Israel to serve God was at best a desire. Speaking in the name of all those who have only law to guide them, Paul cries out, "The law is spiritual; but I am carnal, sold under sin. I do not understand my own actions. For I do not do the good I want, but the evil I do not want is what I do" (Rom 7:14-15, 19). Israel's efforts to keep the law were but the straining of those to pull themselves up by their own shoelaces. This is the problem of every person who has a law to keep and only one's own strength to rely on. That one is condemned to failure from the start.

Even though the law is from God and even when it is most explicit in its requirements, the person's condition (if anything) is worsened. This very knowledge serves only to accentuate guilt, for one must say with Paul, "If it had not been for the law, I should not have known sin" (Rom 7:7). The Apostle even goes so far as to affirm apodictically that in God's plan the law was given to underline the existence and extent of sin (cf. Rom 3:19-20).

These two factors were inherent in the state of Israel under the law, as they are inherent in the life of every person who, Pelagian-like, is trying to live by law alone and one's own strength. The consequence was inevitable. Many Israelites settled for a wretched second-best which only worsened its condition.

Religious officialdom developed a legalism which riveted attention on the mere externals of the law. Passing over the deep spiritual purpose of God's prescriptions, the nation tried to meet the requirements of its vocation by fidelity to practices and taboos. They identified holiness before God with legalistic concern for the material elements of religious observance and for external modes of conduct.

When prompted by a living spirit within the human heart, this legalistic concern was for some a help in keeping God's word. But, in most cases, this strict and exclusive legal puritanism was a hardened shell smothering all true religious spirit. As Paul was to characterize his people, "Israel who pursued the righteousness which is based on law did not succeed in fulfilling that law . . . because they did not pursue it through faith, but as if it were based on works" (Rom 9:31-32).

To this people our Lord came, to those living under a legal system although incapable of fulfilling its charges. He found himself among those who did not really know God or the ways of God, who had deadened life-giving principles into materialistic regulations within reach of their weakness, who centered concern in human rules and paid scant attention to the end of the law or its true spirit.

Speaking of the commandments of God as Israel interpreted them in its rules and regulations, Christ could only repeat mournfully how far distant were these rules from his own understanding of God's law: "It was said to you of old, . . . but I say to you" (Matt 5:21, 27, 31, etc.). He faced, therefore, the mammoth task of giving law a new meaning, by making God known experientially and by filling people with his own life and strength.

THE NEW COVENANT: LIFE THROUGH THE GOSPEL

The gospel, the "good news" of the salvation event, tells how Christ accomplished this task. When St. John writes "The Word became flesh" (John 1:14), he affirms the truth that, in Christ, God at long last became visible to the people. God was no longer an unseen God speaking from afar but was now the God near at hand whom people could hear and see with their eyes and look upon and touch with their hands (cf. 1 John 1:1). God no longer offered a dead written word to manifest the divine self but a "word of life," a living and life-giving word.

St. Paul sums it all up very simply when he writes: In Christ Jesus "the goodness and loving kindness of God our Savior has appeared" (Titus 3:4). Through the coming of God's son into the world, the promise of Jeremiah was fulfilled: "No longer will they have need to teach their friends and kin how to know the Lord. All, from least to greatest, shall know me" (Jer 31:34). The first element of the "good news," therefore, was the truth that the awesome, invisible God who had been manifested at Sinai was now in the midst of the people through the son.

Every word and deed of that son was a living manifestation of God and of God's ways with humans. Christ became the perfect teacher, cutting through the bric-a-brac of human ideas about God and human rules and regulations, to reveal clearly who God is and what God wants. Where human laws were all concerned with means, he emphasized the end and purpose of the law.

Where human laws centered in external proprieties, he stressed the spirit which the law is intended to inculcate. Laws which ran counter to this spirit or killed it were, in his eyes, lethal attacks on the glory of his Father since they obscured or blotted out the radiance of God's saving action.

Where human laws often fettered the heart and so burdened it that people could no longer lift their eyes to God, Christ taught a way of life which made it possible for them to confess: "My eyes are always on the Lord." For this divine teacher, every law had to be alive with the truth of God and had to reflect God's life-giving will for all.

There was nothing antinomian in Christ. He knew too well the will of his Father and lived it too devotedly to absolve humans from following the ways "which God prepared beforehand that we should walk in them" (Eph 2:10). People without law are people with little knowledge of God and of the divine will. Christ, therefore, like another Moses, taught laws (cf. Matt 5–7) and made provision that through all the centuries his representatives would continue to teach them.

But the laws which he taught were all a perfect image of God's will, as only the son of God knows it. Christ knew what is in God and he knew what is in humans, for he himself is both God and human. And so he taught clearly what people must do if they are to become all that God intends. To secure people's perfect conformity with God's will was the purpose of every law he enunciated.

Christ's work, however, involved something more than this role of teacher. If he had come only to make God visible and to authentically teach the human way to God, he would have plunged people into an even worse condition than that of Israel in the old covenant. The stronger the light grows, the more one suffers from it if the eyes are weak. The more clearly God manifested the divine will, the more pitiable would be the condition of those who, through weakness, were constantly prone to follow the urge of their own selfishness.

Lifting the Burden of Sin with Love

If Christ came into the world to lift from people the burden of sin and to unite them to God, he had to do something more than manifest God and unfold God's will through a perfect law. He had to change the whole condition of human beings, strengthening what was weak and giving life to what was anemic. This means that he had to fill them with inward love, his own love for the Father, for love alone makes it possible for people to say with God's son, "My food is to do the will of the one who sent me and to accomplish this work" (John 4:34).

The only power which can bring people to this fidelity is called by Paul "the law of the spirit of life which is in Christ Jesus" (Rom 8:2). He uses the word "law" deliberately to emphasize the all-important truth that the righteousness which the law of the old covenant envisioned is attainable only through the power of the indwelling Holy Spirit whose presence in humans is the consummate fruition of Christ's saving work.

Obviously, as Paul makes clear elsewhere, this "law of the spirit" is unlike any other law, for it is written "not on tablets of stone but on tablets of human hearts" (2 Cor 3:3). Far from being a formulated command which comes to humans from without, the "law of the Spirit" is a loving knowledge within the human heart which enables one to know connaturally what the Creator wills, to desire it with the whole being, and to carry it out with joy and earnestness.

The early apostles were so convinced of the power of this "law of the Spirit" that they wrote to their ordinary Christians words which most of us would be afraid to utter:

> The anointing which you received from him abides in you, and you have no need that anyone should teach you; as his anointing teaches you about everything, and is true, and is no lie, just as it has taught you, abide in him (1 John 2:27).

The "anointing" to which John here refers is the gift of the Holy Spirit who comes to each Christian in baptism. His confidence in the guidance and power of the Spirit dwelling in the baptized is shared by Paul. The claim which Paul makes for his converts, if uttered by someone today, would probably be condemned as an incitement to insubordination:

> The spiritual person (one in whom the Holy Spirit is active) judges all things, but is to be judged by no one. "For who has known the mind of the Lord so as to instruct him?" But we have the mind of Christ (1 Cor 2:15-16).

This empowering of humans with strong, inward love was the second essential element in Christ's saving work. His mission involved not only the illumination of minds by the teaching of a perfect law but also the strengthening of the whole person through the gift of his own spirit: "I am come that they may have life and have it abundantly" (John 10:10).

The New Testament writings tell the story of how Christ fulfilled this purpose. In becoming flesh, the son of God left his Father's house to mingle with people, to take upon himself their humanness, and to become flesh of their flesh, their brother. When, through death and resurrection, he returned to his Father, he appeared before God not only as a beloved son but also as a corporate personality, bearing in his body a permanent blood bond with every person of earth and in his heart an undying love for them. [For the intimate bonding between the risen Christ and the members of the Church, see Chapter 11.]

Adoption Through the Spirit

In receiving him the eternal Father received also a whole new family of people whom Christ "is not ashamed to call brothers and sisters" (Heb 2:11). The only thing still necessary was the deed of adoption. With us, adoption is only a legal fiction, the flourish of a fountain pen signing the contract prescribed by law. How different was God's adoption of us in Christ Jesus.

In this act the incarnate son of God, now the risen Lord of glory sharing in the full power of the Father, showed his boundless love for people, his brothers and sisters, by giving to them his own spirit to be their spirit. Through this gift the new Israel has become the perfect family of God. For the spirit of Jesus dwelling in each member fills the heart with Christ's love and makes each one, in the eyes of the eternal Father, another Jesus. St. Paul describes this historic process of salvation in words which carve an exquisite cameo:

> When the fullness of time had come, God sent the Son, born of a woman, born under the law, to ransom those under the law, so that we might receive adoption. As proof that you are children, God sent the spirit of the Son into our hearts, crying out, "Abba, Father!" So you are no longer a slave but a child, and if a child then also an heir, through God (Gal 4:4-7).

Every Christian, therefore, has received the spirit of Jesus who constantly breathes faith and love into the heart and ceaselessly "bears witness with our spirit that we are children of God" (Rom 8:16). Faith makes Christians cling to the Creator with devoted commitment while love prompts them to do always the things which please God. Bearing Christ's own spirit in their hearts they have "put on Christ" inwardly and outwardly (Gal 3:27), so that if they permit the Spirit to act in them, their souls, like the human soul of Christ, will be limpid pools reflecting without ruffle or ripple the vast expanse of heaven's will.

The lives of these children of God now know only one source of action, "the law of faith" (Rom 3:27), "the law of the Spirit" (Rom 8:2). Nothing is so intransigent as this "law of Christ" (Gal 6:2), for no law is so exacting as love. A hired hand, receiving orders from the employer, may discharge duties with scrupulous care. But such duties are never more than chores performed by one who is an outsider to the family interests. If, however, this employee is adopted into the family by the employer who has come to love and to cherish this person as a child, then the whole picture changes. The estate becomes the adopted child's estate; the home, the child's home; the worker has become a child and a sibling.

The person will now do the same things always done, but in an entirely new way. Future services will come not from the direction of an external command but from the exigencies of love itself. Far from seeking motivation in the orders given or in limited personal interests, the person will work faithfully and full-heartedly because love for the parent and family will both show the way and urge the new family member on with compelling necessity.

This is the character of Christian living, a way of life prompted wholly and empowered by the love which the Holy Spirit dwelling within each person pours into the heart. If Christ's work had not culminated in the gift of the Spirit he would not have saved humanity, for the only source of righteousness before God is the illumination and power which come from the Spirit: "Those who are led by the Spirit of God are children of God" (Rom 8:14).

THE PLACE OF EXTERNAL RULE

Where then is there any place for external rule in a life which flows wholly from inward principle? In other words, does law have any *raison d'être* in the life of the children of God? [Editor's note: Barnabas Ahern delivered this address before the promulgation of the newly revised Code of Canon Law, 1983.]

A moment's consideration of this question provides the answer. In all family life there are things to do, ways of acting to follow, a whole program of conduct to observe. Children must show themselves worthy of their parents' love and vitally concerned about the needs of their family. Even human love has fixed ways of proving itself. If these ways are despised, love dies; if proprieties are neglected, love cools. In the language of St. Thomas Aquinas, full Christian living involves not only activity springing from love, but also careful regard for the *ordines caritatis*—the properties of love.

The knowledge of these *ordines caritatis* is rarely given directly by the Spirit to each Christian as an individual. If such were the case, the divine plan would be nullified, that we live in the Church as members of the body of Christ dependent upon one another, preserving continuity with the Church of the apostles and the Church of the ages. In God's plan, humanity must learn dependence upon the spirit of Christ by experiencing a need for his divergent activities in other members of the Church. Time and again, therefore, the individual Christian—though full of love—will receive illumination and direction from the Holy Spirit only through the action of another.

Hence, Christian life must always have its commandments, precepts, normative directives, and formulated ways of acting. If these are rightly understood, they will be regarded as essential to full Christian living. Certainly they are not the "laws" which a master imposes from afar upon a slave. Far less should they be the merely human dictate of a superior who prefers his or her own way to the ways of God. Rather, they are to be the blueprint of the very form of life which love given by the Spirit prompts the child of God to live.

A parent tells the child to help with the household work, not as though it were a command to a slave or expressing arbitrary will but as describing the very act which a child's love should prompt the parent to do.

In heaven there will be no occasion for laws or precepts; there as perfect children of God, all shall know fully the exigencies and proprieties of love. But here upon earth, where the children of God must walk by faith, they live in dependence upon one another and are safeguarded from thoughtlessness. Our Creator will often remind us by the Church's laws and precepts of all that life in God's family really means.

Practical Conclusions on the Laws of Christian Life

For those members of the Church who are entrusted with the making of laws and precepts, certain guidelines for their labor are immediately evident in the very nature of Christian life as we have described it. These guidelines, we hope, may provide material for fruitful discussion.

The role of lawmaker in the Church is by its very nature an ancillary role. First of all, this function is immediately dependent upon God's will. Not only does the lawmaker owe authority to God but the very enactments must image faithfully God's ways with humanity. Like the supreme teaching authority in the Church, the "stewards" of law and precept are "required to be found trustworthy" in dependence upon God and the divine plan (cf. 1 Cor 4:1-2).

Speaking of the Church's doctrinal magisterium, the conciliar constitution *Dei Verbum* 10 makes clear that this body, in exercising its office as teacher of the faithful, "is not above the word of God but serves it, teaching only what has been handed on, listening to it devoutly, guarding it scrupulously, and explaining it faithfully . . . with the help of the Holy Spirit."

In the same way and for the same reason those with jurisdictional authority are servants of the Word of God; all their enactments must faithfully reflect God's will for the Church and must help people to know and serve God better.

Because the Church is unique as an institution (like Israel of old, wholly from God and wholly for God), its legal code can never be a mere collection of laws; it must be a Torah in which all law is illumined by doctrine. Only in this way will the law of the Church serve its true purpose of bringing all to see that the conduct prescribed reflects the will of God and leads to God.

Any law or precept, therefore, which is not theologically sound, which obscures the nature of God and of Christian life, which distorts the will of God and the divine plan for the life of the Church, is an evil law. Those who make laws or who give precepts without painstaking attention to the ways of God with people deserve the bitter condemnation which Christ poured out upon the Pharisees: "You disregard God's commandment but cling to human tradition" (Mark 7:8).

In the light of this principle, we must examine our Code of Canon Law. The whole mentality of the Church, especially of clerics and lawmakers, is formed by this book. If its perspectives are faulty and if its enactments are defective in mirroring God and God's ways with people, then the Church will continue to suffer from the lawmaking and precept formulation of those whose minds, though faithful to the code, are not faithful to God. What then, shall we say of the obvious weaknesses of the Code?

1. The poverty of its doctrinal orientation: How little there is in this law book to make one God-conscious and aware that the Church is a unique institution. Even the law of Israel was far superior to this code of the new and perfect covenant in bringing all to see the ways of God in the conduct prescribed by the law.

2. Its distortion of Catholic doctrine in its lacunae, vocabulary and enactments, e.g.:

> a. Our Code does not contain a single title on Scripture; it makes no mention of the reading of Scripture by our Catholic people; it gives no indication that Scripture with tradition is "the supreme rule of faith" (*Dei Verbum* 21);
>
> b. By using the phrase *Sedes Apostolica* (Apostolic Seat) for all Roman Congregations it has unwittingly extended to them—in practice—prerogatives which belong personally only to the Roman Pontiff: primacy and infallibility;
>
> c. In giving to the third book, which treats the sacraments, the title *De Rebus* (literally, Concerning Things) it falsifies the very nature of sacraments.

3. Its enactments concentrate on means rather than ends. Contrary to the mind of Christ, too much of our legal system follows the principle: *Finis legis non cadit sub lege* (The end of the law does not fall under the law).

4. The attitude of much of our legislation—*fac hoc* (do this)—does not reflect the revealed doctrine that in Christ people are free and that through the gift of the Holy Spirit, they have the "mind of Christ" (cf. 1 Cor 1:15-16).

5. The basic weakness of our code is that it fails to image the unique character of life in the Church. Unlike the law book of Israel and unlike the moral and jurisdictional directives of Paul, our code represents the mentality and follows the pattern of merely human jurisprudence.

The role of the lawgiver is ancillary. The legislation is commendable only if it is totally dependent on "the law of the Spirit." All Christian life is the work of the Holy Spirit inspiring, strengthening, illumining, and guiding both the Church and the individual Christian. The Spirit of God, therefore, must be allowed full play in the life of the Church.

If jurisdictional authority fails to keep its ears open to the voice of the Spirit speaking through Christian movements and Christian charismata; if in accord with previous usages or "traditional" ways of thinking and acting, it trammels new manifestations of the Spirit or impedes doctrinal, apostolic, or organizational developments; if, thwarting a new directional momentum in the Church universal, it insists that its own local group hold tenaciously to the "old ways," then jurisdictional authority fails in its responsibility, neglecting to follow "the law of the Spirit."

St. Paul emphasizes the respect which authority must have towards manifestations of Jesus' spirit in the Church: "Do not quench the Spirit. Do not despise prophetic utterances. Test everything; retain what is good. Refrain from every kind of evil" (1 Thess 5:19-22).

Final doctrinal decisions and jurisdictional directives rest with those whom "the Holy Spirit has appointed overseers . . . to tend the Church of God" (Acts 20:28). Often enough their enactments will have to rest on a prudential judgment; and, as St. Thomas points out, prudential judgments do not bring certainty. Hence, time and again, the enactments of legislators will later prove to have been faulty.

This failure is a necessary limitation in the lives of all who walk by faith, and not with vision; and so such failure should cause no surprise. But even granting the fallibility of legislators who are human, every precaution must be taken to safeguard the family of God from directives which "quench the Spirit" (1 Thess 5:19).

The very responsibility of rule, therefore, demands on the part of the legislator full recognition of the illumining and often charismatic activity of the Holy Spirit in the Church. Authority must humbly watch for the signs of this activity, the breathing of the Spirit (cf. John 3:8); and, when these signs appear, it must provide for progress by wise enactments and sound encouragement.

Sometimes in the past laws and precepts have repressed the action of the Spirit rather than supported it. What religious order of women ever began its charismatic mission without untold interference from those in authority? For St. Paul, such ill-advised negative repressiveness is a sin against the Spirit.

No Christian writer has defended Christian liberty so forthrightly as Paul, who was convinced that the liberty of the children of God and the liberty of the Spirit are united as effect and cause. He writes: "The spiritual person, however, can judge everything but is not subject to judgment by anyone. For, who has known the mind of the Lord so as to counsel him? But we have the mind of Christ" (1 Cor 2:15-16).

CONCLUSIONS: FUTURE STUDY

In light of the principle that "the law of the Spirit" must be the guide of jurisdictional authority, certain areas merit investigation. We suggest the following:

1. What provisions can be made to safeguard groups in the Church from legislation which makes little allowance for the present activity of the Holy Spirit? I refer to:

> a. Precepts which cripple a group in the fulfillment of its mission;
>
> b. Precepts which limit the rights of individuals as citizens and as children of God;
>
> c. Precepts which, contrary to the spirit of universal legislation and the general practice of the Church, deny to the faithful of a local area the right to exercise activities and to follow practices which are widely permitted elsewhere.

2. Since custom is the ordinary concrete expression of the activity of the Holy Spirit in a group, could we lessen the stringent requirements which are now demanded for the legality of custom?

3. In the past few years we have seen even papal directives pass into immediate disuse because of mass non-observance. Even the *pars sanior* (healthier or more cautious part) of the group to whom the directive was sent (as for example, in the case of *Veterum Sapientia*, spelling out what seminary courses were to be taught in Latin) felt fully warranted in their non-observance. What provision can be made to "legalize" such inaction, so that it will be seen not as people's right to deny authority but rather as people's right under the Holy Spirit of correcting an ill-advised act of authority?

CHAPTER 14

Ecumenism and Revelation

Jerome M. Vereb, C.P.

No one could ever accuse Barnabas Ahern of being lazy. His interests were universal and he pursued them vigorously, whether opera, politics, or theology. He therefore was a good dialogue partner. Friendly, outgoing, loyal, and winsome, he enjoyed human company and his ecumenical activity was one of making friends. A Scripture scholar, following Vatican II he remained in Rome teaching at Regina Mundi and the Gregorian University. He also continued his council-begun service to the Secretariat for Promoting Christian Unity where he moved from consultant of council documents to a promoter of their contents. He joined the Anglican/Roman Catholic International dialogue (ARCIC) where he served for twelve years discussing the themes of Eucharist, ministry, and authority.

Ahern's ecumenical work was furthered by his collaboration in the conversations with Protestant Pentecostals, chaired by Kilian McDonnell, O.S.B., and the late David Du Plessis. Both men admired him and he made his contribution through his unique style which differed only in intensity from his other ecumenical commitment with Anglicans. Here he did not produce papers or even a written *votum* but instead entered into the actual discussion and strove to do that towards which all ecumenical projects are directed: find consensus. He explained, for example, in a session dealing with Marian theology that the Assumption dogma could resemble the Pentecostal concept of "rapture." He was anxious to heal cleavage between one type of spirituality and another. He reminded both dialogues that here were English language phenomena; and in a common linguistic culture there was the possibility of deriving a solution to divisions and misunderstandings. He often cited poetry. After all, who could not relate to Newman's "Lead Kindly Light"? His reference here added just the right tone in a debate.

SOURCE OF ECUMENICAL SENSITIVITY

I have often wondered whence Barnabas Ahern derived his ecumenical sensitivity. After all, he came from a very parochial background; his was a most traditional Roman Catholic piety. He read the lives of nineteenth-century foundresses of religious orders frequently. He prayed fervently to St. Benedict Joseph Labre, whom he greatly admired. He loved to attend devotions to the Sacred Heart of Jesus.

Yet he had lived and studied in the Rome of Pope Pius XII when new ideas slowly emerged in regard to pastoral theology, liturgical refinement, and, of course, the meaning of sacred Scripture, his field of specialization. In the pontificate of Pope John XXIII those ideas burgeoned. In a sense their matrix was "unity," which itself was to develop as the goals of the proposed ecumenical council were to become focused and mature. It is the common view today that the initial ideals of the council did not have the precisely technical ecumenical tone one imagines today. This was to develop only as the suggestions of Paderborn bishop (later cardinal) Lorenz Jaeger were to be brought to the attention of the Pope in 1960. Jaeger had previously engaged himself and his theologians in the work of what he called "controversial theology" since the end of World War II. This substantially was a type of "proto-dialogue" between German Catholics and Protestants but, nonetheless, genuine ecumenical work. Prior to Jaeger's ecumenical proposal, John XXIII's council could more easily have focused on economic, social, or political unity as is brought out in his Peter and Paul encyclical of 1959, *Ad Petri Cathedram*. In the background of all of it was the cold war. Unity as survival was a matter of utmost urgency.

With the establishment of the Secretariat for Promoting Christian Unity and its more focused efforts to deal with divisions in the family of Christendom during the council, Barnabas Ahern became more drawn in. Augustin Cardinal Bea, his former mentor, was nominated the first president of the secretariat and his secretary was Stepan Schmidt, S.J., a classmate of Barnabas from the Pontifical Biblical Institute. In fact, the two were friends and had defended doctoral dissertations at the same time. Through Professor Bea, Ahern had previously become familiar with Protestant contributions to the field of biblical studies and the significance of mutual, even collaborative, efforts at biblical interpretation.

During the time of the council itself, Barnabas assisted Protestant observers, related to the press, served as *peritus* to the American cardinals and bishops, and joined the team of the Secretariat for Christian Unity members and consultors in the review of the council *schemata*. Among these drafts, his principal concern was with the Constitution *Dei Verbum* or "On Divine Revelation." Because of the Protestant emphasis on the primacy of sacred Scripture and the sacrament-like reverence borne for it by the Orthodox members, the proposed drafts had to be carefully presented to the observers for their comments; and in turn their reflections carried back to the appropriate committees.

SCRIPTURE AND TRADITION

As originally presented, the text was based upon the "two source theory" of revelation, i.e., that Scripture and tradition separately were constitutive of the experience of God's self-communication. Further, the language of the two initial chapters was heavily scholastic and too abstruse to satisfy the expectations of Protestant and Orthodox observers. These commented that they could not comprehend such distinctions, let alone imagine how a contemporary secular world could with its materialistic preoccupations and its existential angst. It is here that the unifying theme of the "presence of God" emerged into the finally approved text, to the appreciation of both council fathers and observers. As Roderick A. F. MacKenzie, S.J., explained: "Every single such communication from God is part of a larger pattern, is destined ultimately for the good of all. Revelation by its nature is public. Therefore, it has to be made known to others by the testimony of its recipient. Passed on orally, it becomes tradition; recorded in writing, it becomes scripture."

If revelation is God's self-disclosure and if it carries every person to the threshold of that experience by reason of its necessarily public character, there is already a theme of "oneness" present both in the one God and in the community formed by this exposure to God's dynamic of communication. But there are other themes of unity to be found in the text, themes analogous to the unifying spirit in the Church.

Paragraph 2 speaks thus:

> Through this revelation, therefore, the invisible God out of the abundance of love speaks to human beings as friends and lives among them so that God might invite them and take them into fellowship. This plan is realized by deeds and words having an inner unity. . . .

This introductory statement goes on to speak of the necessary perspective that all persons are part of the history of salvation. Fellowship is guaranteed not only by a common participation in time and space, i.e., history, but also there is a further *providential* character to that history which deepens the historical human experience. Nothing escapes God's eye. Centered in the person of Jesus, himself a figure of history, one's self-understanding becomes relational, first to the Christ and consequently to all those who in turn relate to him. Christ is called the "mediator" who presents history with the "deepest truth about God." The consequence of this experience, "fellowship in providence," provides the Christian with a profound experience of a participant along with others, a so-called team concept. Reading the Scriptures becomes more exciting from this perspective. One is no mere spectator. Albert Outler, an American observer to the council, pronounced himself satisfied with the phraseology here. "We Methodists have long known about fellowship. It is good to see it actively used in Catholic thinking."

ECUMENISM AND UNITY WITHIN THE BIBLE

Paragraph 9 of the Constitution on Divine Revelation refers to an inner ecumenism within the structure of the entire Bible and a dynamic unity between both testaments. In patristic times, Origen had stated that the presence of God in the sacred writings was directly analogous to the actual presence of Christ. In modern times, biblical scholars such as Raymond E. Brown, S.S., and Timothea Eliot, R.S.M., have commented that at a certain moment of exegesis one is taken from the particularities of a specific text, with its own language, history, and archeological references. The scholar is carried away to an experiential awareness of the presence of a spirit which makes Scripture all one. The same God is revealed in each passage of the same book from beginning to end. Said Mother Eliot, "It rushes into you."

The constitution records:

> Hence there exists a close connection between sacred tradition and sacred Scripture. For both of them flowing from the same divine wellspring, in a certain way merge into a unity and tend towards the same end.

Earlier, in paragraph 6, the same text reads:

> Through divine revelation, God chose to show forth and communicate the Divine Self and the eternal decisions of the divine will regarding the salvation of human beings. That is to say, God chose "to share those divine treasures which totally transcend the understanding of the human mind."

Thus "spirit-driven" could be added to other such characteristics like "fellowship-forming" and "providential" which are part of the inherent ecumenism of the Constitution *Dei Verbum*.

Here tradition is seen to be not only a communication of the past but an active forward-moving wave into yet unknown depths of the unexplored or the unanticipated. Sacred Scripture and sacred tradition are so intimately united that it is impossible to separate them. Therefore the counciliar synod at Rome approved the following words:

> For in the sacred books, the Father who is in heaven meets his children with great love and speaks with them; and the force and power in the word of God is so great that it remains the support and energy of the Church, the strength and faith of her children, the food of the soul, the pure and perennial source of spiritual life (par. 21).

This inner relationship quotes Eucharistic-like words and calls up the imagery of the pilgrim people receiving manna, quail, and liquid refreshment in the desert of wandering. Thus, the Scriptures provide a source of common sustenance and everyone is invited to be refreshed at a common oasis. No one has a privileged claim to this food. During the long period of the Byzantine empire the patriarchs of Constantinople reserved copies of the Bible in the tabernacle with the consecrated elements, to impress the significance of the Scriptures as a sacred but common table to which anyone might sit down to find food.

All of the above was best summarized in the words of paragraph 11 which bespeaks the essential unity of God's action:

Those divinely revealed realities were contained and presented in sacred Scripture and have been committed to writing under the inspiration of the Holy Spirit. Holy Mother Church, relying on the belief of the apostles, holds that the books of both the Old and New Testament in their entirety, with all their parts, are sacred and canonical because, having been written under the inspiration of the Holy Spirit they have God as their author and have been handed on as such to the Church herself.

The logical conclusion is that what has been received by the many has been received as by one people, unified by the reception.

WORKING FOR UNITY

I do not know the actual role Barnabas Ahern, biblical scholar, played in the drafting of *Dei Verbum,* nor in its critique and refinement. I do know that in the dialogue sessions with Anglicans and Pentecostals, he quoted it often in Latin. He did the same with the document *Unitatis Redintegratio,* the decree on ecumenism. Obviously he had both of these memorized *in toto* to the amazement of all participants. These together were a source of his own ecumenical spirit and both documents were drafted under an ecumenical character through Cardinal Bea's Secretariat for Promoting Christian Unity. Both are biblically based. Barnabas was present in the drafting.

Further, Barnabas Ahern as a Passionist religious took seriously the motive of the sufferings and crucifixion of Jesus as found in John 17:21, "That they may be one . . . that the world may believe that you have sent me." Here again the evangelical thrust and the cause of unity are so intimately associated that it is impossible to separate them, a thought confirmed by another Johannine prediction: "If I am lifted up I will draw all things to myself" (John 12:32). There is an inherent magnetism to the crucified one whom Barnabas was vowed to imitate in his religious life. It was his personal spirituality.

Since Barnabas began his ecumenical work in 1966, the Secretariat (now Council) for Promoting Christian Unity has opened nine major dialogues on an international level and inaugurated relations with such organizations as the United Bible Society and the World Council of Churches. In many instances, there has been much success. The 1982 document on "Baptism, Eucharist and Ministry" of the Faith and Order subunit of the World Council of Churches stands as a watershed of the possibilities of convergence. However, the present moment sometimes provides a less enthusiastic picture as divisions emerge anew within religious families over ordination and ministry. Barnabas' winning personality always had an appropriate expression in the face of confusion: "Speak well of one another," he said, "work for unity rather than disunity."

Part V
The Presence of Mary in the Bible

Elizabeth, filled with the Holy Spirit, cried out in a loud voice and said, "Most blessed are you among women, and blessed is the fruit of your womb. And how does this happen to me, that the mother of my Lord should come to me? For at the moment the sound of your greeting reached my ears, the infant in my womb leaped for joy. Blessed are you who believed that what was spoken to you by the Lord would be fulfilled (Luke 1:41-45).

Chapter 15

The Infancy Narratives

At last the Advent of Old Testament waiting came to an end, and the moment of fulfillment arrived. The tale of what happened is a woman's story; for it is a woman who entered most intimately into the wonder of Christ's coming, and it is to her—ultimately—that we owe our Gospel. "And the virgin's name was Mary" (Luke 1:27).

There was a day at Nazareth when Mary was like other young girls. Her life was their life; her beauty, their beauty; olive-tinted skin and deep brown eyes, jet black hair swept back and held in place under a long white veil; strong arms browned by the sun and hands roughened with the feel of the water jars. Like the other girls of Nazareth, she could laugh and play and sing and cry. Yet there was something special about her, a spirit that others must have noticed. How often, when she had drawn her day's supply of water at the well and turned toward home, the other women lingering behind at the Ain Sitti Miriam would say to one another, "Isn't Mary such a sweet, thoughtful girl?" It is a pity they had never heard Alice Meynell's poem "The Shepherdess," for certainly they would have recognized her in its words and would have said, "Yes, this is Mary."

> She walks—the lady of my delight—
>   A shepherdess of sheep.
> Her flocks are thoughts. She keeps them white;
>   She guards them from the steep;
> She feeds them on the fragrant height
>   And folds them in for sleep.

How they loved to watch her in the synagogue on the Sabbath as she listened with rapt attention to the solemnly cadenced words of the rabbi reading the Scriptures. She seemed all absorbed in the Word of God as though she were living wholly in that world of the Messiah which the prophets had promised to the *anawim,* the holy ones of Israel. No one ever penetrated into the secret of God's promise as deeply and as vitally as did Mary.

Then one day an angel came to Nazareth, to that village of whitewashed houses clustering on the slopes of the Nebi Sain. When you first glimpse it from a distant hillside, this little town seems like a white rose unfolding its petals against the background of a green bush. It was here the angel came, the same Gabriel who long before appeared to the prophet Daniel in the temple at Jerusalem (Dan 9:21). Just recently, he had appeared once more in the temple, this time to Zachary the priest, promising the birth of John the Baptist (Luke 1:19). But now he bypassed the temple, without even a sidelong glance, to come directly to Mary and to bow low before her who is transcendently holier than the temple.

The story of it all we owe to Mary. It is she who first spoke of the details which we have come to know; it is she, too, who has shared with us her own insight into the fullness of their rich meaning. For the events come to us, not merely as they happened, but as she saw them in the light of the Old Testament promise and as she understood them in the depths of her prayerful soul. Luke himself, who incorporated the infancy narratives into the Gospel, insists on this; several times he reminds his reader that Mary had long pondered these events in her heart before at last she spoke (Luke 1:29; 2:19, 33-35, 48-50). Here was the power of the clean of heart to gaze calmly on the full wonder of God's greatest work and to penetrate deeply into its riches.

AN ANGEL SPEAKS

The angel's first words to Mary were a greeting she could never forget, "Rejoice, O favored one!" Time and again she had heard that salutation in the Scripture readings of the synagogue. Each time the rabbi's voice pulsed with expectancy, for the prophets always used the word *rejoice* to preface their promise that soon the Messiah would come to do his great work. There was, for instance, the pealing cry of Zechariah:

> Rejoice heartily, O daughter Zion,
> Shout for joy, O daughter Jerusalem.
> See, your king shall come to you (Zech 9:9).

These were the very words that now opened the angel's greeting: "*Rejoice*, O favored one!" Mary's soul thrilled with tremendous joy, mingled with fear and awe; for the word *rejoice* alerted her with Israel's ever-expectant hope of the Messiah's imminent coming. But she had never dreamed of the message that now followed. For the angel went on to speak of a child, *her* child, a child who would be the promised king. The words of his solemn announcement were all-revealing; each phrase vibrantly echoed the words that God had once uttered through his prophet Zephaniah:

> Rejoice, O favored one! (Luke 1:28).
> Rejoice, O daughter of Jerusalem! (Zeph 3:14).
>
> The Lord is with you (Luke 1:28).
> The king of Israel, the Lord, is in the midst of you . . . (Zeph 3:15).
>
> Do not be afraid, Mary (Luke 1:30).
> Fear not, O Zion . . . (Zeph 3:16).
>
> Behold, you will conceive in your womb . . . the Son of the Most High . . . (Luke 1:31-32).
> The Lord, your God, is in your bosom (Zeph 3:17).
>
> You shall call his name Jesus (Yahweh-Savior) (Luke 1:31).
> . . . a mighty Savior (Zeph 3:17).

There was no doubt in Mary's mind that the angel was asking her to become the mother of the Messiah-Lord. Familiar as she was with the words of the prophet, she now heard their echo in the words of the angel. She could not have mistaken the meaning of it all. Her mind was rich with the best gifts of the Spirit, and so she saw instantly the identity which the angel's words had forged between the *Lord* of Zephaniah's oracle and the child to be born of her.

SHEKINAH: SYMBOL OF HIS PRESENCE

But all-prudent virgin that she was, Mary had to find out the exact measure of her cooperation; and so she asked, "How shall this happen, since I do not know man?" It would have been easy for Gabriel to reply simply, "God will do everything." But no; Gabriel chooses words that are aglow with revealing light from the Old Testament: "The Holy Spirit shall come upon you and the power of the Most High shall overshadow you." This promise was a flash of light, illumining brilliantly for Mary the full meaning of her maternity. Often before she had heard of the wonder God had wrought for her people during the days of their desert wanderings; often, too, she had lovingly pondered the marvel of it all. As the people moved forward across the wastes of the desert of Sinai, they carried with them the tabernacle where God dwelt. A luminous cloud, the *Shekinah*, was the symbol of God's presence. As the sacred text describes it, "the cloud overshadowed the tabernacle, and the glory of God filled the dwelling" (Exod 40:35). Now Gabriel used these words to speak of Mary herself. Not a cloud but the "power of the Most High" will overshadow her; she is to be the pure ark bearing the *Shekinah* of God's glory, carrying in her immaculate womb the very Son of God. No wonder Gabriel bypassed the altar in the temple at Jerusalem to come to Mary and to bow low in humble reverence. God had chosen her to be the ark bearing divine glory and the *Shekinah* had come to overshadow her. Robert Hawker glimpsed this meaning and gave expression to it in the following beautiful lines:

> She stood, the Lady *Shekinah* of Earth,
>   A chancel for the sky;
> Where woke, to breath and beauty, God's own birth,
>   For men to see Him by.
> Round her, too pure to mingle with the day,
>   Light, that was Life, abode;
> Folded within her fibers meekly lay
>   The link of boundless God.

Mary's cousin Elizabeth glimpses the wonder of it all. When Mary entered the little house at Ain Karem for the mystery of her visitation, Elizabeth's voice thrilled with recognition: "Who am I," she cried, "to have the mother of my Lord come to me?" (Luke 1:43). Mary's heart bounded with joy; for in these words she heard a perfect echo of the cry of King David, as he bowed low before the ark of God and exclaimed wonderingly, "Who am I to have the ark of the Lord come to me?" (2 Kgs 6:9). This was now Elizabeth's outcry. She saw before her not merely a maid become a mother, but the very ark of God bearing within the glory of God.

The joy that filled Mary's heart overflowed in song: "My soul proclaims the greatness of the Lord." She who sings is no longer just a gentle, beautiful girl of Nazareth; no, through motherhood she has become the unique woman, the virgin daughter of Israel who represents all people. Her song is lovely with the humility of humanity itself before its maker. Long before, God had said to Israel, "It was not because you are the largest of all nations that the Lord set his heart on you and chose you, for you are really the smallest of all nations. It was because the Lord loved you" (Deut 7:7). Long before, God had dramatized the story of Israel. On the day of its birth, it lay out upon an open field, a helpless babe weltering in its blood. God passed by and took pity upon it. God loved and nurtured it and made it beautiful with God's own divine gifts. And so, when the babe came to maturity and drew the eye of every admirer, God said to it, "Your reputation for beauty went out through the nations, for your beauty was perfect because of the splendor that I had bestowed upon you" (Ezek 16:14). This is the Israel who sings in Our Lady's *Magnificat.* Her song is our song; and so the Church places it upon our lips day after day. For she is the chosen daughter of Zion, the lovely and lowly representative of all Israel—of all people—and she thanks God for all men and women because God has showed us the greatest of divine favors in giving us his own Son:

> My soul proclaims the greatness of the Lord, and my spirit rejoices
> in God my Savior;
> For he has looked upon his handmaid's lowliness; . . . .
> The Mighty One has done great things for me, and holy is his
> name (Luke 1:46-49).

Mary remained with Elizabeth all during the days of the older woman's waiting. When later she spoke of this period and told its length, it is significant that she chose the very words that occur in the Old Testament to describe the stay of the ark in the house of Obededom: "And the ark of the Lord remained . . . three months" (2 Sam 6:11). "And Mary remained with her about three months" (Luke 1:56). Here was a constant awareness that she was the true ark bearing everywhere the glory of God.

"LORD BECOME SAVIOR"

For her this glory was not just a glowing light, but a *person* rich and real. In him was all the goodness and kindness of God our Savior. Mary heard this in the very name she was to give him, for the angel had said, "You shall call his name Jesus; and he shall save his people from their sins" (Matt 1:21). In Hebrew, this name is pronounced *Yehoshua,* and it is made up of two words: Yahweh (Lord) and Hosea (Salvation). The name Jesus means, therefore, that he is the great

Yahweh, the Lord of heaven and earth, come down to us to be our Savior, our Hosea.

Long before, a prophet of Israel bore the name Hosea. He was a devout man whom God told to marry Gomer, the daughter of Diblaim. This was hardly a happy match for, even from the beginning, the poor wretch must have shown some weaknesses that later led to her undoing. Time and again, she disappointed Hosea by her heedless familiarity with other men. At last, poor Gomer completely fell away. No longer satisfied with a mere illicit love affair, she chose infidelity as her way of life. She left home to sell herself in the slave market for any price. All around, sympathetic neighbors harped on the foolishness of trying to reclaim her. Even her husband Hosea must have been ready to give her up. But then the inexorable Word of God broke through: "Hosea, go yet again and love her" (Hos 3:1). It was the "yet again" of divine love. Obediently, the shamefaced prophet pocketed his coins and went down into the slave market to buy her back. That took a lot of courage. It took heroic love to lead her by the hand back to his own home. For all around he could hear people whispering, "The old fool! Is he crazed by his infatuation?" But God's love for Israel urged him on to show forth this forgiving love of God in his own love for Gomer—to sacrifice his feelings, to throw away his reputation, to give up all that he held dear. Centuries later, this divine love would urge God's Son to descend into the slave market of this world and to buy us back from our degradation with coins of his precious blood. That is why he was to bear the name Jesus. He is the great Yahweh come down from heaven to be our Hosea.

This was the thought that filled Our Lady's mind on the first Christmas night. As she sat in the stable in the shadow of the broken stall, she held her babe in her arms and stroked his forehead with hands like frail white wings of prayer. Then it was that she whispered for the first time his beautiful name. For her, that name was like a seashell drawn from the vast ocean of scriptural prophecy. For they say that when one puts an ear to a seashell, one hears the surging of the sea from which it has come. So when Our Lady pronounced that sacred name, she heard the great sweeping surges of a sea of joy and a sea of pain. To her, it echoed the whole story of what he must do to be truly our Savior. For his whole merciful work of saving peoples everywhere is all contained in his beautiful name Jesus.

Our Lady knew that he was our Savior from living experience. For everywhere she saw and felt the abounding joy which the prophets had promised to all those who would receive him: "You shall draw water with joy from the fountains of the Savior" (Isa 12:1). Everywhere Our Lady saw joy thrilling in every heart. The angel had promised Zachary, "You shall have joy and gladness" (Luke 1:14). In the presence of Jesus and his mother, the little babe in the womb of Elizabeth trembled with joy. Mary herself, in her *Magnificat,* cries out, "My spirit rejoices in God my Savior." On the night he was born, the sky above Bethlehem echoed and re-echoed with the message of the angel, "Behold, I bring you good news of great joy; for there has been born to you today a savior who is Christ the Lord" (Luke 2:10). When the Magi came and found the little babe, "They rejoiced exceedingly" (Matt 2:10). Joy overflowed everywhere—"in good measure, pressed down, and running over" (Luke 6:38). And it all came from the glory of God—the Savior—resting on the ark of Mary's bosom. This is why joy flows through the liturgy of Advent. It is a time of penance and preparation; and yet, the very nearness of the Savior prompts the repeated cry, "Rejoice! Alleluia!"

GLORY HID IN POWERLESSNESS

But, as always before, the gleaming of God's glory was hidden under covers; God must do his saving work through weakness. For men and women of themselves have no strength: "Before him all the nations are as nought, as nothing and void he accounts them" (Isa 40:17). All we can do is to offer God our weakness. Mary knew this truth through and through; so, in every event of the infancy of her child, she saw God at work in weakness; everywhere she saw God's glory gleaming through the cover of human powerlessness. The child in her womb came there without human help; this was all God's work. The divine Infant wrought his first miracle of grace through the weakness of her human voice; he sanctified the Baptist through the word of greeting which she spoke to Elizabeth. The night he was born, the angels told the shepherds that they must expect to find only a feeble little child. Christ, the Lord of heaven and earth, would be wrapped in swaddling bands, God's might in the bonds of human weakness: "This shall be a sign to you: you will find an infant wrapped in swaddling clothes and lying in a manger" (Luke 2:12). The shepherds came to Bethlehem; they saw and reverenced the child; and they told his mother of the sign they had received: power in weakness, God in swaddling bands. For Mary, all this brought fresh light to the insights that were already hers; and so, as Luke adds significantly, "Mary kept in mind all these words, pondering them in her heart" (Luke 2:19).

There was yet a last incident that filled the heart of Mary with deep and lasting insight into the mission of her divine Son and the part that she herself was to play. When forty days had passed, she took him to the temple for his presentation. How proudly she entered the temple court, leaning on the strong arm of Joseph her husband and carrying in her arms the little child she loved. She felt in every fiber of her heart the full, rich meaning of it all. Here was the perfect fulfillment of the words uttered long before by the prophet Malachi:

> And suddenly there will come to the temple
> The Lord whom you seek (Mal 3:1).

She had taken only a few steps when one of those who were truly seeking him came forward to greet them. This was the aged Simeon, whose face gleamed with joy as he lifted the little child into his arms and greeted him as Savior of the world:

> My eyes have seen your salvation
> Which you have prepared in sight of all the peoples
>   (Luke 2:30-31).

Like Elizabeth before him, the old priest saw in Mary the very ark of God; for he saluted the child she bore as "the glory of God's people, Israel" (Luke 2:32).

But Simeon did not stop with words of praise. He had the guideline of Malachi's promise to follow, a promise that foretold not only the coming of the Lord into the temple of the world but also the work of purification which he must perform:

> Suddenly there will come to the temple
> The Lord whom you seek. . . .
> But who will endure the day of his coming?
> And who can stand when he appears?
> For he is like the refiner's fire. . . .
> He will sit refining and purifying [silver],
> And he will purify the sons of Levi (Mal 3:1-3).

It is always interesting to watch a silversmith at work. He puts a piece of metal into his pot, the crucible. Then he sits down; for his work will consume a long time. He applies the fire to the pot until the metal melts and the impurities rise to the surface. Quickly he skims this off; and then, once more, he applies the refining fire. Over and over again he repeats the process until his work is done and the silver is perfectly pure. In this same way, said Malachi, the Messiah-King would sit down as a "refiner and purifier" of silver.

His work of salvation would involve a purification, separating the silver from the dross, the good from the evil. Thus, Simeon saw clearly the destiny of the babe who had come into the temple of the world to save his people. "Behold," he said, "this child is destined for the fall and for the rise of many in Israel, and for a sign that shall be contradicted, and so the thoughts of many minds will be revealed" (Luke 2:34-35). Struggle would be the very law of his life, struggle between the light of God's glory and the darkness of the prince of the world. And, in the tension and strife, Mary would have her part. She would not remain on the sideline, untouched by the fray; rather, she would be drawn into the thick of it to share his suffering. For Simeon was careful to include Mary in the pain-filled destiny of the Savior, her son: "Your own soul," he said to her, "a sword shall pierce."

The words of the old priest fell like hot pellets of lead on the heart of Our Lady, burning it with sorrow and fear—not for herself but for her babe. At the same time, however, they brought strengthening comfort to her. For they revealed that she would always be joined to her child in his whole task as Savior, in its joys and in its sorrows. For her, the words of Simeon brought a reminder of the very words that God had spoken to the Tempter immediately after the sin of our first parents: "I will put enmity between you and the woman, and between your offspring and hers; he will strike at your head, while you strike at his heel" (Gen 3:15). Mary was the "woman," and her babe was her "offspring."

WHAT GOD HAS JOINED TOGETHER . . .

God united them as mother and child at the Annunciation, and they were never to be parted. For what God has joined together, nothing can ever put asunder (cf. Matt 19:6). When she went to visit Elizabeth, he was with her. On the first Christmas night, when the shepherds came to seek him, they saw him nestling in her bosom. The Magi, too, found the child with Mary his mother. When Herod sought to kill him, the angel directed Joseph to take the child and his mother into Egypt. And now Simeon tells her that it will always be so; if he must suffer, her own soul will be pierced. What God has joined together nothing will ever put asunder; they will always be together:

> he the glory of God and she the ark that bore him;
> he the Son and she the Mother;
> he the Savior and she his helpmate;
> he the Mediator and she the Mediatrix;
> he the King and she his Queen.

All this was contained in the glorious promises of the Old Testament. And so, all this found place in Mary's deep, rich understanding of the mysteries of his coming. To her, then, we owe the story of all the events; to her, too, we owe our own insight into what they mean. For our Gospel story comes ultimately from the lovely maid and mother who pondered all these things in her heart:

> She walks—the lady of my delight—
>   A shepherdess of sheep.
> Her flocks are thoughts. She keeps them white;
>   She guards them from the steep;
> She feeds them on the fragrant height
>   And folds them in for sleep.

CHAPTER 16

Mary and the Poor of Israel

As we have seen, there was a day at Nazareth—before she was known as "Queen" or "Mediatrix"—when Mary was simply a lovely young Jewess and nothing more. Faithful child of Abraham and Sarah, daughter of David, she belonged, mind and heart, to those who waited expectantly to welcome the Messiah. Steeped in this faith, her inner life followed a pattern, traced by the prophets, for the holy remnant of Israel which would emerge from the fire-tried centuries to pledge obedience to the promised king. Prophets had dreamed wondrous dreams of this little group, offering to the Messiah the faith of the people Israel, the desires of her seers, the holiness of her just ones. But perhaps it is the prophet Zephaniah who expresses best of all the spirit of the chosen remnant. His eyes alight with vision, he promises in the name of God:

> I will leave in your midst
> *a poor and needy people,*
> Who shall take refuge in the name of the Lord:
> the remnant of Israel.
> They shall do no wrong
> and speak no lies;
> Nor shall there be found in their mouths
> a deceitful tongue; . . . .
> On that day, it shall be said to Jerusalem:
> Fear not, O Zion, be not discouraged!
> The Lord, your God, is in your midst,
> a mighty savior;
> He will rejoice over you with gladness,
> and renew you in his love (Zeph 3:12-13, 16-17).

Mary of Nazareth belonged to this "poor and needy people," her soul steeped as no other in their spirit of humble, trusting dependence. To learn the riches of her inward life, the thoughts that filled her mind, and the secrets of her heart is to study what it meant to be one of Israel's *anawim*—God's "poor and needy."

GOD'S ROLE IN FORMING THE POOR

The concept of the *anawim* has its roots in an earth that was "waste and void," in the primeval darkness that covered the abyss when "the spirit of God was stirring above the waters" (Gen 1:1-2). At that moment, God worked on nothing to produce all that is; and, when finished, "God looked at everything he had made and found it very good" (Gen 1:31). God at work on nothing to produce all that is good: This is the record of every divine deed in Israel's history.

The very origin of this people as the children of Abraham and Sarah called for a miracle, the birth of Isaac from an aged father and mother. And these miraculous works of God continued ever after. It was always the same: God constantly at work to make Israel what he dreamed it should be. For some, it was merely a turn of chance that prepared the land of Egypt for Israel's long sojourn there. But chaste Joseph, with the insight of the pure of heart, recognized God's hand reaching mightily from end to end and sweetly ordering all things (cf. Wis 8:1): "God . . . sent me on ahead of you to ensure for you a remnant on earth and save your lives in an extraordinary deliverance. So it was not really you but God who had me come here" (Gen 45:7-8).

It was God, too, who brought the stay in Egypt to a close. The divine plans called for something better, so God took the initiative, wresting the poor sufferers from the grasp of Pharaoh and leading them out into the freedom of the desert.

Everything was from God—the people, the land, the lawgiver. So, too, Israel's first great prophet was a man of God's making. Samuel came as a gift from heaven to a barren mother who recognized the giver in the gift and made grateful return by consecrating to God forever the boy divinely bestowed. To many, the miracle of Samuel's birth seemed a unique wonder of God's goodness. But for Anna, his mother, it was only one of many similar incidents, all proving that God is always at work to save creation. She rises, then, from the thought of her child to contemplate the greatest wonder of the universal salvation always at hand:

> My heart exults in the Lord;
>   my horn is exalted in my God . . .

> because I have rejoiced in your salvation . . .
> The Lord makes poor and makes rich,
> > he humbles, he also exalts.
> He raises the needy from the dust;
> > from the ash heap he lifts up the poor,
> To seat them with nobles,
> > and make a glorious throne their heritage
> > (1 Sam 2:1, 7-8).

Whatever Israel was, whatever it had, all was God's work; God was ever in the midst of his people to produce good things from nothing and to renew after failure.

"The Lord Alone Their Leader"

The prophets saw this truth energizing the whole course of their nation's history. God had taken part in every incident from first to last:

> He found them in a wilderness,
> > a wasteland of howling desert.
> He shielded them and cared for them,
> > guarding them as the apple of his eye.
> As an eagle incites its nestlings forth
> > by hovering over its brood,
> So he spread his wings to receive them
> > and bore them up on his pinions.
> The Lord alone was their leader (Deut 32:10-12).

The prophet Ezekiel glimpsed the true picture with delicate sensitivity and painted it with the warm glow of consummate artistry. He saw a piteous babe—as discussed in the previous chapter—just born, cast upon the open field. God passed by, and looked upon the poor little thing with love, and lavished upon it a devoted care that brought the child to rich and lovely maturity. As the story continues, however, we see that the time came when faithless Israel sickened and died; its dry bones littered the white sand and bleached under a blistering sun. Once more, God intervened to save: Drawing together the scattered waste, he covered each skeleton with flesh and sinew, and breathed the gift of life: "The spirit came into them, and they lived, and they stood up upon their feet, an exceeding great army" (Ezek 37:10).

Humanly Poor to be Divinely Rich

Thus it always was: God's creative power hovered over an earth that was "waste and void" producing all that is fair and good. In return, God asked for one thing: Let Israel live in constant awareness of her dependence upon him. Time and again, therefore, God reminded the people of Israel of their need for him. Divine is the sovereign will that rules the present; divine is the wisdom that creates the future; divine is the power that makes all reality. Whatever Israel was or might become, it owed all to the simple fact that God's loving gaze had rested upon it.

But it is easy for humankind to forget their benefactor and to despise what they have received. It was a chronic ailment of God's people. They tended to ignore the strong hand that held them up; they seemed to resent their need for support.

The prophets struggled against this spirit of proud self-sufficiency. Sent by God to proclaim divine truth, they sought to dissolve the lie of Israel's self-reliance. Isaiah, greatest of them all, dedicated his whole ministry to the laborious task of shifting attention from humankind to God. The vision he saw in the temple as he gazed on the Lord "sitting upon a throne high and elevated" and heard the seraphim sing "Holy, holy, holy is the Lord of hosts" (Isa 6:1, 3) inaugurated this mission. A sense of divine transcendence marked his soul with living awareness of his own frail creaturehood. Day after day he thundered against everything human that reared in pride before God. Fearlessly, he sang his paeans of humility against "everyone that is proud and high-minded, and everyone that is arrogant" (Isa 2:12).

But in the temple, Isaiah also came to know in a new way the immanence of God. For he heard the angels sing, "All the earth is full of God's glory" (Isa 6:3); all that it contains is of divine making. What comfort in these words! The land of Zebulun and Naphtali might be shrouded in darkness and torn by anguish but God would bring light and joy (cf. Isa 8:22–9:1). Israel would be reduced to a remnant and scattered to a distant nation but, under God's lead, the remnant would return and, through divine power, would once more become a mighty nation (cf. Isa 10:20-21). A charred stump might be the last vestige of a once verdant forest but, from it, a divine shoot would grow (cf. Isa 11:1). The God of power and mercy could produce anything from nothing, so long as men and women were sincere enough to acknowledge their need of God and to "lean upon the Lord, the Holy One of Israel, in truth" (Isa 10:20). This assurance made Isaiah an incorrigible optimist. "By waiting and by calm you shall be saved. In quiet and in trust your strength lies" (Isa 30:15).

His teaching explains the regular reappearance of human goodness in Israel's history. The holy men and women who take part in the story all bowed low before God with that total surrender which enabled God to do great things for them. The later prophets call these blessed ones the *anawim*—"the poor and needy people"; and they refer to their spirit as *anawah*—"lowliness." These words, however, are only suggestive tokens rather than complete titles, for no single word could ever contain a spirit so rich. Nevertheless, at the same time, they are particularly apt terms, for they symbolize perfectly the Isaian formula for gaining God's favor.

THE ORIGIN OF THE POOR

Israel never attached special value to poverty, though it was always a reality in Israel. Poor people always existed in the land and the nation's early laws made prudent provision for their care. According to God's promises, the people had a right to comfort and security. Those who suffered want were considered unfortunate. Far from being something desirable, poverty was looked upon as a lack of the good things God had pledged.

The prophets, however, introduced a new note. The poverty of eighth-century Israel was due not merely to misfortune but also to criminal encroachments of the wealthy. In dealing with poverty, therefore, the prophets of the period—Amos and Hosea, Isaiah and Micah—confronted not only a social problem but also a moral abuse that continued through the following century up to the fall of Jerusalem. The prophets looked upon the poor as innocent victims of evil practice and cruel oppression; naturally, then, they spoke of them with new overtones of sympathy. In comparison with the fraudulent rich, the poor are in the right, and their cause is just. God is on their side and they can lay claim to his special protection. But this does not mean that poverty itself becomes automatic holiness in God's eyes. Jeremiah considered the poor people of his day as reprehensible before God as the rich (cf. Jer 5:4). Even more pointedly, the Wisdom literature always spoke of poverty as an evil to avoid and, often, as evil in its cause.

But the prophets' use of the vocabulary of poverty was never forgotten. They had employed it freely in a religious context; they had spoken of the poor with sympathy and had represented their misery as crying out to God for mercy. Thus, they prepared the way for the transformation of the vocabulary of poverty into a vocabulary of grace. The basis for this transfer is the Isaian principle that God works divine effects only when one recognizes human insufficiency. The occasion for transfer is any personal experience of human powerlessness. The miseries of life and the inability of most to cope with them, the vicissitudes of social struggle and the readiness of the strong to trample on the weak, the instability of the human will and the radical weakness of all things human—these trying and humbling experiences came frequently enough into the lives of God's friends to fill them with poignant awareness of their own poverty and constant need for divine help. They must depend wholly upon their Lord and look to God for everything or perish.

What was more natural, then, than that true Israelites speak to God with the very words that sounded on the lips of the poor? Often enough, these holy ones were poor in physical reality; always they were poor in spirit. And, although external poverty is not a necessary element in poverty of spirit, there is no question that the former often does much to strengthen the latter. Thus M.-J. Lagrange in *Évangile selon saint Luc* seems to make it even an integral part of true poverty of spirit, characterizing "the poor person" in these words: "The poor person . . . is the person of inferior condition, lacking goods of fortune and often mistreated and humiliated, yet who constantly looks to God for help."

Even the earliest heroes of Israel sought God's help as from among the poor. Wealthy Abraham assumed the posture and used the phrases of the mendicant when he pleaded with God for the saving of Sodom (cf. Gen 18:16-23). So, too, a later writer sums up Moses' whole character with a single word that expresses his poverty of spirit: "Moses himself was by far the meekest man *(anaw)* on the face of the earth" (Num 12:3). Holy Anna, pleading for a child, drew God's attention to her share in the misery of the poor: "O Lord of hosts, if you look down on the affliction *(ani)* of your servant . . ." (1 Sam 1:11). God's true friends felt themselves to be really poor before him. Dependence and loving surrender were the breath of their life.

This spirit pulses in every page of the prophet Jeremiah. He is the poor man par excellence, for no prophet equals him in piteous pleading for the help of God. By temperament, his whole being was exquisitely sensitized to pain. A warm-hearted, emotional man, he was keenly alive to love and could feel the opposition of others in every fiber of his soul. Yet God asked him to inveigh against all in Israel. What a fearful vocation for a sensitive man! Poor Jeremiah always felt the heartache of this lifetime struggle, and he cried out: "My sorrow is above sorrow; my heart mourns within me" (Jer 8:18). He needed God in the way a suffering poor man needs a friend to help him in his indigence and to defend him against unjust oppression. Therefore, the harassed prophet used the words of the poor to express his misery and to plead for God's pity.

The Poor in the Psalms

Once Jeremiah had written his personal journal, others also felt free to use his style in their intimate dealings with God. But, above all others, the authors of the Psalms were truly kindred spirits. Causse in *Les "Pauvres" d'Israël* has aptly named the Psalter a "Book of the Poor," not because, as he suggests, it was composed only by the party of the poor after the Exile, but because it is the outpouring of hearts that were steeped in lowly dependence and total surrender. These authors belonged to no particular social class; one at least, King David, must have been wealthy. But they were all conscious of the need for God. A humbling sense of human powerlessness, mingled with strong trust in God, filled their souls with readiness to serve, patience in waiting, and the clinging love of a child. All this is contained in the single word *anawim*—poverty of spirit; it is the theme that pervades the Psalter.

The psalmists were friends of God. More than anything they say, the very way they say it is proof of this. They are so sure of God's love that, at times, they seem Promethean in daring. Fearlessly they lay bare their whole soul because they are certain God will understand. Whatever misery drained them of strength, there was always one thought to sustain them: God was their friend; God would not abandon them. The author of Psalm 22 cried out: "My God, my God, why have you forsaken me, far from my prayer, from the words of my cry?! (v. 1). But, because he was certain of God's friendship, he continued to plead insistently: "Be not far from me, for I am in distress; be near, for I have no one to help me. . . . But you, O Lord, be not far from me" (vv. 11, 19). So, too, the author of Psalm 69 was "sunk in the abysmal swamp where there is no foothold" (v. 2); but he knew that he could always count on his divine friend: "Answer me, O Lord, for bounteous is your kindness; in your great mercy turn toward me. Hide not your face from your servant" (vv. 16-17).

These psalmists needed such confidence, for time and again they were stripped of all human support and felt the full powerlessness of creaturehood. Tasting anguish within and suffering oppression from without, cut off from friends and cruelly betrayed, they sipped the nauseating dregs of human weakness. No heartsick existentialist has reached a deeper nadir of distrust in all things created than the authors of Psalms 10, 22, 38, 88, and many others. God was their only Savior; God was seen to be always at work, striving mercifully and mightily to better the lives of his creatures. On this, the holy ones of Israel reposed their hope. No matter what their need, the psalmists could always count on God to intervene. How or when or where they did not know; but God was the wisdom and power and love, and so in God's own good time all would come well (cf. Pss 36:10; 69:33-37; 86:13; 109:20-31).

This attitude of soul was bound to influence the true Israelites in their dealings with others. The inward spirit of *anawah,* the habit of looking away from humankind to God, permeated even their exterior with the fragrance of peace. The tranquility of complete dependence upon God overflowed in a spirit of meekness and humility. Others might take advantage, or mistreat and even persecute him; human help might collapse and trusted friends turn traitor. Every second psalm describes something of what God's holy ones had to endure. Yet always there was the attitude of acceptance which marks the inveterately poor. Though the psalmists pleaded with God to intervene, they always maintained the silent and calm forbearance of the afflicted poor, certain their powerful protector will soon put in an appearance. To have acted otherwise would have been a lack of trust. Outer life flowed directly from the heart. Rooted distrust of self and unfailing confidence in God radiated the outward tranquility of meekness.

This was the spirit that God looked for in his people, a spirit that found analogy in the experiences of the poor. For the only attitude that rings true to our creaturehood compounds a sense of personal powerlessness with unfailing confidence in the power of God and total surrender to the guidance of divine will.

When the Isaian principle of dependence had transformed the vocabulary of poverty, the prophets following the Exile called this spirit *anawah*—poverty—and those who possessed it the *anawim*—the poor. Whereas Amos, in the eighth century, told his people: "Seek good and not evil that you may live" (Amos 5:4), Zephaniah, in the sixth century, uses the new vocabulary to make the recommendation more pointed: "Seek the Lord, all you meek *(anawim)* of the earth, who do God's will. Seek righteousness, seek humility *(anawah)*" (Zeph 2:3). The later prophet saw clearly that goodness becomes real through poverty of heart. So, too, the author of the last chapters of the prophecy of Isaiah teaches that this spirit alone could win favor from the Lord; for in his pages God's word bears the message: "This is the one whom I approve: the lowly and afflicted one who trembles at my word" (Isa 66:2).

The Poor of the Messianic Age

It was natural, then, for the late prophets to identify the blessed remnant of the future as a group of *anawim*. These holy men and women, so dear to God, were to stand on the threshold of the new age to greet the Messiah and to enter with him into the new kingdom. All that was best in Israel's heritage must be vital reality in their souls. Therefore, above all else, they must possess that spiritual poverty which alone rings true in humankind's dealings with God. Zephaniah was the first to state this explicitly; for it is in his prophecy that God promises: "I will leave in the midst of you a *poor and needy people;* and they shall hope in the name of the Lord" (Zeph 3:12). Later, in the last chapters of Isaiah, the Messiah pledges his mission of mercy to this group: "The Spirit of the Lord God is upon me, because the Lord has anointed me. He has sent me to preach to the meek *(anawim)*, to heal the contrite of heart, . . . to comfort all who mourn" (Isa 61:1-2). Indeed, the Messiah himself would be characterized by this beautiful spirit of the *anawim;* he too would be meek and humble of heart. For just before the light of prophecy dimmed in Israel, Zechariah beheld the future king and sketched this pen-portrait of him: "See, your king shall come to you; a just savior is he, poor *(ani)* and riding on an ass" (Zech 9:9).

All this came to pass.

When at last he appeared, the humble Christ, those who came forward to greet him were the truly poor in spirit—Joseph, Zachary and Elizabeth, Simeon and Anna, the shepherds and the Magi; these formed his court, the holy remnant promised by the prophets. But long before, the divine gaze had rested with special love on Mary, the young Jewess of Nazareth. No other was so truly poor in spirit, so keenly conscious of need for him, so perfectly surrendered to divine will. That is why he chose her to be his mother—the most humble of the *anawim*.

QUEEN OF THE POOR

When the angel brought her God's message and asked her to become the mother of his son, Mary accepted the divine will with total surrender: "Behold the handmaid of the Lord; be it done to me according to your word" (Luke 1:38). This humble acceptance opened her heart to receive the greatest of God's gifts, his own Son. Ever after, it was always the same: Her spirit of *anawah* was the secret of all his favors to her. In her *Magnificat,* we hear the voice of the *anawim* among mingled strains from the song of Miriam and the canticle of Anna and the prayer of Judith:

> My soul proclaims the greatness of the Lord,
>   and my spirit rejoices in God my Savior;
> For he has looked upon his handmaid's lowliness; . . .
> The Mighty One has done great things for me,
>   and holy is his name.
> He has shown might with his arm,
>   dispersed the arrogant of mind and heart.
> He has thrown down the rulers from their thrones,
>   but lifted up the lowly.
> The hungry he has filled with good things,
>   the rich he has sent away empty.
> He has helped Israel his servant,
>   remembering his mercy (Luke 1:46-49, 51-54).

All her life long Mary grew ever more dear to God by growing ceaselessly in the spirit of the *anawim*. May we not say of her what St. Paul has said of her Son: She learned *anawah* from the things that she suffered (cf. Heb 5:8). Everything that God permitted to happen in her life served only to deepen the dependence and to enrich the surrender contained in the first word she uttered: "Behold your handmaid. Be it done to me according to your word" (Luke 1:38). Always, too, this growth in inward life radiated a greater loveliness upon her whole external bearing. Within and without, Mary was ever the fairest of the *anawim*.

Time and again, she had to wait on God, certain of divine will and power to help, but quite in the dark as to when and where. She had to wait on God when she felt Joseph's wonderment about her pregnancy and sensed the problem that lay heavy upon his mind. She was certain that in God's good time all would come well; but, for the moment, it meant keen suffering and inviolable silence—and quiet surrender (cf. Matt 1:19-25).

Even more she had to endure the anguish that goes deepest into the heart because it touches someone who is dearer than life itself. Simeon's prophecy, "Behold, this child is destined for the fall and for the rise of many in Israel, and for a sign that shall be contradicted" (Luke 2:34), pierced her very soul. Again, the hour struck when loss snatched him out of her life. It was a very "poor" mother who sought him, sorrowing; for, that day, her soul agonized with the awareness that everything precious had slipped from her grasp. Of course, she knew that in due time all would be well; but, all the same, the days of search were shrouded in blackness. That is why her *fiat* in those dark hours filled her soul as never before with the surrender of the *anawim* (Luke 2:41-50).

If anything, all her Son's recorded words to her served the one great purpose of deepening this spirit within her. His every sentence steadied her gaze on the will of the Father. Thus, when she found him in the temple, he reminded her that the "Father's business" must always come first (Luke 2:49). When she asked him for the courtesy of turning water into wine for the embarrassed hosts at Cana, he called her attention to the fact that the hour which the Father had assigned had not yet come (John 2:4). Only then did he work the wonder. Later, people spoke to him of his mother and of the bond between him and her (cf. Luke 11:27-28; Matt 12:46-50). But, both times, he made clear that what counted most was the tie that united them in the spirit of the *anawim*—perfect fidelity to the will of the Father.

She needed this spirit in its fullness; for, in God's eternal plan, she was to come closer to him than any other through the most perfect of all surrenders: "Now there was standing by the cross of Jesus his mother. . . . When Jesus, therefore, saw his mother and the disciple standing by, whom he loved, he said to his mother, 'Woman, behold your son'" (John 19:25-26). Never before or after has God asked any creature for such complete detachment from everything human and for such total surrender to divine will. In place of Jesus she was asked to accept John; for him who is all, the human disciple. And Mary, the Queen of the *anawim*, uttered again the perfect word he was waiting for: "Behold the handmaid of the Lord; be it done to me according to your word."

Thus it always was. At every moment, she met him with the full-hearted surrender which is the very essence of the spirit of *anawah*. This is what he asks of all his followers—the spirit that formed the holiness of the Old Testament saints, that inspired the beautiful prayers of the Psalter, and figured so largely in the prophets' dreams for the future. Therefore, on the day when he first drew a blueprint of the ideal Christian character, he sketched with deft stroke the features of the *anawim:*

> Blessed are the poor in spirit. . . .
> Blessed are they who mourn. . . .
> Blessed are the meek. . . .
> Blessed are they who hunger and thirst for justice. . . .
> Blessed are the merciful. . . .
> Blessed are the pure of heart. . . .
> Blessed are the peacemakers. . . .
> Blessed are they who suffer persecution for justice' sake. . .
>   (Matt 5:3-10).

Perhaps, as he spoke these words, he was recalling verses from the Psalms or from the prophets. Perhaps. . . .

But there was a way much more simple. All he had to do was to think of his mother in the poor house at Nazareth and to put into words the beautiful spirit he saw in her—the lowliest and the loveliest of the *anawim.*

Chapter 17

Mary, Prototype of the Church

Although the Apostle Paul spoke only once of the woman who gave birth to Christ (Gal 4:4), he spoke numerous times of that other woman—the Church—who gives birth to Christ in us all. It was on the road to Damascus that Saul, the persecutor, first confronted the blinding splendor of Christ in the Church. The scene is reminiscent of Moses' first contact with God on Sinai: lightning flashed and thunder roared, and a voice whispered eternal truth in these words, "Saul, Saul, why are you persecuting me?" (Acts 9:4).

Years passed before Paul the Apostle understood fully all that these words contained—years of solitude in Arabia, years of suffering and preaching, years of conflict with error. But it was precisely these years of enriching experiences which won Paul a clear insight into the mystery of Christ. He saw "the church in splendor, without spot or wrinkle or any such thing" (Eph 5:27). Thereafter he could boast of total understanding: "When you read this you can understand my insight into the mystery of Christ" (Eph 3:4). For he had come to know the Church with the full flush of personal discovery, so that in his letter to the Ephesians he speaks as though his knowledge of the Church is a new contribution to the deposit of faith.

In a way it was, for his glowing words have enlightened all peoples on "the mystery hidden from ages past in God" (Eph 3:9)—the mystery of Christ living in us, praying and working in us, sharing with us his riches. The fact is, however, that God had previously intimated this wondrous plan. Every prophet of the Old Law had spoken of a searing purification to come and of a small part, "the remnant," which would emerge. These would be "the poor ones" of the new Israel, its *anawim* (cf. Zeph 3:12-17; Zech 13:8-19). Deutero-Isaiah hails them as "the long-lived seed" of the Suffering Servant, children born of God's agency to share divine triumph (Isa 53:1-2). Ezekiel described them as little lambs tended lovingly by the Good Shepherd who claims them as his own (Ezek 34:10-16). All the words of the later prophets pulse with hope in the bright future of this chosen group who will cluster round their Redeemer to receive the riches of redemption. The later psalms throb with the peace and triumph thrilling in their souls. Truly, all the saints and sages of the postexilic period lived in constant vigil, awaiting expectantly the blessed day when at long last the Messiah and his "poor ones" would reap the harvest of victory.

THE GREATEST OF THE *ANAWIM*

Christ fulfilled this Old Testament hope. The first act of his redemptive work was to single out the greatest of the *anawim* and to dower her in the first moment of her conception with all his riches. No wonder this poor maid of Israel cried out, "My soul proclaims the greatness of the Lord, . . . for he has looked upon his handmaid's lowliness" (Luke 1:46, 48). She was the first to taste the fruit of Christ's victory. [Editor's note: See Chapter 16, "Mary and the Poor of Israel."]

But not the only one. The plan of the Almighty One promised that all "the poor and needy" who formed God's Church might share the glory of divine triumph. Christ proclaimed this in the first sermon of his public life, for in the beatitudes he promised the redeemed of all time a full share in God's riches. Summing up the virtues of the Old Testament *anawim* and gazing on his mother as their perfect type and pattern, he cried out, "Blessed are the poor in spirit, for theirs is the kingdom of heaven. Blessed are the meek . . . blessed are the clean of heart . . . blessed," indeed, are all "the poor and needy" of the new Israel (Matt 5:3ff.). Jesus fulfilled this pledge on the first Pentecost when all his "poor and needy" disciples gathered in the upper room to receive the outpouring of the Holy Spirit. And Mary was there, in the midst of the charter members of the Church born on Good Friday, first and greatest of all, yet truly one of them.

This wonder of the *anawim* of the new Israel sharing fully in the riches of Christ is the mystery of the Church. St. Paul pondered it, preached it, lived it, until at last, in his twin letters to the Ephesians and Colossians, he gave it final and mature expression. From all eternity, he tells us, God planned to enclose all people in the heritage of the Divine Word and thus to bestow on them the graces of divine life. In Christ and through him, every member of the Church bears a family resemblance to him in the eyes of the Eternal Father; for God "predestined us for adoption . . . through Jesus Christ" (Eph 1:5). Paul is enraptured by the grandeur of the divine plan. In his epistle to the Ephesians, he pours out his thought in floods of awesome praise that overflow the limits of sentence structure. He is forced to coin words since no superlative is strong enough to bear the weight of "the inscrutable riches of Christ" (Eph 3:8). Indeed, the unique style of this epistle, its grandiose periods and its crescendos of soaring enthusiasm, can be explained only by the exaltation that thrilled Paul's spirit as he contemplated the mystery of Christ's life in the Church.

This single theme of God's wondrous plan dominates all the Marian thoughts of the early fathers. During the 1960s, scholars like Reindl, Arnold, Rahner, and Semmelroth combed the patristic literature of the first four centuries to harvest the first-fruits of Marian theology. Out of these investigations came an insight exceedingly rich in itself, though somewhat unfamiliar to the devotional thought of that decade. These scholars agreed that the fathers of the first four centuries did not highlight the aspects of Marian theology that shine gloriously under the searchlight of the "modern" investigation that began with Venerable Bede. Instead of concentrating on the uniqueness of Mary, these early fathers present her simply as a member of the Church.

THE FIRST MEMBER OF THE CHURCH

The key to their thought is the Pauline mystery of Christ, i.e., the eternal plan of God that his Son incarnate should be the source of all that is good. In this perspective, Mary is the commencement of Christ's redemptive work in the world, the first and greatest member of the Church. Nowhere in the early fathers, not even in St. Irenaeus, is she represented as the causal source of the Church's life. They associate her with Christ as the new Eve, but never do they speak of her as "mother of the living." Instead, she is presented simply as the typical embodiment of what the rest of the Church should be. The teaching of Origen is characteristic. Like St. Paul, he describes the great wonder of Christianity as a rich mystical union between Christ, the Divine Word, and the Church. This union is accomplished in successive moments through the advent of the *Logos* into the world and into the lives of consecutive generations. The union of Christ with Mary, therefore, even though central and decisive, is still only one moment in the univocal process of union that dominates the whole life of the Church.

Thus, it is the penetration of Christ's life into his Mystical Body that provides the dominant theme for the early fathers. For them, God's eternal plan is the paramount consideration; they see all things as energized by the mystery of Christ. The Church is the final term of this mystery and its perfect fulfillment, while Mary is simply its first and greatest member. Certainly these Fathers recognized a continuity between Mary and the rest of the Church. Thus, especially in the Eastern fathers at the end of the fourth century, there is a marked fluidity, almost a "communication of idioms" of equivalence, between Mary and the Church. However, in the Christocentric thought of the fathers, the principle and cause of this continuity is not the spiritual energy of Mary influencing the Church, but the spiritual energy of Christ influencing both. For the writers of the first four centuries, Mary was always "the morning rising" *(quasi aurora valde rutulans)*. For though dawn is joined to day, it does not cause the day. Rather it is the sun which illumines both. And so Mary was regarded simply as the first great work of the Sun of Justice, the perfect type of what he would do in a lesser way in all the *anawim* of the new Israel.

The mystery of Christ, therefore, is the key to early patristic teaching on the relation between Mary and the Church; it is also the clue to liturgical texts which breathe its spirit. For time and again the liturgy reflects this early attitude toward Mary. Instead of isolating her as a cause of the Church's riches, it often treats her simply as one of the Church's members. Thus, in the Confiteor and in the Canon of the Mass, her name is linked to those of Peter and Paul and the other saints as first among them in God's good favor, yet truly one of them. There is no indication of their dependence upon her; all are joined together as sharing Christ's power of intercession before the throne of the Father. Again, the liturgy often uses words which literally refer to someone other than Mary. Thus the previous Mass of the Assumption chose for its gospel the story of the contemplative love of Mary of Bethany (Luke 10:38-42). To some this probably seemed incongruous, but not to those who understood the mystery of Christ. Both Mary the Mother of God and Mary of Bethany are members of the Church, who owe all that they have and are to the same Christ. What is said, therefore, of Mary of Bethany can be said with greater reason of Mary of Nazareth. Her rich share in the treasures of Christ is but the anticipation and type of all the graces of the whole Church.

To contemplate Mary in the light of the mystery of Christ does not obscure her pre-eminence. Though truly a member of the Church, Mary possesses in herself more grace than all others joined together.

She is the masterwork of Christ, the full realization of all his plans for the Church. Thus, the Church itself is already contained in the mystery of Mary, as its first actualization, its prototype and perfect exemplar. She contains eminently all that the Church should be, and so the Church must look to her and imitate her: *Sicut Maria, ita et Ecclesia* (what Mary is, the Church must be).

THE MATERNITY OF MARY

But even more than in her grace, Mary is the type of the Church in her maternity. This, too, flows from the mystery of Christ. The whole plan of God began its fulfillment in the redemptive incarnation of the Divine Word in Mary; it achieves consummation in the new birth of this same Divine Word in the heart of every Christian. For it is only by uniting itself to humankind that the Word accomplishes its mission. It was Mary's privilege to give Christ the physical life whereby he became human. As St. Augustine has expressed it, her womb was the bridal chamber in which the Divine Word and humanity celebrated their nuptials. Through a maternity quite as real, the Church, "mother of all the living," must give Christ a mystical birth in the soul of every person, that all can become Christian, united to Christ and sharing his riches. To each one she must repeat the words of St. Paul: "My children . . . I am again in labor, until Christ be formed in you!" (Gal 4:19).

Thus, the mystery of Mary's maternity is perpetuated and lives again in the maternity of the Church, mother of Christ in each of his members. This is the most striking equivalence between Mary and the Church. They are both mothers of Christ: she pre-eminently as mother of the physical Christ, and the Church secondarily as mother of the mystical Christ. Hence, between Mary and the Church there exists the same relation of identity as between the natural and the mystical body of Christ. That is why St. Clement of Alexandria, contemplating Mary, cries out, "And one alone, too, is the Virgin Mother. I like to call her the Church." And St. Leo, "It is by the same Holy Spirit that Christ is born of the all pure Virgin and that the Christian is born of the womb of the Holy Church." How often, too, this theme recurs in the liturgy. Every thought of Mary's motherhood, in the Masses of Advent and Christmastide, in the Marian anthems, prompts the earnest plea for a new birth of Christ in our own soul through the motherly action of the Church.

For what Mary has done as mother, the Church herself must do—and in the same way. This is another feature of resemblance between the two mothers: both are virgins. They produce the same Christ, one in his physical nature, the other in his members, not through human device or carnal means, but through faith. The Divine Word, received by the faith of Mary and of the Church, is the only source of this maternity. Therefore, when a woman of the crowd praised Mary's physical maternity, our Lord hastened to emphasize Mary's true cooperation through faith (Luke 11:28). How St. Augustine loved to return to this thought: *Beata Maria, Quem credendo peperit, credendo concepit, prius mente quam ventre concipiens* (Blessed Mary begot in faith him whom she conceived in faith, first conceiving in the spirit before she conceived in the womb).

It is this virginal maternity of Mary, a virginity rendered fruitful by her faith, that the Church finds the perfect type and true model of the maternity which she must exercise day after day. Her solicitude in the liturgy for the purity of faith; her emphasis on the fruitfulness of those consecrated laborers who, though virgins, know a long-lived posterity through their work and prayer for the spread of the faith—all this gives eloquent expression to the Church's awareness that she must conform to Mary as type, model, and pattern, if she would share in the fruitfulness of Mary's maternity.

It was left to later ages, however, to illumine the essential aspect of Mary's relation to the Church in the great mystery of Christ. In the 1951 Bulletin of the French Society of Marian Studies, Père Barré, surveying Marian texts from the period of Venerable Bede to Albert the Great, emphasized the first appearance of our modern insight into our Lady's role. Whereas the early fathers saw both Mary and the Church as successive moments in the unfolding of the mystery of Christ, the later fathers sought deeper for the secret of Mary's pre-eminence. Today we bask in the light of their teaching. So great is Mary's share in the riches of Christ that she exerts a real causal influence on the rest of the Church. The ecclesiastical writers of the sixth to the twelfth centuries speak of her real cooperation with Christ in his divine work of redeeming the Church; they see her, as mistress of the apostles, mothering the infant Church; they celebrate her as mother and guardian of the whole Church.

At this period, then, the concept of Mary as the prototype of the Church gained a new richness. She was seen to be the model of the Church, not merely because she anticipated and surpassed the Church in her share of Christ's treasures, but even more because her very fullness is the means Christ uses to sanctify the Church. Hence, she is often spoken of as the *Caput Ecclesiae,* the head of the Church, subordinate to Christ who is the only true Head, yet truly sharing his authority over the other members of the Church. She is regarded also as the *Collum Ecclesiae,* the neck of the Church, since the grace of Christ the Head must pass through her if it is to reach his members. She is not merely a sister to the children of Christ in the Church; even more, she is their mother. The grace-filling influence of her voice on the soul of John the Baptist, at the time of the Visitation, becomes the symbol of what she is always doing in the Church. Indeed, the very action of the Church in mothering souls not merely imitates Mary's divine maternity, but depends on the support of her motherly influence. Only through Mary does the Church become the Mother of Christ in souls. The whole pattern of the Church's life, all its goodness, its guidance, its defense, all that it has and all that it is—all depends upon her mediation.

It is this spiritual maternity that renders Mary the prototype par excellence of the Church. She is the perfect pattern of the body of Christ because, as Pius XII said, she is "the most holy Mother of all his members." This theme enriches the greatest part of our liturgy. The Collects for all Mary's feasts, the very constituency of these feasts, the sequence *Stabat Mater,* and the Marian anthems that conclude the Divine Office—all these reflect the Church's awareness that Mary is truly the type of all her holiness and of all her actions, not merely as the first and greatest member of the Church, not merely as the first among those who share equally in the mystery of Christ, but, above all else, as the mother who contains in herself eminently the very graces which the Church receives only through her mediation.

CONCLUSION

Such is the bond between Mary and the Church. Both are "the poor and needy" of the new Israel who owe all to their share in the mystery of Christ. Both have the same task of bringing Christ into the world. Yet the Church must always look up to Mary as utterly pre-eminent; it must model itself upon her as its prototype; it must honor her as a child honors its mother. For God could have spoken to the Church the words of Dante in the *Paradiso:* "Look now upon the face most like to Christ! For only its radiance can so fortify Thy gaze as fitteth for beholding Christ." And so, in obedience to God, the Church of every age must cry out to Mary with the fullness of complete dependence: Hail, Holy Queen, our life, our sweetness, our hope!

CHAPTER 18

Mary in Church Life Today

Jerome Crowe, C.P.

Friends and colleagues of Fr. Barnabas Mary Ahern, as well as audiences who have listened to his lectures, were aware of his personal devotion to Mary the mother of Jesus expressed in the name he bore as a Passionist religious. By a deliberate decision, some years after his first profession, he requested the middle name, Mary. It comes as something of a surprise, then, to note the limited extent of his written publications on Mary. Almost all are short pieces. They deal with the infancy narrative of Luke, the *anawim* or poor of Israel, the place of Mary in the Church and in the liturgy. Mary is presented in her association with the work of her son, as humblest of the *anawim*, perfect daughter of Zion, incorporating in herself the perfect Israel. A longer, more academic article is a systematic treatment of the Old Testament institution of queen mother which illustrates the position of Mary, queen mother of Jesus, the Messiah king.

MOTHER OF THE CHURCH

The earliest of these articles is the one which most clearly points ahead. An address to the Liturgical Conference of 1954 concerns Mary, the prototype of the Church, anticipating a direction to be taken a decade later by Vatican II. It recalled that the fathers of the first four centuries concentrated not on the uniqueness of Mary but on Mary as member of the Church, the one in whom the Church finds its first actualization and perfect exemplar. Later centuries were to talk of a causal influence exercised by Mary on the rest of the Church so that, in the words of Barnabas Mary Ahern, she is "the Mother who contains in herself eminently the very graces which the church receives only through her mediation."

It is significant that all this material dates from the decade that led up to the council. None of it is the fruit of original research or creative scholarship. They are works of popularization that show the initial impact of Pius XII's encyclical on Scripture studies. They communicate the best recent scholarship, admittedly Catholic, continental, almost all French, and certainly all male. The "new approach" was paying unexpected dividends, enriching the picture of Mary by painting in its biblical background and alerting the reader to the evocative quality of its images and language. Its systematic conclusions simply spelled out in scholarly fashion what the liturgy has already communicated in its own symbolic style to the faith of ordinary folk.

The historical conclusions of these writings were something less than revolutionary. Luke's infancy narrative provides direct access to the events. We owe not only the story but the dialogue itself to Mary who is in a very real way the memory of the Church, a memory charged by her faith-filled pondering of the events. Thanks to Luke we can reconstruct a clear portrait of the "Mary of history," the riches of her inward life as well as the external events as she interpreted them. Even in the decades before Luke it can be shown that the Church was clearly giving to Mary a veneration next in importance to that of her divine son.

DEVOTION-FRIENDLY SCHOLARSHIP

It would be well to recall something of the atmosphere of that decade. As Catholic scholars cautiously explored in the 1950s the freedom of research offered by Pius XII, their study of the historical value of the words and deeds of Jesus triggered very delicate alarm systems in many parts of the world. By 1958, a first-class row had broken out in Rome about the orthodoxy of their methods and their impact on the faith of "ordinary" Catholics. Two lecturers of the Pontifical Biblical Institute, one of them dean of the faculty and director of Barnabas Ahern's doctoral dissertation, were suspended from their posts. They were the first major casualties of this inner-Catholic feuding. Bishops arriving in Rome for the beginning of the council in 1962 were presented, on the steps of St. Peter's, with two competing pamphlets: one condemning the Biblical Institute with all its works, pomp, and exegetical methods; the other fighting to preserve its threatened existence. Only in the course of the council was the air cleared when the Pontifical Biblical Commission issued in 1963 its *Instruction on the Historical Truth of the Gospels*, significant sections of which were then integrated into Chapters 3 and 5 of the Constitution on Divine Revelation.

In this kind of turbulence, the "devotion-friendly" scholarship which Barnabas Ahern conveyed offered a remarkable assurance to audiences of all kinds, lay people and religious, priests, bishops, and cardinals. This was particularly true of his public lectures, where the manifest asceticism of the speaker, his Deuteronomist warmth, and mixture of exposition and exhortation guaranteed to Scripture-hungry audiences that critical scholarship was entirely compatible with traditional Catholic devotion and that its methods, far from destroying or distorting the image of Mary, served only to enhance it. If this was not the pioneer thinking of Congar or Rahner or Lagrange, nor even the original work of Cerfaux or Laurentin, it was stamped with a peculiarly charismatic quality and it responded to another set of needs. It respected the critical, questioning mind, but it touched heart and affectivity. It recognized and confirmed the Catholic instinct that had expressed itself over the centuries in the traditional terms and forms of devotion to Mary.

It is well known that Barnabas Ahern served as scriptural consultant and speech writer to a number of American bishops at the council, but it is much more difficult to do justice to the influence of that "teaching with authority." In one matter, however, and that of central importance to the council's treatment of Mary, he seems to have played a significant part. On the evening of October 28, 1963, the American bishops at the council gathered for their regular weekly meeting. They were addressed by a panel of experts chaired by Barnabas Ahern who dealt with the relation of Our Lady to the Church from the standpoint of scriptural, patristic, and contemporary theology.

After the meeting, many of the bishops said that they had been influenced by the presentations and the speakers and would vote to include the treatment of Mary in the Constitution on the Church rather than devote a separate document to it. On the following day, the council voted 1,114 to 1,074 for its inclusion in the Constitution on the Church. The shape of official teaching about Mary and the context in which the devotion of the faithful to Mary was to be placed was thus determined by an effective majority of twenty votes. It can be argued that his share in creating this majority is the major contribution Barnabas Ahern has made to the ongoing life of the Church.

NOT IMMUNE TO SURPRISE OR ALARM

His last published reflections on Mary appeared in an interview three years after the council in 1968. His words stay very close to the terms of the council itself. Mary must be considered in the life of the Church, as the member who shared eminently in the redemptive work of Christ, who herself embodied and modeled it as the mother who helps us to achieve the Christian ideal by her intercession. We get a glimpse of his inner self in the ease with which he moves with the mentality of the great nineteenth-century saints for whom the love of Mary is part and parcel of Christian living. He returns to his favorite scriptural images and claims that the early Church was gripped by Mary as archetype of both daughter of Zion and queen mother.

It is not altogether too fanciful to imagine him as a kind of John the Baptist figure. Himself representative of the best of a passing era in the devotion to Mary of the Latin Church prior to the council, he shared in its renewal by recalling it to its scriptural sources. He pointed ahead to the direction the council was to take by his appreciation of the ecclesial significance of Mary. Nor was he to be immune to surprise or even alarm when overtaken by the unexpected realities of the era he helped to usher in. The continued study of the biblical sources in the changing situations of the Church fast approaching its third millennium would reveal new images of Mary and submit traditional pictures to further critical scrutiny.

LATER SCHOLARLY DEVELOPMENTS

A decade later a ten-person ecumenical task force set about applying current critical techniques of source criticism, form criticism, redaction criticism, and historical criticism to each of the New Testament passages concerning Mary. Paul's solitary phrase, "born of a woman," refers to Mary simply to establish the true humanity of Jesus. The two appearances of Mary in Mark's Gospel present a negative picture; Mary is bracketed with "his own" who fail to understand Jesus, a group apart from the disciples who are his true family. Matthew softens Mark's picture by removing the contrast between the two families, fleshy and true, and by depicting Mary as the virgin mother who fulfills Isaiah's prophecy.

It is in Luke that the image of Mary comes to full flower. She is the first to hear the Word of God and keep it, the model disciple. These scholars of the ecumenical task force remain unconvinced by the evidence that Luke wishes to portray Mary as daughter of Zion or Ark of the Covenant, though they do see her as spokesperson and representative of the *anawim*. The Fourth Gospel's picture is completely distinctive. At Cana, Mary's faith and understanding remains imperfect and she is not ranked among the disciples of Jesus. It is on Calvary that she becomes mother of the disciple par excellence, a model of belief and discipleship. By his gift of the beloved disciple to Mary as her son and of Mary to him as mother, Jesus brings into being a new community of believing disciples, Jesus' family of faith.

This critical approach rejects the view, presented earlier by Barnabas Ahern, that Luke's narrative is derived from information supplied by Mary. They judge that Luke has built his picture of the Mary of the infancy stories from the Mary of Jesus' public life, where she appears clearly as one who hears the Word of God, not as one who has a clear understanding but as one who seeks to penetrate the meaning of the events in the life of her son in the light of God's Word. Reliable historical information, however, is to be found in the picture, preserved in the Acts of the Apostles, of Mary as member of the first Christian community.

The results of this scholarship for a reconstruction of "the Mary of history" are meager. If the stories of the infancy of Jesus do not stem from Mary, and if she was not present on Calvary (for it is only in John's Gospel that she appears there and John in his Calvary scene may well be dramatizing a theological theme rather than recording historical information), then a "critically assured minimum" would recognize only that Mary did not follow Jesus about as a disciple during his ministry, as other women did, nor understand in any great measure what was happening, but that she was a member of the early community.

On the other hand, these studies make it obvious that the different New Testament writers have presented Mary as a symbolic figure, possibly from the time of Mark but certainly in Matthew, Luke, and John. They have shown that it is possible to pursue the picture of Mary into second-century Christian literature and discern a line of development from earlier to later images. Within four decades of the resurrection, she had become the symbol of the disciple par excellence and virgin. This process, initiated in the Gospels, justifies the continuing symbolization of Mary in the imagination, affectivity, and worship of Christians over the centuries.

Symbols of Self-understanding

This insight has been deepened in new and fruitful ways as contemporary theologians have drawn on the work of philosophers, sociologists, and anthropologists in the area of symbol. They have shown that what a community is attempting to express in its symbols is its understanding of its own self. Though the mystery of its identity eludes capture in conceptual definition, a community finds in an image or person the embodiment of something it recognizes as properly its own. Perhaps the choice of a particular object or person as symbol of the community is the result of an original flash of intuitive genius on the part of one of its members. But still the symbol captures the imagination and compels acceptance because of the way it expresses the characteristics, the ideals, the unique reality of that group. It then evokes from others the same responses as it embodies and stimulates the community to an ongoing, deeper understanding of its being and mission.

HUMBLE DAUGHTER OF THE PEOPLE

The Gospels make it clear that this process was in action in the early Church. Roman Catholics owe far more to Luke than they realize, for it is from the stylized tableaux of his two volumes that our consciousness of our identity as Church is largely derived. It was his intuitive genius that chose Mary as his prime symbol of the believing community. She was surely a long time dead when he wrote, and it can be doubted if he had any more biographical information than the community memory of her as a widow in her fifties or sixties when he proposed her as first and prototypical hearer of the Word of God. She had never been a public figure. She had not followed Jesus in his public ministry; she may well have been bewildered by what was happening. She was not a disciple like Peter or Andrew or the other men or Joanna or Susanna or the other women. She did not follow him to Calvary like Salome or the other two Marys. She had not been with them at the tomb or heralded the resurrection like Mary Magdalene. She was not an apostle like Peter or Paul and exercised no ministry like that of

Prisca or Lydia or Phoebe. If Luke chose this humble daughter of her people as its symbol, it was not because of any function that she fulfilled in the life of Jesus or the early Church but because, in her faith and response to the mysterious action of God in her world, she is what the Church is called to be. So that even the humblest find in her the living image of the faith that lies far deeper than office or ministry or position.

Assertions of the magisterium find their place inside the process started in the Gospels. Modern theologians have analyzed the symbolic nature of declarations of the magisterium concerning Mary. They see the Marian dogmas of the divine motherhood and perpetual virginity of Mary as ultimately statements about the true humanity and divinity of Christ and the efficacy of God's grace. Other Marian dogmas are symbolic statements about the Church, about what it is to be a community of believing disciples, called to respond to the Word of God in the obscurity of faith. The dogmas of the Immaculate Conception and the Assumption not only speak of the special status of Mary, they are also affirmations about the nature of human salvation. They are declarations that God's grace surrounds us all in our entry into this world and in our leaving it.

LIBERATION OF THE OPPRESSED

The rise of liberation theology has brought with it a new approach to the biblical sources and a corresponding transformation in the image of Mary. For the Latin American theologians, the texts are to read not from the detached, objective, critical viewpoint of the scholars from whom they learned, but from the position of economic, social, and political oppression of the poverty-stricken members of the basic Christian communities. Aware of the biases and presumptions of previous interpreters and of exegetical methods that bore the imprint of their first world, their European origins, these theologians developed approaches that were frankly committed, that arose out of their faith commitment to the transformation of society.

The Gospels are concerned with this task. They cannot be confined to any kind of private, individual, interior spirituality. The *Magnificat*, then, comes into its own. It stands out as a central statement concerning God's position on the side of the poor and oppressed, a program of human liberation, a revolutionary manifesto. Its critical revolutionary content is concerned not with the interior, spiritual recesses of the *anawim* but with the economic, social, and political realities of Latin America. Mary's prayer is not for a change of heart but for a change of social structures; not for perfect justice in an eschatological future but for social justice in this world.

From the vantage point of the poor, Mary stands out as a woman of the people. Like them, she observes the religious customs of her time. She is a model of faith and availability, of sensitivity to the plight of the poor and debased. But even more—she is a prophetic voice denouncing injustice, proclaiming the coming liberation of the oppressed, inciting those who hear the ethical indignation she expresses.

MARY IN A GALLERY OF WOMEN DISCIPLES

Feminist theology was born of women's consciousness of another kind of oppression. It unveiled another set of biases and presuppositions, and it produced a new set of critical techniques which were applied to the image of Mary. The traditional image of Mary seemed embedded in the concrete of the patriarchal world from which it came, in the assumptions and biases of its sources in biblical and patristic texts and those of the magisterium, all of which served to reinforce the oppression of a patriarchal culture. How useful could that symbol be in enabling women to come into their own as fully human persons? Is it not rather an ideological weapon which maintains the subjugation of women in the Church?

The traditional symbol was criticized for its ideal of the feminine which is thoroughly patriarchal. Mary becomes a convenient model of passive humility which justifies male domination. She is the subordinate female partner of Jesus in an association that legitimates rather than liberates traditional sex roles. Her image as virgin and mother validates only two roles for women in the Church, those of religious and mother. This image is the creation of a celibate male hierarchy, their kind of "pedestal politics" which elevates that one woman beyond the range of ordinary human existence while it denies their own dignity and equality to other women in the Church.

For some feminist theologians the symbol of Mary was as dead as the patriarchal culture which begot it. Other Christian feminists have taken up the task of retrieving usable elements of the tradition to help them craft an alternative future in a Church of equal disciples. In their task of creating a new consciousness and in their search for models of liberating human relationships, they have attempted to uncover the voices of other biblical women, silenced, ignored, or forgotten in the tradition, such as the women disciples of Jesus. Mary no longer appears as solitary symbol but as one portrait surrounded by a gallery of other women disciples. The image of daughter of Zion has been explored once again to underline her oneness with all humanity. Recent feminist literary analysis of the birth narratives shows that, for all the androcentricity of their origins and viewpoint, they can be seen as undermining the idealogy of patriarchal control.

Feminist study of Marian theology and devotion suggests that Mary has functioned in the imagination and affectivity of many as "the female face of God." Marian devotions have witnessed so many approaches to God in female language and symbols and have provided powerful alternatives to the image of the feminine in the patriarchal tradition. The separation of symbol from cultural matrix is seen in the presentation of Mary as representative of a new liberated humanity for both men and women, the one who participates with God in the creation of an alternative future for humankind.

IN CONCLUSION

The process initiated by the evangelists in their successive portraits of Mary is one of the great examples of the "growth of insight" into the mysteries of God's action spoken of by the council. Far from being the monopoly of theologians or exegetes, this growth is ascribed to "the contemplation of believers" who, like Mary herself, "ponder these things in their hearts," and to "the intimate sense of spiritual realities they experience." The symbol certainly stimulates the intellectual analysis of scholars, yet it also stirs imagination and affectivity. It strikes chords in the subconscious to evoke responses that are expressed in a bewildering variety of cultural forms. Popular devotion to Mary follows its own spirit-guided instinct which these brief pages cannot even begin to discuss. Suffice it to have suggested something of the contributions of Barnabas Mary Ahern to that process both as earnest scholar and as devout believer.

Part VI

The Cross and Suffering

I have been crucified with Christ; yet I live, no longer I, but Christ lives in me; insofar as I now live in the flesh, I live by faith in the Son of God who has loved me and given himself up for me (Gal 2:19-20).

CHAPTER 19

St. Paul and the Apostolate

Several times in 1951 and 1952 a short, stocky, Belgian woman came to the United States to visit the Chicago training center of the community she had founded. Her name was Yvonne Poncelet; her community was the Lay Auxiliaries of the Missions. She was a woman of vibrant joy and an apostle to her finger tips. For her, to be a Christian meant a life of dynamic apostleship for the Church.

She had been quite young when she first heard Father Lebbe preach in the cathedral of Brussels on the need for lay apostles in the mission field. She never saw him again but always kept fresh the memory of his words through constant reading of the epistles of St. Paul. Her own soul matured. At long last, after the passing of ten years, she drafted the first rule of her institute, a rule which breathes the spirit of the great Apostle. In the years which followed, she sent her teams of dedicated Catholic lay women into every mission field, inspiring them with the conviction that their work for the Church was work for Christ. She had learned this truth of the apostolate from St. Paul just as all others will learn it if only they read and reread his writings.

THE UNITY OF PAUL'S SPIRIT

Paul's life work was to preach Christ. There was no dichotomy in his spirit, no rift between an insulated interior life for himself and a detached work of external apostolate for others. Both aspects of his vocation were bound together in unity; apostleship was simply the overflow of inward life.

His real mission began with a soul-stirring event on the way to Damascus. Before that time Paul had been a Hebrew of the Hebrews. How proud he was of his origin in God's chosen people, Israel. Pride pulses in his words every time he speaks of his past. His challenge in Philippians rings a resounding boast:

> Circumcised on the eighth day, of the race of Israel, of the tribe of Benjamin, a Hebrew of the Hebrews; as regards the Law, a Pharisee . . . as regards the justice of the Law, leading a blameless life (Phil 3:5-6).

This very background, however, threw a dark shadow over the claims of the new Christian faith. All his life, Paul had begun each day with the *Shema* (Deut 6:4-9), Israel's profession of faith in the one God. For Paul, this God was unique in his solitary transcendence and awful holiness. No Jew would ever pronounce the divine name Yahweh. It is easy to understand why Paul's soul flamed with anger when he heard Christians claim that one who had died on the cross was truly the Son of God. Hearing this confession of faith, Paul the zealot rose to stamp out the blasphemy, if need be in the very blood of his fellow Jews.

It was this zeal that led Paul to hound the followers of Christ to Damascus. That journey, however, marked for him the point of no return. Near the gates of the city, Christ himself came to Paul in a burst of blinding light. At that moment Saul the Jew came to know that this person is truly God of all. This conviction constituted his faith and created for him a lifetime apostolate. For this man, to believe in Christ meant to make him known everywhere as the living Lord of all. Ever after, Paul would be a "witness of the resurrection" not merely as a historical event of the past but, much more, as a mystery which has meaning in the here and now. The Christ of Paul's faith and of his preaching is the *Kyrios,* the kingly Lord who is "the same yesterday and today, yes, and forever" (Heb 13:8).

All three accounts of his conversion in the Acts of the Apostles (Acts 9:1-19; 22:3-16; 26:2-18) emphasize the following feature of his Damascus experience: He was converted to become both a Christian and an apostle. Paul makes this clear in his own description of his conversion for he presents both aspects as blended in the single call: "When [God], who from my mother's womb had set me apart and called me through his grace, was pleased to reveal his Son to me, so that I might proclaim him to the Gentiles . . ." (Gal 1:15-16).

His Christian life, therefore, was a complete unity. To live as a Christian was to love and to serve, and to serve was to be an apostle.

The compelling logic of it all was a constraint which Paul could not escape: "Woe to me," he writes, "if I do not preach the gospel! If I do this willingly, I have a reward. But if unwillingly, it is a stewardship which has been entrusted to me" (1 Cor 9:16-17). Every one of his letters breathes this compelling devotion; every one expresses the conviction with which he opens his epistle to the Romans: "Paul, the servant of Jesus Christ, called to be an apostle, set apart for the gospel of God" (Rom 1:1).

THE APOSTOLIC SPIRIT OF HIS LETTERS

There is great variety of style and content in his epistles. Many elements have gone into them: Stoic diatribe, Hellenistic cult, the juridic, cultic, and theological thought-patterns of Israel. Paul's background was rich, and he uses every aspect of it to make the Christian mystery meaningful. The style of his composition is generally forthright though sometimes involved; it is quick and nervous yet often sustained and contemplative. All through Paul's letters, however, both thought and style are drawn up into the binding unity of his love for Christ and his desire to preach Christ.

This apostolic note is struck in the very beginning of all his letters. Paul breaks with the convention of the stylized introduction of Greek epistles. Epistolary form presented first the name of the writer, then the name of the one addressed, and finally the simple salutation, *chairein* (greetings). Paul expands this colorless introduction and stamps it with his own cachet. He writes as an apostle with full awareness that his letters will have a large audience even when they are directed to individuals.

He is careful, therefore, to put everything into proper perspective from the very beginning. No matter how commonplace may be the problems which he will discuss, he first lifts the mind and heart of his readers to a level where they will view all things in full Christian light. First, he describes himself for what he really is, "The servant of Jesus Christ, called to be an apostle" (Rom 1:1). Next, he reminds his readers what they are: "God's beloved . . . called to be saints" (Rom 1:7), "holy and faithful in Christ Jesus" (Col 1:2).

This phrase, "in Christ Jesus," is the key to all Paul's letters. Once he has reminded his converts of their membership in the body of Christ he feels free to urge upon them the fullness of Christian living.

LIGHT FROM PAUL'S INAUGURAL VISION

It came naturally to Paul to look upon the Christian vocation as a life "in Christ Jesus." This concept, which shone crystal clear in his inaugural vision, dominated his thought and gave life and direction to his apostolate.

Inaugural visions have always exercised abiding influence on those who receive them. In the temple, Isaiah "saw the Lord seated on a high and lofty throne" (Isa 6:1). The temple was filled with billowing smoke and the Prophet heard the seraphim crying to one another, "Holy, holy, holy is the Lord of hosts!" This vision burned into Isaiah's soul a searing sense of his own creaturehood and of God's lofty transcendence. Every word of his later prophecies is weighted with reverence for God. Often when he speaks of the Lord, he adds the phrase, "the holy one." Each time he speaks of creatures his words are heavy with the feeling of human powerlessness.

The call of Jeremiah was very different. No intermediary but the Lord himself came to lay his fingers upon the Prophet's lips. The intimacy of this inaugural vision pulses all through the prophecies of Jeremiah. He is the apostle of God's merciful love for his wayward people.

In a similar way, Paul's inaugural vision struck the dominant chord of his whole ministry. Near the gates of Damascus, Christ came to him not simply as the risen Lord but also as the Lord who dwells in every Christian heart. Christ's words to Paul were all-revealing, "Saul, Saul, why do you persecute me? . . . I am Jesus the one whom you are persecuting" (Acts 9:4-5). With these words the risen Lord revealed to Paul that he is in some way one with every Christian. This truth was to resound again and again in the writings of the Apostle and to receive classic expression in his words to the Galatians: "All you who have been baptized into Christ have put on Christ. There is neither Jew nor Greek; there is neither slave nor freeman; there is neither male nor female. For you are all one in Christ Jesus" (Gal 3:27-28).

THE CHRISTIAN AND THE BODY OF CHRIST

This truth of the Christian's union with Christ underlies Paul's doctrine on the body of Christ. In order to understand properly this theme, one must remember that Paul the Jew did not look upon us as a dichotomy of body and soul, as did the Greek philosophers. In accord with Hebrew thought-patterns, Paul regarded us as a unity, an animated and personalized body. When, therefore, he spoke of the Christian united to Christ, he thought of this union in a realistic way as binding one body-person to another. To appreciate this concept one should reread the scriptural description of Jonathan's friendship with David: "The soul of Jonathan was knit to the soul of David, and Jonathan loved him as himself" (1 Sam 18:1). For Paul, this friendship was the union of the body-person of Jesus with that of the Christian.

The realism of a similar union between Christ and the Christian was especially impressed upon him through his awareness of the mystery of the Eucharist. Doctor Rawlinson, an Anglican exegete, has done well to stress the influence of the Eucharist in the development of Paul's doctrine on the union of the Christian with the body of Christ. In the Eucharist one sees clearly the realism of the Christian's intimate union with the total Christ.

The reality of this union is a leitmotif which recurs all through Paul's letters binding them into unity. The Apostle uses this truth more than any other to explain the exigencies of Christian life. His first letter to the Corinthians provides an excellent example of the power of this theme to meet every need and to solve every problem.

THE BODY OF CHRIST IN FIRST CORINTHIANS

At Corinth, Paul left behind an enthusiastic community; but this flourishing church soon showed signs of its old weaknesses. As a wide-open seaport town, Corinth provided the "flesh-pots of Egypt" to entice new Christians back to their old ways of sin. Not only that, but hardly had Paul departed when the church broke into factions and cliques. People prided themselves on their extraordinary gifts and boasted of their impressive connections. Paul meets all this weakness with the ringing challenge: Christian life must be lived in Christ Jesus.

In his letter, he treats first the cliques into which the church has broken. Some converts boasted of their friendship with the great orator Apollo; others vaunted their close bond with Cephas; still others preened themselves on their intimacy with Paul. The Apostle, however, recognizes only one bond worthy of the name: "You are in Christ Jesus who has become for us God-given wisdom and justice and sanctification and redemption, so that 'Let him who takes pride, take pride in the Lord'" (1 Cor 1:30-31).

In treating impurity, another problem in the Corinthian church, Paul meets it squarely on the level of its own realism, matching it with the realism of union with Christ. By baptism every Christian belongs to Christ and is intimately united to him as body-person to body-person. How, then, could a Christian seek union with one who would destroy his union with Christ: "Shall I then take the members of Christ and make them members of a harlot?" (1 Cor 6:15).

The third problem of the Corinthian converts is solved in the light of the same principle. They had received impressive charisms, gifts of healing, gifts of speaking with tongues, gifts of prophecy. Like peacocks they strutted about and spread their plumage of colorful charisms. Paul shatters this pride by reminding them that all these gifts are the manifestation of Christ who inspires and rules all. Whatever grace anyone has, he tells them, is all of Christ's giving; all is the work of his Spirit. Because every Christian belongs to the body of Christ, one's role and gifts are seen truly only when they are seen as functions of the body-person of Christ himself (1 Cor 12).

Paul uses this principle in widely assorted circumstances. Even in the most commonplace problems he sought a solution in the reminder, "You are in Christ Jesus." At Philippi two ladies, pillars of the church, were causing disedification by their antagonism to one another. Paul wrote, "I entreat Evodia and I exhort Syntyche to be of one mind *in the Lord*" (Phil 4:2).

Paul uses this same principle to solve a knotty problem in his epistle to Philemon. This letter provides a model of spiritual diplomacy. Philemon's slave Onesimus had run away and had sought refuge with Paul in Rome. The Apostle wrote immediately to recommend kindness; his letter plays on every chord of Philemon's heart, appeals to every motive which could soften the slave-owner's vindictiveness. The Apostle's supreme argument, however, is drawn from the union of the two Christians in the body of Christ. He pleads with Philemon to welcome Onesimus back into his service "no longer as a slave, but instead of a slave as a brother most dear . . . both in the flesh and *in the Lord*" (Phlm 16).

PAUL'S APOSTOLIC RESOURCEFULNESS

The theme of the body of Christ dominated all of Paul's thought; it constantly rose to the surface, therefore, in the work of his apostolate. But, precisely because he was engaged in the apostolate, Paul could easily shift his point of emphasis to become "all things to all people." There was nothing inflexible in his moods or his methods when it came to the work of apostolic ministry. He could easily change his appeal to other motives in order to gain all for Christ. His was the limberness of the truly apostolic spirit.

This fact may provide an explanation for the shifted emphasis in Paul's epistle to the Thessalonians. Here, there is hardly any mention of the doctrine of union with Christ which will figure so largely in his later epistles. Some, in fact, like Dom Jacques Dupont, have suggested that Paul had not yet developed this theme as a dominant guideline of his own thought.

Another explanation, however, is possible. The Thessalonian church was like one of our churches behind the former Iron Curtain. People were suffering persecution; they had little to look forward to in this life. Naturally, therefore, all their hope turned to the parousia, that second coming of Christ when he would appear once more in glory to set all things aright. Paul knew that this motive was helping his converts. As a true apostle, therefore, he does all he can to second this motivation. He thinks the thoughts of his converts, he speaks their language. For the moment he may have silenced the teaching of his own favorite dogma to identify himself with the mind of his persecuted Christians. The theme of this letter, therefore, centers in the prospect of union with Christ not in this life but in the life to come.

The flexibility of the apostolic spirit explains other significant shifts in the doctrinal emphases of Paul's letters. In his first letter to the Corinthians, he shows little regard for *gnosis*, that knowledge which the Corinthians esteemed so highly. He seems, indeed, to be anti-intellectual, curtly critical of the intellectualism which leads to pride: "Knowledge puffs up," he writes, "but charity edifies" (1 Cor 8:1). In reality, this attitude was simply an adaptation to a problem in the Corinthian church. His converts there had fallen under the spell of Judeo-Christians who insisted on the power of knowledge to save. Paul senses danger; his converts might all too easily forget the vital role of charity. To counteract this, Paul steps into the arena armed with strong words to combat an intellectualism which would destroy true Christian values.

This letter to the Corinthians, however, marks only one moment in the development of Paul's thought. Once he has reestablished the balance, once he has shown that knowledge must be infused with charity, he can then move on, as he does in his later epistles, to present the perfect Christian as one who is thoroughly *gnostikos*, full of knowledge, penetrating with deep insight into the mystery of Christ. In the captivity epistles he prays again and again that his converts may ever continue to grow in knowledge.

This is Paul, a true apostle ever ready to adjust and to adapt, to take now one position and now another, according to the needs of those whom he wishes to help.

CHANGING MOODS OF THE APOSTLE

Paul's power of adaptation is manifest not only in the changes of his doctrinal viewpoint but also in the varied patterns of his emotional life. These, too, followed the exigencies of his apostolate. How revealing it is to compare his letter to the Galatians with that to the Philippians.

Paul's love for his converts at Philippi knew no measure. They were his first converts in Europe. When he crossed from Asia Minor into Macedonia these were the first to welcome him. Ever after they held a cherished place in his heart. From them alone would Paul consent to receive a money gift. In writing to them, therefore, Paul lets his heart overflow. His letter is warm with deep affection; it is vibrant with joy. Time and again he repeats the word *chara* (joy); for he can assure his converts, "God is my witness how I love you all in the heart of Christ Jesus" (Phil 1:8).

How different is his letter to the Galatians. In their fickleness they were ready to turn away from the gospel and to accept in its stead the false doctrine of the Judeo-Christians. Paul's rebuke burns like lava. He has not one kind word for them, not one word of commendation. Bitterly he expostulates, "O foolish Galatians! Who has bewitched you? . . . Are you so foolish that after beginning in the spirit you now make a finish in the flesh?" (Gal 3:1, 3). Words like these make clear that Paul's whole emotional life takes tone and color from the needs of the apostolate.

APOSTLESHIP AN OVERFLOW OF INWARD LIFE

The spirit of the apostolate truly gave life and fibre to Paul's whole being. This fact provides the true explanation of the highly personal note in all his letters. He speaks freely of himself and fills his letters with constant reference to his own experiences. He knows well that his "I" is the "I" of every Christian. Whatever he found in himself was a grace which every Christian had a right to because of membership in the body of Christ. When, therefore, Paul writes, "I live, now not I, but Christ lives in me" (Gal 2:20), he speaks not of a unique mystical experience personal to himself alone but of a reality which belongs to every Christian.

Paul, therefore, never asked anyone for anything which he himself had not done: "Be imitators of me," he bids his converts, "as I am of Christ" (1 Cor 11:1). He never taught any truth which he himself was not living. His apostolate was nothing more than his own inward life changing and transforming those around him the way it changed and transformed him: "We the living are constantly being handed over to death for Jesus' sake, that the life also of Jesus may be made manifest in our mortal flesh. Thus death is at work in us, but life in you" (2 Cor 4:11). The price which Paul paid to transform others was a vibrant Christian life in his own soul, a life which overflowed into his preaching and into his writing.

The Apostle has given eloquent expression to the elan which motivated his whole life. While he was in prison at Ephesus (some think at Rome), certain fellow Christians took advantage of his confinement to gain their own converts for the community. This would win for themselves a prestige to rival Paul's. When Paul learned of their activity and saw through to its very human motive, he felt no dismay over the unworthiness of motivation but only thrilling joy at the thought of Christ's gain. His vibrant words ring with the full-hearted and unselfish devotion of the Baptist (cf. John 3:29-30): "What of it? Provided only that in every way, whether in pretense or in truth, Christ is being proclaimed; in this I rejoice, yes and I shall rejoice" (Phil 1:18). How could Paul say anything else? He has written, "For me to live is Christ" (Phil 1:21).

IN CONCLUSION

Familiarity with the writings of St. Paul means a full training in the apostolic spirit. Every page is a transcript from his own heart and bears glowing witness to his love for Christ and to his genius for preaching Christ to all people.

To understand and appreciate this aspect of the Pauline letters, one does not need a scholarly background or scientific preparation. All that is requisite is a heart wide open to share Paul's love for Christ and a will ever ready to do his apostolic work in the world of today.

CHAPTER 20

Begotten Through the Cross

> This decree . . . is buried from the eyes of everyone whose wit is not matured within love's flame. But since this target much is aimed at, and discerned but little, I will declare why such mode was more worthy (Dante, *Paradiso,* Canto VII).

Christianity is the religion of the cross. Its very heart is the mystery of Calvary; all its life-giving activity pulses with the flow of Christ's blood. With unfailing constancy the Church of God administers every sacrament and performs every rite under the sign of Christ's cross, as a continual reminder that all holiness lives through the power of his passion. At the very outset of life, the water of baptism traces the form of a cross on the babe's head to vitalize its soul with the saving grace of redemption. Again, in crucial sickness, it is the cross of anointing which seals the senses with strength. Why the cross? Because Christianity without the cross is a contradiction in terms.

This assertion becomes strikingly clear as one studies the heroes of Christianity, God's saints. No one will ever rob the saints of that common characteristic which is, at the same time, most personal to each: namely, conformity with Christ crucified. To deny to any one of them this most fundamental feature would be to tear from their brow the aureole of sanctity. For, in the plan of divine wisdom, there can be no holiness without likeness to Christ crucified: "Whom he foreknew he also predestined to be conformed to the image of his Son, that he might be the firstborn among the many" (Rom 8:29).

A growing experience of divine ways has familiarized all the saints with this fundamental plan. Each has come to realize, sooner or later, that all spiritual life is lived on Calvary, close to the cross of God's suffering Son. Saints trained in the Ignatian exercises have learned that the mystery of the cross should be "the daily food of our souls." Francis of Assisi, stamped in body with the searing wounds of the Crucified, has left to his followers this glowing reminder that all spiritual life is sealed with total conformity to Christ suffering. Dominicans, dedicated to tireless search for truth, will wander aimlessly until they make their own the method of their towering brother, Thomas, who sought true wisdom in his best loved "Book of Jesus Crucified." Saintly followers of St. Bernard have learned to walk the hard Cistercian way of silent prayer and penance because, like their father, they bear always in their hearts a little bundle of the sufferings of Jesus and breathe deeply of its fragrant strength. All who climb the straight but rugged road to the height of Carmel may expect to find at its summit the joys of transforming union. Yet, the sure guides of Carmel (Teresa of Ávila, John, and Thérèse of Lisieux) all insist that our union will be with the Crucified.

There is no other way of spiritual life than the way that leads to the cross and to union with Jesus suffering: "If anyone wishes to come after me, they must deny themselves, and take up their cross daily and follow me" (Luke 9:23). Those are truly wise who, even from the beginning, take their stand on Calvary. St. Paul knew no other wisdom; therefore, he wrote to the Corinthians, his "little ones in Christ": "And I, brothers and sisters, when I came to you, came not in loftiness of speech or of wisdom. . . . For I judged not myself to know anything among you, but Jesus Christ and him crucified" (1 Cor 2:1-2). The Apostle penned these words with conviction born of experience. He himself had long before reached the summit of perfect love of God. This summit was Calvary. Hence, for him, the life of perfect love was a life of complete union with Jesus suffering: "With Christ I am nailed to the cross. And I live, now not I, but Christ liveth in me. And that I now live in the flesh, I live in the faith of the Son of God, who loved me and delivered Himself for me" (Gal 2:19-20).

Thus it always will be. The fullness of Christian living is to be found only in union with the soul of Christ, the Son of God, suffering and dying on Calvary: "Whom he foreknew, he also predestined to be conformed to the image of his Son" (Rom 8:29).

This necessity has its reason. Christian living is not a haphazard experience, but must be ruled by the wise plan of God, which reaches from end to end mightily and orders all things sweetly (cf. Wis 8:1). To become a saint or a perfect Christian (the two are identical), one must follow the program which God has traced. This plan is very simple, for God is very simple; complexity and ambiguity are altogether foreign to divine ways. The plan is this: We are to live here on earth as children whom God has adopted, and to honor our Creator by offering the loving obedience which Christ Jesus, the only-begotten Son of God, offered on Calvary: "Have this mind in you which was also in Christ Jesus. . . . He humbled himself, becoming obedient to death, even to death on a cross" (Phil 2:5, 8). Through this conformity, a person merits the joy of more perfect recognition in heaven: "If children, then heirs, heirs of God and joint heirs with Christ, if only we suffer with him so that we may also be glorified with him" (Rom 8:17).

The very call to be a child of God through the grace of faith and the power to live this kinship come to us only through the merits of the passion of Christ. On every page of his epistles, St. Paul repeats the truth that the death of God's Son was the purchase price of Redemption: "In whom we have redemption through his blood, the remission of sins, according to the riches of his grace" (Eph 1:7). But it remains for us to work out our redemption by living as a child of God through this grace. This we do by growing in likeness to God's only-begotten Son, suffering and dying on Calvary: "For unto this are you called, because Christ also suffered for us, leaving you an example that you should follow his steps" (1 Pet 2:21).

THE DIVINE PLAN

What concerns us here is this latter feature of God's plan: namely, the total conformity with Christ suffering which is requisite for the holiness of full Christian living. It is of this that St. Paul writes when, concluding his analysis of the divine decree, he urges all Christians: "So be imitators of God, as beloved children, and live in love, as Christ loved us and handed himself over for us as a sacrificial offering to God for a fragrant aroma" (Eph 5:1-2). To love God as father and mother, creator and provider, in the spirit of Jesus suffering and in union with him, is the divine program for all holiness. For full appreciation, we must study this plan in the light of its background.

Before the first pulse of time, only one Being existed, all-wise, all-lovely, all-powerful: a fathomless, shoreless, sea of boundless perfection. Throughout all eternity, as in the beginning, so now, and unto endless ages, this Being contemplates the divine self and breathes a sigh of love and delight. So infinitely perfect is this activity that both divine thought and divine love are one in nature with God, even though each is a distinct person. God contemplating, God contemplated, God loved, in this triune sharing of one and the same Being,

God is infinitely happy. Father, Son, and Holy Spirit find limitless light, love, and joy in self-sharing friendship. Nothing can touch or increase their infinite bliss.

However, even from the timelessness of eternity, God dreamed of pouring out divine goodness upon others. Not to obtain greater joy (for what could add to the infinite fullness of divinity?), but for the glory of radiating holy perfection, God planned a world of persons who would know the bliss of calling him Father. God's own happiness would be neither greater nor less; but in a torrent of generosity, others would be enriched through the granting of divine fellowship. God is like that—infinite love, a sun that warms all it touches, without itself receiving increase. And so, from all eternity, God decreed that one day we should come into being to receive a share in the kinship of the divine Word and to be enwrapped in the love that is the Holy Spirit.

Even more, God planned to come and be present so completely that this world of divine making would be able to return full measure of glory "pressed down and running over" (Luke 6:38). This is the consummate mystery of divine wisdom (Eph 3:9). From all eternity, God foresaw that sin would mar creation and disrupt the peace of the human family. God, therefore, decreed that the eternal word and divine Son should become human in order to retrieve all through the total surrender of his human nature. This self-sacrifice of the incarnate Word would be the supreme outpouring of God's goodness and, on our part, the abiding tribute of perfect glory. In all ages it would be the unique source and measure of all human sharing in the life of God.

THE PLAN GONE AWRY

This was a tremendous plan, worthy of God; and the story of its accomplishment is written on every page with love. Anyone who reads its earlier incidents is tempted to suspect that God's first venture in love was only tentative—and a failure. Certainly it appears to be that. God created us and, through grace, adopted us as a favorite child. But what a prodigal! All through the devious history of the Old Covenant these wayward children roamed a wild way, with only an occasional half-hearted return to the bosom of their parent who could but whisper piteously: "Children I have raised and reared, but they have disowned me! An ox knows its owner, and an ass, its master's manger; but Israel does not know, my people has not understood" (Isa 1:2-3). God is always the loving parent; but, to limited human vision,

God seems so feeble and shortsighted in training these first little ones. And thus, what seems to us God's "first" plan proved a failure. Those whom God had adopted became so unmanageable that, at long last, God almost had to disown them.

But even before the final break, God seems to have considered another plan. While doing everything to salvage his first venture, God was at the same time getting ready another scheme. The work of preparation was long and hidden. Yet, time and again, God let drop hints of One who would come to make all things new. At length, preparation issued into fulfillment. For, "when the fullness of time had come, God sent his Son, born of a woman, born under the law, to ransom those under the law, so that we might receive adoption" (Gal 4:4-5).

Bound by limits of past and future, even in thought, we must thus speak of a "first" plan that failed and "another" plan that succeeded. But God must smile at the limitations of our concepts; we find it so hard to understand the mystery of divine condescension. Of course God's plans are unchanging; of course divine will knows no repentance. From the very beginning God had planned a masterpiece of love, and this plan was perfect in its unity. But it is hard for us to realize the utter simplicity and overall providence of divine wisdom. With the changeless consistency of eternity, God knew but one person: "Before the foundation of the world. . . . God destined us for adoption through Jesus Christ" (Eph 1:4-5). Through Christ, and in Christ, all would receive the grace of adoption: yes, all! Even the long delay in the coming of the Son had its part in God's program. Where sin had abounded, the loving gift of God's grace might more abound.

This plan is vital with unity. From all eternity, God has decreed to pour out upon us the fullness of infinite love, granting us a share in the life of his own Son: "God gave us eternal life, and this life is in his Son" (1 John 5:11). To show the greatness of divine love, God permitted the ugly meanness of sin; to manifest divine mercy, God permitted misery and ingratitude. Light after darkness, cheery warmth after piercing cold, repletion following hunger, it is always contrast that gives the best appreciation of true worth. When, at last, the goodness and kindness of God our Savior appeared, it was rich in meaning because "we ourselves also were sometime unwise, incredulous, erring, slaves to diverse desires and pleasures, living in malice and envy, hateful and hating one another" (Titus 3:3). Only when we had first rejected all the rich gifts of God and rebelled against his loving advances, only then would we appreciate the infinite mercy of a parent who "so loved the world that he gave his only-begotten Son" (John 3:16) to suffer and die for wandering, ungrateful children. Therefore, it was not merely an afterthought that prompted God to send the only-begotten Son, nor was this a second venture to remedy the failure of the first. God does not deal in afterthoughts; divine decrees are changeless. Planning everything just as it happened, God "chose us in him before the foundation of the world" (Eph 1:4).

OUR ADOPTION

The story of our adoption tells a deed of infinite love, selfless, self-squandering, self-sacrificing. With the wonderful calm of an inspired writer, St. Paul describes it in his brief note that "God sent his Son, born of a woman, born under the law, to ransom those under the law, so that we might receive adoption" (Gal 4:4-5). This means, first of all, that God stooped down an infinite distance to enclose the fullness of divinity in weak human flesh: "For in him [Christ Jesus] all fullness was pleased to dwell" (Col 1:19). The only-begotten of the Father emptied himself of all the glory that was really his and dimmed the luster of his Godhead under our flesh with its piteous human weakness. In a word, God took the all of us, save sin, that we might have the "all" of God.

To accomplish this plan, God became another Abraham; but this time no angel intervened to stay the sword of sacrifice (Gen 22). For God sent his beloved Isaac not merely to bear the burden of our flesh; even more, he sent him to pay our full debt and to mount the cross. In this, God's love pours out in overflowing measure. Now God can truly say: "What is there that I ought to do more to my vineyard, that I have not done to it?" (Isa 5:4). God sent the eternal word, a beloved Son, to become a member of our sinful family that, by bearing our penalty in his flesh, he may change us into the family of God: "For our sake he made him to be sin who did not know sin, so that we might become the righteousness of God in him" (2 Cor 5:21). Christ Jesus, our only healthy brother, would be cauterized in the fire of God's wrath that we, who were sick unto death, might be healed. This is the insoluble paradox of God's infinite love. At the moment when Christ would die under the weight of our sin, we would begin to live the divine life of children beloved by God.

The painful cautery itself is a complete revelation of God's love. The flesh of the victim was weak like ours; his feelings were delicately sensitized to every bruise and wound; transcending light filled his human mind with an infused knowledge of God's attributes and the stark vision of all sin. Every part of his human nature was finely tempered to feel suffering: "For this reason, when he came into the world, he said: . . . 'A body you prepared for me'" (Heb 10:5). Born to be the Savior, Jesus was divinely prepared to feel in every member of his body, and every fiber of his soul, the pain that would heal the rottenness of our sin. Flesh of our flesh, he had to bear the burden of our iniquity. He was brother to a worldwide family of criminals. It was for him to stand alone, in our place, before an all just God whose power makes mountains smoke and the earth quake (cf. Ps 104:32). Do we wonder, then, that his body should quiver and his soul cry out in pain?

His constancy, however, never failed. Divine justice racked his body, tore his soul, and pierced his heart; yet, "like a lamb led to the slaughter or a sheep before the shearers, he was silent and opened not his mouth" (Isa 53:7). In this, the infinite love of God becomes visible to our eyes. The human soul of Christ suffered all with sweet patience, because it images in a human way the inaccessible light of God's tender love. St. Catherine of Siena once saw this soul of Christ in a vision; she describes it in one word, *nettezza* (limpidity). Like a clear, motionless sea, the soul of Christ suffering on the cross mirrors the boundless love of God which sent him to us. He suffers all in silence and in full, devoted acceptance because divine love has overflowed into the ocean bed of his human soul. Christ is not merely a victim for sin; he is an eager, willing victim, heartbroken with devotedness: "Who loved me and delivered himself for me" (Gal 2:20). In him, all the goodness and kindness of God has appeared.

The passion of Christ is thus the living symbol and final proof of God's limitless love: "In this way the love of God was revealed to us: God sent his only Son into the world so that we might have life through him. In this is love: not that we have loved God, but that he loved us and sent his Son as expiation for our sins" (1 John 4:9-10). Certainly there were other ways to redeem us. A word of pardon, a single sigh or tear of the God-man, any one of these would have been enough. Yet God passed them all by and, instead, plunged his own Son into a sea of suffering where waves of fire would wash him up, a corpse, on the shores of death. Here divine mercy seems to exhaust the infinite ingenuity of divine wisdom; even the generosity of God can reach no greater breadth nor length nor height nor depth (cf. Eph 3:18). Our adoption as children through the death of God's Son speaks with eternal eloquence of the burning love in our Father's heart.

THE ATTRACTION OF THE CROSS

Calvary, then, must needs be the center of the world. As the sickbed of a dying mother draws the children to whom she has given life, so the cross is the magnetic center of all true children of God. Christ himself promised it would be so. His was the strong, hopeful confidence that, once mounted on the cross, he would have compelling claim on every heart: "And I, if I be lifted up from the earth, will draw all things to myself" (John 12:32). This confidence has never been disappointed. Even as in the bosom of the Trinity the divine Word with his Father breathes forth the Person of love, the Holy Spirit, so too, here on earth, the least knowledge of him in his sufferings breathes love into the soul. Once we have tenderly contemplated Christ on the cross, we can never again turn away our gaze. The silent Sufferer draws "all things" with irresistible attraction.

One day at prayer, St. Paul of the Cross found himself plunged into the sea of the Savior's sufferings. There he understood, as never before, that the passion is a work entirely of love. Ever after, his prayer consisted in clothing himself with the sufferings of Christ and in yielding himself to be immersed in the ocean of God's love; he knew no other practice. In the same way, all the saints have come to feel, sooner or later, the magnetic drawing of the passion of Christ. Each has discovered, in contemplating Jesus crucified, the living, throbbing proof of God's infinitely tender love; and, in the light of this understanding, they have realized how full and unfailing must be the return: Love is repaid by love alone. Therefore, each saint has labored to make his/her own the spirit of the apostle St. Paul: "For the love of Christ impels us. . . . He indeed died for all, so that those who live might no longer live for themselves but for him who for their sake died and was raised" (2 Cor 5:14-15).

But still another drawing power is to be found in the magnetism of Christ's cross. For divine wisdom knows no limit, and divine love knows no bound. This loving wisdom, then, has vitalized the cross with yet another appeal to draw our souls. God has arranged that his Son, even in dying, should show us how to live. Silently suffering in every nerve of his body, shedding every drop of his blood, draining every possibility of interior agony, Christ hangs before the eyes of all as a perfect example of a devoted child, lovingly obedient to the will of the Father. Every true child of God, then, must contemplate Jesus crucified in order to become like him: "Whom he foreknew he also predestined to be conformed to the image of his Son" (Rom 8:29).

Does this mean that everyone must become a stigmatic and feel in one's own flesh the lash of the whips and the burn of the nails? No; outward resemblance to Christ is not necessary. Pain and trial will come, it is true. Suffering is a commonplace in every life; it spares no one. But endurance of pain in soul and body, even though necessary, is not the chief element in conformity with Christ crucified. Endurance of pain was not the chief element in his passion. Rather, Christ gave glory to his Father through the loving obedience which accepted full heartedly the divine will that he suffer and die. In the same way, it is chiefly by imitating these interior dispositions of the heart of Christ that a person relives the passion in one's own life. To accept all suffering, and to perform every duty with Christ's devoted obedience to the will of God, is truly to be conformed to his image. Such inward conformity is the best fruit of loving attention to Christ on the cross. It is this which sanctifies suffering and gives life and meaning to every act of human virtue. For, through this inward resemblance to Christ suffering, we live fully our own glorious life as children of the heavenly creator.

The true child of God is, then, the model in whom we see ourselves as we should be; Christ, as human, is the only way of our going. Through his death on the cross, he became head of a mystical body whose members share in his status as child. But this incorporation, like any other, involves a process of assimilation; if it is to be real, it must mold the members into a true likeness to their head. Accordingly, conformity with Christ in his sufferings will always be the measure of our incorporation into him. A person shares in the kinship which Christ died to give, in proportion as the redeeming passion is relived in one's own soul. "Thus there is a double movement in the christian universe. And the movement by which it mounts upwards to God is only a consequence of the primary movement by which God descends to it. And the more it opens itself to the movement by which God gives Himself, the more is awakened in it the movement by which it gives itself to God" (Jacques Maritain, *Science and Wisdom* [New York: Scribner, 1940] 19–20).

This is the paradox of exchange which Mother Church loves to contemplate: *O admirabile commercium*! Here is the master stroke of divine wisdom: The true Son of God suffers and dies that, through conformity with his sufferings, we may live the full spirit of his adoption. When we meditate prayerfully on this plan of God, we receive the conviction which gave spirit and life to the soul of St. Paul: "I count all things to be but loss for the excellent knowledge of Jesus Christ my Lord; for whom I have suffered the loss of all things, and count them but as dung, that I may gain Christ and may be found in him . . . that I may know him . . . and the fellowship of his sufferings, being made conformable to his death" (Phil 3:8-10). [Editor's note: See Chapter 21 for a full development of this passage.]

The young Carmelite of Dijon, Sister Mary Elizabeth of the Trinity, recently beatified by Pope John Paul II, was one who thoroughly understood this plan; she has translated it into the practical resolution which dominated her life: "I must study this divine model, so thoroughly identifying myself with him that I can incessantly show him forth in the sight of the Father."

CHILDREN OF GOD: CHRIST AND OURSELVES

This insistent need for conformity with Christ crucified rests on obvious reasons. Never was anyone so manifestly a child as Christ in the hours of his suffering and death. His heart was vibrant with loving obedience. Pain and opprobrium, anguish of soul and torture of body, all this Jesus accepted in silent love, seeing only the hand of his Father in the fist that struck or the word that wounded. Each new penalty he accepted with an unhesitating "Yes, Father." Each new decree of divine justice echoed in his soul with an act of perfect submission: "Father, not my will but yours be done." His was the will of a devoted child, soft like wax under each breath of God's flaming spirit, hard like steel to work God's will. His perfect obedience knew no wavering. For him, the human instruments of the passion were but the shadows of God's hand lifted in justice to strike the Son of his heart; and the Son, so tender in his devotion to the Father, did not recoil. Never before or after has God received so rich a token of filial love. Truly "Christ loved us and handed himself over for us as a sacrificial offering to God for a fragrant aroma" (Eph 5:2).

How different it is with even the best of God's other children! All have so much to learn from the perfect sonship of Christ suffering. No matter how long one lives, one never outgrows the rule of divine wisdom: "Let this mind be in you which was also in Christ Jesus. . . . He humbled himself, becoming obedient unto death, even to the death of the cross" (Phil 2:5-8).

It is also through Christ crucified that we learn the attributes of God: "Whoever has seen me, has seen the Father" (John 14:9). In his light we see light (cf. Ps 36:10). Looking upon him we can read in the wounds furrowing his body the holiness and justice of God and the strong power of God's love which surpasses all knowledge. For the human soul of Christ was like the crystal sea which stands before the throne of God, mirroring the divine attributes (cf. Rev 4:6). His every thought was a vital communion with the Godhead. Divine truth was reflected in his humility; God's long-suffering found a perfect human image in his patience; God's mercy kindled the flame of Christ's pity for his followers. In the suffering of Jesus we find a perfect human reflection of the fullness of God.

Here, then, is the inexorable rule of our kinship. In order to live as a child of God, we must image the soul of the Crucified. We have no other way: "Those who belong to Christ have crucified their flesh with its passions and desires" (Gal 5:24). This conformity with Christ involves a practical program of *agere contra*. Pride, anger, petty selfishness, softness, meanness, and a host of other deliberate evils, little and big, must be crushed and strained out, before our soul mirrors limpidly, like the soul of Christ, the image of God. St. Paul urges this program of conformity with his usual vigor:

> You have taken off the old self with its practices and have put on the new self, which is being renewed, for knowledge, in the image of its creator. . . . but Christ is all and in all. Put on then, as God's chosen ones, holy and beloved, heartfelt compassion, kindness, humility, gentleness, and patience (Col 3:9-12).

Only when this conformity with Christ crucified has been achieved through faith and love and suffering, does God utter over us the blessing of full adoption: "This is my beloved one, in whom I am well pleased" (Matt 3:17).

With most of us, such close conformity is the work of a lifetime. Even a casual examination of the human heart uncovers a host of wayward thoughts and desires without kinship to the thoughts and desires of Christ suffering. This humiliating contrast is proof through bitter experience that we must still work hard to realize St. Paul's formula of perfect conformity: "Let this mind be in you which was also in Christ Jesus" (Phil 2:5).

His human mind was bathed in infused light which illumined at once the beauty and goodness of God and the ugly filth and defiant nothingness of sin. The vision tortured his mind, racked his heart, and nauseated his whole being. Because God meant so much to him, the heart of Christ broke at the thought of humanity's mean, cruel ingratitude in rejecting so good a Father. Because he saw so clearly the lovely holiness and perfect purity of God, his soul sickened to death before the stench and filth of sin, the very sin which holds so real an attraction for even good people.

BEGOTTEN THROUGH THE CROSS

Perfect conformity with Christ crucified is above human power. God himself must illumine our minds with the same divine light as filled the human mind of the suffering Son. This light brings cleansing pain and a love that burns. "When this loving contemplation illumines man and woman, who are impure and weak, it illumines them according to their nature. It plunges them into darkness and causes them affliction and distress, as does the sun to the eye that is weak; it enkindles them with passionate yet afflictive love, until they be spiritualized and refined by this same fire of love" (St. John of the Cross, *Dark Night of the Soul,* 1:438).

In this light, the child of God gazes anew on the Crucified and is transformed into a living sorrow—to cleanse its sin-poisoned depths. The soul conceives a hatred of sin, as uncleanness. It was this piercing light which filled the soul of Mary Magdalene at the foot of the cross. Motionless, she gazed lovingly upon the Crucified, while ineffable holiness beat its searching rays upon her. In this light she understood, as never before, what sin means to God.

In this same light of contemplation, a person realizes as never before that all spiritual life is a process of vital growth into the image of Christ on the cross. For now an all-merciful Father compels one to draw near to the Crucified. Everything seems to wage war on the poor soul, so that it may know, within and without, "fellowship of his sufferings" (Phil 3:10). Through these trials, a person comes to appreciate the mystery of the cross in a new way. For always, according to St. John of the Cross, "the purest suffering bears and carries in its train the purest understanding" (*Points of Love*, 3:255). Saint Claude de la Columbière was experiencing this conforming power of the cross when he wrote: "Since I have been ill, I have only learnt one thing; and that is that we cling to ourselves by many imperceptible threads and if God did not do it for us, we should never break them: We do not even recognize them." So it is with everyone; we learn best through suffering.

It is this new knowledge, learned in the light of God, which most helps a person to live this kinship with strong purpose of will. Now Christ crucified becomes "all in all." One sees the fullness of God gleaming in the God-man's soul and learns from him what it means to be a child of God. This surpassing knowledge brings high courage and the inflamed desire to become like him, to have fellowship with him in suffering, and to be configured to his death (Phil 3:10). For now we fully realize the plan of God, who loves as offspring those who are one with Jesus, the true Son on the cross.

The great St. Teresa knew this truth by personal experience; and so she has written: "His Majesty can grant us nothing more precious than a life conformed to that of his well beloved Son. And I am absolutely convinced that these graces (of transforming union) are intended to strengthen our weakness and to render us capable of supporting great sufferings after the example of this Divine Son. Do we not see that all those who have come nearest to our Lord Jesus Christ are those who have endured the greatest tribulations. Let us consider those of his glorious mother and his glorious apostles" (*The Interior Castle*, ch. 4, 6–7).

Mere mention of the sorrowful Mother Mary teaches in a single word our absolute need for conformity with Christ crucified. After him, she is God's best-loved child. Therefore, she, more than any other, has shared the sufferings of the Son. More perfectly than any other, her heart and soul are molded into perfect conformity with his. In suffering and death, Christ sought only the will of his Father; so, too, Mary standing near the cross breathed the whole spirit of her life into a loving acceptance uttered silently in the depths of her soul: "May it be done to me according to your word" (Luke 1:38). Jesus, Mary: they share but one heart; for on Calvary, in the fire of suffering, these two hearts have fused.

St. Brigid, in her *Revelations,* speaks of the close intimacy she felt with Jesus in his passion and the mutual sharing of sorrow that united them together. It is the same with all God's true children. A saint begins to love God in earnest on that day when he/she mounts the hill of Calvary to stand with Mary beneath the cross. There, contemplating Christ crucified, one begins to understand the boundless reality of divine love. There, too, sharing really in Christ's sufferings, one lives the full spirit of a vocation as child of God. Life and pain and sin have an entirely new meaning when seen from the vantage point of Calvary. This life seems empty, pain becomes precious, and sin sickens the soul with loathing when one feels sorrow with Christ who is full of sorrow, a broken heart with Christ heartbroken, tears and interior pain for the great pain that Christ has suffered.

The writings of St. Paul are alive with this spirit of devotedness to the suffering Christ. This, indeed, was his whole life: "I have been crucified with Christ; yet I live, no longer I, but Christ lives in me; insofar as I now live in the flesh, I live by faith in the Son of God who has loved me and given himself up for me" (Gal 2:19-20). The one desire of Paul's life was to share in the sufferings of Christ and to be configured to his death (Phil 3:10). These sufferings of the God-man provided the chief theme of all his preaching (1 Cor 2:2) and the way of life which he proposed to his best-loved converts (Phil 2:5-8). It was his glory to bear in his own body the marks of Christ's wounds and to shoulder his cross (Gal 6:14, 17); it was his comfort to abound in the sufferings of his master (2 Cor 1:5). For his was the supreme hope that, through bearing the death of Jesus in his body, the life also of Jesus, true Son of God, would be manifest in his mortal flesh (2 Cor 4:10-11). It is little wonder, then, that St. John Chrysostom could write of him: "Cor Pauli, cor Christi," the heart of Paul is one with the heart of Christ.

This is true also of all the saints; all were predestined by God to conformity with his Son. Many, indeed, have left to the Church touching expressions of their devotedness. It is refreshing to instance some of these. St. Bernard, who ever bore the sufferings of Christ in his heart and on his lips, uttered the conviction: "The most sublime philosophy which I have in this world is to know Jesus and him crucified." St. Margaret Mary exulted in her large share of the Savior's sufferings: "Oh, what happiness to be able to share here on earth in the anguish, the bitter torments, the dereliction of the Sacred Heart!" St. Bonaventure, true son of St. Francis, prayed: "Grant that I may always see thee crucified for me." To St. Catherine de' Ricci, the simple sight of a red rose would instantly recall the memory of the redeemer. The Curé d'Ars spoke of the cross as the gift which God reserves for his friends and insisted that "all who would serve God must love the cross." A single glance at Jesus scourged revitalized completely the spirit of St. Teresa; she never forgot this great grace. And therefore, in one of the most striking passages of her autobiography, she appeals for a continual remembrance of him. In the same way, St. Paul of the Cross expressed a deep personal conviction and revealed the ceaseless practice of his own life when he urged the members of his little Congregation always to keep alive in their heart the memory of Christ's passion. To Saint Philippine Duchesne God gave failure upon failure; her long life never knew a moment of felt success. Nevertheless this experience, though crushing, brought deep peace, for the thoughts of Mother Duchesne rested always in the humble, suffering heart of Jesus.

This attraction is most remarkable in the history of Sister Mary Elizabeth of the Trinity. Dominated by the gift of wisdom, the young Carmelite found her heaven on earth through a devoted realization of the indwelling of God in her soul. At the same time, her thought of Christ crucified became more and more frequent. As she herself wrote, the one ideal of her life was "to enter into the movement of his divine soul" and, like St. Paul, "to fill up in her body for the Church what was lacking of the sufferings of Christ." She longed to go to the passion of her death in order to be a co-redemptrix with him. For her, the transforming union meant complete conformity with the soul of the Son of God suffering on the cross, as M. M. Philipon, O.P., develops in his *The Spiritual Doctrine of Sister Elizabeth of the Trinity*.

This same love of the cross is found in the lives of the great servants of God who, living close to our own day, have not yet received the aureole of sanctity. Abbot Marmion loved every feature of the whole Christ; however, his thoughts turned with preference to the passion as the summit and crowning point of Christ's life on earth. The great-souled Benedictine found in it the holy of holies where one is transformed into a child of God. For Mother Janet Erskine Stuart, too, the sufferings of Christ were the favorite theme of meditation. Each season of the liturgical cycle claimed attention; yet it was always with yearning that she returned to the passion of Christ, finding time for this thought each day, even though the morning meditation had been devoted to some other mystery. Charles de Foucauld, the knight errant of the hidden life, found the secret of his penance and prayer and the guide of his wanderings in the vision of the Man on the cross.

IN CONCLUSION

Such examples of devotedness to Christ crucified are as many as there are saints. For there is no other way of holiness but to be united with him on the cross and to reproduce in one's own life the dispositions of heart which were his under the sufferings which brought us kinship. The rule admits no exception: "Whom he foreknew, he also predestined to be conformed to the image of his Son" (Rom 8:29). Here we are face to face with the master plan of God's wisdom: Divine adoption is ours through the sufferings of the only-begotten of God; and only through conformity with this same suffering Son of God do we live in full filial love for God. It is for children of God to accept this plan which God has traced. They are to remain in spirit on Calvary, in the company of Mary, the sorrowing mother, there to contemplate the Crucified with love and to become like him. No task could be sweeter or easier.

This conformity brings its own rich reward. For on this new child in Christ Jesus, God pours out the fullness of divine love. St. John of the Cross has described this in unforgettable words:

> With such great reality of love does God communicate with the soul in this interior union that no affection of a mother who so tenderly caresses her daughter nor love of a brother, nor affection of a friend is comparable to it. For so great is the tenderness and reality of this love wherewith God caresses and exalts this humble and loving soul, that in very truth God subjects the divine self to it in order to exalt it. God seems the servant and the soul God's master. God is as solicitous in granting it favors as though God were the soul's slave and the soul were God. So profound is the humility and sweetness of God (*The Spiritual Canticle*, st. 27, 1).

Here is the touch of experience. John of the Cross describes what he himself has tasted. And well he deserved this sweetness of God's love. For when Christ crucified appeared to him and asked what favor he wished in return for his long years of service, did not the little friar whisper back, "To suffer and to be despised"? This is, and ever must be, the one great cry of all the saints; for each is a child through the cross.

CHAPTER 21

Sharing in His Sufferings

Through conversion, St. Paul gained a new spiritual life. On the road to Damascus, he received from the risen Christ the messianic gift of the Holy Spirit who, ever after, inspired and ruled his activity as that of a true son of God. For the Apostle this meant, in the expressive phrase of Philippians 3:10, that he had come to know Christ, "and the power of his resurrection." But that was not all. He affirms in the same breath that, through conversion, he came to know also "the sharing of his sufferings." This significant addition is in accord with the polarity of all Pauline thought which joins death and resurrection as two inseparable aspects of the same salvific mystery, whether in the life of Christ or in the lives of Christians.

It is not easy, however, to determine the precise application of this death theme to the enigmatic phrase, "the sharing of his sufferings," for the context does not define or explain its authentic meaning. Paul, moreover, has spoken so rarely of the historical details of the passion that the expression, "sufferings of Christ," fails to command the unanimous interpretation accorded to words of obvious meaning.

Due to this uncertainty, the controverted phrase needs to be studied in the light of Paul's general doctrine, especially as it is found in the great letters to the Corinthians, Galatians, and Romans. For when he wrote Philippians, Paul had already advanced beyond the limitations of the early *kerygma*—the apostolic preaching in the first year after Pentecost—and even beyond the limitations of his own doctrine in his first letters, those to the Thessalonians. During the first months at Corinth, Paul went through a maturing process which virtually developed his thought and significantly influenced his preaching. This enrichment is reflected in the letters which followed. Their fullness constitutes the background of his words in Philippians. Hence, a review and examination of relevant themes in the Pauline corpus will help greatly to explain his affirmation that conversion brought him to know Christ and "the sharing of his sufferings."

PAUL'S EARLY DOCTRINE ON SUFFERING: 1 AND 2 THESSALONIANS

The doctrine on suffering in First and Second Thessalonians reflects the teaching of the early Church as enunciated in Acts 14:22: "It is necessary for us to undergo many hardships to enter the kingdom of God." In accord with this truth, Paul takes it for granted that the Christian lives in a climate of suffering. He insinuates this belief in an opening phrase of his first letter to the Thessalonians and frequently alludes in both letters to the sufferings borne by himself and his Thessalonian converts. Thus, he employs many forms of *thlipsis*, a Greek word more and more frequently used for those tribulations which usher in the glorious risen Christ.

Such suffering is not a mere accident; rather, it is a necessity imposed by divine decree, for in First Thessalonians Paul parallels his earlier statement in Acts with the equivalent phrase, "we are *destined* for [affliction]" (1 Thess 3:3). Although the struggle between good and evil will break out in titanic fury at the end of time, even now it has already begun: The "Tempter" is active; the "mystery of lawlessness" is at work (cf. 2 Thess 2:1ff.). Hence, for Paul, there is no break in continuity between the sufferings of the present moment and the eschatological crisis of the final age of the world.

This explains the rich joy which the Thessalonians and Paul himself experienced in their trials. Looking forward eagerly to the imminent coming of Christ, they were able to identify their trials as a share in the tribulations of the "last age." Hence, their hope was something more than ordinary hope; it was an attitude of patient and persevering waiting in the midst of trials. In the New Testament, this virtue is always, at least implicitly, connected with messianic salvation, for it represents the power of hope to endure in the midst of sufferings which lead to final reward. The patient endurance of trials, therefore, fills the Christian with joy, for it brings the conviction that such fidelity in the midst of messianic tribulations provides a pledge of salvation at the time of the parousia or the second coming of the Risen Lord.

This doctrine of the letters to the Thessalonians might lead one to conclude that Paul's teaching on suffering is identical with that of

Judaism of his day, i.e., the patient endurance of trial is really a blessing, for it is only by passing righteously through the messianic throes that one will enter the messianic kingdom. Fragmentary references in these letters show, however, that Paul thinks of suffering in a *Christian* light. Trials are the continuation of the tribulations which Christ himself inaugurated. What is more, these references, when coupled with other doctrinal elements in these letters, suggest a concept which Paul will develop later: The bond between the sufferings of the Christian and Christ is based on intimate union.

Imitators of Christ

In Thessalonians, Paul speaks of the suffering Christians as "imitators" of the suffering Christ. As St. John Chrysostom points out, the term of comparison in 1 Thessalonians 1:6 is suffering with joy: "You became imitators of us and of the Lord, receiving the word in great affliction, with joy from the Holy Spirit." A second text which is more casual in its reference to Christ, centers the comparison in suffering alone: "For you . . . have become imitators of the churches of God that are in Judea in Christ Jesus. For you suffer the same things from your compatriots as they . . ." (1 Thess 2:14). To explain this bond it would suffice to invoke the dominant theme of these letters with regard to suffering and to conclude that the conformity between the suffering Christ and the suffering Christian arises from their common adherence to the design of God that all who attain messianic glory must pass through messianic trial. There are indications, however, that Paul's concept of imitating Christ involves a more intimate bond.

It is significant that the word "imitator" always denotes moral effort in the New Testament. It reflects the saying of Jesus: "If anyone wishes to come after me, let them deny themselves, and take up their cross, and follow me" (Mark 8:34). We see a close connection with the concept of disciple following master. This theme of master-disciple is actually found in First Thessalonians, where Paul makes clear that the precepts governing Christian life have come from God through and in Christ Jesus (1 Thess 4:2ff.; 5:18). Jesus is, therefore, the mediator of God's will and the master of all who are subject to it. It is noteworthy that, to express this role of Christ, Paul uses the phrase "in Christ Jesus" which recurs throughout these two letters and which, at least in the following letters, frequently refers to an intrinsic bond.

Even in the present letters, moreover, Paul shows Christ forming his disciples by actual influence from within. He writes in First Thessalonians: "May the Lord make you increase and abound in love . . . so as to strengthen your hearts, to be blameless in holiness before God . . . at the coming of our Lord Jesus" (1 Thess 3:12-13). In his first letters, therefore, Paul's concept of imitating Christ in suffering may be based not only on the duty of the Christian to follow the same divine will that imposed messianic suffering on the Savior, but also on the intrinsic necessity of living the pattern of life that flows inevitably from inward communion with him who, while on earth, suffered the trials of the Messiah.

There is also another suggestive element in these early letters. Paul asserts that the joy of suffering with which the Christian imitates Christ is a gift of the Holy Spirit. "You have become imitators of us and of the Lord . . . with joy from the Holy Spirit" (1 Thess 1:6). This is significant, for the Holy Spirit is present in the Christian as God's permanent gift (cf. 1 Thess 4:8). The way is thus prepared for the subsequent letter to the Romans, wherein Paul teaches that Christians have reason to rejoice in trial since they can rely on the ever present Spirit to strengthen their resistance and to fulfill their hope (Rom 5:3-5).

The Divine Gift of Endurance

There is yet a last phrase to suggest that, even in Thessalonians, Paul anticipated his later doctrine on the profound influence of Christ in all Christian suffering. He writes: "May the Lord direct your hearts to the love of God and to the endurance of Christ" (2 Thess 3:5). As it stands, the phrase is open to several interpretations.

James Everett Frame in *Epistles of St. Paul to the Thessalonians* suggests that it refers to Christ not only as the supreme model but also as the efficient cause of the Christian's patience. Paul, therefore, asks here that his converts may be strengthened with an endurance that is both inspired by the example of Christ and actually bestowed by him.

B. Rigaux, O.F.M., in *Les Épîtres de Saint Paul aux Thessaloniciens* and M. Zerwick in *Graecitas Biblica,* while accepting Frame's explanation, enrich it by interpreting the phrase in the light of Paul's doctrine on the union of Christ with his members. Seen in this light, the patience which Paul requests for his converts is truly "Christ's endurance," not only because he bestows it but also because he, as the "Body," must claim whatever belongs to his members. There is much to recommend this thoroughly Pauline interpretation. Not only is it warranted by Paul's allusions in Thessalonians to the bond between Christ and his followers, it is also a corollary of the words spoken to

Paul in his inaugural vision: "Saul, Saul, why are you persecuting me? ... I am Jesus whom you are persecuting" (Acts 9:4-5).

Such allusions to a distinctly Pauline explanation of suffering, though precious, are only fragmentary and incidental; as such, they leave much room for discussion. The fact is that, in these first two letters, Paul does not emphasize the role of Christ in *present* life and suffering. His attention is fastened on the parousia or final coming, and his thought is strongly colored by the eschatological outlook of late Judaism and early Christianity. Hence, it may be that in Thessalonians he is content to emphasize only that aspect of the bond between Christ and the Christian which is based on God's will ordaining trial both for the Messiah and his followers as the necessary means for entering the kingdom.

SUFFERING IN THE GREAT PAULINE LETTERS: FROM RESURRECTION-PAROUSIA TO DEATH-RESURRECTION

Passing now to the period of the great letters of First and Second Corinthians, Galatians and Romans, we notice a marked shift of emphasis from the outlook and teaching of Thessalonians. Paul's own experience offers the probable reason for this new development. Leaving Thessalonica, he went to Athens where, in his address at the Areopagus, he followed the pattern of his earlier preaching (Acts 17:16-31). Not only did he develop the theme of resurrection-parousia, but he also embellished his words with oratorical devices. This method of preaching met with signal failure so that, coming to Corinth immediately afterwards, he feared even worse (1 Cor 2:1-3). But now he deliberately altered the theme of his discourse to emphasize the role of the death of Christ in God's plan for salvation. He also changed to a simple style of preaching and addressed especially the less promising elements of the population.

Fruitful Ambient for Divine Activity

As the months passed, Paul witnessed a phenomenon which made a deep impression upon him. He had already seen at Thessalonica that spiritual fruitfulness was possible even under a storm of suffering. Now, at Corinth, he came to see that suffering and human weakness provide the climate that is most conducive to the activity of God's saving power. He was not slow to grasp the implications of this experience. It squared perfectly with the Isaian picture of redemption. Salvation did not depend upon human strength but only upon God, so that all glory belongs to God alone:

> The haughty eyes of humankind will be lowered,
> the arrogance of all will be abased,
> and the Lord alone will be exalted on that day.
> By waiting and by calm you shall be saved,
> in quiet and in trust your strength lies (Isa 2:11; 30:15).

This principle of "salvation through God alone" pervades biblical thought, appears frequently in nonbiblical Jewish literature, and finds some of its most beautiful expressions in the hymns of Qumran. In one of these hymns, as translated by Menahem Mansoor, we read:

> For I know that truth are the words of thy mouth and in thy hand is righteousness, and in thy thought is
> All knowledge; and in thy power is all might and all glory is with thee. In thy wrath are all judgments of affliction,
> But in thy goodness there is abundance of forgiveness, and thy mercies are on all thy favored children. For thou hast made known to them thy true counsel,
> And through thy marvelous mysteries thou hast enlightened them. And for the sake of thy glory, thou hast cleansed men and women from transgressions so that they may consecrate themselves
> For thee . . . (1QH 11:7-11).

Paul himself recognized this principle at work in the unfolding of the divine plan at Corinth. Human weakness and human contradiction provided the ambient for fruitful divine activity, that all might recognize and give glory to the true author of salvation. At Corinth, the Apostle came to see in a new way that all people must become aware of their own human powerlessness if they are to make room for the power of God. Trial and weakness, therefore, because they lead to such awareness, are both a preparation for and a sign of God's work.

Human Weakness, Divine Glory

Paul returns to this theme time and again in the first three chapters of First Corinthians. He identifies it as the governing principle in the divine choice of the crucifixion of Christ for the work of salvation; God has chosen what is humanly "weak" and "foolish" to accomplish

God's greatest mercy, that we might see clearly how fully the power and wisdom of salvific activity is entirely divine. In this new emphasis on the death of Christ as interpretative of the nature of the salvific plan, Paul delivered the very "testimony of God" (1 Cor 2:1). He focused attention on the human "weakness" of the way in which Christ attained messianic glory and so demonstrated that salvation is wholly God's work and wholly a work of love.

The Apostle saw this principle of power-in-weakness directing also the extension of salvific activity through his own preaching: "It was the will of God through the foolishness of the proclamation to save those who have faith" (1 Cor 1:21). The same principle was at work in the selection of the first converts: "God chose the foolish of the world to shame the wise, and the weak . . . and the lowly and despised . . . and those who count for nothing" (1 Cor 1:27-28). Moreover, to counter the arrogance of the Corinthians who were preening themselves as though they had attained the fullness of salvation, Paul emphasized the fact that the apostles in whom God's power is most active experience an acute feeling of human insufficiency and suffer great trials constantly.

Nowhere, perhaps, does Paul express this reaction so poignantly than in Second Corinthians: "We hold this treasure in earthen vessels, that the surpassing power may be of God and not from us. We are afflicted in every way, but not constrained; perplexed, but not driven to despair; persecuted, but not abandoned; struck down, but not destroyed; always carrying about in the body the dying of Jesus, so that the life of Jesus may also be manifested in our body. For we who live are constantly being given up to death for the sake of Jesus so that the life of Jesus may be manifested in our mortal flesh" (2 Cor 4:7-11).

Thus, always and everywhere, God manifests divine power in a context of human weakness. The reason remains ever the same: We must learn that all spiritual strength comes from God alone and can be used only with divine help, "so that, as it is written, 'whoever boasts, should boast in the Lord'" (1 Cor 1:31).

Christian Unity with Christ

The shift of emphasis in First Corinthians from resurrection-parousia to death-resurrection is accompanied by new attention to the riches and requirements of Christian life *here on earth.* Succeeding letters will concentrate more and more on this, until, in the later captivity letters, Paul's attention rests almost entirely on the anticipated resurrection which union with Christ brings even in this life. But these subsequent developments are already contained substantially in the teaching of First Corinthians. There he writes of the Christian's present union with Christ and of the dynamic activity of the Spirit whom he bestows. "Avoid immorality," he demands. "Every other sin that a person commits is outside the body, but the immoral person sins against their own body. Do you not know that your body is the temple of the Holy Spirit within you whom you have from God, and that you are not your own? For you have been purchased at a price. Therefore glorify God in your body" (1 Cor 6:18-20).

This doctrine of First Corinthians, however, is not complete; it must be complemented by the teaching of Romans and Galatians. For, in these two letters, Paul penetrates the involvements and applications of union with Christ which come to the Christian through the Spirit at the moment of baptism.

To appreciate the doctrine of these letters, one must keep in mind that Paul is the "witness of the resurrection" par excellence. In his account before King Agrippa of the miraculous event on the day of his conversion, he recalls Christ's words, "I have appeared to you for this purpose, to appoint you as a servant and witness of what you have seen [of me] and what you will be shown" (Acts 26:16). Paul remained true to this awareness of the Savior. Christ was always, for him, someone present and living. His constant allusion to Christian life as life "in Christ" serves as the classic emblem of his own conviction that Christians have been incorporated by baptism into the body of the risen Christ.

Equally fundamental in his thought is the truth that Christ died and rose again, not merely as an individual but as the embodiment and representative of all people. The Hebrew conception of "corporate personality," essential for understanding Old Testament messianic prophecies, is essential also to Paul's concept of the role of Christ. Like Adam, Christ too is a "corporate personality," a new Adam. Paul writes: "For just as in Adam all die, so too in Christ shall all be brought to life. . . . Just as we have borne the image of the earthly one, we shall also bear the image of the heavenly one" (1 Cor 15:22, 49). Through the law of solidarity, Christ's death and resurrection are efficacious for all: "We have come to the conviction that one died for all; therefore, all have died" (2 Cor 5:14).

The efficacy of Christ's redemptive act takes effect in the individual through the rite of baptism which is at once "a tomb and a womb." At baptism, according to Paul's thought, the body-person of the

Christian is united to the body-person of Christ. [This doctrine has been explained in detail in Chapter 11.] Here we sense the physical realism of Old Testament thought which always considered the "body" not a part of the person, in contrast to the soul, but the whole person as a concrete reality. The body, consequently, has an important role in the Old Testament prophecies of the final salvation. In Paul's thought, therefore, baptismal union takes place between two real, physical persons, the individual Christian and the individual glorified Christ.

These factors serve to explain the Apostle's words on the union of the baptized with the death of Christ: "Are you unaware that we who were baptized into Christ Jesus were baptized into his death?" (Rom 6:3). In the simple realism of Paul's thought, baptism so unites the body-person of the Christian to the body-person of the glorious Christ that he, who died and rose again as a corporate personality, is able to share with his members the salvific effects of his death and resurrection.

DEAD TO SIN AND LIVING FOR GOD

For Paul, as C. H. Dodd expresses it in *The Epistle of Paul to the Romans,* "the whole sacrament is an act by which the believer enters into all that Christ did as our representative, in that he was delivered up for our sins and rose again for our justification." Paul explained what it meant to share through baptism in the effects of Calvary. Christians are freed from subjection to the law, from the shackles of the "body of sin," from servile obedience to the world, from the death of sin. In a word, they are liberated with the "freedom wherewith Christ has made us free" (Gal 4:31).

In order to understand Paul's conception of this truth and its application to Christian life, it is necessary to keep in mind an essential doctrine—that the death of Christ was a death of obedience and love. It brought an end to his bondage "in sinful flesh . . . under the law" (Rom 8:3). His death, however, was not merely a negation of contact with the world; it was prompted and accompanied by an interior act of consummate obedience to God and of ardent love for humankind inspired by the Holy Spirit. Christ's death was, above all else, a visible expression of the surrender of his whole humanity to the will of the Father who sent him to die out of love for all people (Rom 5:6-8). The dynamism of such a death, vital with love and obedience, could never die. Once he had passed through death and escaped the limitations of life on earth, this abiding spirit found full and necessary expression in the messianic glorification of the Savior rising from the dead. Far from being a mere extrinsic reward, Christ's glorious resurrection and salvific activity as messianic Son of God are the vital products and full flowering of the love and obedience which filled his soul in its passage through death.

This aspect of Christ's death-resurrection helps to explain a striking feature of St. Paul's doctrine on baptism. For him, sacramental death marks the point of departure for an altogether new life, in which the Christian ever remains "dead to sin and living for God" (Rom 6:11). This is possible only because, in baptism, the Christian shares the very Spirit of Christ which endures forever in the body-person to which the new member is united. If, therefore, baptismal incorporation brings death to the old life through the power of Christ's death, it is because the Spirit who prompted the loving obedience of his death now becomes active in the new member, transforming him radically from the carnal state of egoism to the spiritual state of God-mindedness. "Yet I live, no longer I, but Christ lives in me; insofar as I now live in the flesh, I live by faith in the Son of God who loved me and gave himself up for me" (Gal 2:20).

This concept of baptism influences the whole Pauline program of Christian life. Because the baptized always remain members of the body of Christ, the power of his Spirit is ever present to keep them centered in God and dead to sin and to self. Life in Christ requires this: "You too must think of yourselves as [being] dead to sin and living for God in Christ Jesus" (Rom 6:11).

The Gift of the Spirit and the Temptation of the Flesh

It is in chapter 8 of Romans that Paul penetrates deeply into the workings of this death principle. He makes clear that the Holy Spirit, received in baptism, is always active in Christians, guiding them with vital inspirations that deliver them from the tyranny of sin and death; for "the inclination of the Spirit is life and peace." Because the Spirit is the "Spirit of Christ," its every gift conforms the baptized to the image of the Son. This means that "they who are led by the Spirit are children of God"; for the Spirit infuses into them the Son's love for the Father. This love always inclines to the Father's will; and so, by its very nature, it is a principle of opposition to the "flesh." "The wisdom of the flesh is hostile to God, for it is not subject to the law of God, nor can it be." "Flesh," in Paul's language, includes everything in humankind hostile to God.

Flesh turns us from God, and leads to sin and death. But, by conserving and strengthening in the baptized the Son's love for his Father, the Spirit leads the Christian to wage ceaseless war on the deeds of the flesh. In every conscious act the Christian must continue, through the power of the Spirit, to sacrifice all resistance which still remains in the flesh. Hence Paul writes, "We are not debtors to the flesh, to live according to the flesh. For if you live according to the flesh, you will die, but if by the Spirit you put to death the deeds of the body, you will live" (Rom 8:12-13). It is this principle which gives originality to the moral and ascetical doctrine of St. Paul.

The Apostle treats the same theme in Galatians, where he clearly attributes to the activity of the Holy Spirit the elimination of all that is evil in Christ's members: "Live by the Spirit and you will certainly not gratify the desire of the flesh. . . . Those who belong to Christ [Jesus] have crucified their flesh with its passions and desires. If we live in the Spirit, let us also follow the Spirit" (Gal 5:16, 24-25). The word "crucified" is not a mere figure. Baptism gives a share in the death which loving fidelity to God's will produced in Christ, so that Paul could write, "I have been crucified with Christ" (Gal 2:19). This continuance of the baptismal contact with the risen Savior fills the member of his body with the strong love that crucifies whatever is hostile to the will of God.

Christian life, therefore, involves an enduring paradox. The Christian, on the one hand, lives on an eschatological plane, sharing the risen life of the Savior and his love for the Father. Paul writes in the name of every Christian, "I live, no longer I [now not I], but Christ lives in me" (Gal 2:20). On the other hand, the activity of the Holy Spirit has not yet transformed the whole of humankind, or the whole of our world. Therefore, the "now" of life upon earth combines the present temporal level with the final eschatological moment. As long as Christians are in the world they must carry a "body of death"; they are always able to "yield their members to sin as weapons of iniquity"; they are constantly surrounded by "the wisdom of the flesh that is hostile to God." Hence, though they have truly "clothed themselves with Christ" through baptism, a weakness is always present to solicit a return to the earthly ways of the old self.

BETWEEN THE ESCHATOLOGICAL AND THE TEMPORAL

Paul was vitally aware that in the present life the Christian shares only imperfectly in Christ's redemption. The Apostle, therefore, recognized a constant tension between the two orders, eschatological and temporal. This awareness is reflected in his letters; his language ceaselessly varies in them from the indicative mood of simple declaration, when he enunciates the truth that the Christian lives Christ's own life, to the imperative mood of command, when he urges his converts to fulfill the exigencies of the heavenly life. On the one hand, for example, he states the fact, "Our old self was crucified with him"; yet immediately he goes on to command, "Therefore, sin must not reign over your mortal bodies" (Rom 6:6, 12).

The actual process of dying is always a painful experience, for it involves separation from that to which nature clings. The death of Christ himself was painful beyond measure; he had come "in the likeness of sinful flesh" and underwent real suffering when he had to part with it, in passing through the door of death to heavenly life. Once his passion was over and he had risen from the tomb, this "death was swallowed up in victory" (1 Cor 15:54); for the love and obedience that filled his soul in the moment of death gained power to effect every good. In the application of this efficacy to his members upon earth, however, Christ must often renew the painful experience of mortal suffering. It is characteristic of his Spirit to separate his members from whatever does not accord with God's will—even though it be something as intimate as one's own "flesh" and as homelike as the "world." The daily "dying" of the Christian, therefore, is a prolongation of Christ's own death, just as the abnegation characteristic of Christian service is truly a sacrifice. Such experiences renew in the member that state of death which love and obedience produced in Christ. It is his Spirit, received in baptism, who inspires and rules all.

In Romans and Galatians, Paul affirms an intimate bond between the death of Christ and the inevitable conflict and suffering in each Christian's life. This bond rests on the truth, often repeated in these letters, that the principle of death in both cases is one and the same. Because they are intimately united by baptism as body and member, both Christ and the Christian share the same Holy Spirit whose activity inspires the death which loving obedience to God enjoins.

A study of the doctrine on suffering in Romans and Galatians must take into account Paul's statement in chapter 8 of Romans. In these verses he brings together the theme of Romans on union with Christ in suffering and an earlier theme of Thessalonians, union with him in the eschatological tribulation.

This text concludes Paul's analysis of the death principle which the baptized receives from Christ. Paul has identified it as the activity of the Holy Spirit, who infuses the life and love of the glorious Son of God, putting to death all that is inimical to God's will and insuring by his very presence the certainty of glorious resurrection. Paul then describes this *terminus* of Christian experience: "The Spirit itself bears witness with our spirit that we are children of God, and if children, then heirs, heirs of God and joint heirs with Christ, if only we suffer with him so that we may also be glorified with him. I consider that the sufferings of this present time are as nothing compared with the glory to be revealed for us" (Rom 8:16-18).

JOINT HEIRS WITH CHRIST

The thought here is clear enough. Christian adoption, Paul asserts, leads inevitably to full reward through the sufferings which are intimately connected with life in Christ. He has already introduced in chapter 5 the theme of tribulation, as it develops virtue and leads to glory through the activity of the Holy Spirit. Now, in chapter 8 he analyses the contents of this earlier statement and shows that Christian suffering, which has its source in the Spirit's constant war on the flesh, is the necessary consequence of all union with Christ. Furthermore, Paul carefully identifies the "sufferings of this present time" with the tribulations which precede the final, eschatological coming of the Lord. This quasi-technical expression in the Pauline vocabulary—sufferings *of this present time*—refers to the period of tension and trial between the two appearances of Christ. As the Apostle has shown before and as he repeats here, the share which the Christian has in the messianic trials insures an even greater share in the messianic reward.

Because Paul describes the "sufferings of this present time" as a "suffering with Christ," the question arises, what is the nature and measure of the Christian's union with Christ while that person passes through the tribulations which Christ's death inaugurated?

As it stands, the term "suffering with" could be interpreted as focusing attention on a bond between the sufferings of Christians and the *historical* passion of the Savior. Though the Apostle has spoken of such a bond in First Thessalonians, he has left this theme undeveloped in his following letters. Indeed, the only feature of Christ's earthly life on which he centers attention is his death—and this because it constituted, with the resurrection, the unique cause of salvation. Hence, in treating this death he does not ordinarily delay over external aspects but views it constantly in its redemptive role. He sees it, on the one hand, as the necessary counterpart of the resurrection. Christ's passage from this world made possible his full messianic activity of Savior. On the other, he traces the involvements of Christ's death in the lives of his members; they share its efficacy through the activity of the Holy Spirit. As James Moffatt observes in *The First Epistle of St. Paul to the Corinthians,* "For the Apostle, what was vital was not the Lord as a heroic individual; it was Christ dying and rising as one who bore in his own person the destiny of God's chosen people, Christ living as the Lord and Spirit in whom they actually shared and reproduced his death and resurrection within their own experience."

This estimate of Paul's doctrine is particularly relevant in interpreting the phrase "suffering with," or, as the Greek expresses it, *sym-paschomen*, "co-suffering." All similar compounds, in fact, referring directly to union between the Christian and Christ, must be similarly interpreted: co-dying; co-buried; co-rejoicing. It is noteworthy that the Apostle limits these expressions to union with Christ in the salvific mysteries of his death and risen life; he never extends this phraseology to the incidents of the Savior's earthly life, so as to speak of co-praying with Christ, co-fasting, or co-conquering temptation. This significant restriction is consonant with the whole burden of Paul's doctrine in Romans and Galatians. In these letters he teaches that baptism, by uniting the Christian to the Savior, confers a share in his death-resurrection. This union constitutes the essential redemptive experience of Christ the "corporate personality." Life begins with baptism, what happened before that moment matters little.

A SHARE ALSO IN SALVATION

Thus, the Christian is not only *in* Christ but also dies and lives *with* him. It is this latter aspect which finds rich expression in Paul's writing. We have already seen that it is the Spirit, received in baptism, who makes the Christian die to all that is apart from God; like Christ and in Christ, the Christian lives unto God. Hence, because both body and member share the same principle of life and death, Paul not only claims for Christ all that his member is and has, but he also attributes to the member a true share in the salvific death-resurrection of the Savior.

This must be kept in mind in analyzing the phrase "we co-suffer *with* him." To interpret the term, as some have done, as affirming primarily an identity or bond of *resemblance* between Christian suffering and the suffering of the passion does not accord with Paul's many uses of this compound: *co*-dying; *co*-buried. Paul consistently applies these expressions to inner union with Christ's death-resurrection in their salvific efficacy. Moreover, references to the historical sufferings of Christ are so incidental and so apart from the consistent Pauline motif of death-resurrection that their presence does not suffice to alter the obvious Paulinism of Romans 8:17: If we co-suffer, we will also be co-glorified.

The denial that the historical sufferings of Christ are the primary term of reference does not exclude this reference altogether. The fact is that Paul's thought includes, by implication, a bond of resemblance between Christian suffering and the Savior's passion. For Christian suffering flows from the presence in the individual of the Holy Spirit and so is always characterized by the fruits of that person's activity: charity, joy, peace, patience (Gal 5:22). Paul, accordingly, has explicitly pointed out that Christians must manifest the dispositions of Christ in meeting the trials of life. He has also expressed the desire that "the endurance of Christ" may characterize the sufferings of his converts (2 Thess 3:5). He was certainly aware, therefore, of the bond of resemblance between Christians and the suffering Christ; and he has spoken of this in his letter to the Thessalonians: "You became imitators . . . of the Lord, receiving the word in great affliction, with joy from the Holy Spirit" (1 Thess 1:6).

This theme, however, does not come to the fore in the death-resurrection couplet of Romans 8:17-18. Here, he merely repeats what he has developed earlier: Christians, because they are incorporated into the body of Christ, share not only his life but also his death (Rom 6). It must be noted, nonetheless, that the juxtaposition of verses 17 and 18 adds a real contribution. Each verse sheds light upon the other. "If children, then heirs, heirs of God and joint heirs with Christ, if only we suffer with him so that we may also be glorified with him. I consider that the sufferings of this present time are as nothing compared with the glory to be revealed for us." The second verse with its rich background in First and Second Thessalonians, shows how real the trials involved in suffering with Christ are; the other verse stresses the intimate bond which unites the Christian to Christ. The Christian today undergoes the tribulations of the final messianic age, an age which opened with the Savior's death. Through this juxtaposition of themes, the divine plan of messianic reward through messianic suffering finds its due place in the Christology which dominates all of Paul's thought.

SECOND CORINTHIANS: PAUL'S OWN STORY

In the highly personal Second Letter to the Corinthians, Paul does not enunciate new themes; but, as a master in complete possession of the doctrine affirmed in the other great letters, he shows the vital influence of these principles, especially in the apostolate. The attack of critics upon his apostolic authority and his mode of procedure as a minister of the gospel forced him to reflect on the antinomy of his public life. In every respect it manifested both divine force and human weakness. He treats this theme from every angle in the two apologetic sections: 1:12–7:17 and chapters 10–13. Apostolic labor, like Christian life itself, must follow the rule of thumb for all divine activity: power through weakness so that all glory may belong to God alone.

Throughout this letter, Paul constantly emphasizes that, though the apostle is the bearer of God's power, this treasure is held in an earthen vessel. Apostolic life involves struggle and suffering; it leads to inward tension and outward persecution. Paul's own endeavor to bring the light of God to all people involved a corresponding experience of human weakness. This aspect of his apostolate had been foretold of him from the beginning; the Lord said to Ananias: "I will show him what he will have to suffer for my name" (Acts 9:16). And suffer he did. "Whoever would write the story of Paul the apostle," as J. Schneider observes, "must write the story of his sufferings." His intimate self-revelation in Second Corinthians is a tale of suffering from within and from without. Yet so certain was Paul that this weakness was the human concomitant of divine power acting in him and through him, that the experience of human limitations was for him a cause of joy: "About myself I will not boast, except about my weaknesses" (2 Cor 12:5).

He recounts a personal experience in which God himself confirmed the conviction that divine power works through human frailty. Paul was suffering from a "thorn in the flesh" and prayed for deliverance. God answered: "My grace is sufficient for you, for power is made perfect in weakness." Paul draws the obvious conclusion in words which echo chapter 1 of First Corinthians: "I will rather boast most gladly of my weaknesses, in order that the power of Christ may dwell in me. Therefore, I am content with weaknesses, insults, hardships, persecutions, and constraints, for the sake of Christ; for when I am weak, then I am strong" (2 Cor 12:9-10). In this letter, he also sums up in a brief statement the teaching that Christ himself had to follow the pattern which marks all divine activity—power through weakness:

"For indeed he was crucified out of weakness, but he lives by the power of God" (2 Cor 13:4).

Divine Encouragement in the Face of Affliction

But in Second Corinthians Paul does more than merely reiterate and apply the "power-weakness" theme of the first letter. He here unites to it the vivid coloring of the principles enunciated in Romans and Galatians on the union of the Christian with Christ. Several passages are noteworthy. The first of these passages is 2 Corinthians 1:3-7:

> Blessed be the God and Father of our Lord Jesus Christ, the Father of compassion and God of all encouragement, who encourages us in our every affliction, so that we may be able to encourage those who are in any affliction with the encouragement with which we ourselves are encouraged by God. For as Christ's sufferings overflow to us, so through Christ does our encouragement also overflow. If we are afflicted, it is for encouragement and salvation; if we are encouraged, it is for your encouragement, which enables you to endure the same sufferings that we suffer. Our hope for you is firm, for we know that as you share in the sufferings, you also share in the encouragement.

Paul here repeats the familiar theme that afflictions abound in Christian life, and especially in the apostolic ministry. In accord, however, with the fundamental antithesis of death-resurrection, he affirms that such suffering brings its corresponding measure of comfort: "As Christ's sufferings overflow to us, so through Christ does our encouragement also overflow." Such encouragement, it must be noted, is not merely personal; whatever the apostle experiences is of benefit to his converts. "If we are afflicted . . . [or] if we are encouraged," all serves to strengthen the Corinthians for the endurance of the same sufferings which the apostles sustain. Paul, therefore, is confident that because the Corinthians share his sufferings, they will share also the encouragement which he has received.

The trials and sufferings of which he speaks are those that afflict both the apostle and his converts in the first days of a Christian community, for the Corinthians are true sharers in the tribulations which the founder of their Church endures. He describes his apostolic sufferings, in which the Corinthians share, as the "sufferings of Christ." It seems unlikely that the phrase refers only to an *extrinsic* bond based on

Christ's command or the exigencies of his service. Rather, the dominance in Paul's doctrine of the *intrinsic* bond between the Christian and Christ strongly suggests that this expression contains richer meaning.

The Corinthians truly belong to Christ who, through his Spirit, is the efficient principle of all Christian experience in the lives of his members. This aspect, which is the immediate consequence of baptismal union with Christ, is the quality which gives richest value to the sufferings of both apostle and converts. Indeed, it is because the *sharing of their sufferings* is really a *sharing of the sufferings of Jesus* that Paul applies the death-resurrection theme of all his thought to establish the certainty that consolation will follow upon trials.

It is legitimate to conclude, therefore, that 2 Corinthians 1:3-7 belongs to the thought-pattern already enunciated in Romans: "If children, then heirs: heirs of God and joint heirs with Christ, if only we suffer with him so that we may also be glorified with him." Both passages affirm an objective and necessary bond between suffering-consolation and suffering-glory. At the same time, these passages refer the trials of Christians directly to Christ, calling them "the sufferings of Christ" and "suffering with Christ." The parallelism of these texts emphasizes that Paul sees verified through the whole course of Christian life the union with Christ in his death-resurrection which was first realized through baptism. Baptismal union between the body and its members necessarily involves a life process. The Holy Spirit leads the Christian to renew constantly the death of Christ in order to continue living with his life. It is with this context in mind, therefore, that Paul speaks of Christian trials as "the suffering of Christ."

The Paradox of Christian Life

Another striking example of the death-life theme is in chapter 4 of Second Corinthians. Paul has just spoken of the light which he received as an apostle to communicate to others. He goes on to affirm that the power of his ministry is wholly God's, for the elements of his own temporal life contribute little to its efficacy. "We hold this treasure in earthen vessels, that the surpassing power may be of God and not from us." His own experience made him vitally aware of this duality: "In all things we suffer tribulation, but we are not distressed; we are sore pressed, but we are not destitute; we endure persecution, but we are not forsaken; we are cast down, but we do not perish." His interpretation of the profound meaning of these vicissitudes is significant. He traces these antitheses to his union with Christ, whose death is the source of apostolic suffering and whose life is the source of apostolic strength. For he sums up all by portraying apostles as "always bearing about in our body the dying of Jesus, so that the life also of Jesus may be made manifest in our bodily frame. For we the living are constantly being handed over to death for Jesus' sake, that the life also of Jesus may be made manifest in our mortal flesh."

These words indicate that more than an external bond links the human weakness and suffering of the apostles to Christ. The daily trials of apostolic life borne for Christ are identified as a bearing about of "the dying of Jesus." This latter expression refers to the state of death which is the enduring effect of baptismal death with Christ. This Paul has already indicated in chapter 6 of Romans where he stated that those who have sacramentally died with Christ must ever after consider themselves dead. Because this state of death involves a constant dying to the deeds of the flesh, it issues necessarily in the activity of self-denial and mortification. But, whether considered in its primary meaning as a passive state of death or in its derived sense of active mortification, this "dying" of the Christian is truly that of Christ, because his Spirit is the effective principle who constantly renews the Savior's death in all the members of his body.

In these verses Paul also states in parallel clauses that the suffering of the apostolic life is inseparably connected with the Apostle's manifestation of the life of Christ: "in order that the life also of Jesus may be manifest." Paul speaks here of the actual effects of the labor and suffering of his apostolate. For the manifestation of life takes place in an earthly state and benefits the Corinthians in the present life. The force of the verb "to be made manifest" cannot be overlooked. Though scarcely appearing outside the New Testament, it shows there an almost technical meaning, referring to the first or second coming of Christ, with faithful disciples sharing his glory. Its use in the present case expresses the truth that the life which the apostle diffuses is the life of the risen Christ, "the power of his resurrection." At the same time it suggests that apostolic activity is an anticipated share in the resurrection.

In Paul's eyes, the apostolate is but an extension to others of the life of Christ who already lives in his apostle. Its purpose is to form Christ in all people, that he may live in them just as he lives in Paul. Apostolic labor, therefore, follows the same law that governs the personal development of every Christian: life accompanied by death. Paul expressed the pattern of apostolic life this way: "Death is at work in us, but life in you."

In the apostolate, the "zone of fulfillment" for Christ's power is enlarged. This means an equally extensive zone of opposition. The apostle has to enter into conflict with a wider "world"; that one must "crucify" sin and the hostile flesh in the life of every convert. All this involves struggle and suffering, which Paul can truly call the "dying of Jesus," since he who dwells in the apostle and acts upon him through his Holy Spirit provides the effective principle for such struggle. To make Christ live in all converts, therefore, the apostle has to endure the death that Christ underwent to share his life with the world. The principle of death is always one and the same; only the time and manner of its application differs.

The Psychological Aspect of Christian Unity

A few verses later in chapter 4 of Second Corinthians, Paul presents another aspect—the psychological—of the union between Christ and his members. Though it is true that Paul does not here speak explicitly of suffering, he brings into sharp focus, nonetheless, the active, psychological influence of the principle which accounts for all Christian suffering.

In the other great letters Paul has already shown why all Christians must endure trial and struggle; through the indwelling of Christ's Spirit they share ontologically in the dynamic love-principle of Christ's activity. He now affirms that the very love which the Savior manifested in his life and ministry and which he now continues in his glorious life provides, also, the dynamic psychological impulse of the Christian apostolate: "The love of Christ impels us, once we have come to the conviction that . . . he indeed died for all, so that those who live might no longer live for themselves but for him who for their sake died and was raised" (2 Cor 5:14-15).

Such fullness of ontological and psychological sharing in the inward spirit of the Savior is required by the very nature of the apostolate, for both Christ and his apostle are engaged in the same work of reconciliation under the guiding inspiration of God's love: "All this is from God, who has reconciled us to himself through Christ and given us the ministry of reconciliation, namely, God was reconciling the world to himself in Christ. . . . so we are ambassadors for Christ, as if God were appealing through us" (2 Cor 5:18-20). This charge and its motivation in love flow from the inward bond between Christ and his members, the bond to which Paul has attributed the whole of Christian suffering.

The same thought of union with Christ in his death-resurrection underlies one of the concluding passages of Second Corinthians. "Since you are looking for Christ speaking in me," Paul states, "he is not weak toward you but powerful in you. For indeed he was crucified out of weakness, but he lives by the power of God. So also we are weak in him, but toward you we shall live with him by the power of God" (2 Cor 13:3-4).

THE LAW OF CHRISTIAN LIFE

Paul here stabilizes the "power-weakness" theme of First Corinthians as the law of Christian life; he also identifies it with the intrinsic bond which unites Christians to Christ and gives them a share in his death-life.

Paul deals with the antinomy of his ministry: Though personally weak, he is conscious of bearing the power of Christ. Such an experience is inevitable. For the Savior himself had to follow the law that governs all divine activity in this world: "He was crucified out of weakness, but he lives by the power of God." Therefore Paul, too, must follow this rule, not merely because it is a law of God's salvific activity, but especially because he lives by the very principle that produces death-life in both the body and its members. Whatever weakness or power the apostle experiences in doing God's work, all is both "in Christ" and *with him* through "the power of God."

This passage is a particularly felicitous conclusion to Second Corinthians, since it blends so well the themes of the two preceding letters. It offers a consummate apologia for the "weakness" of the apostolic ministry. It shows that the "power-weakness" theme of all God's activity applies with special force to the Christian, who, through intimate union with Christ, shares the death-life principle which leads both the body and the member through suffering to glory.

THE LATER LETTERS

The study of Paul's teaching on suffering in his later captivity and pastoral letters strongly corroborates the thesis that, in composing First Corinthians, Galatians, Romans and Second Corinthians, he was already in possession of the basic tenets of his full doctrine. The later letters to Timothy and Titus or to the Colossians and Ephesians make essentially no new contribution. Written in face of new developments and new problems in the community, they merely give fresh expression or application to doctrine which he had previously taught. This assertion is pointedly true of his teaching on Christian suffering, which is limited in extent and almost commonplace when compared with his treatment of this theme in Second Corinthians.

An apothegm in Second Timothy recalls substantially an earlier statement on the inevitability of suffering in Christian life. "All who want to live religiously in Christ Jesus," Paul wrote to Timothy, "will be persecuted" (2 Tim 3:12). Such struggle is represented as the consequence of the Christian's share in the life and power of Christ, for to live with him means to die to all that is hostile to God. This principle, as applied to baptism in Romans, is echoed in Colossians, where the sacramental death of baptism is called "the circumcision of Christ" and consists in putting off the "body of flesh" through incorporation into Christ who died in his "body of flesh" to save us (Col 2:11).

The consequent lifelong war against the flesh which faces every Christian is proposed anew in Colossians and Ephesians. This struggle, as we read in Second Timothy, is particularly acute in the lives of apostles. The power of Christ, however, can always be counted on to sustain loyalty and to strengthen patience. Endured in this spirit, suffering is a true favor from God. From the beginning of his ministry to its close, Paul saw in Christian trials a preparation for and a guarantee of heavenly reward. Near the moment of "being poured out in sacrifice," Paul wrote to Timothy: "I have competed well; I have finished the race; I have kept the faith. From now on the crown of righteousness awaits me, which the Lord, the just judge, will award to me on that day, and not only to me, but to all who have longed for his appearance" (2 Tim 4:7-8).

"The Afflictions of Christ"

Thus, the teaching of the captivity and pastoral letters is thoroughly consonant with Paul's previous doctrine. There is one statement in the Letter to the Colossians, however, which calls for special study.

Colossians 1:24 has a certain mysteriousness due in great part to the uncertain meaning of the phrase which Paul employs. It reads: "Now I rejoice in my sufferings for your sake, and in my flesh I am filling up what is lacking in the afflictions of Christ on behalf of his body, which is the Church."

In the first part of this verse, Paul declares that he rejoices in the sufferings which he bears for the Colossians. Here we meet elements which are frequent in Paul's writings. He has often mentioned the suffering he endured for his converts, and he has spoken of joy in suffering as a characteristic trait of all Christian spirituality.

The second part of the verse makes specific reference to his teaching on the Church as the body of Christ, for he expands the limited phrase "for your sake" into the wider one "for his body, which is the Church."

The fundamental question, however, centers in what Paul means by the phrase: "the afflictions of Christ." He has consistently spoken of the afflictions of *Christians;* never, except in four passages, has he joined the word to Christ's name (Col 1:24; Rom 8:17-18; 2 Cor 1:4-5; 4:8, 10). Never, in fact, has any form of this expression been employed by Paul to refer to any aspect of Christ's earthly life. This is especially significant in view of the frequency with which he employs it to designate the sufferings of Christians. Finally, as we have seen, there is nothing in the immediate context or in the background of Pauline doctrine to urge the interpretation of "the afflictions of Christ" as referring primarily to a bond between Paul's trials and the historical sufferings of the passion. Paul's phraseology finds full explanation in the light of his earlier doctrine on baptismal union with Christ. Because Christ is the Body in which the member lives and functions, his Spirit is the principle of all death-life and the prime mover in all Christian struggle. It is, above all, under this aspect that the trials of the Christian, and especially of an apostle, are the "afflictions of Christ."

There is nothing to indicate that Paul means anything else in Colossians 1:24. The immediate context of this verse is typically Pauline, while the verse itself seems to be inserted almost as a casual aside in the development of Paul's thought. It is not likely that a sentence, so incidental to his theme, would contain a new truth which he has never affirmed before. On the contrary, the verse bears marked resemblance to earlier texts and admits an interpretation thoroughly consonant with his usual doctrine. He has constantly asserted that the apostolate involves both a work to be done and sufferings to be borne if the body of Christ is to be built up and the life of Christ to be diffused to new members. But, as there is a term to the development of the body of Christ, so there is a corresponding exigency to supply what is still lacking in apostolic labor and suffering. As a minister of the gospel, Paul has received the commission to fulfill this need by preaching and by suffering. Such apostolic labor and trials are truly the "afflictions of Christ" because they are endured in his service and because his Spirit is the life-principle of his members.

The Heart of Pauline Doctrine

A long search through the writings of St. Paul brings us now to the heart of his doctrine on Christian suffering. We read in his letter to the Philippians: ". . . to know him and the power of his resurrection and [the] sharing of his sufferings" (Phil 3:10).

The very word order of this verse parallels the events of his conversion, as set down in Acts. Its first element was his meeting with the risen Christ on the road to Damascus. This contact illumined his mind and aroused the first stirrings of new life; in shining truth, Paul came "to know Christ in the power of his resurrection." But, immediately after this experience, he learned that suffering was to fill his life: "I will show him what he will have to suffer for my name." His surrender to the risen Christ, although life-giving, involved also a share of suffering. In the story of his conversion, therefore, two elements are essential: vivifying contact with the Lord of glory and a declaration of the necessity of suffering. In the order of actual occurrence, the first preceded the second.

Paul's aim in Philippians, however, is not merely to summarize the incidents of his conversion. He is here writing an apologia for Christianity itself so that, although he speaks of his own conversion, he brings to light the excelling "gains" of which every Christian can boast. Paul understood well that his "I" is the "I" of every Christian and that the new life which he received through conversion is the same reality which every Christian possesses through baptism. He speaks, moreover, of the benefits of life in Christ from the vantage point of rich experience and mature understanding.

THE "GAIN" OF CHRISTIAN LIFE

It is clear from the climactic rise in the verses that Paul singles out the parousia-resurrection as the ultimate "gain" dominating all motives, ". . . to know him and the power of his resurrection and [the] sharing of his sufferings by being conformed to his death, if somehow I may attain the resurrection from the dead" (Phil 3:10-11).

Hope for final union with Christ has been a theme throughout the whole letter. To reach this union necessitates previous labor and suffering. The Jews, with their doctrine of the messianic tribulations, recognized that one attained to glory only through suffering. For Paul, to attain the ultimate Christian reward, one had to live and to suffer in the Christian way. The "gain" of Christianity consisted not only in the excelling *end* at which it aimed—resurrection in and with Christ—but also in the excelling *way* whereby it reached that goal—life in and with Christ.

A Christian enters on this way through conversion-baptism. At that moment, the new member is united to the body of Christ and receives the gift of the Spirit. The Spirit vivifies what was dead by infusing the very life of the risen Christ which will one day manifest its full vitality in the parousia-resurrection. As with Paul on the way to Damascus, so too with the Christian in baptism, the first "gain" of conversion is "to know Christ in the power of his resurrection."

But there is another essential "gain" which Paul describes as "the sharing of his sufferings." To urge his converts to firmness in the faith, Paul reminds them that their suffering is a sign of salvation, for it is a gift of God like faith itself. There is no question that he sees a strongly active element in the suffering of which he speaks. For he has previously described the activity of the Philippians as a worthy strife and immediately afterwards explains their suffering with the parallel phrase, "yours is the same struggle."

"Sharing of his sufferings," therefore, could be interpreted as referring to the Christian's share in the passion of Christ. As we have already seen, however, Paul has spoken so rarely of a parallelism between Christian suffering and the historical sufferings of Christ, that it does not seem likely he would highlight such a feature in this condensed statement of the essential elements of Christian life. The reproduction in the Christian of the historical sufferings of Christ, whether by mystical identity or by physical similarity, can hardly be called an essential or even primary element in Pauline doctrine.

On the other hand, the phrase, "sharing of his sufferings," could refer to sufferings that are borne for Christ, in his cause. But to limit the content of the phrase to this meaning alone—that is, to a merely external bond between Christian suffering and Christ—does not accord with the demands of Pauline thought. Paul is here speaking of life in Christ and of the fullness of its "gains." He has just referred to the activity of the Holy Spirit which constitutes the "power of Christ's resurrection"; immediately afterwards he speaks of conformity to Christ's death which leads to resurrection from the dead, a conformity which is effected by the Spirit of Christ working within the baptized. Both of these themes are related essentially to Paul's rich concept of life in Christ. It seems likely, therefore, that the intermediary phrase is also of the same nature.

This inference is wholly consonant with a truth that has emerged clearly from our review of Paul's doctrine: the truth, namely, that Christian suffering has deep theological roots in his teaching on union with Christ. This doctrine, as we have seen, supposes that every Christian receives at baptism the efficacy of the salvific death and resurrection once accomplished in the body of Christ to which the Christian is now united: "Are you unaware that we who were baptized into Christ Jesus were baptized into his death?" (Rom 6:3). This "gain" of Christian life may be viewed both as it exists in the first moment of conversion when it is simply life-with-Christ, and also as it exists in the lifelong process of preparation for the ultimate goal of parousia-resurrection. When Paul speaks of this second aspect, he always sees it as a process involving trial and suffering. For, after baptism, the Christian must continue to live in the "flesh" and to deal with the "world," both of which form an ambient hostile to the love of God and the life of the Spirit. If, therefore, the members of Christ are to live the risen life of the Savior, they must be crucified to the "world"; they must put to death the "deeds of the flesh." In a word, baptismal death with Christ must be renewed constantly throughout earthly life if one is finally to attain the ultimate goal of parousia-resurrection with Christ.

CONCLUSION

The "gain" of Paul's conversion, therefore, and of every Christian in baptism, consists not merely in momentary death with Christ, but in the fact that it inaugurates a lifelong *state of death,* through the power of the Spirit, to the world, to the flesh, and to sin, both in Paul's own life and in the lives of all whom he must gain for Christ. This Christian experience constitutes the *sharing of his sufferings.*

This phrase means, undoubtedly, that such suffering is borne for Christ and is incurred in laboring for his cause. It means, too, that such suffering is supported in the spirit of his virtues. But, according to the rich Pauline concept, all this is true because the bond between Christian suffering and Christ himself is rooted in the bond that unites body and member. Such suffering is truly "Christ's," because the love which impelled him to die is the very same love which the Spirit infuses into his members, so that they die daily to all that is opposed to God.

It is significant that Paul speaks here of "knowing the sharing of his sufferings" rather than simply "knowing his sufferings." The word "sharing" introduces into this phrase the spirit of the whole letter. Throughout, he has shown himself vitally conscious of the part which all Christians play in working and suffering for the gospel; several times, in fact, he has used the word "sharing" to express the close bond that unites them and to describe the share which the Philippians have contributed. Now, in 3:10, with graceful allusion to the part which his converts play, Paul speaks of his sufferings as a sharing of Christ's immense suffering. For truly his own daily experiences of "dying" formed but a share of the vast *sufferings of Christ* which all Christians, and especially apostolic laborers, must bear in order to bring the body of Christ to full measure.

"Sharing in Christ's sufferings" is, therefore, a reality in all Christian living. If Paul here refers the phrase to himself, it is because every Christian can make the same boast and must follow the same example. For everyone life in Christ is vital with the activity of the Holy Spirit who daily renews in the members of Christ's body the love and obedience which inspired the Savior to undergo the passage of death. This experience involves every Christian in a crisscross of two levels—life in Christ and life in the flesh. Tension and struggle are inevitable. But always the resultant suffering is truly a share in the *suffering of Christ*, for the glorious Savior claims as his own the sufferings which the dynamic presence of his Spirit occasions in his members.

CHAPTER 22

The Death of Jesus and the Birth of a New World: Matthew's Theology of History in the Passion Narrative

Donald Senior, C.P.

Barnabas Ahern, C.P., was my teacher and provided much of the inspiration for my own commitment to biblical scholarship. It is with a sense of gratitude and no little poignancy that I take up the topic of this chapter.

In the turbulent and wonderful years since Vatican II, an event on which Barnabas left a significant mark, the link between experience and theology has become a rallying cry. The most recent and most forceful proponents of that link have come from churches and theologians who know the bitter reality of chronic economic and political oppression. Such Christians have reminded the whole Church that a theology not rooted in experience or praxis or one not capable of informing experience is not a theology worth retaining.

Most of Barnabas' writings antedate the flowering of liberation theology. But his biblical interpretation was characterized by a strong link between Christian life and its intellectual reflection. His involvement in the Vatican Council and his devoted promulgation of the biblical renewal flowed from his deep love for the Church and his conviction that theology and theologians should be at the service of God's people. It was his destiny to serve the Church at a time of extraordinary transition whose reverberations we still experience. He played a significant role in helping a new Church to birth and personally experienced both the joys and anxieties of that birthing.

All of this leads me to honor Barnabas by reflecting on the passion narrative of Matthew's Gospel. Matthew's church, too, had experienced change without precedent and the passion story helped his community put that change into a perspective of faith. As a devout Christian and as a Passionist, Barnabas reflected constantly on the sufferings of Christ and wrote and spoke about the passion throughout his active ministry. In his memory, I dedicate this reflection on the passion story in Matthew's Gospel.

THE JEWISH-CHRISTIAN COMMUNITY OF MATTHEW'S GOSPEL

The passion narrative of Matthew holds a commanding position in the Gospel narrative and proclaims some of Matthew's most important theological motifs. I would like to focus on one that may have particular significance at this turbulent stage in our world history, namely, Matthew's affirmation that through the death and tragedy of the passion a new age and a new people are born.

Much recent scholarship has concentrated on deciphering the relationship of Matthew's community to Judaism. A generation ago, W. D. Davies' magistral work on the Sermon on the Mount understood Matthew as a Christian response to the Jewish reform movement of Jamnia, as Judaism attempted to redefine itself in the wake of the Jewish revolt and the destruction of Jerusalem in A.D. 70. More recent interpreters, such as Alan F. Segal, have added nuance to this thesis, suggesting that the evidence for a clearly defined and formal "reform movement" at Jamnia is less compelling than once thought. Yet few scholars would deny that Matthew is concerned to understand the vital relationship between his Christian community and its roots in Judaism. That concern was undoubtedly intensified by growing tension and bitter disputes between Matthew's Jewish Christian community and at least some important groups within Judaism. Matthew, indeed, according to J. Andrew Overman and others, may have thought of his community and its emerging Christian heritage as the truly faithful way of Israel—thus the Gospel's perspective is not that of an "outsider" looking in (i.e., between distinct "Christian" and "Jewish" perspectives) but of an internecine struggle for identity within Judaism itself. Only later would a decisive rupture occur.

What is clear in all of this is that Jesus' rejection by a significant portion of the Jewish religious leadership and the subsequent apparent failure of the Christian movement to persuade the majority of Jews about the validity of Christian faith in Christ became for Matthew's Christians not simply a difficult historical experience but a profound religious issue. Ulrich Luz, in his recent major commentary, states that Matthew's Gospel is best understood "not (as) a Christian answer to 'Jamnia' but a Christian answer to Israel's rejection of Jesus, an attempt to understand this 'no' from a fundamental perspective." Precisely because of their adherence to the sacred heritage of Judaism, Matthew's Christians found rejection and censure by the teachers of Israel difficult and that experience gives the Gospel's portrayal of the Jewish leaders its bitter edge.

At the same time, Matthew's Jewish Christians had to grapple with another unexpected turn in history. A growing number of Gentiles were attracted to the Gospel and entering the community. As we know from Paul's letters and the traditions in Acts, this influx was a source of consternation for some Jewish Christians. On what terms were the Gentiles to be accepted and how much of the Jewish law would be required? The overall thrust of Matthew's narrative, with its affirmation that Jesus' ministry was initially confined to Israel (10:5; 15:24) and yet in the final resurrection appearance open to the nations (28:16-20), evidently intends to provide some perspective on this issue.

Thus, the challenge for Matthew's community was to establish its own self-identity, not in the serenity of peaceful discussion but in the crucible of rejection, suffering, and unexpected change. As Gregory Stanton writes, Matthew's Gospel is a "foundation document" for his readers, attempting in part to assist his Jewish Christian community grasp their self-identity in a time of profound change.

The passion story plays a capital role in all of this. It is obviously the end result and climax of the opposition that Jesus meets in his ministry. Yet, precisely at the same time that one dream appears to die, a new people and a new age are born. As Jesus breathes his last breath in crucifixion, the old world is torn asunder and the dead rise again while a Gentile soldier and his company acclaim Jesus as God's Son (27:51-55).

A study of Matthew's passion narrative clearly shows that these are the major and characteristic concerns of the evangelist. The Gospel of Matthew and its passion narrative contain a rich and varied message, not reducible to a single dominant motif. Yet an analysis of Matthew's literary activity in the passion story demonstrates that the rejection of Jesus by Israel and the death of Jesus as marking a new moment in history are his trademarks.

Both redaction criticism with its attention to sources and the evangelist's editorial characteristics and more recent literary critical methods which emphasize the narrative unity of the Gospel help at this point. The passion stories of Mark and Matthew are strikingly similar. Most scholars contend that Matthew used Mark's Gospel as one of his major sources. Assuming this to be the case, the vast majority of Matthew's "interventions" in the Markan narrative are precisely around the issues we have noted. And the themes that dominate in the passion story find their root and development throughout the "plot" of Matthew's Gospel.

THE REJECTION OF JESUS BY ISRAEL

Opposition to Jesus begins long before the passion narrative. In Matthew's infancy narrative "all of Jerusalem" is frightened by the Magi's report of the star (2:3) and, while "all the chief priests and scribes" are able to brief Herod on the location of Jesus' birth in Bethlehem, they do not offer homage to the new king as the foreigners are determined to do (2:4-6).

Opposition breaks out in the open during Jesus' public ministry. The leaders take offense at some of his healings (9:3) and his association with sinners (9:11). Hostility seems to increase as Jesus' ministry continues; Jesus is branded as being in league with the prince of demons (12:24) and validating signs are demanded of him (12:38; 16:1). He and his disciples are accused of "breaking the tradition of the elders" (15:2). The Pharisees begin a plot to destroy him (12:14).

On his part, Jesus denounces the leaders as "hypocrites" whose piety is a sham (6:1-18). They are part of an "evil and adulterous generation" (12:39) and are filled with "evil spirits" (12:45).

By the time Jesus reaches Jerusalem and encounters the "chief priests and elders of the people" this opposition has reached the boiling point. The discourse in chapter 23 of Matthew's Gospel is a scorching indictment of the leaders, acknowledging the teaching authority of the scribes and pharisees "who sit on Moses seat" (23:2) but bitterly attacking their hypocrisy and abuse of their teaching authority, accusing them of being "blind guides" who make their converts "twice as much a child of hell as yourselves" (23:15).

With this type of preparation in the Gospel, the bitter harvest of the passion comes as no real surprise. In Matthew's Gospel the leaders are one dimensional—representative of implacable opposition to Jesus and his mission. The passion story of Mark had already stressed the active role of the religious leaders in securing the death of Jesus; Matthew intensifies this motif. He expands the opening verses of the passion story, having the leaders gather in assembly to launch their conspiracy against Jesus (26:1-5). Judas the betrayer plays an important role in Matthew's narrative because he becomes the tool of the religious leaders. They pay Judas "thirty pieces of silver" (26:15), a vivid detail unique to Matthew, one that recalls Zechariah 11:12 where the shepherd is paid the wages of a slave and, at the same time, prepares for the tragic story of Judas' death (27:3-10). Driven by remorse (but not repentance), Judas returns the pieces of silver to the leaders. They refuse this "blood money" but Judas casts the pieces of silver into the temple where the leaders must retrieve them and then decide to buy the potters' field as a place to bury strangers (27:3-10). Matthew's macabre tale is full of irony; the blood money ultimately returns to condemn the priests who paid it to the traitor in the first place. All of this is in accord with God's word in Scripture, as Matthew evokes through a citation that combines Zechariah 11:13 about the blood money and Jeremiah 19 concerning the potter's field.

A key moment of opposition is the "trial" before the Sanhedrin. More explicitly than in Mark's version, Matthew has the assembly take a formal verdict against Jesus: "When morning came, all the chief priests and the elders of the people conferred together against Jesus in order to bring about his death" (27:1).

But for Matthew's narrative the summit of opposition and rejection on the part of Israel is the notorious text of 27:24-25. Matthew's version of the Roman trial prepares for this text by underscoring the clear choice that faces the leaders and now the people as a whole. Over and over, Matthew uses the word "choose" (27:17, 20, 21). According to a variant reading, accepted by the NRSV, Matthew identifies Barabbas as "Jesus the one called Barabbas" who stands as a clear, haunting alternative to "Jesus the one called the Christ." The leaders press the crowd to reject Jesus and to choose Barabbas, while in pointed and ironic contrast the Roman governor Pilate and even his wife (who has a unique cameo appearance in Matthew's passion story, 27:19) plead for his innocence.

The terrible moment of choice comes in 27:24-25. Matthew draws on biblical symbolism and language to dramatize the choice. Evoking the ritual in Deuteronomy 21:7 for declaring oneself innocent of murder, Pilate washes his hands: "I am innocent of this man's blood; see to it yourselves" (27:24). In response, the "whole people" accept responsibility for Jesus' death: "His blood be on us and on our children" (27:25). Here, too, Matthew draws on some stock biblical language for his characters (see Lev 20:9-16; 2 Sam 1:16 and similarly Josh 2:19-20).

The interpreter of Matthew's Gospel must be attentive here and first read the text as it is, not as later interpretation would have it. There is little question that Matthew intends the phrase *pas ho laos* ("all of the people") to be a collective term for Israel as a whole and not simply as an alternative for the "crowds" *(ho ochloi)* to whom, up to this point, Matthew has given a fairly passive role in the narrative. Matthew uses the term "the people" some fourteen times in his Gospel and consistently in a collective sense (see, for example, the repeated phrase the "elders of the people"). The emphatic *"all* the people" simply underscores the comprehensive scope of this phrase. In the context of 27:25 this means that whereas before only the leaders had condemned Jesus (27:1) now the leaders have successfully swayed all the people to join them in rejecting Jesus.

Also problematic is the phrase "on us and on our children." Later anti-Jewish interpretations of the Gospel have taken this as a sign of a perpetual curse upon the Jewish people. The destruction brought about by such an interpretation is incalculable and, at the very least, warns the Christian interpreter to read and proclaim this text with utmost care and prudence. In fact, there is no suggestion in the wording of the text of unlimited temporal responsibility: i.e., that "on our children" means on all of our children forever and ever. If, in fact, the evangelist wanted to express this he could have drawn on a frequent biblical expression "forever and ever."

At face value, the phrase "on us and on our children" may simply emphasize the comprehensive span of the word "people": i.e., "We, that is adults and our children with us, accept this responsibility which Pilate refuses." If, on the other hand, the term "and on our children" is to be understood generationally, then the text could literally mean: "We, that is this generation, and our children, that is *the next generation"* accept this responsibility. In this case, responsibility for Jesus' death extends to one generation, the generation in fact that would experience the destruction of Jerusalem.

There is evidence in the Gospel that Matthew—in concert with other New Testament authors—understood the tragedy of Jerusalem's destruction during the Jewish revolt of A.D. 66–70 as a consequence of the rejection of Jesus (texts such as 21:41 and 23:38 may reflect such a perspective). Obviously such a theological interpretation on the part of the evangelist is not without its problems, too, but at least it does not support a theory of the perpetual guilt of the Jewish people for all ages. For a world sick from genocide any theology of retribution, even a limited one, may be abhorrent. However, some moderating context is put on Matthew's theology when we recall that this theological perspective was not developed by someone outside of Judaism looking in, but by a Jewish Christian swept up in the anguish of the division and suffering within Judaism itself. A great prophet such as Jeremiah did not hesitate to predict in bitter and vindictive tones the destruction of Jerusalem and its temple and other apocalyptic Jewish traditions would do likewise. Matthew stands in this robust and tormented theological tradition.

For Matthew, therefore, one fundamental historical and theological reality was the baffling fact that Jesus' ministry and the subsequent mission of the Jewish Christian community had been for the most part rejected by God's own people. The passion story and its dramatic choice of the people lays this before the reader. On one level Matthew assigns the cause for this to the moral failures of Jesus' opponents. In the Gospel's view they represent all of the wrong values and the wrong choices: they do not believe in Jesus; they lack integrity; they are failed moral guides. They become, in effect, a negative example for the Christian reader of the Gospel. Here is what a true disciple of Jesus is *not* to be.

But Matthew recognizes a deeper and more mysterious causality at work in Israel's rejection of Jesus and the gospel message. In some strange and impenetrable sense, the rejection of Jesus falls within God's providence; "all of this has taken place so that the scriptures of the prophets may be fulfilled," as the Matthean Jesus notes at the moment of his arrest (26:56). Every dimension of Jesus' life as presented in Matthew's Gospel falls under the canopy of scriptural fulfillment and is therefore God's doing. Even Judas' terrible act of betrayal fulfills God's prophetic word (27:9-10).

A THEOLOGY OF HISTORY

The deeper mystery of Israel's rejection of Jesus brings us to another fundamental perspective of Matthew in the passion story, namely, his theology of history. It is here that Matthew's Christology comes into play.

Throughout the Gospel Matthew portrays Jesus as the fulfillment of God's promises to Israel, indeed as the Savior of the world. Declared both "Son of David" and "Son of Abraham" in the opening words of the Gospel (1:1), Jesus is conceived by the power of the Spirit (1:20) and God's angel declares that he will "save his people from their sins" (1:21). He is "God with us," the "Emmanuel" promised by Isaiah (1:23).

Every page of Matthew's subsequent narrative reaffirms Jesus' powerful messianic identity and his fulfillment of God's promises. Through his teaching and healing Jesus inaugurates the very rule of God expected for the end-time. Matthew presents Jesus' redemptive mission as having explosive force—at first contained within Israel but ultimately bursting out to engulf the whole world and beginning a new age of history.

Tentative contact with Gentiles early in the Gospel are signs of the ultimate scope of Jesus' mission and its profound historic significance. The Magi come "from the east" to offer homage (2:1-2). A Roman centurion exemplifies startling faith in Jesus (8:5-13), drawing from him a vision of the future when "many will come from east and west and will eat with Abraham and Isaac and Jacob in the kingdom of heaven." The bold faith of a Canaanite woman compels Jesus to heal her daughter, despite his protest that his mission is "only to the lost sheep of the house of Israel" (15:24). These are signs of what direction the Christian mission must ultimately take. Matthew hints at that by portraying Jesus' first entrance into his public ministry as a fulfillment of Isaiah 9:1-2: ". . . Galilee of the Gentiles—the people who sat in darkness have seen a great light, and for those who sat in the region and shadow of death light has dawned" (Matt 4:15-16).

It is significant that in Matthew's Gospel these encounters with Gentiles usually take place as a counterpoint to rejection or lack of response on the part of Israel. The Magi offer homage to Jesus while Herod and his Jerusalem court attempt to destroy him. In praising the Centurion Jesus laments, "Truly I tell you, in no one in Israel have I found such faith" (8:10) and while many will come from east and west to eat at table in God's kingdom, "the heirs of the kingdom will be thrown into the outer darkness" (8:12). Jesus' journey into Tyre and Sidon and his encounter there with the Canaanite woman follows upon a sharp conflict with the Pharisees and scribes (15:1-20).

For Matthew, the opening to the Gentiles comes mysteriously in the wake of the failure of the mission to Israel. Matthew emphasizes this in his version of the parable of the vineyard. Because the tenants of the vineyard reject God's long line of messengers and finally reject and kill the son, the vineyard is taken away from them and given "to other tenants." Matthew drives the message home by having Jesus address the chief priests and Pharisees at the conclusion of the parable: "Therefore I tell you, the kingdom of God will be taken away from you and given to a people that produces the fruits of the kingdom" (21:43). Although the genre of the Gospel does not permit the evangelist to reflect on this paradox in an explicit way, as Paul can do in Romans 9–11, there is a strong similarity in their theological perspectives here.

This prepares us for the drama of the passion. We have already noted how in his passion narrative Matthew highlights Israel's rejection of Jesus, both on the part of the leaders and ultimately the people themselves. Matthew correspondingly emphasizes the burst of new life that paradoxically is born in the midst of baffling and inexplicable tragedy. The key scene is 27:51-53, another of the rare instances where Matthew has substantially altered Mark's presentation. In Mark's account, Jesus' death instantaneously triggers two dramatic events—the tearing of the temple veil signaling the end of the temple "made by hands" (Mark 15:38) and the centurion's acclamation, "Truly this man was God's Son!" (15:39).

Matthew builds on Mark's account. Between the tearing of the veil and the centurion's testimony he injects a series of cosmic events. In response to Jesus' death not only does the temple veil tear in two but so, too, the earth shakes, the rocks split and the very tombs of the dead break open. From the abode of the dead come forth the "holy ones" of Israel now alive and ready to enter the holy city of Jerusalem triumphantly (but Matthew adds, only *after* Jesus' own resurrection). To this extraordinary display the centurion and "those with him" (a Matthean addition) respond: "Truly this man was God's Son" (27:54) and from a distance the women who had remained faithful to Jesus also witness this burst of new life (27:55).

There have been numerous discussions about the possible origin of Matthew's material but the overall significance is clear. The evangelist draws on stock apocalyptic motifs found in such texts as Ezekiel 37:11-14 and Daniel 12:1-2—earthquakes, splitting of rocks, opening of tombs—to affirm that the death of Jesus marks the turning point of world history. The new age of salvation promised by God and longed for by Israel begins with the death and resurrection of Jesus. The unlikely community of faithful Jews (the women who stand by Jesus' cross) and converted Gentiles (the centurion and his companions) are the nucleus of a new people.

The finale of Matthew's Gospel is a necessary sequel to all this. The discovery of the empty tomb (where Matthew also refers to an apocalyptic earthquake; 28:2) and the final appearance of the Risen Christ to his disciples confirm Matthew's historical perspective. The age of resurrection has come with Jesus as the first born Son of God. He returns triumphantly to his community, with "all authority in heaven and on earth . . . given to me" (28:18). Where earlier in the Gospel the limits of the old age had confined Jesus' mission to Israel, it now breaks out in the new age to embrace all the nations (28:19). The disciples are empowered to proclaim the gospel throughout the world and the Risen Christ will remain with the community until the final consummation of the world and the return of all things to God (28:20).

IN CONCLUSION

As many interpreters have suggested, Matthew writes to give perspective to his community. His Christians stand at a turbulent moment in history. The rejection and death that Jesus experienced in his lifetime seems to have been repeated in the failure of the Jewish Christian mission to Israel. The strength and coherence that Matthew's Jewish Christians drew from their Jewish heritage seemed in peril not only from questions of legitimacy raised by Jewish leaders past and present but also by the influx of Gentile converts who had little or no appreciation of the sacred tradition and practices of Judaism.

It would be understandable if a community such as Matthew's would choose to withdraw from the field, to protect itself from hostility and chaos by erecting a religious and psychological barrier between itself and the rest of the world. But Matthew draws on the deepest well of Christian faith, one whose streams also course through the heart of the Hebrew scriptures. God is faithful and despite—and even more astoundingly *through*—the experience of suffering and death new life is born. Jesus' own death and resurrection had proclaimed this fundamental pattern of salvation and Matthew's community was experiencing it themselves. Instead of withdrawal Matthew's Gospel urges his community to recognize God's abiding presence within history and to courageously enter into mission to the world.

And what of Israel in all this? Does Matthew consider the leaders and the people who adhere to them as a lost cause? Or does he, like Paul, believe that God's tenacious love for Israel will ultimately prevail? The question is difficult and interpreters have been divided about the answer. My own view is that Matthew does not give up on Israel despite his bitter estimate of its response to the gospel. He concludes Jesus' denunciation of the scribes and Pharisees in chapter 23 with this telling prophecy: "Jerusalem, Jerusalem, the city that kills the prophets and stones those who are sent to it! How often have I desired to gather your children together as a hen gathers her brood under her wings, and you were not willing! See, your house is left to you, desolate. For I tell you, you will not see me again until you say, 'Blessed is the one who comes in the name of the Lord'" (23:37-39). ". . . you will not see me again *until* . . .": the words and tone of this prophetic woe end with a promise. If Israel repents, then God's messenger will be seen again.

This is stock biblical theology and one that Matthew espouses. Just as the "holy ones" of Israel are the first fruits of Jesus' redemptive death, so the people of Jerusalem (and by extension, Israel itself) will yet experience the divine visitation. If through the passion of Jesus a new people and a new age are born, through the passion of Israel God will also bring redemption. Undoubtedly Matthew saw this in terms of Jewish acceptance of Jesus as the messiah but from our contemporary vantage point who can predict the manner in which God brings life from death—for both Christian and Jew.

Part VII
Mystical Life and Life After Death

I will go on to visions and revelations of the Lord. I know someone in Christ. I know someone in Christ who fourteen years ago was caught up to the third heaven—whether in the body or out of the body, I do not know; God knows. And I know that this person—whether in the body or out of the body, I do not know; God knows—was caught up into Paradise and heard ineffable things, which no one may utter. . . . Therefore, that I might not become too elated, a thorn in the flesh was given to me, an angel of Satan, to beat me, to keep me from becoming too elated (2 Cor 12:1-7).

CHAPTER 23

The Indwelling Spirit: A Foretaste of Heaven

The presence of the Holy Spirit in the souls of the just has ever been a living source of happiness for all people of good will. In every age, earnest Christians have found in this doctrinal truth a sweet foretaste of life in heaven. Fifty years ago, in recognition of its power to sanctify souls, Pope Leo XIII sought to renew this conviction by a forceful and inspiring expression of the doctrine of divine indwelling in his encyclical *Divinum illud munus.* Therein he set forth the full content of St. Thomas' terse and rich summary of the Church's teaching on grace: "Grace is nothing less than the beginning of glory" (cf. *S. Th.*, Ia IIae, q. 69, a. 2; IIa IIae, q. 24, a. 3; *De Veritate,* q. 14, a. 2).

This doctrine also received comprehensive expression under the inspired pen of St. Paul in his letter to the Ephesians 1:13-14. [Editor's note: The reading of these verses evolved within various Catholic translations: from (1) the Challoner edition of the Douay-Rheims (1914); (2) to the Confraternity version from the Latin Vulgate (1941); (3) to its successor, the New American Bible, translated from the original languages, in its earlier (1970) and revised (1986) forms. Barnabas Ahern wrote this article for the *Catholic Biblical Quarterly* (April 1947), critiquing the Confraternity version of 1941 from the background of the Greek text of the Epistle and of other ancient sources. He strongly influenced later translations. In this copy of his article, we leave intact the Confraternity version, but for the convenience of readers we quote the modulations in translation:

> *Challoner-Douay-Rheims* version, 1914: You were signed with the Holy Spirit of promise, who is the pledge of our inheritance, unto the redemption of acquisition, unto the praise of his glory.
> *Confraternity* version, 1941: You . . . were sealed with the Holy Spirit of the promise, who is the pledge of our inheritance, for a redemption of possession, for the praise of his glory.

New American Bible, 1970: You were sealed with the Holy Spirit who had been promised. He is the pledge of our inheritance, the first payment against the full redemption of a people God has made his own, to praise his glory.
New American Bible, 1986: You . . . were sealed with the promised holy Spirit, which is the first installment of our inheritance towards redemption as God's possession, to the praise of his glory.]

Frequently, in his epistles, St. Paul asserts the fact that through grace the Holy Spirit dwells in the souls of the just (cf. Rom 5:5; 1 Cor 3:16-17; 6:19-20; 1 Thess 4:8); often, too, he describes the activity of the Holy Spirit in the justified soul (cf. Rom 8:16, 26; 2 Cor 5:1-5; Gal 4:6-7). But, in this verse of Ephesians, he combines both elements of the doctrine in a concise and suggestive description of the indwelling Holy Spirit as "the pledge of our inheritance."

It is clear that the Greek word for "inheritance" here signifies the beatific vision of God considered as our future reward. But the other member of this figurative expression, "the pledge," in Greek, *arrabon*—indeed, the very key-word of the phrase—is not equally intelligible, especially since the *pignus* of the Latin Vulgate text is admittedly inadequate to express its full meaning. In this single word, St. Paul has concentrated all the richness of his own concept of the indwelling Holy Spirit. Therefore, this concise and vivid expression of our faith merits careful study.

PHILOLOGICAL STUDY

As with many other words, the history of this term, "pledge" or *arrabon*, presents a fixed, though evolving signification. It is constant in basic content, though, of course, it takes on a new connotation when applied to varied fields of activity.

Semitic Background

According to the authority of ranking lexicographers, the Greek word *arrabon* is of undoubted Semitic origin. More probably, as Julius Furst-Victor Ryssel suggested, it found entrance into the Greek language through the influence of Phoenician traders, who used it in the sense of *surety* or *pledge*.

In Hebrew the consonants 'rb were used to form the roots of many words, covering such various significations as *raven* and *to be sweet*.

One of these uses, denoting a *pledge* or *surety*, makes its first appearance in Genesis 38:17, 18, and 20, under the substantive form ʿrbon. In this passage, the sacred writer narrates that Judah gave Tamar his ring, bracelet, and staff as a *pledge (ʿrbon)* for the kid he owed her. Later, on fulfilling his part of the contract, he demands the return of the *pledge*. If we exclude a doubtful reading in Job 17:3, this is the only instance of the use of ʿrbon in the Old Testament; though, in three other texts, it does appear in cognate forms, with the same basic signification of *pledge-guarantee* (1 Sam 17:18; Prov 17:18; 2 Kgs 14:14). Accordingly, its biblical signification is easy to define: a real and precious article, distinct from the object of contract, offered by the debtor to his creditor as a guarantee of future payment.

After this first-known use in Hebrew literature, the root ʿrb recurs frequently, but always as a verb. It always preserved the basic notion of *surety* or *guarantee*, though in the living language of the Hebrews, it often found new applications. Accordingly, in the twenty-two instances of its use in the Old Testament, ʿrb presents such accidental differences in meaning as to offer surety for the debts of another (Prov 6:1; 11:15; 17:18; 20:16; 22:26; 27:13), to guarantee the safety of another (Gen 43:9; 44:32; Job 17:3; Ps 119:122; Isa 38:14), to mortgage (Neh 5:3), to transact business (2 Kgs 18:23; Isa 36:8; Ezek 27:9, 27), to ally with (Ezra 9:2; Ps 106:35; Prov 20:19; 24:21), and to share (Prov 14:10). But, as has been remarked, these differences of meaning are merely accidental; in final analysis, the primary concept of ʿrb, namely, *to guarantee with a pledge,* underlies all particular applications of this notion to various fields of activity. Not once, however, in all these Old Testament examples does the term express explicitly that form of pledge which is most familiar to us, the partial payment of a money debt.

Greek Vocabulary

At a very early date, the substantive form of the Semitic root ʿrb became a loan-word in the Greek language. Some authorities, as mentioned already, attribute its adoption by the Greeks to the influence of Phoenician traders—a plausible suggestion, since commercial transactions would have presented frequent occasions for its use.

In the Greek language, however, the term took on a meaning over and above the basic *pledge* concept of ʿrb. Thus, extrabiblical literature of earlier and later date presents unmistakable reference to the use of this word in the sense of *earnest money* or partial payment.

The first known Greek use of the word occurs in *Oration* 8, *De Circo*, of Isaeus (ca. 375 B.C.), who employed it in the technical sense of *earnest money*. He is followed a few years later by Aristotle who also used it, in *Politics*, I, 11, to designate deposits on the full price. About 300 B.C., the word appears again in Menander, the comic dramatist.

The next instance of its use is biblical, found in the Septuagint Greek translation of Genesis 38:17, 18, and 20. Here it is used for the first and only time—to correspond with the equivalent Hebrew ʽ*rbon*. Accordingly, the Greek word is a mere transliteration and therefore represents the *pledge* concept in its narrow signification.

This restricted meaning, however, is not the only one to be found. In extrabiblical literature, contemporary with and subsequent to the Septuagint, it designates something more than a *guarantee*. It is, as Alfred Plummer pointed out, "an installment, i.e., a delivery of a small portion, whether of money or of goods, as an earnest that the remainder would be delivered later."

In fact, the signification of the Greek *arrabon* in the texts collected by Professors Moulton and Milligan from literature of this period is almost always the concept of *earnest money*. These references drawn from a period of history contemporary with St. Paul present a distinct form of business guarantee. There is, of course, a basic similarity between this *earnest money* and the *pledge* concept represented by the Semitic ʽ*rbon*, for both are practical expedients intended to facilitate contracts and transactions: In fact, *earnest money* is but a special application of the *pledge* guarantee. For the *pledge*, in its basic concept, signifies any form of guarantee. As such, it may be an article entirely distinct from the object of contract, to be returned to the debtor on fulfillment of the obligation. *Earnest money*, on the other hand, represents a real part of the object of contract, given in advance, both to insure final full payment and, also, to contribute to it. In modern parlance, it is a partial payment over which the creditor exercises complete and inalienable dominion.

We conclude, then, that the Greek word possesses a twofold meaning: (1) an advance partial payment or earnest money properly so called, or (2) a pledge guarantee which can be taken back when the buyer has fulfilled the contract.

STUDY OF *ARRABON* IN EPHESIANS 1:14

What meaning, then, did St. Paul intend to convey when he described the Holy Spirit as the "*arrabon* of our inheritance"? Did he conceive the role of the Holy Spirit in the soul as confined to the narrow limitations of the noncommittal *pledge,* a mere guarantee of God's fidelity to promises made? Or did he regard the divine indwelling as a real but incomplete foretaste of eternal life, a *part-payment* or first installment of our inheritance?

The fact that the Latin Vulgate employs the word *pignus* or "pledge" as the translation of the Greek word is by no means a final determinant of accurate interpretation. For though St. Jerome retained this reading in his translation, still, in his commentary on Ephesians, he declared the other interpretation to be preferable. Moreover, it is certain, on the authority of St. Augustine's *Sermo* 23:8, that the manuscripts of the old Latin version were divided over the variant readings, *pignus* (pledge) and *arrha* (earnest money). Finally, the Syriac Peshitta translates the Greek word by *rhabuno,* which is closer in meaning to *arrha* (part-payment) than to *pignus* (pledge). It is obvious, then, that accuracy of interpretation requires a fresh study of the text.

The Context of Ephesians 1:14

In the first fourteen verses of Ephesians, St. Paul describes for his Gentile converts at Ephesus the divine plan of salvation and its actual execution. In verses 3-7, he details this plan as it existed from all eternity in the mind of God; in verses 8-14, he explains its actual fulfillment in time through the restoration of all things in Christ. In the concluding verses of this introduction, 13 and 14, the Apostle becomes more specific, narrowing his scope to the concrete realization of the designs of God in the lives of the Ephesians. Having received the gospel of salvation favorably, they have believed in Christ and have been sealed with the gift of the Holy Spirit.

This is not a reference to the charismatic gifts of the Holy Ghost. Rather, since St. Paul here speaks to Gentile converts as a whole and not to a select number, it is clear that he had in mind a privilege shared in by all Christians, namely, the indwelling of the Holy Spirit who brings peace, grace, divine adoption, and the right to eternal glory.

This passage contains an implicit reference to the sacrament of baptism. It is only with the infusion of baptismal grace that the Holy Spirit begins its supernatural indwelling in the soul of the Christian.

The Text

It is this mention of the indwelling Spirit that brings the Apostle to introduce the descriptive phrase now under discussion: "You also

. . . were sealed with the promised holy Spirit, which is *the pledge of our inheritance,* toward redemption as God's possession, to the praise of God's glory."

In this figurative designation, two features in the role of the indwelling Holy Spirit are clearly indicated:

1. "The pledge of our inheritance." According to the explicit meaning of this phrase, the presence of the Holy Spirit in the soul bears close connection with a future "inheritance." The indwelling of this divine person guarantees the obligation which God has predestined. In proof of divine fidelity, God has sealed the soul with his own Holy Spirit, a divine surety that the state of filial adoption which the soul now enjoys will one day reach consummation in the complete inheritance of glory. This divine pledge, then, points forward to that full "redemption as God's possession" in heavenly beatitude.

This concept of the Holy Spirit as God's guarantee to bestow on his adoptive children the fullness of promised reward in heaven occurs frequently in the epistles of St. Paul. He has expressed it at length in the Letter to the Romans 8:9-24. In this passage, the "pledge" of Ephesians 1:14 is substituted by another appropriate figure, "the first-fruits of the Spirit." Both comparisons bear the same connotation. For, in the words of G. G. Findlay, "what the earliest sheaf is to the harvest and what the pledge is to a contract, that the entrance of the Spirit of God into a human soul is to the glory of its ultimate salvation."

In the present instance, therefore, *arrabon* denotes a guarantee of fidelity to obligation. Because God has sent the Holy Ghost into the soul of the Christian, God has pledged to pay the full inheritance of heaven.

2. "The promised holy Spirit." These words present a second element which expands the signification already assigned to *arrabon*. For St. Paul identifies this particular pledge with God's own Holy Spirit. This Spirit is itself God and, therefore, the very object of that full beatitude which God has guaranteed to confer. Accordingly, this pledge, identical in nature with the object of full payment, will endure even when complete recompense has been made. Recognition of this fact suggests a deeper and richer implication in the word *arrabon*. This divine pledge must be more than just a guarantee.

The fact that this *pledge* is the very Spirit "promised" eliminates a merely static presence of the Holy Ghost in the soul. For the Apostle refers to the promise made by Christ himself at the Last Supper (John 16:5-15; 25-26). There, in revealing the future mission of the Holy Ghost, Christ represented the Spirit as vitally active in the soul of all people, consoling, strengthening, bestowing peace and joy. Moreover, St. Paul himself was very familiar with this activity of the Holy Ghost; he knew it by personal experience. That is why he could describe so graphically how even here on earth the Spirit of God fills the Christian soul with a portion of the joy and happiness of heaven (cf. Rom 8:14-17, 26-27; Gal 4:6-7).

However—and this element is fundamental in any true explanation of the passage—the indwelling Spirit is only the *part-payment* of a fuller gift in the future. It is true that the object of future reward is identical with the foretaste of that reward now possessed. Yet present possession is only partial, restricted by our present situation. Accordingly, the distinction between full and part payment arises not from the object itself but from the manner in which it is possessed. On earth, God can be known only by faith, a medium of possession which St. Paul has described as imperfect and obscure; but, with the bestowal of full reward, the divine object, previously possessed imperfectly on earth, will emerge from obscurity into the light of vision (cf. 1 Cor 13:12; 2 Cor 5:6-8; 1 Tim 6:16; Heb 11:1).

Therefore, the inheritance of the future and its foretaste in the present differ not in object, but only in degree. Pope Leo XIII has given classic expression to this truth in his encyclical *Divinum illud munus:* "This marvelous bonding, called divine inhabitation, differs only in its condition or degree from that heavenly state where God completes the soul's beatitude." A truly active presence of God in the soul, but a presence recognized only in the obscurity of faith—this is the role of the indwelling Holy Spirit. The Spirit is at once a *guarantee* and a *part-payment* of our inheritance, a "pledge" in the rich, twofold meaning of the word.

Accordingly, this phrase expresses the culminating point of the beautiful introduction to the Epistle. Previously, the Apostle described how God has predestined souls to be divine children, in accord with the purpose of the heavenly will formed in the depths of eternity (vv. 3-6). As such, they are true heirs who have already received rich blessings from the inheritance (vv. 7-10), though the richest part of it, the full possession of God in beatific glory, is not yet attained. However, through the gift of the Spirit, God has set a seal upon the divine promise, for it is this very same Spirit who fills the predestined soul with grace and charity. Its presence, when perceived in faith, diffuses true joy, thus constituting at once a guarantee and a foretaste of heaven. The Spirit is a true *arrabon* or "first installment" in the fullest sense.

EARLY CHURCH COMMENTARIES

The interpretation of the Greek word *arrabon* in Ephesians 1:14 as a rich metaphor expressive of the twofold concept of *guarantee* and *partial payment* does not rest merely on an independent study of the text. Independent exegesis of sacred Scripture counts for nothing unless it merges with the full stream of traditional interpretation. The proposed explanation is of value only because it is supported by the authority of commentators possessing deep insight into the hidden secrets of sacred Scripture. Their concordant interpretation of *arrabon* gives a true understanding of its deep meaning.

St. Jerome. As remarked before, this holy doctor retained the term *pignus* or pledge in his Latin Vulgate translation of Ephesians. Elsewhere, however, he found fault with those Latin translators who had previously inserted *pignus* in place of the more exact *arrhabo* or partial payment. The reason he alleges for his dissatisfaction is significant: *pignus* is inadequate to express the full meaning truly demanded by the text and adequately represented only in the wider content of *arrhabo*.

St. Augustine. Though this saint never wrote a commentary on Ephesians, still several times in his homilies, he introduced and explained the verse under consideration (cf. *Sermo* 23, 8; *Sermo* 156, 15; *Sermo* 378). In a like spirit of vigorous criticism he echoes the complaint of St. Jerome:

> The codices which have *arrha* are by far preferable to those with *pignus*.... For in the case of *pignus*, the pledge is taken back when the object is delivered for which the pledge was given.... Therefore, *arrha* is far more exact than *pignus*. For when you give a sum of money to make good a contract you are arranging, you pay something of the price itself. This will be an *arrha*, not a *pignus*; for it is simply to be completed, not to be taken back (*Sermo* 23, 8–9).

Thus, in the opinion of St. Augustine, the word *pignus* is inept to express the rich twofold meaning demanded by the thought of St. Paul. The deep significance of the divine indwelling finds adequate expression only in the full connotation of *arrha*. The saint repeats this observation each time he comments on this verse.

St. John Chrysostom. The prince of Pauline exegetes is equally insistent in his *In Epistolam ad Ephesios* on the apt use of *arrabon* in the present instances; for an *arrabon*, he says in substance, is part of the whole which one day will be given to faithful Christians in its completeness. He then continues this interpretation and goes on to confirm it with a homily on the reason why so many Christians fail to appreciate the indwelling Holy Spirit as a foretaste of heavenly glory. Spiritual sloth blinds their eyes and hinders them from beholding the heavens open and the Lord Jesus standing in majesty.

Subsequent Commentators. The interpretation of *arrabon* in this text has been so consistent that no school of exegesis deviates from the traditional analysis proposed by the earliest Fathers. At most, we may note in individual exegetes some particular elaboration or happy turn of phrase which emphasizes with striking clarity the original thought of St. Paul.

Thus, Theodore of Mopsuestia, the friend and follower of Chrysostom, paraphrases *arrabon* by another apt figure in perfect accord with its full meaning—"a sample taste." Theodoret of Cyre, whose brief commentaries on the Pauline epistles are real gems, bears out the basic interpretation of St. John Chrysostom by assigning a reason for the indwelling of the Holy Spirit—"that it may make us members of God's household." In like manner, Theophylact merely repeats the homiletic elaboration of St. John Chrysostom on this text. Finally, St. John Damascene faithfully reproduces the accepted interpretation by ascribing to the indwelling of the Holy Spirit a beginning of our perfect adoption even here below on earth. Through the Spirit, the Christian becomes the possession of Christ and of God.

Many commentators find other accidental shades of meaning in the term. Thus Theodoret of Cyre and Cornelius à Lapide extol the divine nature of the *arrha* as a unique indication of the greatness and splendor of the Christian's full reward. In this they merely stress a detail already expressed in St. Jerome's commentary: *Si autem arrhabo tantus, quanta erit ipsa possessio!* (If partial payment is such, how great the full possession!) Again, John Gagnaeus and Cornelius à Lapide emphasize that feature of the material pledge demanding its careful preservation in order to be of credit in securing final and full payment. Finally, some exegetes, as St. Thomas and Cornelius à Lapide, are so explicit and detailed in their interpretation that they identify the specific concept of *arrha* or partial payment with charity, which endures forever, and the specific concept of *pignus* or pledge with transitory faith and hope. Yet, whatever may be the accidental shades in presentation, all commentators bear testimony to the rich and twofold signification of *arrabon* in the present text.

IN CONCLUSION

Analysis of the Greek word *arrabon* discovers in it a twofold meaning. The first denotes the simple concept of a *pledge-guarantee*, enforcing the obligation of payment without, however, contributing to that end. The second meaning includes a double concept, namely that of *guarantee*, rendering final payment obligatory, and that of *part-payment*, previously admitting the creditor to a share in the fruits of final payment. This latter concept is now familiar in its modern application of the installment plan. [Editor's note: Hence the translation of the revised edition of the NAB: "first installment."]

Careful examination of St. Paul's use of this word in Ephesians 1:14, shows that the great Apostle intended that *arrabon* should here convey the rich and full signification of its twofold meaning. This interpretation has been confirmed by the traditional exegesis of this text consistently and vigorously proposed by all commentators from the beginning.

Therefore, the profound theological treatises and inspiring devotional studies which have been written of late on the benefits of vital realization of the indwelling of the Holy Spirit in the soul are in the full stream of traditional thought. This concept was familiar to the earliest Christians, who heard it repeated again and again in the epistles of St. Paul, teacher of the nations. Indeed, this present study has made clear that, in the metaphor used in Ephesians 1:14, St. Paul has given to this doctrine of the divine indwelling a rich tessera which, for wealth of connotation, cannot be surpassed.

If it is difficult for us to realize in our own souls the experience which made this concept so vivid and vital in the mind of St. Paul, let us hearken to these words of St. John Chrysostom who knew so well the teaching and the mind of his beloved master:

> Those who truly partake of the Spirit know that it is a foretaste of the inheritance. Such a one was Paul, who had tasted here below the delights that are above. For this very reason, he pressed on and labored to leave the things that are here.... If we all were partakers of the Spirit as we should be, we too would see the heavens open and would gaze on him who stands there (*In Epistolam ad Ephesios, Hom.* 2).

This reproof from the mouth of St. John Chrysostom, faithful disciple of Paul, strengthens all people of good will for complete detachment from the things of the world. Only this attitude can bring a lively realization of all that the indwelling Holy Spirit can and should mean in the life of the true Christian.

CHAPTER 24

With Christ After Death

Catholic thought today has registered its own emphasis in eschatology, the end-time or final age. The popular mind centers attention on the definitive judgment which launches the soul at death upon an eternity of joy or of anguish. In this frame of reference, the apocalyptic events of the end-time claim little interest. For most people the general judgment is only consequential and secondary, a mere ratification of the preliminary decision which is far more important.

It may come as a surprise, then, to learn that the Christians of New Testament times did not share this outlook. Their preoccupation centered in the parousia, the Greek word designating the apocalyptic return of Christ as judge and savior of the universe. The interest in the final restoration was so dominant that it tended to withdraw attention from the immediate aftermath of death.

This outlook of the early Church was the consequence of its biblical and Jewish background. Christ and the Judeo-Christian community made their own the eschatology which Hebrew thought had formulated after the long and intricate processes of its development. Even now, it is difficult to trace the devious course which led from the early belief, in collective and worldly retribution, to the postexilic hope of otherworldly reward both for the collected people of God and for the individual. The course of development was so complex that the Jews never produced a universally accepted eschatology. We cannot speak of a Jewish *dogma* of retribution after death even in our Lord's own day. The Sadducees, with no belief in reward after death, could and did attain to the highest positions in temple and state.

THE ESCHATOLOGY OF THE PHARISEES

The theology of the Pharisees, however, dominated the scene. These respected leaders taught the doctrine of an apocalyptic end-time and the bodily resurrection of the just as it is enunciated in the biblical books of Daniel and Second Maccabees or in nonbiblical books like Enoch or the Psalms of Solomon. As George Foot Moore has well noted, the thesis of the Pharisees was the natural consequence of God's revelation: "On the premises of Scripture, the only logical way in which the Jews could conceive the fulfillment of God's promises to the righteous was that they should live again upon earth in the golden age to come and share in the salvation of Israel. The resurrection seems, indeed, so necessarily the consequence of the whole teaching of Scripture concerning the salvation of the righteous and their great reward that it is not strange that the Pharisees found it explicit or by intimation in all parts of the Bible" (*Judaism*, 2:313–14).

Jesus accepted this doctrine and made it his own, thus giving certainty to the essential feature of final retribution. His synthesis of the highest developments in Old Testament revelation stands as a basic assumption in all New Testament thought.

The essential features of the doctrine of Jesus and the Pharisees bring to the fore three elements which had remained constant in Hebrew thought on retribution despite the many changes which preceded its final formulation. For, in all stages of its development, this doctrine shows three characteristics which are inherent to biblical thought. These dominant elements must be kept in mind if we are to understand the teaching and spirit of our early Christian sources.

Psychosomatic Unity

First of all, every biblical theory of retribution provides for the human being as an animated and personalized body and not as a dichotomy of body and soul as in the Greek system. Whether in the early concept of reward and punishment on this earth or in the later development of retribution in an after-life, the *whole* person is always involved. Biblical men and women lived always as animated bodies, and so as bodies they had to be rewarded. No people ever had so keen a sense of human psychosomatic unity as did the Semites.

Membership in the People of God

Second, every Hebrew theory of retribution looks primarily to the social group. With historical origins in a close-knit tribal society and with divine origin in a covenant between God and God's people, Israel never lost sight of the fact that it must live as a people. Even when the individual emerges in the theology of Jeremiah and Ezekiel, the devout Israelite finds fulfillment and mission in the nation's destiny to glorify God as a corporate personality (cf. Jer 31:29-34; Ezek 18). A markedly personal note characterizes the postexilic piety of the *anawim* [Editor's note: See Chapter 16 for an extended study of the *anawim* or poor ones]; in their prayer, however, these poor and lowly ones remain always aware of membership in the *Qehal Yahweh*, the community of the Lord. This corporate consciousness of Israel is the very context in which they lived. It is the background of their piety and the support of their confidence.

The Bible, therefore, is alien to the subjectivism and atomistic individualism of our age. The hopes of individuals may be fired with the flame of their own personalities; their fulfillment always includes the collectivity. Whether retribution is on this earth or in a world to come, whether reward involves the whole nation or only the just, Hebrew thought always centers in the social group.

Primacy of God's Glory

Third, every theory of retribution always gives first place to God and God's glory. In the beginning, men and women were content to die after a long and blessed life on earth and to pass into the namelessness of the grave, called Sheol, happy in the thought that their people would continue to dwell on the land and to glorify God. When this confidence was shattered by the nation's infidelity, the Jewish people had to seek another theory of retribution to safeguard God's glory. Divine honor was one of the motives which drove Israel from one theory to another until at last it reached the perfect eschatological dream which envisioned endless glory for God through endless praise offered by the risen just.

These three themes dominated the retribution thesis of the Pharisees. The end-time would bring full reward in the presence of God to the resurrected nation and to the righteous individual. The nation of the just would thus glorify God forever. This belief rings through the confession of faith uttered before Antiochus by the Maccabee martyrs (2 Macc 7:9ff.).

THE EVOLUTION OF SHEOL: REWARD AND PUNISHMENT AFTER DEATH

Late Hebrew thought knew also that reward and punishment begin in some way immediately after death. The justice of God and the survival of Israel required this. In the literature written during the gap of time between the Old and New Testament, Sheol ceased to be merely an abode of the dead, without distinction in reward and punishment. It became instead a provisory stage where the dead anticipate their future lot. One part of this resting-place is called Paradise, for there the just enjoy felicity; another part, called Gehenna, is a place of punishment for the wicked.

This late development in Jewish eschatology lacks the clearness and certainty of the Pharisee thesis on retribution at the end-time. The Hebrew mind, with its compelling sense of human unity, found it difficult to conceive of reward and suffering for a disembodied spirit. Whatever is positive in this picture of humankind's lot during the interim period between the Old and New Testament seems to borrow shape, tone, and color from the picture of the final drama.

Christ adopted this doctrine of the Pharisees on the end-time, sharpening its focus and stabilizing its certainty through his own teaching and that of his apostles. We turn to the Gospels first; though they are among the latest compositions of the early Christian Church, they are true to the teaching and emphases of Jesus himself.

BRIDGING TWO WORLDS

During his earthly life, Jesus was engaged in building a bridge between the worlds of the Old and New Covenants. It was his task to herald the fulfillment of Old Testament hopes and to manifest himself as the full and perfect embodiment of all that God had promised. Humankind had to see in him the eminent source of all salvation and the consummation of age-long expectancies.

He made clear that his kingdom would enjoy moments of growth and would suffer moments of waning. At the same time, however, he did look forward to playing a special role in the future, eschatological consummation. Jesus did not limit his vision to a "realized eschatology"—as though every hope had already been "realized" in his earthly life and resurrection.

Jesus spoke also of the immediate aftermath of death, making his own the Pharisees' doctrine on the interim period. It is to Luke that we are indebted for the memory of these words of Jesus. This is significant. Luke the Greek, writing for Greeks, takes care to record the doctrine which matches their interest in the fate of men and women when life on earth comes to an end.

From Paradise to Union with Christ

To Luke we owe Jesus' parable of the Rich Man and Lazarus (Luke 16:19-31). Jesus speaks here of reward and punishment after death, painting his picture as the Pharisees did with the colors of final retribution, yet scaling down the perspective to accord with the interim period. The picture was a common one. In renewing it and making it his own, Jesus confirmed belief in reward and punishment following immediately upon death.

Luke makes a more important contribution in recording Jesus' words to the thief on the cross: "Today you will be with me in Paradise" (Luke 23:43). This promise serves as a guide to our own doctrine on the interim period. Jewish thought had focused attention on a place of bliss described in terms of earthly pleasure: the food of life, living water, shade, rest, light; this they called Paradise. In his messianic proclamation from the cross, Jesus effects a transition from the Jewish hope of Paradise to the Christian hope of union with Christ: "You will be *with me.*" These words make clear that, even immediately after death, the righteous person enjoys the companionship of the king of the messianic realm.

We are also indebted to Luke for the revealing incident of Stephen's death. This account, in Acts 7:54-60, makes clear that even though the thought of the parousia dominated the mind of the early Christian writers, they possessed at the same time a concept of union with Christ at death. As L. Cerfaux points out, it is the Christ of the parousia whom Stephen beholds. The circumstances of the vision, however, indicate that Christ's presence is meaningful here and now. Christ does not "sit" at the right hand of the Father in the role of judge. Instead, he "stands" in an attitude of expectant welcome. The words which Stephen utters, "Lord Jesus, receive my spirit," are the very words which Jesus used to surrender himself into the bosom of his Father (Luke 23:46). "And when he said this, he [Stephen] fell asleep." The real meaning of the cliché, so frequent in Jewish literature, must be gleaned from the context. There is no question of "awakening" only at the final resurrection. Even at the moment of death, Stephen lives in some way "with Christ."

St. Paul hardly made any real advance beyond these contributions of St. Luke. In his eschatology, as in his anthropology, he is a Pharisee of the Pharisees; he knows and accepts what is best in Jewish thought. There is great value, however, in studying his contribution. As the theologian of the Church, he saw clearly what Christianity had done to sharpen the focus of Old Testament revelation and to illumine it with the light of Christ. Secondly, his letters are the earliest writings of the New Testament period, not written like the Gospels to keep alive the words and teachings of Jesus, but to show the full mind of the Church in Paul's own day. In reading his epistles, therefore, we come to grips with flesh and blood Christianity between A.D. 50 and 60—with its attitudes and interests.

The Promise of the Parousia

In these letters, the parousia comes frequently to the fore, not only in the beginning of his ministry (it is the whole burden of Thessalonians) but also at its close. In dying, Paul looks forward to "that day": "From now on the crown of righteousness awaits me, which the Lord, the just judge, will award to me on that day, and not only to me, but to all who have longed for his appearance (2 Tim 4:8).

In the captivity epistles, Paul's attention to the mystery of Christ leads him to concentrate on anticipated eschatology. As we have seen in the previous chapter, through the *arrabon* or first installment of the indwelling Spirit (Eph 1:14), Christians have already begun their future life. If anything, however, this foretaste serves to whet the desire for that day when, through resurrection, the whole person shall be with the Lord.

This prospect of a rich personal experience provides only a partial reason for the magnetism of the parousia. The last day drew the mind of Paul much more because it represented the salvation of the whole body of Christ for the glory of the Father. For Paul, the Hebrew, salvation had to include the note of solidarity and further the glory of God. For Paul, the Christian, this meant the resurrection of the whole body of Christ for the glory of the Father: "Then comes the end, when he hands over the kingdom to his God and Father. . . . When everything is subjected to him, then the Son himself will [also] be subjected to the one who subjected everything to him, so that God may be all in all" (1 Cor 15:24, 28).

In Paul's judgment nothing could compare with the final consummation. For, up until the parousia, death would reign; and for Paul, death is not a mere biological fact but a tyranny, a penalty for humankind's offense which lay heavy not only upon the living but also in some way even upon the dead. The symbol and effect of sin, death was a power hostile to God which would continue to blight humanity even until the very end: "The last enemy to be destroyed is death" (1 Cor 15:26). Paul's lack of interest in the immediate aftermath of death, and his yearning for the parousia make clear that in his judgment even those who have died in the Lord still lack something.

In this regard it is significant that, when the Thessalonians mourn their dead, the Apostle does not comfort them with the reminder of a consummation in glory already achieved. He is content simply to point out that the living will have no advantage over the dead at the time of the parousia. He says nothing more than this to reconcile his readers to the fate of those who have already died. For Paul the Hebrew, death stripping a person of their body stood in open hostility to the full consummation of God's glory and humankind's definitive salvation.

This attitude is fundamentally biblical and Hebrew. Paul's yearning for the parousia echoes the hope of the author of Daniel for the total eschatological victory over sin (cf. Dan 9:24-25). The Apostle shares fully the ardent longing of the prophet who looked beyond the "seventy weeks" to the definitive defeat of all evil and the total realization of all good.

Death, the Doorway to Life

There is, however, another essential element in Paul's teaching, and this is formally Christian. It is this aspect of his doctrine which illumines death with truly Christian light. Through an act of supreme generosity Christ has made himself one with the human solidarity which lies under the burden of sin and death. As a man, incorporating in himself all that is human, he went through death in order to change the whole meaning of death. On Calvary, he faced all the horrors of a death which sin had made terrible. He endured the experience dreaded by all people as God's worst punishment, and thus he himself underwent God's judgment on the fallen human race.

It was precisely by this act that Christ took the bitter sting out of death (cf. 1 Cor 15:56-57). Because he was God's own son, death *had* to be for him the doorway to life, the return to the bosom of his Father.

Previously death was the consummation of our separation from God; in Christ it became the way of God. Previously it was the symbol of sin separating humankind forever from the living God. In Christ, it became the supreme manifestation of loving obedience which promised immediate access to God.

Such a death, the death of God's own son, beloved by the Father and totally devoted to the Father, contained a compelling right to glorious risen life with the Father. "He humbled himself, becoming obedient to death, even death on a cross. *Because of this* God greatly exalted him" (Phil 2:8-9). The connective "Because of this" marks the consequence not of mere promise but of inherent necessity. Resurrection was contained in the very nature of this death as the life of the flower is contained in the seed.

For Paul nothing could be more definitive than the death-resurrection of Christ. His passage from life in this world broke the tie which bound him to "flesh," the solidarity of earthly existence, with its inherent qualities of weakness, mortality and distance from God. Death swept him out beyond everything which bore the blight of life upon earth—the flesh and the law, sin and suffering, earthly weakness and death itself. Through resurrection he began an entirely new life in which he could give full play to the love and power which is his as messianic Son of God: "We know that Christ, raised from the dead, dies no more; death no longer has power over him. As to his death, he died to sin once for all; as to his life, he lives for God" (Rom 6:9-10).

Life in Jesus Christ

There is another factor equally essential to Paul's thought. The death-resurrection of Christ is of benefit not only to Christ but to all Christians. He died and rose again as a corporate personality, bearing all people in himself to the Father. The Hebrew conception of corporate personality underlies Paul's whole concept of the role of Christ. Like Adam, Christ embodies and represents all people; he is the new Adam (cf. 1 Cor 15:22, 45-49). Through the law of solidarity, therefore, his death and resurrection are efficacious for all: "We have come to the conviction that one died for all; therefore, all have died" (2 Cor 5:14). The experience of Christ, like the life in Adam, has power to extend and to renew itself in every person. That is why Paul can write in the name of every Christian: "I have been crucified with Christ; yet I live, no longer I, but Christ lives in me" (Gal 2:20).

Paul is not speaking of mere external imitation—"As Christ . . . so the Christian." His thought rests not on the level of external concomitance but on the deeper level of organic functioning. He speaks of the experience which he describes as life "in Christ Jesus."

In the Pauline vocabulary, this phrase means a real and psychosomatic union between Christ and the Christian. Through baptism the neophyte is so united to the risen body-person of the Savior that she shares the very life of Christ and becomes capable of extending the influence of his personality: "All of you who were baptized into Christ have clothed yourselves with Christ. There is neither Jew nor Greek, there is neither slave nor free person, there is not male and female; for you are all one in Christ Jesus" (Gal 3:27-28).

This union is both real and dynamic, bringing a vital share in the redemptive mysteries of Christ's own death and resurrection. What Christ has done in his body in dying on the cross and in rising from the dead is shared and reproduced in the Christian. The union between them is as exclusive and communicative as that of man and wife. This truth comes to clearest expression in Romans 7:4: "In the same way . . . you also were put to death through the body of Christ, so that you might belong to another, to the one who was raised from the dead in order that we might bear fruit for God."

The Christian does not merely assent psychologically to the redemptive activity of Christ, as some would hold. If that were the case, Calvary would be nothing more than another Sinai, and our justice would no longer be the gift of Christ but the wages of our own tedious human effort which always fails. To this latter suggestion Paul would have only one answer—*mē genoito*! (Certainly not!) [Gal 2:17]. It repeats the fundamental error of the Judeo-Christians which Paul strove against throughout his ministry. He himself knows no other way of justice except that which he describes in Philippians 3:8-10: "I have accepted the loss of all things and I consider them so much rubbish, that I may gain Christ and be found in him, not having any righteousness of my own based on the law but that which comes through faith in Christ, . . . depending on faith to know him and the power of his resurrection and [the] sharing of his sufferings."

All this becomes possible through the gift of the Spirit which Christians receive when they are united to the body-person of Christ in baptism. For the Spirit renews in the member of Christ the very death which the Savior died on the cross (death to the flesh and to sin); at the same time it vitalizes the Christian with the very life which

Christ himself now lives in glory. This share is so real that Paul does not hesitate to write: "We were indeed buried with him through baptism into death, so that, just as Christ was raised from the dead through the glory of the Father, we too might live in newness of life" (Rom 6:4).

THE FUNDAMENTAL LAW OF CHRISTIAN GROWTH

This sharing in the mysteries of Christ is real yet not static. All during our days upon earth we must live *en Christo* (in Christ) while at the same time continuing his human life *en sarki* (in the flesh). The crisscross of these two levels leads inevitably to tension and contradiction. Humankind is constantly drawn to assume again the "mind of flesh" (Rom 8:5) which represents primarily a denial of human dependence on God and a proud confidence in itself. For St. Paul, therefore, *sarx* implies much more than our English word *flesh*; *sarx* is humankind with all its faculties in rebellion against God. To react against this the Christian must often renew the baptismal death to sin and to *sarx* (cf. Rom 6:12ff.).

Life with God, too, must know its constant deepening and increase. If Christians have "clothed themselves with" Christ at baptism, they must ever continue to "clothe themselves" more and more throughout the course of life upon earth. The mystery of Christ's resurrection once shared in is to be lived always more intensely. Christian life, therefore, knows a fundamental law of growth. The conformity to Christ which gives new shape and new vitality to the whole personality at baptism, is to grow constantly until at last it becomes perfect conformity through the parousia-resurrection.

It is unfortunate that Paul's words on bodily resurrection in 1 Corinthians 15 have so often been considered apart from the consistent doctrine of the rest of his epistles. This has led to the mistaken notion that the final change will have in it something quasi-magical. Many indeed think of resurrection only as a physical resuscitation. They have overlooked Paul's words on the bond between resurrection and the indwelling Holy Spirit (Rom 8:11). This Spirit is always at work preparing Christians for the parousia by perfecting their likeness to Christ. The glorious moment of bodily resurrection, therefore, is but the last and consummate stage of that conformation to Christ which has been going on all during life.

We are now in a position to estimate the full Pauline perspective on death and the parousia. As a Jew and as a Christian, Paul could not think of humankind's perfect salvation except in terms of the full glory of God, the full redemption of the solidarity, the full conformity of all people to Christ through the parousia-resurrection. Obviously, therefore, his best thoughts always rested on the end-time of perfect consummation. Whatever took place before that was simply the development of the Christian's first conformation to Christ through baptism.

Père Feuillet has pointed out what is essential in this perspective: "Paul is interested above all in two crucial moments of our participation in the risen life of Christ: baptism which inaugurates this sharing and the parousia which consummates it. Baptism makes us one with Christ in his death and resurrection; the glorious parousia places the final seal on our conformity to him. All that takes place between these two moments does not establish any really new relation to Jesus."

PHYSICAL DEATH: ONE STEP IN THE PROGRESSION

Physical death, therefore, claims no special attention in Paul's letters. In his eyes it does not bring that full life with God which only the *total* person can know. For this, resurrection is necessary, the resurrection of the individual and of all the people of God. Death, therefore, marks only one more moment in the progressive conformation to Christ which is life's whole purpose.

He conceives of it only in the line of the progressive mortification of *sarx* which began at baptism. Paul envisages all Christian existence as a death realized in principle on Calvary, commenced in fact for each Christian at baptism, continued all through life, and completed by death "in Christ" at the term of one's earthly existence.

Death, therefore, is significant in Paul's mind not because it marks the consummation of entry into a new solidarity (only the parousia could do that) but because it marks, for the Christian, the dissolution of the old solidarity of *sarx*. Even this significance, however, must be qualified. The dissolution is only partial; for the solidarity of the *sarx* is bound up with "this age" rather than with this earth. Even those who have died in Christ must still await the "redemption of the body" and the restoration of all things.

We cannot say, however, that Paul was indifferent to the experience of death. He spoke of it twice, and both times with an awareness that death is a blessing. In Philippians 1:21-23 the Apostle, faced with martyrdom, expresses his longing for death and speaks of it as "a gain": "For to me life is Christ, and death is gain. If I go on living in the flesh, that means fruitful labor for me. And I do not know which I shall choose. I am caught between the two. I long to depart this life and be with Christ, [for] that is far better. Yet that I remain in the flesh is more necessary for your benefit."

The most obvious remark one can make on these words is to note that were it a question of choice between life and the parousia, instead of between life and death, Paul would not have experienced this uncertainty in making a choice. In the present instance he inclines towards death. His reasons appear in the very words he employs. He sees death as a departure from the world of *sarx* and therefore the last stage in his baptismal death to sin and weakness. This means conversely an intensification of his life "with Christ." From now on, he would walk uninterruptedly in that "newness of life" which has been his since baptism. Death, therefore, is a true "gain" rendering definitive his baptismal death with Christ and intensifying his baptismal life with Christ.

The fact remains, however, that death is not the parousia. It affects only Paul and not the solidarity. It brings the dissolution of *sarx* for Paul but not for the world. It lends new intensity to his personal life with Christ; but it does not bring life to the *whole* person. Death, therefore, leaves much to be desired. And so, apart from this single fervent wish here, Paul centers his attention throughout the rest of this epistle on the parousia.

This same spirit pervades Paul's second word on death—in 2 Corinthians 5:1-10. In this passage, moreover, he makes explicit the perspective which governs all his thinking. He begins with the mention of resurrection and ends with the reminder of judgment. The parousia is always to the fore in his thought. He is aware, though, that life has its immediate term in death when one leaves the body "to be at home with the Lord." Interpreted in the light of Paul's constant and fervent devotion to Christ this phrase has overtones of a rich personal companionship, which becomes all the more constant once *sarx* is laid aside. To lay aside *sarx*, however, means to lay aside the body also. This prospect fills him with dismay. He frankly confesses that it takes courage to face this ordeal, for "to be unclothed" ruptures the securities of life as one knows it; death, even at its best, is an exile.

CONCLUSION

Once more Paul has sketched his scale of values. No matter what death may achieve in intensifying life with the Lord, it cannot match the full and rich consummation of the parousia. It is now clear that early Christian thought laid little emphasis on death and its immediate aftermath; interest centered chiefly in parousia. It was the task of later theology to illumine the interim period between death and final consummation. This it did by focusing the light of precise philosophy on the data of revelation to formulate a full thesis on the beatitude of the soul immediately after death.

Unfortunately, the modern mind (the product of nineteenth-century subjectivism and individualism) has so concentrated on the "salvation of the soul" at death that it no longer adjusts easily to the complementary perspective of the parousia. The vision of the early Church, however, is the very perspective most needed in our day. The salvation of all people and the glorification of the total person through resurrection are divine answers to excessive individualism. The salvation of the body corporate and the renewal of family ties before the Father on the last day provide a living hope which gives moment and meaning to our present ecumenical efforts.

The ultimate glory destined by God for the whole world is one of the best incentives to true Christian humanism. It is in the light of the parousia that we come to understand best of all our duty to develop the world's resources, to foster ours and each other's talents, to lift human life from an inferior to a higher level. This is not merely a matter of social obligation or of civic pride; it is rather the working out of God's plan for the consummation of all things at the parousia. For what will this final consummation mean except that once more the whole world which God created will come completely under the control of Christ, Christ completely under his Father, giving into God's hands the family and the Kingdom divinely perfected?

CHAPTER 25

Christian Perfection, Contemplation, and Purgatory

In the late forties, a new translation brought to light a long-lost spiritual classic. This is the *Treatise on Purgatory* of St. Catherine of Genoa, translated by C. Balfour and H. D. Irvine. The appearance of this work was timely, not only for its teaching on purgatory, but especially for its contribution to the moot question of the relation between Christian perfection and contemplation. European theologians have long discussed this problem. But, as yet, no definitive solution has been reached. All that has emerged from prolonged study and debate are three conflicting views, each solidly probable.

THREE POINTS OF VIEW

One group of theologians, headed by Fathers Garrigou-Lagrange, O.P., and Saudreau, argue that the full flowering of the mystical life is the only normal development of the interior life. Hence, only those who have first passed through all the stages of infused prayer, at least equivalently, are perfect souls. In other words, the fire of infused contemplation must first sear both sense and spirit before a soul normally reaches heroic sanctity. Father Garrigou-Lagrange has given final expression to his thesis in vigorous words: "According to St. John of the Cross," he writes in *Christian Perfection and Contemplation,* "the full perfection attainable in this life is found only in the transforming union, or the spiritual marriage."

A great number of spiritual writers find it difficult to accept this theory of a universal call to contemplation. Such theologians as Monsignor Farges in *Mystical Phenomena* and Father Poulain, S.J., in

The Graces of Interior Prayer deny that infused contemplation is the only way to Christian perfection. They insist on the reality of a nonmystical way which leads to perfection as securely as the parallel mystical way. Hence, these scholars argue that it is possible for a soul to attain heroic sanctity without receiving the graces of infused contemplation and without passing through those mystical trials of sense and spirit which are always the concomitant of infused light.

There is yet another theory which Cuthbert Butler, O.S.B., explains and defends in his work, *Western Mysticism.* This theory resolves the extreme divergences of the previous two schools and, from elements of supposed truth in each, compounds a third thesis. Dom Butler agrees with Father Garrigou-Lagrange in teaching that infused contemplation is necessary for Christian perfection. However, he swings toward the other school in his insistence that a soul need not reach the higher degrees of infused contemplation nor pass through all the mystical purifications.

These theologians deserve grateful commendation for their devoted study of this question. However, in fairness, we must admit that the relation between Christian perfection and infused contemplation still remains an open problem—and also an important problem, since any final solution will involve many practical effects. For, if the theory of the universal call to contemplation is wholly embraced by the Church, then the attainment of sanctity will exact some very searching requirements. Father Garrigou-Lagrange was not slow to recognize this practical element in the controversy. Hence, one of his strongest arguments rests on this challenge: "The problem is a serious one. Is not the ideal of perfection notably lessened by maintaining that we can reach the full, normal development of Christian life without passing under one form or another through the passive purifications, which belong to the mystical order, and without being raised to infused contemplation, that dark and secret initiation into the mystery of God present within us?"

Consequently, any work which can throw light on this vital question is of real value. For this reason, we welcome the translation of St. Catherine of Genoa's brief *Treatise on Purgatory.* It is true, this little book never once mentions the word *contemplation;* but it does give clear, precise knowledge of God's requirements for Christian perfection.

ONE WOMAN'S EXPERIENCE AND REVELATION

Neither the worth nor authorship of this spiritual classic has ever been disputed. The great Italian mystic drew its contents not only from her own experience of soul purification, but also, no doubt, from her revelations. Father Pourrat's praise of the work is brief, but unqualified. He writes in *Christian Spirituality:* "Her treatise is remarkably accurate in doctrine, and theologians, no less than mystics, have given it their attention."

The work opens with an admission that the *Treatise* owes its origin to the fact that Catherine "found herself, while still in the flesh, placed by the fiery love of God in purgatory" (ch. 1). Thus she came to understand "what purgatory was like and how the souls there were tormented." She has related her experiences in the seventeen short chapters of this monograph on the nature of purgatory. Moderation and restraint strike the keynote of the entire composition. Again and again Catherine asserts "that neither arguments nor figures nor examples can make the thing clear as the mind knows it to be in effect" (ch. 5). Accordingly, the saint does not labor to arouse sense impressions; her whole concern is with the substance of truth. Certainly, if Dante has been described as St. Thomas Aquinas in verse, Catherine represents the angelic doctor at work on a mystical treatise. In this brief study we find all the limpid clearness and moderation of the *Summa.*

The relevance of the *Treatise on Purgatory* to the problem of perfection and infused contemplation is not immediately evident. Any conclusion in this matter will be reached only by inference from a cumulative argument. However, we do believe that such an inference can be reached validly. For, when studied with an eye to the problem of infused contemplation, the *Treatise* does yield three pertinent considerations. Taken together, these considerations form a basis for the inference which St. Catherine herself seems to have drawn. We shall review these three elements, one by one.

Cleansed to Immaculate Purity

The first essential element revealed by the *Treatise* requires that souls in purgatory be cleansed to immaculate purity before entering heaven. St. Catherine shows herself most exacting in stating the requirements of true holiness. Frequently she stresses the truth that only a completely purified soul can dare to approach infinite purity. "God stands before us," she says, "with open arms to receive us into divine glory. But well I see the divine essence to be of such purity, greater far than can be imagined, that the soul in which there is even the least note of imperfection would rather cast itself into a thousand hells than find itself thus stained in the presence of the Divine Majesty" (ch. 8).

Apparently Catherine did not think that our earth offered a congenial home for this perfect purity. She never forgot that humankind is in a fallen state. And so her picture of the ordinary soul (in ch. 11) is deeply shaded with dark hues. "So many hidden imperfections are in the soul, that, did it see them, it would live in despair" (ch. 11). Indeed, Catherine seems to take it for granted that most souls will need the fire of searching purification if they are to recover the baptismal innocence which ineffable purity demands. For eternal life exacts the fullness of perfect works; and there are so few who always measure up to the requirement which Catherine has enunciated: "If a work is to be perfect it must be wrought in us but not chiefly by us, for God's works must be done in God and not wrought chiefly by humankind" (ch. 12).

Certainly, then, Catherine of Genoa does not barter heaven for a cheap price. She has little sympathy with half-hearted righteousness and smug mediocrity. And self-satisfaction in one's spiritual state would have a hard time of it under her careful scrutiny, for she herself had felt too keenly the pain of God's own probing. Therefore, with the strong conviction born of experience and revelation, she made bold to address these words of reproach to the people of our world. The passage is too important to abbreviate:

> I would fain send up a cry so loud that it would put fear in all men and women on the earth. I would say to them: "Wretches, why do you let yourselves be thus blinded by the world, you whose need is so great and grievous, as you will know at the moment of death, and who make no provision for it whatsoever?"
>
> You have all taken shelter beneath hope in God's mercy, which is, you say, very great, but you see not that this great goodness of God will judge you for having gone against the will of so good a Lord. God's goodness should constrain you to do all God's will, not give you hope in ill-doing, for divine justice cannot fail but in one way or another must needs be fully satisfied.
>
> Cease to hug yourselves saying, "Near the hour of my death I will confess my sins and then receive plenary indulgence, and at that moment I shall be purged of all my sins and thus shall be saved." Think of the confession and the contrition needed for that plenary indulgence, so hardly come by that, if you knew, you would tremble in great fear, more sure you would never win it than that you ever could (ch. 15).

These words of the saint might be open to question, if they were spoken only by her lips. But divine truth has confirmed them. Like

Catherine, Christ himself has warned all people that only "the clean of heart" shall see God.

Purification by *Divine Ray*

Second, St. Catherine writes that souls in purgatory are purified chiefly by the "divine ray" of infused knowledge and love of God. In describing the nature of purgatory and in analyzing its cause, the *Treatise* explains and demonstrates the thesis once enunciated by Père de la Taille, S.J., in *Contemplative Prayer:* "Purgatory, if both contemplative and non-contemplative have to pass through it, will make things equal even as regards the process of union. There, both will be contemplatives."

Even a casual reader will remark a close resemblance between the *Treatise on Purgatory* and the pages in which St. John of the Cross, St. Thérèse, and John Tauler tell the experiences of their own mystical life. Certainly souls in purgatory are kindred spirits to our own great contemplatives. Their absolute forgetfulness of every creature, even of self, their total abandonment to the divine will, that craving for God which causes in them a chiaroscuro of rapturous delight and gnawing pain—all these elements in their cleansing are identical with the mystical experiences realized here on earth by Saints Catherine of Siena, Thérèse, Bernard, Bruno, Gemma Galgani, and even Catherine of Genoa herself. Like these great saints and mystics, "the souls of purgatory can no longer will nor desire save with the pure will of pure charity" (ch. 1).

The chief cause of the soul's purification in purgatory, as stressed in the *Treatise,* is that same supernatural knowledge of God which flows into the soul, even in this life, through the light of infused contemplation. St. Catherine describes it thus: "I see, too, certain rays and shafts of light which go out from that divine love towards the soul and are penetrating and strong enough to seem as though they must destroy not only the body but the soul, too, were that possible" (ch. 10). This light purifies because it illumines the soul with an infused knowledge of that "uniting look" with which God draws it into the divine. In one of the most beautiful passages of the *Treatise,* Catherine describes this infusion of loving knowledge and explains how, in purifying the soul, it causes both exquisite joy and unspeakable pain:

> I perceive there to be so much conformity between God and the soul that when God sees it in the purity in which divine majesty created it God gives it a burning love, which draws it to himself, which is strong enough to destroy it, immortal though it may be, and which causes it to be so transformed in God that it sees itself

as though it were none other than God. Unceasingly God draws it to himself and breathes fire into it, never letting it go until he has led it to the state whence it came forth, that is to the pure cleanliness in which it was created.

When with its inner sight the soul sees itself drawn by God with such fire, then it is melted by the heat of the glowing love for God, its most dear Lord, which it feels overflowing it. And it sees by the divine light that God does not cease from drawing it, nor from leading it, lovingly and with much care and unfailing foresight, to its full perfection, doing this of pure love. But the soul, being hindered by sin, cannot go whither God draws it; it cannot follow the uniting look with which God would draw it to himself. Again the soul perceives the grievousness of being held back from seeing the divine light; the soul's instinct too, being drawn by that uniting look, craves to be unhindered. I say that it is the sight of these things which begets in the souls the pain they feel in purgatory (ch. 9).

All during the period of purgatory, therefore, this infused knowledge of God acts as the chief agent of purification, for the awareness of infinite purity convinces the soul "in regard to sin and righteousness and condemnation" (John 16:8). This light reveals so strongly the attributes of God that "the soul in which there is even the least note of imperfection would rather cast itself into a thousand hells than find itself thus stained in the presence of the divine majesty" (ch. 8). At the same time, this knowledge of God is a cause of great joy, always increasing as the process of purification lengthens: "Day by day," Catherine says, "this happiness grows as God flows into these souls, more and more as the hindrance to divine entrance is consumed" (ch. 2).

We may conclude, then, that if the mystic undergoes purgatory here on earth, the soul in purgatory receives purification in the divine fire of infused contemplation. Both receive, in their own way, the full effects of that loving knowledge which St. John of the Cross has described so well in *Dark Night of the Soul:* "It enkindles [contemplatives] with passionate yet afflictive love, until they be spiritualized and refined by this same fire of love; and it purifies them until they can receive with sweetness the union of this loving infusion after the manner of the angels.... But meanwhile they receive this contemplation and loving knowledge in the distress and yearning of love."

The Gift of Infused Contemplation

The final element to be considered in our cumulative argument is the capacity of St. Catherine of Genoa to share in the purification of the poor souls in purgatory through her own gift of infused contemplation. The strength of this light blinded the saint with the cleansing dark night of sense and spirit. This she explains in the last chapter of her *Treatise.*

Her own sufferings were the perfect counterpart of the torments of the souls in purgatory. Catherine was left without power to enjoy anything, spiritual or temporal; all things became to her "hateful and abhorrent." Her only comfort was the thought of God. "My happiness," she wrote, "is that God be satisfied, nor could I suffer a worse pain than that of going outside God's ordinance, so just I see God to be and so very merciful" (ch. 17).

The cause of this experience was the infused knowledge of God which she received. It is the "loving fire" of this "light of God" which works all suffering and all virtue in her soul. For infused contemplation always entails great suffering for the soul not yet purified. As St. Catherine herself has said: "The more the soul knows God, the more it esteems God and the more sinless it becomes, so that the hindrance in its way grows yet more terrible to it, above all because the soul which is unhindered and wholly recollected in God knows God as the Lord truly is" (ch. 17).

Thus, the latter years of Catherine's life provide an eloquent commentary on the passage in which St. John of the Cross describes the purifying and strengthening effects of the grace of infused contemplation. "When this loving contemplation," he says, "illumines us, who are impure and weak, it illumines us according to our nature. It plunges us into darkness and causes us affliction and distress, as does the sun to the eye that is weak; it enkindles us with passionate yet afflictive love, until we be spiritualized and refined by this same fire of love."

Catherine herself was the first to see the necessity of this soul-searching purification. For she knew well her own weakness; only the fire of God could burn away the accumulated rust of guilt. In her own soul she was convinced of a real need for the special action of God to cleanse "whatever in her needed cleansing, to the end that when she passed from this life she might be presented to the sight of God, her dear love" (ch. 1).

IN CONCLUSION

These three considerations render the *Treatise on Purgatory* a valuable contribution to the problem of the relation between Christian perfection and infused contemplation. It is true, the *Treatise* does not solve this problem finally; but, at least, it does lend greater probability to one of the theories previously proposed.

To appreciate this probability, we must take into account the certain conclusions which the book presents. First, it emphasizes the truth that there can be no perfect purity of mind and heart. At the same time, it takes for granted that fallen humankind cannot, by unaided efforts, attain this purity. It requires a very special help of God. This is the whole purpose of purgatory. In this state, the light of infused knowledge and love cleanses the soul of all rust of sin. These are conclusions which all theologians readily accept.

Does the *Treatise on Purgatory* authorize a further deduction? Does it contain any definite teaching on the process of sanctification in this life? The present writer thinks it does. For, in tracing the odyssey of all human weakness (ch. 11), St. Catherine says of *every* soul: "It stays so sullied and so turned to self that all the divine workings of which we have spoken are needed to recall it to its first state in which God created it; without them it could never get back thither." In these words, the saint gives expression to a conviction which pervades the entire *Treatise*. If any soul in this life is to be purified to perfect holiness, then, like the souls in purgatory, it too needs the cleansing fire of infused contemplation.

Therefore, the *Treatise on Purgatory* gives new strength to the thesis that infused contemplation is the normal way to perfect purity, both in this life and in the next. As Father de la Taille has pointed out in a letter to Father Bainvel, S.J., there are bounds to the psychological make-up of fallen humankind, even when this is supernaturalized by ordinary grace. It is a moral impossibility for the soul, with its ordinary psychological apparatus, to produce and to sustain that overflowing love of God which is absolutely requisite for perfect purity and perfect union. Only an infused and luminous knowledge of God, creating a new and ultra-human state of soul, can bring a soul to perfect purity and maintain this condition. This is the mind of Catherine of Genoa: "If a work," she says, "is to be perfect it must be wrought in us but not chiefly by us, for God's works must be done in God and not wrought chiefly by humankind" (ch. 12).

All men and women, then, who are striving for a pure, wholehearted love, should ardently desire this infused light and humbly pray God for strength to support its afflictive and blinding brilliance. It is our very helplessness which makes this grace so necessary. Without it, the perfecting of humankind will lack that strong help which comes from the infused knowledge of God's goodness and the soul's misery. The practice of the love of God and of real humility, fervor in God's service and generosity, a spirit of true mortification and detachment, real zeal for souls—these virtues will never be fully strong and pure until God has given the light of contemplation. For, in this life, contemplation alone brings that knowledge of God so needful for perfect love and perfect purity. It is for this knowledge we must ask, for, as St. Catherine says so well: "The more the soul knows God, the more it esteems God and the more sinless it becomes" (ch. 17).

CHAPTER 26

Mystical Life Today

Costante Brovetto, C.P.

This short reflection will attempt to give an account of some positive developments in Catholic spirituality despite the difficulties inherent in the prevailing culture as the twentieth century reaches its close.

The Church has accepted legitimate secularization and recognizes the proper autonomy of the temporal order as willed by the creator. The Second Vatican Council taught in the Constitution on the Church that "eschatological hope does not lessen the importance of earthly pursuits but, rather, provides added motives to work at them." This remains true even where an arrogant secularism floods over the world seeking to reduce the horizons of human life to the confines of immanentism and a hedonism without limits. The devastating consequences for the well being and even the survival of humankind are such that in all camps we have an about-face, as can be seen in the growing concern with our ecology.

A further symptom, a return to the sacred, despite the fact it is marred at times by extravagant cults, indicates "a new hunger and thirst for the transcendent and the divine" as noted in the report from the 1985 Synod of Bishops. We have witnessed increased studies in spirituality in Catholic circles as well as the rise of spiritual movements with large followings. Here we see theology following the trend of the times developing along experiential lines.

The condemnation of modernism in 1907 by Pius X safeguarded theology from reducing itself to an immanent religious experience. Since then there occurred a revival of interest in genuine religious experience. Schools of theology embraced a variety of positions. However, we think it would be safe to say that the position that held for a profound unity in the spiritual journey and a normal culmination in an authentic experience of God prevailed. Exceptional mystical phenomena were given a very secondary consideration. New horizons were opened to Christians immersed in secular society. After 1950, mysticism received a more adequate reception as a participation in the mystery of Christ.

Reacting against the "Death of God" movement, energetic, audacious thinkers proposed an authentic, strong experience of God known beyond dispute. In this experience one enters personally into the sphere of the transcendent, beginning to live an "eternal life." As a matter of fact the gift that God offers to us in grace and the transcendental yearning of humans for the immediate presence of God is activated in such a way that its fulfillment is the beatific vision in which God possesses us without any mediating created reality.

Perhaps this is the best and most comprehensible way to speak to people of today of the future life, or at least what pertains to the "intermediate period" which will last until we are called to the final resurrection. Pope Leo XIII when treating our union with Christ and the divine paraclete dwelling in us directed his eyes to that blessed vision in which this mystical union will achieve its fullness in heaven: "The marvelous union, the Indwelling, differs from that in which God embraces and rejoices in the saints only by reason of our state and condition."

According to the Congregation for the Doctrine of the Faith, an essential point in thinking of the status of people after death is to believe "in the fundamental continuity which exists by virtue of the holy Spirit, between the present life in Christ and the life to come." For the saints, the life of faith is such. Thus, St. Catherine of Genoa in her mystical experience describes the quality of purification undergone in purgatory by those who need to come to full beatitude. [Editor's note: See Chapter 25 of this book, "Christian Perfection, Contemplation and Purgatory."]

At this point, we wish to offer a short essay based on the doctrine of a spiritual master whose greatness and relevance has come to light in our times—St. Paul of the Cross. With the publication of his retreat diary and letters in 1924, he was "discovered" as a mystic. We will concentrate on his frequent use of the texts of St. John the evangelist. St. Paul of the Cross made use of the Johannine texts in accord with the works of John Tauler with whose writings he was quite familiar. Johannine spirituality anticipates and places eschatology in the present.

While not excluding a "last day" yet to come, Jesus assures the disciples that he and the Father will come to them every time they have an experience of the spirit. We will examine this anticipation of eternal life in current terms in order to throw some light on the mysterious period of the life to come.

CERTAINTY OF FAITH: JESUS BRINGS US TO WHERE HE IS

St. Paul of the Cross declares that he wishes to speak in "the language of faith." He distrusts superficial experiences, but willingly welcomes persons who desire a life of deep union with God. His ordinary procedure is to bring together various passages of the gospel, weaving them into a description of our spiritual journey. Here is an example from his letters:

> Jesus speaking to his loved ones says: "Father, where I am, there I will my servant to be." My servant is in the bosom of the Father, and the soul united to God in pure and holy love, is where God is, "in the bosom of the Father," and there feeds on love, a love that makes the servant Godlike.

The way in which St. Paul of the Cross merges the two Gospel texts is significant. In John 17:24, Jesus prays that his followers share his glory. In John 12:26, the promise is joined to a challenging condition—Whoever loves one's life, loses it, and whoever hates one's life in this world will preserve it for eternal life. "Whoever serves me must follow me, and where I am, there also will my servant be." The logic of John is clear: The glory of Jesus and of the disciple is the glory of the cross!

So the bosom of the Father is the mystical place *par excellence*. Paul of the Cross constantly uses this language and once more depends on John:

> Be assured that the divine shepherd will lead you as his beloved sheep to his sheepfold. And what is the sheepfold of this gentle shepherd? It is the bosom of the Father, so it is to this most holy and divine bosom that he brings his sheep for their repose.

The Gospel of John presents the human experience of Christ in a dramatic way: Jesus has come from the Father and returns to the Father by way of the cross. However, Jesus never leaves the heavenly home which is the font of divine life: "I am in the Father, and the Father is in me" (John 14:10). The believer is brought to this home by accepting and following the pathway taken by Jesus. Thus one lives habitually in eternity, considering the cross exclusively as the path of entry into the heart of God:

> Lose sight of heaven and earth, the sea and the strand; lose sight of all things created, and allow that drop of the spirit which God granted you to lose itself in its origin which is God. In lofty recollection the soul passes, I would say, beyond time and loses itself in eternity; for in God time does not exist, all is eternal. To make this flight of love, you must pass through the door that is Christ, as he says in the gospel. The door is Jesus Christ, our Lord, and his most holy passion—a work entirely of love. The one who passes through this divine door finds oneself where Jesus is: in the bosom of the Father.

St. Paul of the Cross describes this passage as a real plunging "into the abyss of divinity" yet warns us "not to try to understand this happening." It is an experience of faith illuminated by interior grace: "Jesus will teach you, if you remain in your nothingness." We have echoes here of John speaking of our access to the transcendent divine life: "No one has seen God . . ." (John 1:18).

THE NEW AND DIVINE BIRTH

The passage of which we are speaking is often styled "mystical death" by St. Paul of the Cross. The expression has a large range of applications. In his well-known booklet "The Mystical Death or Holocaust of the Pure Spirit of the Religious Soul" the expression is used for religious profession. There are many "crucifying" factors which can contribute to the mystical death of one who has undertaken the spiritual journey. At this point we will not delay over these. The experience of one who definitively abandons the self to the creator in imitation of Jesus in his dying is to be seen not primarily in the category of suffering but in the contemplative aspect of a death in one world and entry into another. The spiritual terms are detachment, separation, annihilation:

> Entirely crucified with your divine spouse through a mystical death to all that is not God, with a continual separation from all created things, and entirely hidden in the bosom of the heavenly

> Father, in true interior solitude, living no longer in oneself, but in Christ Jesus!
> All your effort should be knowledge of your nothingness and of the true all that is God!

Anyone who has such an experience shuts out any consideration of self, the world around, even the religious world in which one lives. All human values are set aside, "closing off in the sight of our horrible nothingness: having nothing, able to do nothing, knowing nothing." A truly new life cuts away from everything, since one's only worth is to be born anew from the bosom of the Father in a divine birth with and in the Son.

Mystical death is the passage of a person from the empirical and deluding truth about self to the ultimate and beatifying truth one finds in God. In reality we are more "true" in God than we are in ourselves. Paul of the Cross liked to say that to experience this we had "to enter into the depth of Tauler." He shared with Tauler the ancient spiritual tradition which reemerged so strongly in the Rhenish-Flemish School of the fourteenth century. This tradition did not permit the soul of faith to limit itself to functioning on a merely moralistic, emotional, cultic love, but insisted it must reach its ultimate truth in that "depth" of self that cannot be perceived experimentally insofar as it coincides with the "bosom of God." A person finds oneself in the plan God had for one from all eternity. If and when one accepts this plan and embraces it, just as Jesus did, one is "reborn," perfect, at peace and happy:

> In the divine bosom of the Father, in the sacred silence of faith and holy love, one will be reborn in the divine word, Christ Jesus, to a new life of love, a Godlike life, a holy life.

The theme of the divine birth is also Johannine. In the prologue of his Gospel, John tells us that believers are born of God (John 1:13), and this is not a figure of speech but a reality, even if "what we shall be is not yet revealed" (1 John 3:2). Jesus will tell Nicodemus that it is necessary to be reborn from above (John 3:6), as a new creation from the spirit, as Barnabas Ahern noted in "The Indwelling Spirit: A Foretaste of Glory." [See Chapter 23 of this book.] On the level of faith, there is only one divine blueprint for humanity—Jesus Christ crucified. "Those predestined to glory are first of all predestined to be conformed to Christ on the cross" (Rom 8:29). Thus, for one who is reborn mystically, the very consciousness of one's being ("memory" as seen by Augustine constitutes the foundation of our identity) coincides with the "memory of the Passion!" And this, paradoxically, is the blessed life of eternity already begun. J. Ratzinger in *Introduction to Christianity* puts it well following the thought of the fourth evangelist: "the being united to Christ, made possible by faith, is already a beginning of resurrected life which has conquered death. The dialogue begun in faith is already life: a life which can never be cut off by death."

GODLIKE LIFE — FORETASTE OF BEATITUDE

> One who is mystically dead thinks only of living a Godlike life. Mystical death in Christ brings with it a new life of love, a divine life, since it unites us to our supreme good through love.

The adjectives *deiforme* (godlike) and *deifico* (divinizing) as used by St. Paul of the Cross are links to ancient tradition, especially that of the Eastern Church. Christians are "sharers of the divine nature" (2 Peter 1:4). They are "one" in God, as are the Father and the Son (John 17:21), that is, in one and the same spirit.

> In that divine embrace, God so unites God's self to the soul in love that the soul seems to be one spirit with God . . . whoever is joined to the Lord becomes one spirit with God (1 Cor 6:17), so said St. Paul who had experienced this.

The close resemblance between this godlike life and that of the life to come with the beatific vision is clear. In describing both aspects, St. Paul of the Cross used the classic metaphor of the droplet immersed in the immensity of the sea. Is it possible to sketch some aspects of this experience in a way that will be understood today? Saint Paul of the Cross seems to have preferred the Johannine metaphor of the eschatological banquet.

Perhaps, in the light of the Petrine text (1 Peter 2:2), ". . . like newborn infants, long for pure spiritual milk," Paul of the Cross did not hesitate to describe the newborn soul as feeding on holy love in the bosom of the Father, an ingenuous characterization of God as "Father-Mother"—solicitous and most tender. "Repose in the bosom of the heavenly Father and grow strong there feeding yourself on the sacred milk of divine love." Here life feeds at its origin, in that eschatological climate that Jesus refers to when, going beyond the cult practiced at this or that temple, he reminds the Samaritan woman how the Father wishes to be adored (cf. John 4:23). "The place of prayer is in the spirit of God. You ought to stay in a true internal solitude, reposing with the most intimate part of your spirit in the bosom of the heavenly Father, adoring God in spirit and in truth, and there receive all that God wishes to give you. If you do this, the divine spirit will clothe you with virtue and make you live a Godlike life."

Joy in doing the will of God is the experiential foundation of divinized life. It grows in a contemplative way and understands step by step that all contingent events are simply what God has willed for us from all eternity and are always for our good.

> The loving soul is pleased that in everything the divine will is accomplished, feeding in this way on the divine will, just as Jesus said that his food was the will of his Father, and this—not merely in things according to one's taste but even more in suffering. Whatever happens is for the best—sin excepted. Hence the loving soul rejoices in the divine will in all that happens, for that will can wish only what is best.

To find a delightful flavor in the divine will everywhere: Here is the nucleus of the wisdom of the cross which prevents the godlike life from exempting itself from cruel reality into which it infuses something of eternity.

> On the feast of the cross, always prepare for yourself a solemn banquet, feeding on the divine will after the pattern of our crucified love. Oh, how sweet this food! It is spiced in many ways, with pains of body and spirit, with contradictions, calumnies, and insults. Oh what a pleasant taste to the palate of the spirit when tasted in pure faith and holy love, "in silence and in hope" (Isa 30:15).

BEATITUDE OF THE "IN-BETWEEN TIME"

The experience of the divine nativity can provide the theologian with a basis for saying something about the happiness beyond this world as it is experienced by the separated soul. "Soul" is accepted today as the "human ego," the spiritual entity endowed with consciousness and will as it continues to exist awaiting its completion through reunion with the body.

We do not pretend to have discovered clear concepts in the spirituality of St. Paul of the Cross. However, we do perceive the clarity of his heavenly life in the frequent use he made of brief prayers of praise as though he were already living in the unveiled presence of God.

For the cause of the beatification and canonization of St. Paul of the Cross, Brother Bartholomew testified:

> Often he would break out in fiery bursts of prayer, and with hands joined and eyes fixed on heaven: *Gratias agimus tibi propter magnam gloriam tuam* (We give thanks to you on account of your great glory), repeating the chant, as he would say, of paradise. Or again, *Benedictio, et claritas, et sapientia et gratiarum actio, honor et virtus et fortitudo Deo nostro in saecula saeculorum. Amen.* (Blessing and clarity, wisdom and thanksgiving, honor and virtue and strength to our God forever and ever. Amen). Then he would add the *Gloria Patri, et Filio et Spiritui Sancto* . . . (Glory to the Father, and to the Son, and to the Holy Spirit . . .). Paul wrote: "A holy soul has said—'Sing the *Sanctus* when you have crosses!'"

The cross and glory! In this holy Passionist there comes a moment in which the inebriation of the spirit is often expressed with respect to the Eucharist, in which he recalls the cry of Jesus: "Let the one who is thirsty come to me and drink" (John 7:37), so indicative of the full gift of the spirit.

> What a treasure is holy communion! This is the font of love, of holiness. "Let the one who is thirsty come to me and drink." Drink and quench your thirst; drink rivers of divine love, drink seas—but let them be rivers and seas of fire!

In the Eucharist we touch immortality: "This is the bread that comes down from heaven, so that the one who eats it does not die. The one who eats this bread will live forever" (John 6:53, 58). One who has found true identity in a new birth in Christ is never deprived of one's "body" even if one is "asleep" in the Lord. It is the Body of Christ! "God in you and you in God. . . ." God feeds on your spirit and your spirit feeds on the spirit of God: *Cibus meus Christus et ego eius* (My food is Christ, and I am his).

In this divine work there can be no deception, for it is the work of faith and love. "Sleep on the bosom of the savior in peace, receiving what God gives. When you sleep this divine sleep in Jesus Christ, you learn more than all the wise ones of the world." Paul of the Cross is thinking of John at the Last Supper resting on the bosom of the Savior (John 13:25), and he shared his secrets. Here is the special secret: Even here on earth we are in Christ and form with him one body. In heaven we will know in all its depth what it means to live with and in the risen Body of Christ, which grows toward its final perfection, completing itself in the history of redeemed humanity (cf. Col 1:24). Jesus Christ and as many as are living in him continue to be the active participants in this growth. This glory of the cross has historical happiness with regard to us, to whom the risen one shows himself as the lamb slain in the Eucharist (cf. Rev 5:6). The eschatological victory is being laboriously completed until God is all in all (cf. 1 Cor 15:28), and the lamb will be the eternal temple and the light of the city of saints (cf. Rev 21:22).

IN CONCLUSION

In this short essay we have limited ourselves to a few incomplete indications. We hope that persons of good will would find here a pathway to an experience of God that is not illusory because it is founded on Christ crucified. The divine birth leads to the birth of a new world. Those who are reborn, in the language of St. Paul of the Cross, are "separated from the world and are free of its slogans." They radically reject every false value. They "receive the heavenly light with the acquisition of true wisdom and work for the kingdom, leaning on the weakness of each other in the likeness of Jesus Christ," until the end of the world.

Part VIII
In Recognition

Now I will praise those godly persons,
   our ancestors, each in their own time; . . .
Or counselors in their prudence,
   or seers of all things in prophecy; . . .
Authors skilled in composition,
   and forgers of epigrams. . . .
Composers of melodious psalms,
   or discoursers on lyric themes;
Stalwart persons, solidly established
   and at peace in their own estates—
All these were glorious in their time,
   each illustrious in their day.
Some of them have left behind a name
   and people recount their praiseworthy deeds
   (Sir 44:1-8).

CHAPTER 27

Barnabas M. Ahern, Churchman

Bishop Paul M. Boyle, C.P.

My privileged invitation to contribute to this project honoring Fr. Barnabas Mary Ahern, C.P., requested that I consider his vital involvement in the Church of some thirty years ago. It is a distinct pleasure to participate. Because I am writing from a mission location, outside the United States, I do not have access to sources, not even to Barnabas' own writings (except for one article). This chapter, therefore, is a recollection. Nevertheless, I feel a degree of confidence since I write from almost fifty years of close friendship with Barnabas, half of them living with him. If my deep love and profound admiration color my vision and cloud my judgments, I readily admit this weakness which I share with very many others.

* * * *

Catholic life today is essentially what it has always been. Now as always one's striving for holiness is guided by the word of God and gains momentum through prayer and the sacraments. The apostolate too, works for the end it has always pursued, to make the whole world one in Christ.

This sameness, however, is not monolithic. . . . All living things adjust to the world around them. So too, the Church. It shapes the dimensions of its service to the framework of the present time; it takes tone and color from its present surroundings.

Essentially the same yet perennially contemporary, the Church faces now as always the challenge of a contemporary world. If spiritual life is to be vital and apostolate effective, men and women of the Church must keep their finger on the pulse of life around them.

Father Barnabas wrote these words for *Perspectives* in 1962, admirably summarizing his deep and peaceful conviction that the Church remains the same while continually adapting to the ever changing reality in which it lives. [Editor's note: Chapter 4 of this book, drawn from another published work of Father Barnabas, further develops these ideas.] In this he was anticipating by more than a quarter of a century the declaration *On the Interpretation of Dogmas* by the International Theological Commission that "a contemporary interpretation of dogmas must take into account two, at first sight, contradictory principles: the abiding validity of the truth and the actuality of the truth" (October 1989).

Barnabas was convinced that our modern passion for the real was being used by the Holy Spirit in bringing Catholics to test all things in a relentless search for truth. He was well aware that this devouring search can lead to an unwarranted iconoclasm that "can destroy not only the rind but the fruit, not only the shell but the nut-meat which it encases." But as long as it is the search of the Church it "is bound to bring out what is richest in the Church's life."

Undoubtedly, one of Barnabas' most powerful contributions before and during Vatican II was his striking ability to manifest the dynamic action of the Holy Spirit in the process of rethinking and reexpressing traditional Catholic beliefs and practices to attain more clearly and convincingly the goals presented in the Scriptures. He always strove to demonstrate how the approaches accepted by the council were an enrichment of perennial Catholic teachings. In doing so, he was instrumental in preparing many to accept, with conviction and enthusiasm, the orientations proposed by the Vatican Council.

In that same article in 1962 Barnabas articulated some principal concerns of the Church to which all Catholics must be committed: "to ecumenism, to the revival of liturgy, to the renewal of sacred studies, to the activation of the laity, to the mission-mindedness of the Church, to its yearning for peace, to its awareness of all life as sacramental." During several decades Barnabas devoted his considerable creativity and energy to promoting these concerns. With varying degrees of success Vatican II brought the Church closer to the attainment of most of these goals.

SCHOLARSHIP

For the first half of this century the American Catholic Church was almost totally dependent upon European scholars for ideas. After

World War II, however, scholarship began to bud in the United States. Perhaps the liturgical movement, led by the monks of St. John's Abbey and, later, by Notre Dame University, was the first flowering but Scripture studies were not far behind. There were, of course, scholars in other fields, like John Courtney Murray in the area of religious freedom. But genuine scholarship was just beginning to unfold in America during the decade before Vatican II.

Barnabas Ahern was in the forefront of Catholic scriptural scholarship during that time. He was one of the first Americans to obtain a doctorate in sacred Scripture from the Pontifical Biblical Institute, Rome. He did so with the highest honors. He believed in scholarship for its own sake and supported and appreciated those who provided pure research. In talks to seminary faculties, clergy, and seminarians, he was eloquent and challenging in his promotion of the best in scholarship. While his chief concern was the sacred sciences, he urged a well-rounded education in science and the humanities.

Long before the council he asked for and received a rescript from the Holy See allowing him to pray the psalms of the Roman Breviary in the original Hebrew. He loved the Hebrew and Greek languages. Entering his room one was often confronted with his enthusiasm at some new insight from a comparison of the Hebrew text with the Greek Septuagint. In addition to his knowledge of biblical languages, he was fluent in French, Italian, and German. He kept *au courant* of developments in Scripture studies by reading scholarly journals and monographs in various languages.

For Barnabas, study of the Scriptures meant also a careful scrutiny of the fathers of the Church and the teachings of theologians, especially St. Thomas Aquinas. For many years he would spend an hour or so daily studying the writings of Thomas Aquinas. Likewise, during a few years he spent some time almost each day studying Denzinger's *Enchiridion Symbolorum,* a collection of official teachings of the Church. Even when he ceased this as a regular practice, he would frequently return to this compilation to study Church teaching. This study of sources was not a passive reading for information but a search to understand the texts, to interpret them, to harmonize them with other information. He had a keen awareness that "it is the one spirit working throughout all of the history of salvation" and, as a result, he appreciated that "the inner coherence of the tradition constitutes a fundamental criterion" *(On the Interpretation of Dogmas).* Barnabas liked to discuss these teachings with friends, to explore with them various aspects and possibilities. He found these discussions helpful in clarifying and sharpening his appreciations and insights. He was eager to share with others his love for the magisterium of the Church, the writings of the fathers, and the works of theologians.

Some have claimed that Barnabas knew the Bible by heart but this is a great exaggeration. He did indeed know the Scriptures very well. In particular, he had a marvelous facility for recalling details in the sacred texts and relating them to other minor incidents in the Bible. At the end of the 1940s and early in the 1950s, he received several mysterious telephone calls asking him for names of biblical personages related to Moses. Without looking at the Bible, he was able to give several. Each call was followed by a generous donation. Finally, after several years, a grateful owner informed Father Barnabas that he was naming a family of thoroughbred race horses. When preparing homilies or conferences, I would sometimes explain to him my need for an apt quote or better, some incident. He was almost always able to suggest something pertinent.

LITURGY

Although Barnabas was not a liturgist, he was enthusiastic about the goals of the liturgical movement. Frequently he spoke and wrote to further these objectives. He gave numerous lectures at different liturgical gatherings of religious communities, dioceses, regional groups, and national conventions. He published articles in liturgical magazines, especially in *Worship*. Naturally, his point of view was always some doctrine of sacred Scripture as applied to daily life in and through communal worship.

His interest was constantly in making the liturgy a source of life and action. No one would have thought of Barnabas Ahern as a leader in the liturgical movement but whenever liturgical leaders thought of someone to enlighten or inspire others about the liturgy, his name was among the first to come to mind. His lectures and writings did indeed serve to promote interest in and appreciation of the liturgical movement.

LAITY

No one could be even remotely associated with the liturgical movement without developing an awareness of the role of the laity in the life of the Church. Besides, Chicago in the two decades before

Vatican II was the center of American Catholic thought and action regarding lay involvement. It was only natural, then, that Barnabas was deeply involved in efforts to promote the spirituality and apostolic activity of the laity. He was, moreover, close to Chicago priests who were leaders in the various groups and organizations of Catholic Action.

Barnabas was frequently called upon to give lectures to diocesan, regional, and national gatherings of clergy, religious, and laity on Catholic Action. His most frequent theme when speaking of the laity was the universal call to sanctity. Using different scriptural approaches, he developed the point that as members of the body of Christ we are all called to perfection. While this seems commonplace to us today, it was a stirring message a decade before the council. Occasionally, Barnabas also conducted seminars in the Chicago area with small groups of lay men and women, usually professional or business people. He became spiritual director to many of these participants.

ECUMENISM

Controversy or even apologetics were not Barnabas' style. He preferred an approach that concentrated on the beauty of the goal to which we are all called. In this way, he stressed the fundamental points that unite all Christians. The universality of God's love for all and the salvation offered us through the cross of Christ were truths appealing to all Christians. Prior to Vatican II there was not much ecumenism, particularly on a public or organized level, but Barnabas did have many contacts with Protestant groups. Several times he was invited to talk to Protestant church gatherings. His appreciation of the Scriptures and the riches of God's love for us was an inspiration to these groups.

Barnabas had a particular predilection for Jews. Although I am not aware of any lectures he gave to Jewish groups, he did have a number of Jewish friends. Whenever Barnabas met a Jew, he would talk about the riches of Jewish spirituality. Recalling the tremendous faith of the holy men and women in Israel's history, he would speak of the traditions of daily prayer in Judaism. Quite frequently the reaction was: "You know more about my religion than I do." Often these people asked if they could come to speak with Barnabas later, so enthusiastic were they about his appreciation for their history and spirituality.

It was during Vatican II, however, that Barnabas' ecumenism blossomed. In contact with men of great knowledge and profound faith,

Barnabas developed a deep admiration for these Christian leaders. He found them an inspiration and he longed to share with them the insights and appreciations of his own beliefs. His postconciliar years of service as a member of the Anglican-Roman Catholic International Commission were a treasured experience. As his ecumenical interests grew, he became more concerned with the theological refinements of a doctrine. He was utterly opposed to carelessness or superficiality about God's truth. He was anxious that believers explore together to make sure they have the same understandings of God's revelation.

SPIRITUALITY

God's word is life-giving. Probably this could summarize Barnabas' basic understanding of Scripture. Whenever he spoke about Scripture, he inevitably spoke of the life this word intends to give. His appreciations in this regard were particularly impressive.

When the modern Catholic Scripture movement began in the United States, a few popularizers shocked or otherwise upset audiences by broad generalizations or over-simplifications. When Barnabas presented an interpretation, there was little danger of upset or shock, as the explanation was seen to fit so perfectly into the life-giving purpose of the passage. If an interpretation was new or different, it was presented as a more convincing challenge to an already understood Christian goal. It was shown to provide a keener appreciation of a known Christian truth.

Undoubtedly the most convincing aspect of Barnabas' presentation of spirituality was his utter sincerity. His lived experience of the truths he was expressing was a powerful dynamic. In listening to his words, one had a strong sense of someone speaking from personal experience.

For Barnabas, our understanding of doctrine is guided by the power and presence of the Holy Spirit in the Church and in the hearts of individual Christians. Because of this, he saw the charism and testimony of saintly men and women as a gift of the Holy Spirit to the Church. He studied the lives and writings of the great saints of history, especially women like St. Catherine of Genoa and St. Brigid of Sweden. He was also powerfully attracted to humble figures like St. Rose of Lima, St. Peter Claver, and St. Benedict Joseph Labre. Outstanding Christian leaders of our era especially impressed him, women like St. Madeleine Sophie Barat, Catherine McAuley, and Janet Erskine Stuart.

His conversations and lectures were salted with interesting incidents from the lives of holy men and women. Every new canonization and beatification was a source of delight to him and he was eager to read the lives of these heroes. For him they were sources of inspiration, manifestations of the activity of the Holy Spirit in the different situations of our world. In this same spirit he cherished his close friendships with some of the outstanding priests, religious, and laity of his day. He found their dedicated zeal and contact with reality an inspiration. Their experience and expertise in a variety of fields provided him with precious nuggets of examples and insights that he cherished and used in his lectures.

APOSTOLATE

Barnabas was, in every sense of the word, a Scripture scholar, completely dedicated to the study and implementation of the Word of God. He recognized the need for pure research and readily acknowledged the rich contribution such scholars make. He was acutely aware of the need for a scholarly, scientific approach to revelation and theology, but he was even more sensitive to the fact that revelation and doctrine are primarily salvific. They are intimately and inseparably linked to the Church's life. His study and presentation of revelation and dogma were concerned with their soteriological meaning and role. As the International Theological Commission was to formulate it, revelation and dogmas "are to protect the community of the Church against errors; heal the wounds of error; and contribute to growth in living faith."

Theoretical scholarship was not Barnabas' métier. He was, to the marrow of his bones, an apostolic man, a preacher. Barnabas felt compelled to share with others, to proclaim by every means possible, the good news of the gospel. In carrying out this task, his talents were as outstanding as were his knowledge of and love for the Word of God. In the years before and during the Vatican II Council he spoke to innumerable groups and organizations throughout the United States and Canada. During many years such lectures were several a week. He was invited to address meetings in many parts of Africa, Asia, Australia, India, and Europe. Most of these overseas workshops were for bishops, priests, or religious, but he also conducted sessions for various organizations of laity. He used every opportunity available to him: conversations, confessions, spiritual direction, classroom, group discussions, conferences, homilies, retreats, conventions, articles. Apart from classroom presentations, his lectures in a typical year would have averaged well over a hundred. Often they would have totaled several hundred. And for many years he spent one afternoon a week visiting the sick in Chicago hospitals and sanitariums.

His sermons and lectures were always well written with vivid and powerful images. Extensive reading and a phenomenal memory enabled him to cite passages from poetry, plays, novels, films, and current songs. Those who knew Barnabas were often amazed and amused by his brief but telling allusions to modern plays, novels, films, and songs. These friends and confreres knew that while Barnabas did enjoy classical literature, especially poetry, he never saw a movie or read a current novel. His insightful and pithy references were gleaned from reviews or from conversations with artistic and literary friends. All reality had a sacramental value for Barnabas, so he was alert to and interested in all that was current.

Some of his Scripture peers and religious confreres lamented what they considered an excess of apostolic zeal. They wanted Barnabas to devote more time to scholarly pursuits, especially producing scholarly writings. A glance at the bibliography of his published works will show that his writings were not what one could properly call popular writings. They were, in general, scholarly efforts to address topics of vital interest for the life of the Church.

Only with great difficulty could Barnabas say no to any invitation to speak, whether it was to address a group of married couples, a class of high-school students, an altar society, or a regional or national convention. His zeal was not confined to large or prestigious groups. Wherever he was stationed, a large number of priests, religious, and laity came to him for confession or spiritual direction. Particularly during his years in Chicago, the number of people who came to see him or called was formidable.

SECOND VATICAN COUNCIL

Barnabas was in the hospital in Louisville, Kentucky, when his provincial, Very Rev. James Patrick White, C.P., flew down from Chicago to inform him that he had been appointed an expert or *peritus* to the Vatican Council. The provincial was deeply concerned about Barnabas' health and sought assurance from his doctor that he was strong enough to go to Rome. I was present when Barnabas was told of his appointment. It was generally assumed that his appointment was the result of a request by Albert Cardinal Meyer, Archbishop of Chicago, himself a professor of sacred Scripture.

It would take someone closely involved in the Second Vatican Council to evaluate the contribution Barnabas made. I have heard a variety of strong claims but am not able to verify them. Moreover, often a claim is based on the experience of one or another person and projected onto others. Some have assured me that Barnabas was a decisive influence in convincing the American and African hierarchies on several points. An Asian cardinal told me he thought Barnabas was the single most influential *peritus* for English language bishops. From bishops in various parts of Asia, Africa, and North America, I have received an impressive assortment of testimonials to the insight and inspiration provided by Father Barnabas during the council years. At this late date it probably would be hard to sort out the facts. Moreover, Barnabas was extremely reluctant to discuss his activities during the council.

IN CONCLUSION

It is neither possible nor important to evaluate the contribution Barnabas made to furthering the concerns of the Church before and during the Vatican Council. He was committed to the pursuit of these goals with all his heart and energy. For many thousands of readers and listeners he offered new appreciation of the Word of God relative to the needs of the contemporary world.

By his stirring words and, even more tellingly, by his striking example, he inspired many to a more enthusiastic and generous commitment to these goals. In every fibre of his being he was a man of the Church.

Barnabas M. Ahern's Bibliography

Compiled by Kenneth O'Malley, C.P.

BOOKS AND MONOGRAPHS

"The Power of His Resurrection and Fellowship in His Sufferings: An Exegetical and Doctrinal Study of Philippians 3:10–11." Doctoral thesis, Pontifical Biblical Institute, Rome, 1958.

The Epistles to the Galatians and to the Romans. New Testament Reading Guide 7. Collegeville: The Liturgical Press, 1960.

Life in Christ. Doctrinal Pamphlet Series 18. New York: Paulist Press, 1962. Translated as *Vida en Christo.* Teologia para todos 37. Santander: Sal Terrae, 1967.

New Horizons: Studies in Biblical Theology. Collection of 11 essays. Edited by Carroll Stuhlmueller, C.P. Notre Dame, Ind.: Fides Publishers, 1963.

The Formation of Scripture. Chicago: Argus Communications, 1967.

Men of Prayer, Men of Action: Christian Spirituality Today. Faith & Life Series. New York: Bruce Publishing Co., 1971.

The Priest and Sacred Scripture. United States Catholic Conference Publications Office, 1972.

Problemas de la iglesia hoy. Biblioteca de Autores Cristianos, 1975.

Jesus the Priest, Source and Model of Consecrated Service. Daughters of St. Paul, 1978.

Pentateuch. A Commentary. Private Notes.

Mary, Queen of the Poor. St. Louis, Mo.: Pio Decimo Press, 1960. Reprint from *Cross and Crown.*

EDITED WORKS

"The Church as the Body of Christ." *The Church as the Body of Christ.* Edited by R. S. Pelton. Notre Dame, Ind.: University Press, 1963: 45–65.

"St. Paul and the Holy Scripture." *Paul, Trumpet of the Spirit.* Edited by Sr. Emily Joseph Daly, C.S.J. Paterson, N.J.: Anthony Guild Press, 1963: 147–54.

"The New Testament Idea of the Church." *Studies in Salvation History.* Edited by C. Luke Salm, F.S.C. Englewood Cliffs, N.J.: Prentice-Hall, 1964: 196–214.

"Union with Christ after Death." *Studies in Salvation History.* Edited by C. Luke Salm, F.S.C. Englewood Cliffs, N.J.: Prentice-Hall, 1964: 215–31.

"The Biblical Way of Life/The Spirituality of the Bible." *Protestants and Catholics on the Spiritual Life.* Edited by Michael Marx, O.S.B. Collegeville: The Liturgical Press, 1965: 3–19.

"Scriptural Aspects of Dei Verbum: Vatican II, An Interfaith Appraisal." A cura di J. H. Miller. Notre Dame, 1966: 54–67.

"Le dimensioni escatologiche della Chiesa: La Teologia dopo il Vaticano II." A cura di J. H. Miller. Brescia, 1967: 365–73.

"Law and the Gospel." *Law for Liberty, The Role of Law in the Church Today.* Edited by James E. Biechler. Baltimore: Helicon, 1967: 93–108.

"The Loss That Is Gain." *Contemporary Spirituality.* Current Problems in Religious Life. Edited by Robert W. Gleason, S.J. New York: Macmillan, 1968: 247–57.

"The Pauline Spirit — An Inspiration for Action." *Christian Action and Openness to the World.* Edited by Joseph Papin. Villanova, Pa.: Villanova University Press, 1970: 2:7–21.

"Maturity: Christian Perfection." *Maturity and Vocation.* Edited by James Walsh. London: *The Way,* 1972. Suppl. Vol. 15:3–15 (Spring 72).

"The Risen Christ in the Light of Pauline Doctrine on the Risen Christian, [I Cor 15:35–37]." *Resurrexit.* Edited by E. Dhanis. CV, 1974: 423–39.

"The Fellowship of His Suffering." *A Companion to Paul.* Readings in Pauline Theology. Edited by Michael J. Taylor, S.J. New York: Alba House, 1975: 37–64.

"Sacra Dottrina del ministerio pastorale contemporaneo." *Probleme della chiesa, oggi.* Edited by Joseph Ratzinger. 1976: 125–44.

"Light from St. John of the Cross on the Knowledge Theme in the Letters of Paul." *The Papin Festschrift — Wisdom and Knowledge, II.* Edited by J. Armenti. Villanova, Pa.: Villanova University Press, 1976: 201–5.

"Christian Holiness and Chastity." *Declaration on Sexual Ethics. Commentaries.* Washington: United States Catholic Conference, 1977: 111–19. Also in *L'Osservatore Romano*, [English] (February 19, 1976): 4–5.

"Law of the Spirit of Holiness." *The Spirit of God in Christian Life.* Edited by Edward Maletesta. New York: Paulist Press, 1977: 3–23.

PERIODICAL ARTICLES

"Staff or no Staff?" *Catholic Biblical Quarterly* 5 (1943): 332–37.

"Textual Directives of the Encyclical Divino Afflante Spiritu." *Catholic Biblical Quarterly* 7 (1945): 340–47.

"Our fellow-priest, Ezekiel." *Homiletic and Pastoral Review* 46 (1946): 338–43.

"A Patron for the Assistant Pastor." *Homiletic and Pastoral Review* (August, 1946): 839–45.

"Tolle, Lege!" *American Ecclesiastical Review* 115 (1946): 81–88.

"Suggestions for Interior Living." *Review for Religious* (November, 1946): 373–79.

"The Indwelling Spirit, Pledge of Our Inheritance (Eph 1:14)." *Catholic Biblical Quarterly* (April, 1947): 179–89.

"Christian Perfection, Contemplation, and Purgatory." *American Ecclesiastical Review* (February, 1948): 81–90.

"Sons Through the Cross." *Cross and Crown* 1 (March, 1949): 25–42.

"Can the Psalms Again Be Popular Prayers?" *Proceedings — National Liturgical Week* (Esberry, Mo., 1953): 117–25.

"Presenting Our Lady to Youth." *Catholic High School Quarterly Bulletin* (April, 1954): 41–48.

"Mary, Proto-Type of the Church." *National Liturgical Week* (1954): 43–51.

"A Scripture Workshop." *The Passionist* (September, 1954): 417–25.

"Exodus, Then and Now." *Bridge* 1 (1955): 53–74.

"The Sacred Passion in the Old Testament." *Proceedings — First National Congress of Confraternity of Passion* (1955): 7–14.

"On Teaching Osee. Panel discussion with D. M. Stanley and R. T. Murphy on the Methods of Teaching Scripture." *Catholic Biblical Quarterly* 17 (1955): 35–53. *Lumen* 4 (1955): 279ff.

"The Goals of Passionist Student Formation as Aims of Professors." *The Passionist* (July–August, 1956): 340–46.

"St. Thérèse of the Holy Face." *Review for Religious* 17 (1958): 257–70.

"The Power of His Resurrection and Fellowship in His Suffering. An Exegetical and Doctrinal Study of Phil 3:10–11." Thesis Defense. *Verbum Domini* 37 (1959): 26–31.

"The Loss That Is Gain." *Spiritual Life* 5 (1959): 298–308.

"Mary and the Poor of Israel." *Cross and Crown* 11 (1959): 278–91.

"The Scriptures and Preaching." *Proceedings — Second Annual Convention of the Catholic Homiletic Society* (Chicago, 1959): 24–29.

"The Fellowship of His Suffering, (Phil 3:10)." *Catholic Biblical Quarterly* 22 (1960): 1–32. Abstract from doctoral dissertation.

"Jewish and Christian Requiem." *Worship* 34:10 (1960): 606–10.

"Gathering the Fragments." *Worship* 35:1 (1960): 32–35.

"The Infancy Narratives — Our Lady's Contribution to the Gospels." *Cross and Crown* 12 (1960): 398–408.

"St. Paul and the Apostolate." *Perspectives* 6 (1961): 13–16.

"The New Catholic Approach to the Interpretation of Sacred Scripture." *Proceedings — Archdiocese of Chicago Clergy Conference* (February, 1961): 3–10.

"Mother of the Messiah." *Marian Studies* 12 (1961): 27–48.

"Gathering the Fragments: Of Fear and Scholarship." *Worship* 35:3 (1961): 160–65.

"Gathering the Fragments: Of Resurrection Theology." *Worship* 35:5 (1961): 293–98.

"Gathering the Fragments: The Lord's Supper." *Worship* 35:7 (1961): 424–29.

"Gathering the Fragments: Of Qumran Literature." *Worship* 35:10 (1961): 652–56.

"For Christ in the Church." *Sponsa Christi* 32 (June, 1961): 261–68.

"Concept of Union with Christ after Death in Early Christian Thought." *Proceedings — Catholic Theological Society of America* 16 (1961): 3–21.

"Concept of the Church in Biblical Thought." *Proceedings — Society of Catholic College Teachers of Sacred Doctrine* 7 (1961): 32–61. Reprinted in *Guide* 166 (1962): 3–12.

"The Christian Union with the Body of Christ in Corinthians, Galatians, and Romans." *Catholic Biblical Quarterly* 23 (1961): 199–209.

"Light and Power Through the Spirit." *Student World* 1 (1962): 42–52.

"Realismo del Cuerpo Místico." *Selecciones de Teología* 1 (1962): 17–22.

"The Objectives of Clerical Training in 1962." *The Passionist* (March, 1962): 21–27.
"Search for the Real." *Perspectives* 7 (1962): 134–37.
"Sacred Scripture." *The Critic* 21:1 (August–September, 1962): 27–30+.
"Gathering the Fragments: Bible Study in the United States." *Worship* 36:2 (1962): 100–106.
"Gathering the Fragments: Père Lagrange." *Worship* 36:4 (1962): 242–48.
"The Lord's Freedman." *Way* 2 (1962): 166–76. Reprinted in *Theology Digest* 11 (1963): 19–20.
"Gathering the Fragments: Mary in Scripture and Liturgy." *Worship* 36:6 (1962): 386–91. Reprinted as "Our Lady in Liturgy and Scripture." *Our Lady's Digest* 17 (1963): 286–91.
"Contemporary Scriptural Developments." *Proceedings — Society of Catholic College Teachers of Sacred Doctrine* 8 (1962): 115–22.
"The Gospels in the Light of Modern Research." *Chicago Studies* 1 (1962): 5–16.
"Study Aids for the Bible Today." *Bible Today* 7 (October, 1963): 38–43.
"Who Wrote the Pauline Epistles?" *Bible Today* 12 (April, 1964): 754–60.
"The Charity of Christ." *Way* 4 (1964): 100–109.
"The Witness of Sacred Scripture to the Collegiality of the Apostles and Bishops." *Bible Today* 13 (October, 1964): 858–63.
"Report from the Council." *Bible Today* 14 (November, 1964): 942–44.
"The Paschal Mystery." *Clergy Review* 50 (1965): 137–42.
"The Book of the People of God." *Clergy Review* 50 (1965): 39–44. Condensed in "The Bible and the People." *Catholic Digest* 29 (1965): 82–84.
"Sacramentality. Its Biblical Background." *Chicago Studies* 4 (1965): 67–78.
"The Scriptures and the Preaching." *Japan Missionary Bulletin* 19 (Tokyo, 1965): 311–15.
"On Divine Revelation." *Homiletic and Pastoral Review* 66 (1966): 557–65.
"The Spirit and the Law." *Way* 6 (1966): 219–29.
"The New Testament and Today's Christian." *National Catholic Reporter* 3 (February 8, 1967): 7.
"Christ, the Cosmos and Modern Colossians." *Bible Today* 38 (November, 1968): 2631–4.
"Mary and the New Church: Interview by H. Cargas." *Sign* 47 (May, 1968): 20–22.

"Outline for Formation Workshop." *Sister Formation Bulletin* 17 (September, 1971): 8–11.
"Ambassadors for Christ: Pauline Principles for Apostolic Renewal." *Way Supplement* 13 (Summer, 1971): 14–25.
"Joy in Weakness." *Way* 11 (1971): 120–27.
"Il significato del Sangue nella Sacra Scrittura." *Fonti Vive* 17 (1971): 127–35.
"Maturity: Christian Perfection." *Way Supplement* 15 (Spring, 1972): 3–15.
"Theology in a Missionary Perspective." *Seminarium* 25 (1973): 937–50.
"The Wisdom of the Cross Today: Jubilee Congress in Rome." *L'Osservatore Romano* [English] (August 14, 1975): 6.
"While We Were Still Enemies, [Rom 5:10]." *Way* 15 (1975): 255–65.
"Sacred Doctrine and the Formation of Christians." *Our Sunday Visitor* 64 (June 15, 1975): 1+.
"The Minister's Responsibility for Sacred Doctrine." *Our Sunday Visitor* 64 (June 29, 1975): 1+.
"The Minister's Duty to Promote Sacred Doctrine." *Our Sunday Visitor* 64 (June 29, 1975): 1+.
"Sacred Doctrine: The Bond of Unity and Charity." *Our Sunday Visitor* 64 (July 13, 1975): 1+.
"The Living Word of the Pastoral Ministry." *Our Sunday Visitor* 64 (July 13, 1975): 1+.
"Un congresso sulla Croce di Cristo. Roma, 13–18 ottobre, 1975." *Ministero Pastorale* 50 (1975): 131–34.
"Jesus the Priest, Source and Model of Consecrated Service." *L'Osservatore Romano* [English] (February 19, 1976): 7–8.
"Charity: Foundation for the Moral Virtues." *Our Sunday Visitor* 64 (May 1, 1976): 14–15.
"Beyond the Declaration on Sexual Ethics." *Our Sunday Visitor* 64 (April 25, 1976): 1+.
"La maturita cristiana e la croce." *Parole di Vita* 21 (1976): 86–96. Also in *La Sapienza della croce oggi: atti del congresso internazionale, Roma, 13–18 ottobre, 1975*. (Torino Leumann: Elle Di Ci, 1976) 2:9–17.
"El tema de la liberación et la Sagrada Escritura." *Salmaticensis* 24 (1977): 495–510, 589–600.
"By the Grace of God: St. Luke's Story of the Sinful Woman in the House of Simon the Pharisee." *Way* 17 (1977): 3–11.
"Pauline Mysticism." *Way* 18 (1978): 3–12.
"Human Wisdom and Spiritual Power." *Way* 20 (1980): 243–52.

"A Servant of Christ Jesus. Fr. Eugene Maly." *Bible Today* 18 (1989): 416.
"Biblical Doctrine on the Rights and Duties of Man." *Gregorianum* 65 (1984): 301–17.
"The Zacchaeus Incident [Luke 19:1–10]." *Bible Today* 25 (1987): 348–51.

SPOKEN RECORDINGS

The Formation of Scripture (six lectures). Chicago: Argus Communications, 1966.
The Gospel of St. Luke. Chicago: Argus Communications, 1966.
Scriptural Background for Three Major Themes of Vatican II. Chicago: Argus Communications, 1966.
Themes from St. Paul. Chicago: Argus Communications, 1970.
Sacramentality: Sign and Symbol. Chicago: The Center for Pastoral Ministry, n.d.
The Faith Experience of the Preacher: An Address. Washington, D.C.: Word of God Institute, n.d.

ARTICLES ABOUT BARNABAS AHERN

Diekmann, Godfrey. "Welcome, Father Barnabas." *Worship* 34 (1960): 604–6.
Nugent, V. "Minutes of the 19th Annual Convention: Cardinal Spellman Award." *Proceedings — Catholic Theological Society of America* 19 (1964): 225–38.
Osiek, Carolyn. "Jacob's Well: Feminist Hermeneutic." *Bible Today* 24 (1986): 18ff.

Index of Names

Abraham, 14, 22, 36, 46–49, 63, 183, 184, 188, 227, 272
Alfrink, Bernard Cardinal, 25, 99

Bea, Augustin Cardinal, 27, 28, 164, 165, 168
Bultmann, Rudolf, 14, 23, 44, 64, 65, 97, 132

Catholic Biblical Quarterly, xv, 4, 77, 279, 335–337
Cerfaux, Canon, 40, 123, 129, 138, 204, 293

Dibelius, Martin, 23, 64, 97, 132
Dupont, Jacques, 100, 219

Ecole Biblique, 6, 38, 105, 107–109
Egypt, 21, 36, 47–63, 106, 149, 181, 184, 217

Harnack, Adolph, 132

Israel, 5, 6, 14, 21, 29, 34, 36, 42, 43, 47–63, 70, 80, 82, 83, 85, 91, 109, 124, 134–138, 148, 149, 151, 152, 154, 156, 159, 160, 174, 175–178, 180, 181, 183–193, 195, 196, 198, 201, 202, 214, 215, 225, 266–275, 290–292, 327, 336

Jacob, 22, 47–50, 63, 272, 340

Jerusalem, 4–6, 38, 43, 60, 68, 104–106, 108, 136–138, 144, 146, 174–176, 183, 187, 266, 268, 270–273, 275

Kierkegaard, Sören, 47, 95

LaGrange, Père M.J., 4, 35, 37, 38, 43, 66, 68, 104–109, 188, 204, 302, 303, 337
Lyonnet, Stanislaus, 7, 100, 131

Meyer, Albert Cardinal, xix, 15, 21, 24, 26, 27, 331
Moses, 20–22, 24, 26, 29, 37, 48, 50–55, 57, 60, 62, 70, 77, 82, 149, 154, 188, 195, 268, 326

Nairobi, xxii, 11–13, 18

Pharoah, 184
Pontifical Biblical Commission, xviii, 10, 15, 17, 204
Pontifical Biblical Institute, 7, 164, 203, 325, 333
Pope Leo XIII, 279, 285, 312
Pope Pius XII, xi, 33, 38–40, 42, 44, 61, 78, 104, 123, 164

Rahner, Karl, 16, 24, 28, 80, 100, 113, 197, 204

342 *Index of Names*

Red Sea, 21, 50, 53, 57, 59, 60, 62, 63
Revue Biblique, 38, 106–108

Secretariat for Promoting Christian Unity, 163, 164, 168
Sinai, 21, 48–52, 55–57, 61, 130, 133, 141, 148, 153, 176, 195, 297
St. Benedict Joseph Labre, 75, 164, 328
St. Bernard, 223, 235
St. Catherine of Genoa, 302, 303, 307, 312, 328

St. Cyril of Jerusalem, 60
St. John Chrysostom, 62, 235, 240, 286–288
St. John of the Cross, 233, 237, 302, 306–308, 335
St. Paul of the Cross, xxii, xxiii, 10, 11, 133, 229, 235, 312–314, 316–319
St. Thomas Aquinas, 16, 157, 304, 325

Tertullian, 59

Williams, Tennessee, 78, 95

Index of Topics

anawim, 6, 14, 174, 184, 187, 189–196, 198, 202, 206, 209, 291

baptism, 53, 57–60, 62, 70, 72, 126–128, 131, 136, 141–143, 155, 168, 218, 222, 245–249, 251, 255, 259, 261–263, 283, 297–300

Christology, 18, 252, 271
church, xii, xviii, xix, xx, xxii, xxiv, 5, 6, 9, 11, 15–18, 21, 23–29, 33, 34, 38–41, 44, 50, 56–59, 65, 67–73, 75, 76, 78–80, 82, 83, 91, 95–97, 99–103, 105–107, 109–115, 117–119, 121, 123, 126, 128, 132, 133, 136–148, 150, 155, 157, 158, 159–161, 165, 167, 168, 177, 195–205, 207–209, 213, 217–219, 222, 230, 235, 236, 239, 254, 260, 265, 266, 279, 286, 289, 292, 294, 301, 303, 311, 316, 323–331, 334, 335, 337, 338
community, xii, xxi, 11, 12, 14, 15, 18, 28, 29, 43, 44, 59, 64–66, 68–73, 82, 104, 132, 134–138, 144, 145, 165, 206–208, 213, 217, 221, 254, 259, 266, 267, 271, 273, 274, 289, 291, 329
covenant, 21, 48, 50–55, 57, 62, 91, 148, 150, 153, 154, 159, 206, 225, 291
criticism, xviii, 14, 37, 39, 40, 64–66, 68, 71, 79, 97, 106–108, 132, 205, 268, 286
cross, xv, xxi, xxii, xxiii, 5, 10, 11, 22, 55, 59–62, 103, 106, 133, 193, 211, 214, 222–224, 227–231, 233–237, 240, 273, 293, 296, 297, 302, 306–308, 312–319, 327, 333, 335, 336, 339

Dei Verbum (Constitution on Divine Revelation), 15, 150, 158, 159, 165, 166, 167, 168, 204, 334
Divino Afflante Spiritu, xi, xii, 4, 33, 38, 40, 42, 44, 104, 123, 335

eschatology, 27, 102, 289, 290, 292, 294, 312
eucharist, 56, 61, 100, 127–129, 131, 141–143, 163, 168, 217, 318, 319
exile, 37, 48, 51, 86, 149, 189, 190, 300
exodus, 14, 21, 22, 46, 47, 49–59, 61–63, 130, 336

gentile, 28, 67, 68, 70, 99, 267, 274, 283
gnosis, 219

343

344 *Index of Topics*

Greek, 38, 59, 72, 73, 77, 124, 126, 128–130, 136, 142, 143, 145, 215, 216, 239, 251, 279–283, 286, 288–290, 293, 297, 325

heilsgeschichte, 43, 44, 98, 101
history, xxii, 4, 5, 14, 16, 28, 36, 37, 40–44, 46, 47, 51, 53, 60, 64, 69, 77, 83, 98, 101, 105, 108, 110, 117, 125, 146–149, 151, 166, 184, 185, 187, 203, 206, 225, 236, 265–267, 271–274, 280, 282, 319, 325, 327, 328, 334

infancy narrative(s), v, 173, 174, 268, 336

kerygma, 135, 139, 146, 238
koinonia, 128, 142

Last Supper, 55, 70, 100, 284, 318
Lumen Gentium (Dogmatic Constitution on the Church), 79

Mediator Dei, 61
messiah, 44, 67, 72, 134–137, 174, 175, 181, 183, 191, 196, 202, 241, 242, 275, 336
mystical, xxiii, 10, 11, 57, 58, 63, 88, 123, 124, 131, 197–199, 221, 230, 262, 277, 302–304, 306, 311–316

paradox, 227, 230, 248, 255, 273
Passion, xviii, xxiii, 7, 10, 14, 15, 23, 54, 59, 74, 90, 95, 97, 99–102, 134, 138, 222, 224, 228–231, 234–236, 238, 249, 250, 252, 260, 262, 265–269, 271, 273, 275, 314, 316, 324, 336
Passover, 47, 51, 55, 61, 130, 147
Pentateuch, 35, 37, 51, 149, 333
Pharisee, 214, 292, 294, 340
pneuma, 96, 125
prayer, xi, xviii, xix, xx, xxi, 1, 4, 10–13, 17–19, 26, 49, 63, 71, 72, 74, 76, 78, 82, 85, 88, 89, 98, 178, 189, 192, 200, 209, 223, 229, 236, 291, 302, 303, 306, 316, 318, 323, 327, 333
prototype, 195, 199–202

resurrection, xxiii, 7, 11, 13, 42, 58, 68, 88, 100, 101, 125, 130, 131, 134, 135, 146, 155, 206, 207, 214, 238, 242, 244–247, 250–252, 254, 255, 256, 258, 261–263, 267, 273, 274, 290, 292, 294, 296–301, 312, 333, 336, 337

sacrament, 27, 58–61, 70, 101, 102, 137, 143, 146, 147, 159, 165, 222, 246, 283, 323
salvation, xi, 15, 31, 44, 46, 47, 80, 88, 90, 98, 101, 111, 113, 135, 141, 150, 153, 156, 166, 167, 177, 180, 181, 184, 185, 208, 239, 242, 243, 244, 246, 250, 251, 254, 262, 273, 274, 283, 284, 290, 292, 294, 295, 299, 301, 325, 327, 334
sarx, 125, 126, 298–300
Sermon on the Mount, 53, 266
shekinah, 50, 56, 175, 176
soma, 7, 125, 127, 128, 131, 141, 142
spirit, xviii, xix, xxiii, 1, 7, 11, 14, 15, 17, 22, 23, 25, 27–29, 35, 37, 38, 43, 44, 66, 67, 69, 71–78, 83, 89, 90, 95–103, 107, 108, 109, 119, 121, 125, 127–130, 134, 135, 137, 142, 151–158, 160–162, 165–168, 171, 173, 175, 177, 179, 183–194, 196, 197, 198–200, 210, 213, 215, 218–221, 224, 225, 229–231, 234–236, 238, 240, 241, 245–252, 255–257, 259–264, 272, 279, 280, 282, 283–288, 290, 292–294, 297, 298, 300, 302, 303, 308, 310, 312, 313–318, 324, 325, 328, 329, 334, 335, 337, 338
suffering, xix, 6, 49, 76, 81, 87, 88, 114, 146, 181, 189, 190, 192, 195, 211, 219, 222–224, 228–236,

239–242, 249–264, 267, 271, 274, 292, 296, 308, 314, 317, 334, 336
symbolism, 54, 59, 61, 269
synagogue, 173, 174

temple, 86, 88–90, 136, 137, 140, 143, 174, 176, 180, 181, 186, 193, 216, 245, 269, 271, 273, 289, 316, 319
torah, 82, 85, 86, 88–91, 149, 150, 159

Tubingen school, 34
typology, 47, 52–59, 61, 62

Vatican II, xi, xix, xx, xxiii, 9, 15–17, 20, 21, 29, 80, 83, 87, 91, 325, 327, 329, 334, 340

Yahweh, 14, 47–52, 56, 77, 86–88, 90, 148, 149, 175, 177, 178, 291

zeitgeist, 23, 78, 79, 82, 95, 97, 99, 101, 102

Index of Biblical Passages

Genesis
1–11	14
1:1-2	184
1:31	184
2:24	126
3:15	181
12–25	36
12:1-3	46
18:16-23	188
19:36	107
22	227
38:17-18	281, 282
38:20	281, 282
43:9	281
44:32	281
45:3	99
45:7-8	184

Exodus
12:14	51
15	84
19–24	148
32	151
33:9-10	54
34:6-7	91
40:35	176

Leviticus
11:45	149
20:9-16	270
21	85

Numbers
12:3	54, 188
21:4-9	57

Deuteronomy
6:4	138
6:4-9	214
7:7	177
18:9-14	87
21:7	269
28:21-24	86
32:10-12	185
34	21
34:4	22
34:5	22

1 Samuel
1:11	188
2:1	185
2:7-8	185
9:9	83
17:18	281
18:1	217
28:8-25	87

2 Samuel
1:16	270
6:11	177
24	86, 87

Index of Biblical Passages

Kings
- 17:22 — 86

2 Kings
- 6:9 — 176
- 14:14 — 281
- 18:23 — 281

Ezra
- 9:2 — 281

Nehemiah
- 5:3 — 281

2 Maccabees
- 7:9ff. — 291

Job
- 17:3 — 281
- 19:25 — 41
- 29:14 — 127

Psalms
- 1 — 149
- 6:4 — 89
- 6:6 — 89
- 10 — 190
- 18 — 149
- 22 — 189, 190
- 24:10 — 49
- 34:26 — 127
- 36:10 — 190, 231
- 38 — 190
- 69 — 189, 190
- 78:49 — 87
- 86:13 — 190
- 88 — 190
- 91:5-6 — 87
- 92:1 — 127
- 95:7-8 — 43
- 104:32 — 228
- 105 — 51
- 106:35 — 281
- 109:20-31 — 190
- 113 — 51
- 118 — 149
- 119:122 — 281
- 139:7-12 — 74

Proverbs
- 6:1 — 281
- 11:15 — 281
- 17:18 — 281
- 20:16 — 281
- 20:19 — 281
- 22:17–23:11 — 36
- 22:26 — 281
- 24:21 — 281
- 27:13 — 281

Wisdom
- 8:1 — 184, 223
- 16:5-13 — 57

Sirach
- 39:1-6 — 1
- 44:1-8 — 321

Isaiah
- 1:2-3 — 225
- 1:5-6 — 88
- 2:11 — 243
- 2:12 — 186
- 5:4 — 227
- 6 — 79
- 6:1 — 216
- 6:1-3 — 186
- 7:3 — 80
- 8:1-4 — 80
- 8:13 — 80
- 9:1-2 — 272
- 12:1 — 179
- 21:1-4 — 84
- 30:15 — 81, 187, 243, 317
- 30:18 — 81
- 35:5-6 — 90
- 35:10a — 90
- 38 — 88
- 38:14 — 281

40:7	96
40:17	179
46:3-4	58
51:9-10	49, 127
53:1-2	196
53:7	228
53:11-12	146
55:10-11	46
61:1-2	191
66:2	191

Jeremiah

3:1-12	48
3:22	87
4:19-21	84
5:4	187
8:18	189
8:18-23	87
10:11	76
26:8	25, 101
30:12-17	87
31:29-34	291
31:34	153
33:6	87

Ezekiel

5:11-17	273
16	48
16:14	177
18	291
27:9	281
27:27	281
34:10-16	196
37:10	185
37:11-14	273
44:25	86
47:1-12	46

Daniel

7	146
7:13-14	146
9:21	174
9:24-25	295
12:1-2	273

Hosea

2:16	50
2:16-25	52
3:1	178
5:13-14	87
6:1-2	87, 88
6:4	88
7:1	87
11:1	53
11:4	87
12:6-7	49
13:14	87
14:5	87

Amos

3:8	84
4:10	87
5:4	190

Micah

4:6-7	89
7:14-15	63

Habakkuk

2:4	80
3:5	87

Zephaniah

1:12	48
2:3	191
3:12-13	183, 191
3:12-17	195
3:14	175
3:15	175
3:16-17	175, 183
3:19-20	89

Haggai

2:13	86

Zechariah

2:3	191
9:9	174, 191
11:12-13	269
13:8-19	195

Index of Biblical Passages   349

Malachi
  3:1-3   180

Matthew
  1–28   265–275
  1:19-25   192
  1:21   177
  1:31   52
  2:10   179
  2:15   53
  3:13-17   53
  3:17   232
  4:1-11   53
  5–7   53, 154
  5:3ff.   196
  5:3-10   194
  5:17   150
  5:21   152
  5:27   152
  5:31   152
  7:24-27   145
  7:28-29   54
  8:10   70
  11:29   54
  12:46-50   193
  13:11   146
  16:17-20   145
  17:1-8   54
  18:15-18   145
  18:19-20   145
  19:6   181
  28:20   143

Mark
  1:9-11   53
  1:12-13   53
  1:30   69
  4:11   146
  4:40   67
  7:8   159
  8:29   67
  8:34   240
  9:1-7   54
  10:11   70
  15:38   273
  15:39   67

Luke
  1:6   150
  1:14   179
  1:19   174
  1:27   173
  1:28   175
  1:29   174
  1:30   175
  1:31-32   175
  1:38   192, 234
  1:41-45   171
  1:43   176
  1:46-49   177, 192, 196
  1:51-54   192
  1:56   177
  2:10   179
  2:12   179
  2:19   174, 180
  2:30-32   180
  2:33-35   174, 181
  2:34   193
  2:41-50   193
  2:48-50   174
  2:49   193
  5:29   71
  6:38   179, 225
  9:23   223
  10:38-42   198
  11:27-28   193, 200
  16:19-31   293
  23:46   293
  24:32   15

John
  1:13   315
  1:14   56, 153
  1:18   314
  1:36   55
  2:4   193
  2:13   55
  3:5   57

3:6	315	2:38	136
3:8	161	2:42	128, 135, 136
3:14-21	57	2:46	136
3:16	227	2:46-47	135
3:19-21	56	3:1-11	138
3:29-30	55, 221	3:12-16	135
4:20	137	3:20	136
4:23	316	3:24ff.	135
4:34	154	4:1-22	135
6:4	55	4:8ff.	138
6:30-31	56	4:8-12	135
6:53	318	4:36-37	22
6:58	318	5:3-11	138
7:37	318	5:17ff.	135
7:39	151	5:29-32	135
8:12	56	5:32	135
8:24	55	7	134
8:28	55	7:47-48	136
8:56	47	7:54-60	293
8:58	55	8:1	137
10:10	155	8:4-6	137
11:55	55	8:5	137
12:26	313	8:12	137
12:32	168, 229	8:14	137, 138
13:1	55	8:17	137
13:19	55	9:4	138, 141
13:25	318	10:15	70
14:9	231	10:38	69
14:10	314	11:19-20	137
14:26	71	11:24	22
16:5-15	284	11:26	137
16:8	307	13:33	134
17:21	168, 316	20:28	160
17:24	313	28:31	13
19:25-26	155		
19:36	55	*Romans*	
25–26	284	1:1	215
		1:3-4	140
Acts		1:7	215
1:15ff.	138	1:16-17	140
1:22	135	1:17	80
2:14-26	138	3:19-20	152
2:29-36	135	3:27	156
2:36	134	4:17	46

Index of Biblical Passages   351

5:3-5	241	1:30	126
5:5	280	1:30-31	142, 217
5:6-8	246	1:31	244
6	252	2:1	244
6:3	246, 263	2:1-2	140, 223
6:3-4	59	2:1-3	242
6:4	298	2:2	235
6:3-11	130, 131	2:15-16	155, 161
6:6, 12	249	3:1ff.	139
6:9-10	296	3:16-17	143, 280
6:11	247	3:17	140
6:12ff.	298	4:1-2	141, 158
7:4	126, 297	6:15	125, 218
7:7	152	6:17	125, 142
7:12, 14	149	6:18-20	245
7:14-15, 19	151	6:19-20	280
8	130, 249	8:1	219
8:2	154, 156	9:15	145
8:3	246	9:16-17	215
8:5-6	96, 298	10:1-2	57
8:9-24	284	10:2	59
8:11	298	10:4	56
8:12-13	248	10:11	61
8:14	157	10:16	128, 142
8:14-17	285	10:16-17	131, 136
8:16	156, 280	10:17	128, 142
8:16-18	250, 252, 260	11:1	221
8:17	224	11:16	140
8:26	280	11:24-30	131
8:26-27	285	12	218
8:29	222, 223, 229, 236, 315	12:13	128, 129
		12:27-28	144
9–11	273	13:12	285
9:5	140	15:3	139
9:31-32	152	15:5	145
10:4	150	15:22	245, 296
10:9-10	136	15:24	294
12:4, 8	144	15:26	295
		15:28	294, 319
1 Corinthians		15:45-49	296
1:12	145	15:49	245, 296
1:15-16	160	15:54	249
1:21	244	15:56-57	295
1:27-28	244	6:17	316

352 Index of Biblical Passages

2 Corinthians

1:3-7	254, 255	3:24	150
1:4-5	260	3:27	126, 131, 142, 156, 216, 297
1:5	235		
3:3	154	3:28	99, 127, 131, 142, 216, 297
3:6-7	151		
3:14	151	4:4	195
3:18	141	4:4-5	148, 226, 227
4:7-11	244	4:4-7	156
4:8	260	4:6-7	280, 285
4:10	260	4:19	199
4:10-11	235	4:31	246
4:11	221	5:16	248
5:1-5	280	5:22	252
5:1-10	300	5:22-23	75
5:6-8	285	5:24	232
5:14	125, 245, 296	5:24-25	248
5:14-15	229, 257	6:2	148, 156
5:18-20	257	6:14	235
5:20	143	6:17	235
5:21	227		
6:16	143	*Ephesians*	
12:1-7	277	1:4	227
12:5	253	1:4-5	226
12:9	18	1:5	197
12:9-10	253	1:7	224
13:2-4	144	1:13-14	279
13:3-4	258	1:14	294
13:4	254	2:10	153
		3:4	195
Galatians		3:8	197
1:1	139	3:9	195, 225
1:15-16	214	3:17-19	77
1:18	144	3:18	228
2:6	138	5:1-2	224
2:11	139	5:2	231
2:11-14	144	5:3-4	78
2:17	297	5:25-32	126, 142
2:19	248	5:27	195
2:19-20	211, 223, 235		
2:20	127, 221, 228, 247, 248, 296	*Philippians*	
		1:21-23	300
3:1	220	3:8-10	297
3:3	220	3:10-11	7, 238, 364
		4:8-9	93

Index of Biblical Passages 353

Colossians
- 1:2 — 215
- 1:5-7 — 140
- 1:19 — 227
- 1:24 — 259, 260, 319
- 2:6-7 — 140
- 2:11 — 259
- 2:17 — 57, 151
- 3:9-12 — 232
- 3:11 — 143

1 Thessalonians
- 1:6 — 240, 241, 252
- 2:4 — 140
- 2:13 — 140
- 2:14 — 240
- 3:3 — 239
- 3:12-13 — 241
- 4:2ff. — 240
- 4:8 — 241, 280
- 5:12-13 — 144
- 5:18 — 240
- 5:19 — 161
- 5:19-22 — 160

2 Thessalonians
- 2:1ff. — 239
- 3:5 — 241, 252

1 Timothy
- 6:16 — 285

2 Timothy
- 2:8 — 139
- 3:12 — 259
- 3:14-16 — 31
- 4:7-8 — 259
- 4:8 — 294

Titus
- 3:3 — 226
- 3:4 — 153

Philemon
- 1:8 — 220

- 1:18 — 141, 221
- 1:21 — 221
- 1:25 — 12
- 2:5-11 — 140, 231, 232, 235, 296
- 3:3-8 — 145
- 3:5-6 — 214
- 3:8-10 — 231
- 3:10-11 — 233, 234, 261
- 16 — 218

Hebrews
- 1:3 — 58
- 2:11 — 156
- 3:1–4:13 — 61
- 5:8 — 192
- 10:5 — 228
- 11:1 — 285
- 13:8 — 57, 63, 214

1 Peter
- 2:2 — 316
- 2:9 — 58
- 2:21 — 62, 224

2 Peter
- 1:4 — 316

1 John
- 1:1 — 153
- 1:3 — 145
- 2:27 — 145, 155
- 3:2 — 315
- 3:11 — 145
- 4:6 — 145
- 4:8 — 81
- 4:9-10 — 228
- 5:11 — 226

Revelation
- 1:5-6 — 63
- 2:7 — 56
- 2:17 — 56
- 3:17 — 46

4:6	232	21:3	63
5:6	319	21:6	63
15:2-3	62	21:22	319

BS 511.2 .A37 1996
Ahern, Barnabas M.
A voice crying out in the desert